CliffsTestPrep®

Military Flight Aptitude Tests

CliffsTestPrep®
Military Flight Aptitude Tests

by

Fred N. Grayson, M.A., 1st Lt. USAF (Ret'd)

Contributing Authors

Elaine Bender, M.A.

Richard Branch

Michael DeMarci

Thomas G. Franco II

Michael Hamid, Ph.D.

Jo Palmore, M.S.

Deborah Grayson Riegel, M.S.

Barbara Tepper

Mark Weinfeld, M.S.

Douglas R. Lang, CFI; CFII; MEI; AGI; IGI; Pilot, ExpressJet Airlines

WILEY

Wiley Publishing, Inc.

About the Author

As an independent book developer and publisher, Fred N. Grayson has published hundreds of books in conjunction with many major publishers. In addition, he has written and/or coauthored dozens of books in the test-preparation field.

Publisher's Acknowledgments

Editorial

Project Editor: Marcia L. Johnson

Senior Acquisitions Editor: Greg Tubach

Copy Editor: Kathleen Robinson

Technical Editors: Brian Proffitt, Douglas R. Lang

Composition

Proofreader: Betty Kish

Wiley Indianapolis Composition Services

CliffsTestPrep® *Military Flight Aptitude Tests*

Published by:
Wiley Publishing, Inc.
111 River Street
Hoboken, NJ 07030-5774
www.wiley.com

Copyright © 2004 Wiley Publishing, Inc. New York, New York

Published by Wiley Publishing, Inc., New York, NY
Published simultaneously in Canada

Library of Congress Cataloging-in-Publication Data available from publisher

ISBN: 0-7645-4103-X

Printed in the United States of America

10 9 8 7 6 5

1B/SY/QS/QV/IN

Table of Contents

PART II: FULL-LENGTH PRACTICE TESTS

This *CliffsTestPrep Military Flight Aptitude Tests* offers you a complete guide to test preparation for three military flight aptitude tests to help you qualify to become a military aviator. All the military services need pilots and navigators, whether for fixed-wing planes or helicopters. The tests included in this book help you study for the tests you have to take to qualify for pilot training.

To become a pilot, a navigator, or have any other flight career in the military, you have to pass one of the tests for that branch of the service: Air Force, Army, Navy, Marines or Coast Guard. This book is an in-depth study guide to help you familiarize yourself with the types of questions you will encounter, depending on which branch of the service you plan to enter.

The tests in this book include the Air Force Officer Qualifying Test (AFOQT), Army Alternate Flight Aptitude Screening Test (AFAST) and the U.S. Navy and Marine Corps Aviation Selection Test Battery (ASTB). Each test is different, although some question types overlap. We review all the types of questions you will encounter, so regardless of the test you plan to take, you will be fully prepared.

The Organization of This Book

To make it easier to study, the book is divided into two basic sections. The first section details all the types of questions on all the exams. We include a description of the questions that you will encounter, an analysis of how to answer them to achieve the highest possible scores, and then offer you samples of each so that you will be completely familiar with the questions. The second section of the book contains three sample tests—one for each of the three military flight aptitude tests.

We recommend that you take the time to review each section of the exam that you plan to take. Pay particular attention to the directions because they can often be somewhat complicated. Because all portions of the tests are timed, you don't want to spend additional time reading and rereading the directions, trying to decipher them. You should be able to go right for the questions, with only a brief glance at the directions to make sure they are the same as those you've studied here—although it is not likely that they will change.

About the Tests

All the tests that are currently being given are multiple-choice tests. Depending on which test you are taking, you have anywhere from two to five answer choices. These are not easy tests, as you can imagine. However, the multiple-choice format should give you an advantage; if you don't know the correct answer, you can always try to use the process of elimination to narrow the odds in your favor.

Let's look at the format of the tests.

Air Force Officer Qualifying Test (AFOQT)

The AFOQT measures aptitudes and is used to select applicants for officer commissioning programs, such as Officer Training School (OTS) or Air Force Reserve Officer Training Corps (Air Force ROTC). The test assesses aptitudes required of student pilots, navigators, students in technical training, and officers in general. You are required to complete all sections of the test regardless of the program for which you are applying. The test can only be taken twice, although that restriction might be waived. However, you have to wait at least 180 days between tests, and the most recent AFOQT scores are the ones that count—whether you do better or worse the second time. These scores never expire.

The complete AFOQT contains 380 test items divided into 16 subsets and requires approximately 5 hours to administer.

The following is a brief description of each subset:

- **Verbal Analogies:** Measures your ability to reason and see relationships between words. (25 questions/8 minutes)
- **Arithmetic Reasoning:** Measures your general reasoning ability. It is concerned with your ability to arrive at solutions to problems. (25 questions/29 minutes)
- **Reading Comprehension:** Measures your ability to read and understand paragraphs. (25 questions/18 minutes)
- **Data Interpretation:** Measures your ability to interpret data from graphs and charts. (25 questions/24 minutes)
- **Word Knowledge:** Measures your verbal comprehension, involving your ability to understand written language. (25 questions/5 minutes)
- **Math Knowledge:** Measures your functional ability in using learned mathematical relationships. (25 questions/22 minutes)
- **Mechanical Comprehension:** Measures your ability to learn and reason with mechanical terms. This test has pictures of mechanisms whose functions call for comprehension. (20 questions/10 minutes)
- **Electrical Maze:** Measures your ability to choose the correct path from among several choices. (20 questions/10 minutes)
- **Scale Reading:** Measures your ability to read scales, dials and meters. (40 questions/15 minutes)
- **Instrument Comprehension:** Measures your ability to determine the position of an airplane in flight from reading instruments. (20 questions/6 minutes)
- **Block Counting:** Measures your ability to "see into" a 3-dimensional stack of blocks and determine how many pieces are touched by certain numbered blocks. (20 questions/3 minutes)
- **Table Reading:** Measures your ability to read tables quickly and accurately. (40 questions/7 minutes)
- **Aviation Information:** Measures your knowledge of general aeronautical concepts and terminology (past and current). (20 questions/8 minutes)
- **Rotated Blocks:** Measures your spatial aptitude, that is, your ability to visualize and manipulate objects in space. (15 questions/13 minutes)
- **General Science:** Measures your verbal comprehension in the area of science. (20 questions/10 minutes)
- **Hidden Figures:** (Template matching) Measures your perceptual reasoning using visual imagery and short-term memory. (15 questions/8 minutes)

Test Table

Test	Number of Test Items	Time (in Minutes)
Verbal Analogies	25	8
Arithmetic Reasoning	25	29
Reading Comprehension	25	18
Data Interpretation	25	24
Word Knowledge	25	5
Math Knowledge	25	22
Mechanical Comprehension	20	10
Electrical Maze	20	10
Scale Reading	40	15
Instrument Comprehension	20	6
Block Counting	20	3
Table Reading	40	7

Test	Number of Test Items	Time (in Minutes)
Aviation Information	20	8
Rotated Blocks	15	13
General Science	20	10
Hidden Figures	15	8
Totals	**380**	**196**

The test actually takes about 4 1/2 hours, including breaks.

Test results are given in five areas: Pilot, Navigator, Academic Aptitude, Verbal and Quantitative (Math). Following are the scoring requirements.

Pilot: This composite measures some of the knowledge and ability considered necessary for successful completion of pilot training. The Pilot composite includes subtests that measure verbal ability, knowledge of aviation and mechanical systems, ability to determine aircraft altitude from instruments, knowledge of aeronautical concepts, ability to read scales and interpret tables, and certain spatial abilities.

- Pilot score of 25
- Navigator score of 10
- Combined Pilot and Navigator score of 50
- Verbal score of 15
- Quantitative score of 10
- No minimum Academic score

Navigator: This composite measures some of the knowledge and ability considered necessary for successful completion of navigator training. It shares many subtests with the Pilot composite. Subtests that measure verbal ability, ability to determine aircraft altitude, and knowledge of aeronautical concepts are not included. However, subtests measuring quantitative aptitudes, some spatial or visual abilities and knowledge of general science are added.

- Pilot score of 10
- Navigator score of 25
- Combined Pilot and Navigator score of 50
- Verbal score of 15
- Quantitative score of 10
- No minimum Academic score

Verbal: (All candidates must achieve a minimum score of 15.) This composite measures various types of verbal knowledge and ability. The Verbal composite includes subtests that measure the ability to reason and recognize relationships among words, the ability to read and understand paragraphs on diverse topics and the ability to understand synonyms.

Quantitative: (All candidates must achieve a minimum score of 10.) This composite measures various types of quantitative knowledge and ability. The Quantitative composite shares subtests with the Navigator-Technical composite discussed previously and includes subtests that measure the ability to understand and reason with arithmetic relationships, interpret data from graphs and charts, and use mathematical terms, formulas and relationships.

Academic Aptitude: (No minimum score required.) The Academic Aptitude score, which is a composite of the Math and Verbal sections, is used as part of the Field Training selection process. This composite measures verbal and quantitative knowledge and ability. The Academic Aptitude composite combines all subtests used to score the Verbal and Quantitative composites.

Each of the five scores are percentile based, meaning that they range from 1–99. Statistical analysis indicates average scores are in the 40s for each of the areas. It is highly recommended that individuals interested in being pilots strive to achieve scores in the 70s or higher.

U.S. Navy and Marine Corps Aviation Selection Test Battery (ASTB)

The Bureau of Medicine and Surgery developed these tests in conjunction with the Naval Aerospace Medical Institute to evaluate those interested in pursuing a career in aviation. Until recently, this test had six sections, but the Biographical Inventory, which was to be a predictor of training attrition, has been eliminated. Studies indicated that this was no longer a valid predictor.

You may take this test as many times as you wish, although there is a waiting period of 30 days between the first time you take the test and the second. You must then wait at least 180 days for all subsequent retests. When you pass the test, the scores are good for life. You must pass this test to become an aviator.

The four sections of the test are:

- **Math/Verbal Test (MVT):** This is a 35 minute/37 question test of general intelligence, which includes both mathematics and verbal questions. Those who have low scores on this test tend to have difficulty in the academic portions of training.

- **Mechanical Comprehension Test (MCT):** This is a 15 minute/30 question test of your ability to perceive physical relationships and solve some practical problems in mechanics.

- **Spatial Apperception Test (SAT):** This test measures your ability to perceive spatial relationships from differing orientations. The test has 35 questions, and you have 10 minutes to complete them. It is given to those individuals applying for aviation training.

- **Aviation and Nautical Information Test (ANT):** This is a measure of your aviation and nautical knowledge, helping to determine your interest in naval aviation. The test has 30 questions, and you have 15 minutes to complete them. It is given to those individuals applying for aviation training.

Test Table		
Test	**Number of Test Items**	**Time (in Minutes)**
Math/Verbal	37	35
Mechanical Comprehension	30	15
Spatial Apperception	35	10
Aviation and Nautical Information	30	15
Totals	**132**	**75**

The Navy, Marine Corps and Coast Guard use the complete results of this test battery as a primary selection instrument for aviation programs. The scores are weighted and four scores are derived:

1. **Academic Qualifications Rating (AQR)** (scoring range: 1–9). This score is a predictor of your performance in the academic portions of ground school training.

2. **Pilot Flight Aptitude Rating (PFAR)** (scoring range: 1–9). This score is a predictor of flight grades in primary flight training.

3. **Flight Officer Flight Aptitude Rating (FOFAR)** (scoring range: 1–9). This score, like the PFAR, is a predictor of flight grades in primary flight training.

4. **Officer Aptitude Rating (OAR)** (scoring range: 20–80). This is a composite score derived from the combination of the five tests.

For the Navy, you must meet the following minimum scores:

AQR—3

PFAR (pilot)—4

FOFAR (info)—4

OAR—40

For the Marine Corps, you must meet the following minimum scores:

AQR—4

PFAR (pilot)—6

FOFAR (info)—6

OAR—40

However, to be competitive, applicants should have scores of 5 or higher on the AQR and 6 or higher on the PFAR and FOFAR.

A new test called the Automated Pilot Examination (APEX) is being developed and will be similar to the paper-and-pencil ASTB. It will be completely computerized and is currently being tested at several testing sites. For the government, the advantage is in diminishing the amount of necessary paperwork, and for the applicant, the advantage is that scores will be available much faster. The test will be a computer-administered test, but will eventually become a computer-adaptive test. In a computer-adaptive test (CAT), the student is presented with a question of medium difficulty. If it is answered correctly, the next question is more difficult. If it is answered incorrectly, the next question is slightly easier. In essence, the test adapts to the applicant's answers.

At this point, however, only the computer-administered test is available. You might be given the computer version, rather than the paper-and-pencil version. One of the advantages of this test is that you are able to get your scores almost immediately, rather than waiting several weeks.

Army Alternate Flight Aptitude Screening Test (AFAST)

The AFAST is used to select men and women for training to become Army helicopter pilots. This is not an intelligence test, but rather a test that measures those special aptitudes and personality characteristics that are predictive of success for this type of training.

This exam has seven sections, with a total of 200 questions. Each test has separate time limits and directions, and as we said earlier, it's important to understand these directions clearly BEFORE you take the test so that you don't waste time trying to decipher them during the actual exam. In some of the subtests, a portion of wrong answers is counted against right answers. However, it is suggested that you make every effort to answer the questions as best you can, unless you really have no idea. Later in this book, we cover techniques in answering multiple-choice questions, and these pointers can help you make educated guesses to improve your odds of answering the questions correctly.

The tests:

- **Background Information Form:** This section has 25 questions about your background, and your time limit is 10 minutes.
- **Instrument Comprehension Test:** This section has 15 questions, and you have 5 minutes to answer them.
- **Complex Movements Test:** You have 5 minutes to answer 30 questions.
- **Helicopter Knowledge Test:** This test is made up of 20 questions about helicopter flight, and you have 10 minutes to complete them.
- **Cyclic Orientation Test:** This test is made up of 15 questions that test your ability to recognize simple changes in helicopter position. You have 5 minutes to answer these questions.

- **Mechanical Functions Test:** This is a test of general mechanical principles with 20 questions to be answered in 10 minutes.
- **Self-Description Form:** This form is made up of 75 questions dealing with your interests, likes and dislikes. You have 25 minutes. There is no pass/fail on this test.

Test Table		
Test	**Number of Test Items**	**Time (in Minutes)**
Background Information Form	25	10
Instrument Comprehension Test	15	5
Complex Movements Test	30	5
Helicopter Knowledge Test	20	10
Cyclic Orientation Test	15	5
Mechanical Functions Test	20	10
Self-Description Form	75	25
Totals	**200**	**70**

The next part of this book covers the various types of questions you'll encounter in each of the different examinations.

PART I

SUBJECT AREA REVIEW

This part includes the following subject area reviews:

- Verbal Review
- Mathematics Review
- Mechanics Review
- Science Review
- Spatial Relations Review
- Aviation Review
- Personal Information Review

Measuring verbal ability—knowledge of words and reading comprehension— is one of the best ways to predict academic and vocational success, particularly for positions of leadership. The review sections that follow give you the information you need to score well on the verbal sections of the AFOQT and the ASTB tests.

Verbal Analogies

Verbal analogy tests measure your ability to reason and see relationships between words.

Practice Questions

Directions: Choose the answer that best completes the analogy developed at the beginning of each question.

1. TOOL is to DRILL as POEM is to:

   A. SONG
   B. MACHINE
   C. SONNET
   D. BIRD
   E. NOVEL

2. TALK is to SHOUT as DISLIKE is to:

   A. SCREAM
   B. DETEST
   C. FRIGHTEN
   D. CONTRIBUTE
   E. ADMIRE

3. CONDUCTOR is to ORCHESTRA as SHEPHERD is to:

   A. FILM
   B. CANINE
   C. CONTROL
   D. FLOCK
   E. GENERAL

4. OBSTINATE is to COMPLIANT as OBLIVIOUS is to:

   A. CONSCIOUS
   B. CAREFREE
   C. FORGETFUL
   D. INTUITIVE
   E. NATURAL

Answers and Explanations

1. **C.** An example of a kind of tool is a drill, and an example of a kind of poem is a sonnet.

2. **B.** To talk intensely is to shout, and to dislike intensely is to detest.

3. **D.** The function of a conductor is to lead an orchestra, and the function of a shepherd is to lead a flock.

4. **A.** The opposite of obstinate is compliant, and the opposite of oblivious is conscious.

Word Knowledge and Reading Comprehension

Word Knowledge appears on both the AFOQT exam and the ASTB exam. The formats of the exams differ slightly, however. On the AFOQT exam, you are given a word and then asked to find the synonym from five choices (A–E). On the ASTB exam, three different types of questions test your vocabulary knowledge. The first type of question is a sentence with a missing word, and you are asked to choose the missing word from among four choices (A–D). The second type of question is a little more complex. You are given a brief quotation that contains a word that is used incorrectly. You are asked to select, from a choice of five words, the word that would replace the incorrect word and would correctly convey the meaning of the quotation.

Word Knowledge

Let's look at the different question types. The first question is the type you will find on the AFOQT.

> 1. CIRCUMVENT
>   A. get over
>   B. go under
>   C. get through
>   D. go around
>   E. go easily

The correct answer is **D**, go around. This type of question is not tricky. It requires, however, a strong vocabulary. (*circum = around, vent = go*). The AFOQT has a total of 25 questions of this type.

The second type of question is from the ASTB. The question consists of a sentence in which one word is omitted. Select the choice that best completes the sentence.

> 2. Paul was able to _____ the complainer with a look of contempt.
>   A. squelch
>   B. offend
>   C. assail
>   D. expel

The correct answer is **A**. To squelch is to silence. This satisfies the meaning of the sentence.

The final type of question is also from the ASTB and is a little more complex. The following quotation contains a word that has been misused. It is not in keeping with the meaning of the quotation. You must first determine which word is incorrect, and then select, from the choices given, the word that would be more appropriate for that quotation.

> 3. "Even while their components vary from culture to culture, rites of adulteration convey status in a new social grouping on the participants."
>   A. maturity
>   B. ceremony
>   C. initiation
>   D. consumption

The correct answer is **C**. The word *adulteration* is incorrect. It means to make something impure by adding a foreign substance. *Initiation,* which means the process of being admitted to something, fits the meaning of the sentence.

The first two types of questions really just require you to understand the vocabulary. This last section requires a little more thought on your part. You are required to first identify the word that is misused, and then substitute the correct word.

The ability tested in the Word Knowledge portion of the AFOQT and ASTB exams is your command of language—in other words—your vocabulary. Of course, by this point in your life, you might think that you have learned all the words you will ever learn or that it is impossible to improve your vocabulary. On the contrary! If you are diligent and put your mind to it, you can improve your vocabulary in several ways. The following are three ways that definitely help:

1. Read, read, read. Pick up a newspaper, a magazine or a novel and make note of words you do not understand. Make a list or put them on note cards. First, try to figure out the meaning of the words by looking at the context in which they are used. Make an educated guess. If you are still not sure, look up the meaning of the words in a dictionary and write them out in a notebook or on note cards. Then try to make up your own sentences using the words.

2. Learn a new word every day or every other day. You can get into the habit of looking up a new word in the dictionary every day. Write out the word and its definition on a piece of paper. Then write out a sentence using the word. This helps you visualize it. Don't pick words that are too technical or specialized (such as medical/scientific terms or proper names). Try using this new word in conversation.

3. Words are made up, generally, of prefixes, roots and suffixes. Many prefixes and roots have a Latin or Greek origin. If you can familiarize yourself with some of these, you can arrive at the meaning of some words by breaking them down. The following section offers you some common prefixes, roots and suffixes to help you tackle words you are unfamiliar with in the Word Knowledge section.

Prefixes

To break down words you do not understand or to help you recognize why a word means what it means, you should become familiar with prefixes. Prefixes come at the beginning of words and can affect their meaning.

As an example, let's look at the word *synonym*. This word is made up of the prefix *syn* plus the root *nym*. If you know that the prefix *syn* means *with/together* or *same,* and that the root *nym* means *name* or *word,* you can conclude that the word *synonym* means *same word*. And that's what it means!

Let's look at another example. The word *circumvent* is made up of the prefix *circum* plus the root *vent*. If you know that the prefix *circum* means *around,* and that the root *vent* means *go* or *come,* you can conclude that the word *circumvent* means *go around*.

What follows is a list of common prefixes that are often found at the beginning of certain words. Following the prefix is the meaning of the prefix and a word using the prefix (with a rough definition in parentheses following the word). Try including a word of your own in the space provided for each prefix. If you cannot come up with your own word, refer to a dictionary for help.

Prefix	Meaning	Word (Definition)	Your Example
ab-	away from	abnormal (away from normal)	
ad-	to, toward	adjoin (join to)	
a-, an-	not, without	apathy (without feeling)	
anti-	against	antiviolence (against violence)	

(continued)

Prefix	Meaning	Word (Definition)	Your Example
ambi-	both	ambidextrous (both hands)	
bene-	good	benign (good or harmless)	
circum-	around	circumvent (go around)	
con-	with, together	connect (come together)	
contra-	against	contradict (speak against)	
com-	with, together	communion (coming together)	
de-	down, away	descend (move down)	
dis-	apart, not	discontent (not content)	
e-	out of, from	eject (throw out)	
ex-	out of, from	exclude (leave out)	
hyper-	over	hyperactive (overactive)	
hypo-	under	hypodermic (below the skin)	
inter-	between	interconnected (connected between)	
il-	not	illegal (not legal)	
in-	not	indiscreet (not discreet)	
in-	into	ingest (take into the body by mouth)	
im-	not	impossible (not possible)	
im-	into	imbibe (drink in)	
ir-	not	irrational (not rational)	
mal-	bad, evil	malign (speak badly of)	
ob-	against	obstruct (build against)	
omni-	all	omniscient (knows all)	
peri-	around	periscope (view around)	
post-	after	postgraduate (after graduation)	
pre-	before	precede (go before)	
pro-	for, forward	proceed (move forward)	
re-	again, back	reconvene (get together again)	
retro-	back	retrogression (step back)	
se-	away from	seduce (lead away)	

Prefix	Meaning	Word (Definition)	Your Example
sub-	under	subhuman (below human)	
sur-, super-	over, above	supersonic (above sound)	
sym-, syn-	together, with	sympathy (feeling with or for)	
trans-	across	transatlantic (across the Atlantic)	

Roots

Along with prefixes, roots are central to the meanings of words. If you familiarize yourself with some common roots, you might be able to better recognize certain words or at least get a general feel for several words. By studying the following list of roots, you will be better equipped to break down many words and make sense of them!

Following is a list of roots, their meanings, a word using the root, and a space in which you can write a brief definition in your own words.

Root	Meaning	Word	Your Definition
ami, amic	love	amicable	
anthrop	human, man	anthropology	
arch	chief or leader	patriarch	
auto	self	autobiography	
aud	sound	audible	
brev	short	brief	
bio	life	biography	
cap	take, seize	capture	
ced	yield, go	intercede	
corp	body	corporal	
cred	believe	credible	
culp	guilt	culpable	
chron	time	synchronize	
crac, crat	rule, ruler	democracy	
dic	speak, say	dictate	
duc, duct	lead	deduce	
demo	people	democracy	
equ	equal	equity	

(continued)

Root	Meaning	Word	Your Definition
grad, gress	step	progression	
graph	writing, printing	biography	
ject	throw	inject	
luc	light	elucidate	
log	study of	geology	
mono	one	monotone	
man	hand	manual	
min	small	minority	
mit, miss	send	emit	
mort	death	mortal	
mut	change	mutate	
nym	word or name	pseudonym	
nov	new	renovate	
pac	peace	pacify	
pel, puls	push	compel	
pot	power	potent	
port	carry	portable	
path	feeling	apathy	
phil	like, lover of	philosophy	
quer, quis	ask	query	
scrib	write	manuscript	
sed	sit	sedentary	
sent	feel	sensory	
sequ	follow	sequel	
son	sound	unison	
spir	breathe	inspire	
tang, tact	touch	tangible	
vac	empty	vacant	
ven	come, go	intervene	
ver	truth	verify	
vert	turn	introvert	

Root	Meaning	Word	Your Definition
vit	life	revitalize	
voc	call	evocative	

Suffixes

Suffixes come at the end of words and usually change the part of speech (noun, adjective, adverb and so on) of words, which also subtly changes the meaning. Becoming familiar with suffixes might help you get a sense of the meaning the word is *conveying,* even if you are not sure of what the definition of the word is exactly.

Let's look at a word with different suffixes to see how the part of speech or the meaning can change. For example, the word *sedate* means to *calm* or *relax.* The following sentences contain words that are made up of the root word *sedate* but have different suffixes attached to the end:

> The doctor prescribed a sedat*ive* [something that sedates] to calm her nerves.

> The speech was delivered sedat*ely* [in a sedate manner].

> The dog was under sedat*ion* [in a state of sedation] for the long trip.

> Many office workers live a sedent*ary* [relating to nonactivity] lifestyle.

As you can see, in each of the sentences, the word *sedate* means generally the same thing, but the part of speech changes. However, you can get a sense of *how* the word changes if you know what the suffix means.

What follows is a list of common suffixes that you might encounter at the ends of certain words. Try applying these suffixes at the ends of words you know (or words from the preceding lists) to see how the part of speech or the meaning of the word changes.

Suffix	Meaning	Your Example
-able, ible	capable of or susceptible to	
-ary	of or relating to	
-ate	to make	
-ian	one relating to or belonging to	
-ic	relating to or characterized by	
-ile	relating to or capable of	
-ion	action or condition of	
-ious	having the quality of	
-ism	quality, process or practice of	
-ist	one who performs	
-ity	state of being	
-ive	performing or tending to	
-ize, ise	to cause to be or become	
-ly	resembling or in the manner of	

(continued)

Suffix	Meaning	Your Example
-less	without	
-ment	action or process or the result	
-ology	study of	
-y, -ry	state of	

Reading Comprehension

Reading comprehension questions appear on both the AFOQT and the ASTB. A variety of different question types appear, but the essential element of all the question types involves reading a passage carefully and answering questions based *only* on the information included.

Practice Questions

For questions 1–4, choose the answer that means the same as the capitalized word.

1. GRAPHIC

    A. unclear
    B. detailed
    C. large
    D. childish

2. INDISPENSABLE

    A. trashy
    B. ridiculous
    C. necessary
    D. uninvited

3. CONCOCT

    A. make up
    B. throw away
    C. go through
    D. walk around

4. SONIC

    A. relating to the sun
    B. relating to the moon
    C. relating to sound
    D. relating to the earth

Questions 5–8 consist of sentences in which one word is omitted. For each question, select the lettered choice that best completes the thought expressed in the sentence.

5. The committee voted to _____ the membership requirements, but the board of directors overruled the vote, and the requirements remained in place.

    A. consider
    B. remember
    C. rescind
    D. enhance

6. He tried to budget his funds, but his _____ for gambling led him into debt.

    A. talent
    B. predilection
    C. consideration
    D. distaste

7. After the cake collapsed in the oven, the cook decided the recipe needed to be _____.

    A. increased
    B. fermented
    C. consolidated
    D. amended

8. Pouring water on burning grease does not put out the fire; instead, it _____ the danger.

    A. quenches
    B. improves
    C. exacerbates
    D. expiates

Questions 9–12 consist of quotations containing one word that is incorrectly used, and is not in keeping with the meaning that each quotation is evidently intended to convey. Determine which word is incorrectly used. Then select from the lettered choices the word that, when substituted for the incorrectly used word, best helps to convey the intended meaning of the quotation.

9. "When a reader tells me my novel makes a political statement, I am distressed, because such a remark complies literature with propaganda."

   A. corrupts
   B. communicates
   C. compares
   D. confounds

10. "His baseball-oriented parents, his work ethic, and his reluctant competitive nature made it possible for Cal Ripken, Jr., the best shortstop of his era, to break the record for consecutive games played."

   A. relentless
   B. persuasive
   C. moderate
   D. contest

11. "Applicants for insurance disclose personal information to our company; state and federal laws regulate the uses of this information for any purpose, and therefore we instruct our employees to understand the importance of restraining the confidentiality of personal information supplied by you to our company."

   A. permitting
   B. maintaining
   C. complicating
   D. forwarding

12. "Arguments, in the academic sense of the term, provide a device for exploring a controversy or dispute, a tool for isolating issues in contention, and a way to evaluate different possible outcomes; furthermore, they shape and mangle each arguer's position."

   A. manipulate
   B. clarify
   C. reply
   D. obscure

Questions 13–16 require you to answer each question on the basis of the information contained in the accompanying quotation or passage. The AFOQT questions have five choices; the ASTB has four.

13. "Careful designing that complements the lot and the house as well as the planting of shrubs and trees in the proper season will guarantee successful landscaping and increase the curb appeal for a house on the market."

   The preceding quotation best supports the statement that appearance of one's property

   A. can make or break the potential sale of a house
   B. depends on how many shrubs and trees are planted
   C. should be improved to enhance property when a house is for sale
   D. depends on a talented horticulturist and a landscape architect

14. Panthers refer to two different types of animals—the leopard and the concolour. Concolours are called by many other names: Cougar, puma, mountain lion, and panther are just a few. In fact, the panther has more dictionary names than any other known predator.

   Which of the following is *not* mentioned as another name for the concolour?

   A. cougar
   B. mountain lion
   C. bobcat
   D. panther
   E. puma

15. Thomas Alva Edison is one of the most well-known inventors in history. He is most famous for inventions like the phonograph, the motion picture camera and the light bulb. However, even Edison failed in a few attempts at invention, namely in trying to develop a better way to mine iron ore during the late 1880s and early 1890s. He was tenacious in his attempts to find a method that worked, but he eventually gave up after having lost all the money he had invested in iron ore mining projects.

This passage is mainly about

A. Edison's successful inventions
B. the light bulb
C. iron ore mining
D. Edison's foolish inventions
E. Edison's invention attempt in iron ore mining

16. In an age that stresses the importance of water conservation, many plants exist that require less water than other more traditionally grown plants. To optimize water usage efficiency, experts recommend watering such plants during the cooler times of the day.

One can conclude from the preceding statements that water-efficient plants should be watered

A. at 12:00 noon, when the sun is at its hottest
B. at 6:00 a.m. when the sun has just risen
C. at 10:00 a.m. when the day is warming up
D. at 3:00 p.m. before the sun goes down
E. at 6:00 a.m. and at 3:00 p.m.

Answers and Explanations

1. **B.** *Graphic* (graph = written or drawn) means described in vivid detail or clearly drawn out, so *detailed* would most closely mean *graphic*.

2. **C.** *Indispensable* literally means not dispensable (able to be thrown away). So if something is *indispensable,* it is necessary; you cannot do away with it.

3. **A.** *Concoct* means to create or come up with, like in the sentence, "The two boys concocted a plan to skip school." *Concoct* most closely means *to make up.*

4. **C.** *Sonic* means *relating to sound* (son = sound).

5. **C.** The word *rescind* means to repeal, or to revoke.

6. **B.** The word *predilection* means inclination toward, or preference for.

7. **D.** The word *amended* means changed.

8. **C.** The word *exacerbate* means to make worse, or to increase the severity.

9. **D.** The word *complies* is incorrect. The writer is distressed, so the quotation intends to convey the idea that literature should not be thought of as propaganda. *Confounds,* which means fails to distinguish between, best expresses the sentence's meaning.

10. **A.** The word *reluctant* is incorrect. A reluctant person is unwilling to do something. *Relentless,* which means steady and persistent, describes the kind of person who could break a record.

11. **B.** The word *restraining* is incorrect because to restrain means to put limits on. The quotation is intended to reassure people that information will be kept confidential. Therefore, *maintaining* is the word that would convey the intended meaning.

12. **B.** The word *mangle,* meaning to ruin, is incorrect. The quotation is about the advantages of argument. Replacing *mangle* with *clarify* expresses that idea.

13. **C.** **A** is incorrect because it is too extreme; the quotation does not indicate that a lack of landscaping prevents the sale of a house. **B** is wrong because the passage does not reveal how many plants are called for; no number is required. **D** is incorrect because the quotation does not include a requirement for professional assistance.

14. **C.** The only name not listed in the paragraph as another name for the concolour is bobcat.

15. **E.** The third sentence states that Edison had a few failed inventions, and the rest of the selection elaborates on the iron ore mining invention attempt.

16. **B.** The selection states that such plants should be watered during the cooler parts of the day. Choice **B,** 6:00 a.m., is the coolest time of day listed.

This section reviews all the skills you need to do well on the math portions of the AFOQT and the ASTB tests, including plenty of examples. There are also practice problems for you to try so that you can be sure you've got a handle on these types of questions.

Arithmetic Reasoning and Mathematics Knowledge

Several basic arithmetic and mathematics sections appear on the AFOQT, AFAST, and ASTB exams. For example, the AFOQT exam includes the sections "Arithmetic Reasoning" and "Mathematics Knowledge." The ASTB exam has a combined "Math and Verbal" section. The following is a brief review of arithmetic and mathematics, covering some basic information that will come in handy on any of these tests.

While you might not have to know everything that we present in this section, it would be a good idea to review most of this material. In addition, take all the arithmetic and mathematics tests in this book to get a better understanding of what you know and what might require more studying.

The Numbers of Arithmetic

Whole Numbers

The numbers 0, 1, 2, 3, 4 and so on are called *whole numbers*. The whole number system is a *place value* system; that is, the value of each digit in a whole number is determined by the place it occupies. For example, in the number 6,257, the 6 is in the thousands place, the 2 is in the hundreds place, the 5 is in the tens place, and the 7 is in the ones place.

The following table contains a summary of whole number place values:

Ones	1
Tens	10
Hundreds	100
Thousands	1,000
Ten-thousands	10,000
Hundred-thousands	100,000
Millions	1,000,000
Ten millions	10,000,000
Hundred millions	100,000,000
Billions	1,000,000,000

For example, the number 5,124,678 would be read five million, one hundred twenty-four thousand, six hundred seventy-eight.

Write the number thirty million, five hundred seven thousand, three hundred twelve.

30,507,312

Write in words the number 34,521.

Thirty-four thousand, five hundred twenty-one

Rounding Whole Numbers

When you need only an approximate value of a whole number, the following procedure can be used to round off the number to a particular place:

Procedure for Rounding Whole Numbers:

1. Underline the digit in the place being rounded off.
2. If the digit to the right of the underlined digit is less than five, leave the underlined digit as it is. If the digit to the right of the underlined digit is equal to five or more, add one to the underlined digit.
3. Replace all digits to the right of the underlined digit with zeros.

Rounding whole numbers often helps you determine the correct answer to a multiple choice question more quickly.

Round off the number 34,521 to the nearest hundred.

Because we are rounding to the nearest hundred, begin by underlining the digit in the hundreds place, which is a five:

34,<u>5</u>21

Now, look to the right of the underlined digit. Because the number to the right of the five is two, leave the five as it is, and replace all digits to the right of the five with zeros.

34,500 is rounded to the nearest hundred.

Round off the number 236,789 to the nearest ten-thousand.

Because we are rounding to the nearest ten-thousand, begin by underlining the digit in the ten-thousands place, which is three:

2<u>3</u>6,789

Now, look to the right of the underlined digit. Because the number to the right of the three is six, increase three by one, obtaining four, and replace all digits to the right of this four with zeros.

240,000 is rounded to the nearest ten-thousand.

Fractions

A fraction is made up of two numbers, separated by a line that is known as a fraction bar. Typically, a fraction is used to represent a part of a whole. For example, in the following diagram, note that five out of eight pieces of the diagram are shaded:

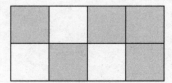

In this case, the fraction ⅝ could be used to represent the fact that five of the eight equal pieces have been shaded. In the same way, the fraction ⅜ could be used to represent the fact that three of the eight pieces have been left unshaded.

When the number on the top is *less than* the number on the bottom, fractions are said to be *proper*. Thus, the fractions ²⁄₉, ⅝ and ³⁄₇ are proper fractions. The value of a proper fraction is always less than one.

When the number on the top is either *equal to or greater than* the number on the bottom, fractions are called *improper.* For example, the fractions ⁵⁄₂, ⁷⁄₄ and ¹¹⁄₅ are improper. If the number on the top is greater than the number on the bottom, the value of the fraction is greater than one. If the number on the top and the number on the bottom are equal, such as in ⁸⁄₈, the value of the fraction is equal to one.

A *mixed number* is a whole number together with a fraction, such as 7½ or 3⅝. The mixed number 7½ represents the number seven plus the fraction ½. As we see later, every improper fraction can be written as a mixed number and vice versa.

Classify the following numbers as proper fractions, improper fractions or mixed numbers: ⁸⁄₉, ⁶⁄₆, 5⅔, ⁶⁄₄, ¹¹²⁄₁₁₃.

The numbers ⁸⁄₉ and ¹¹²⁄₁₁₃ are proper fractions, the numbers ⁶⁄₆ and ⁶⁄₄ are improper fractions, and 5⅔ is a mixed number.

Decimals

The numbers 10, 100, 1,000, 10,000 and so on, are called the *powers of 10*. Fractions like ⁷⁄₁₀, ⁵⁹⁄₁₀₀ and ³²³⁄₁₀₀₀, which have powers of 10 on the bottom, are called *decimal fractions* or *decimals*.

Decimals are typically written using a shorthand notation in which the number on the top of the fraction is written to the right of a dot, called a *decimal point*. The number on the bottom of the fraction is not written, but is indicated in the following way: If the number to the right of the decimal point contains one digit, the number on the bottom of the fraction is 10, if the number to the right of the decimal point contains two digits, the number on the bottom of the fraction is 100, and so on. Therefore, ⁷⁄₁₀ = .7, ⁵⁹⁄₁₀₀ = .59 and ³²³⁄₁₀₀₀ = .323. The decimal .7 is read "point seven" or "seven tenths." In the same way, .59 is read "point fifty-nine" or "fifty-nine hundredths."

Write the following fractions using decimal notation: ³⁄₁₀, ¹⁵⁷⁄₁₀₀₀, ⁷⁄₁₀₀.

³⁄₁₀ = .3, ¹⁵⁷⁄₁₀₀₀ = .157 and ⁷⁄₁₀₀ = .07

Note that in the last example, a 0 must be placed between the decimal point and the 7 to indicate that the number on the bottom is 100.

Write the following decimals as fractions: .7, .143, .079.

.7 = ⁷⁄₁₀, .143 = ⁴³⁄₁₀₀₀ and .079 = ⁷⁹⁄₁₀₀₀

A number that consists of a whole number and a decimal is called a *mixed decimal*. The number 354.56, for example, represents the mixed number 354⁵⁶⁄₁₀₀.

Write the following mixed numbers as mixed decimals: 76.3, 965.053.

76.3 = 76³⁄₁₀, 965.053 = 965⁵³⁄₁₀₀₀

Percents

A *percent* is a fraction whose bottom number is 100. Percents (the word percent means *per hundred*) are often written using a special symbol: %. For example, ⁶⁷⁄₁₀₀ can be written 67%, and ³⁄₁₀₀ can be written 3%. Note that, just as every percent can be written as a fraction, every percent can also be written as a decimal. For example, 51% = ⁵¹⁄₁₀₀ = .51, and 7% = ⁷⁄₁₀₀ = .07.

A quick way to rewrite a percent as a decimal is to move the decimal point two places to the left and drop the percent sign. Thus, 35% = .35. In a similar way, to write a decimal as a percent, move the decimal point two places to the right and put in a percent sign. Thus, .23 = 23%

Write the following decimals as percents: .23, .08, 1.23.

.23 = 23%, .08 = 8%, 1.23 = 123%

Write the following percents as decimals: 17%, 2%, 224%.

17% = .17, 2% = .02, 224% = 2.24

Arithmetic Operations

Addition, subtraction, multiplication and division are called the *fundamental operations of arithmetic*. To solve the word problems that are asked on the "Arithmetic Reasoning" section of the AFOQT test, you need to be able to add, subtract, multiply, and divide whole numbers and decimals. In this section, the techniques of doing this are reviewed.

Addition of Whole Numbers

When numbers are added, the result is called the *sum*. The first step in adding whole numbers is to line them up, placing ones under ones, tens under tens, hundreds under hundreds and so on. Then, add each column of numbers, beginning with the ones and moving to the tens, hundreds, thousands and so on. If the sum of the digits in any column is 10 or more, write down the last figure of the sum as a part of the answer, and then "carry" the other figures into the next column.

For example, suppose you are asked to add 37, 64 and 151. Begin by lining up the numbers in columns as shown:

$$\begin{array}{r} 37 \\ 64 \\ +151 \\ \hline \end{array}$$

Now, add the digits in the ones column: $7 + 4 + 1 = 12$. Because this number is more than 10, write the 2 below the ones column in the answer, and carry the 1 over to the tens column.

$$\begin{array}{r} \overset{1}{}37 \\ 64 \\ +151 \\ \hline 2 \end{array}$$

Now, add the 1 (that you carried over) to the other digits in the tens column: $1 + 3 + 6 + 5 = 15$. Put the 5 below the tens column, and carry the remaining 1 to the hundreds column:

$$\begin{array}{r} \overset{11}{}37 \\ 64 \\ +151 \\ \hline 52 \end{array}$$

Because $1 + 1 = 2$, the final answer would be 252:

$$\begin{array}{r} \overset{11}{}37 \\ 64 \\ +151 \\ \hline 252 \end{array}$$

Add 235, 654 and 12.

$$\begin{array}{r} 235 \\ 654 \\ +12 \\ \hline 901 \end{array}$$

Addition of Decimals

Adding decimal numbers is also very straightforward. Simply line up the decimal points of the numbers involved, and add as you normally would. Suppose, for example, you wish to add 23.31, 19 and 3.125. Begin by writing the numbers in a column, lining up the decimal points:

```
  23.31
  19.
+  3.125
```

Note that the number 19 is a whole number, and, as such, the decimal point is to the right of the number; that is, 19 and 19.0 mean the same thing. If it helps you when you add these numbers, you can fill in the missing spaces to the right of the decimal points with 0's as placeholders:

```
  23.310
  19.000
+  3.125
```

Now, position a decimal point in the answer directly below the decimal points of the numbers in the problem:

```
  23.310
  19.000
+  3.125
       .
```

Finish by adding as described previously:

```
  23.310
  19.000
+  3.125
  45.435
```

Some problems on the test ask you to add money. Of course, to add money, just line up the decimal points, as shown previously, and add the money. For example, expenses of $23.25, $52.35 and $97.16 would lead to a total expense of:

```
  $23.25
  $52.35
+ $97.16
 $172.76
```

Add 23.56, 876.01, 34 and .007.

```
   23.56
  876.01
   34
+    .007
```

If you like, before doing the addition, you can put in some 0's so that all the numbers have the same number of digits:

```
   23.560
   76.010
   34.000
+    .007
  933.577
```

If Brian buys three items priced at $3.45, $65.21 and $143.50, how much has he spent?

To find the answer to this problem, we need to add the three amounts spent:

$$
\begin{array}{r}
\$ \ \ \ 3.45 \\
\$ \ 65.21 \\
+\$143.50 \\
\hline
\$212.16
\end{array}
$$

Subtraction of Whole Numbers

When two numbers are subtracted, the result is called the *difference*. The first step in subtracting two whole numbers is to line them up, placing ones under ones, tens under tens, hundreds under hundreds and so on. Then, subtract each column of numbers, beginning with the ones and moving to the tens, hundreds, thousands and so on. If, in any step, the digit on the top is smaller than the digit on the bottom, add 10 to the digit on top by borrowing 1 from the figure directly to the left. If the sum of the digits in any column is 10 or more, write down the last figure of the sum as part of the answer, and then carry the other figures into the next column.

Let's take the following problem as an example:

$$
\begin{array}{r}
567 \\
-382 \\
\hline
\end{array}
$$

The first step is, of course, to subtract two from seven. Because seven is bigger than two, no borrowing is necessary, so this step is easy:

$$
\begin{array}{r}
567 \\
-382 \\
\hline
5
\end{array}
$$

Now, we need to subtract the numbers in the tens column. Note that 6 is smaller than 8, so we need to borrow 1 from the 5 to the left of the 6. This makes the 6 into 16, and, by borrowing the 1 from the 5, it becomes 4, as shown:

$$
\begin{array}{r}
^{4}\cancel{5}67 \\
-382 \\
\hline
5
\end{array}
$$

Next, we can subtract the 8 from the 16, which leaves us with 8. Finally, in the hundreds column, subtracting the 3 from the 4 leaves us with 1:

$$
\begin{array}{r}
^{4}\cancel{5}67 \\
-382 \\
\hline
185
\end{array}
$$

Remember that if you would like to check the answer to a subtraction problem, you can add the difference (that is, the answer) to the number you are subtracting, and see if you get the number you subtracted from. Because 185 + 382 = 567, we know we have the correct answer.

Subtract 534 from 893.

$$
\begin{array}{r}
^{8}8\cancel{9}3 \\
-534 \\
\hline
359
\end{array}
$$

Subtraction of Decimals

Just as with addition of decimals, begin by lining up the decimal points of the two numbers involved. Then, place a decimal point for the answer directly below the decimal points of the two numbers. For example:

$$
\begin{array}{r}
265.01 \\
-\ 127.5 \\
\hline
.
\end{array}
$$

When performing a subtraction, it certainly helps to write in extra 0's so that both numbers have the same number of digits to the right of the decimal point.

$$
\begin{array}{r}
265.01 \\
-\ 127.50 \\
\hline
137.51
\end{array}
$$

Of course, to subtract monetary amounts, line up the decimal points and subtract as usual. For example:

$$
\begin{array}{r}
\$324.56 \\
-\ \$\ 34.07 \\
\hline
\$290.49
\end{array}
$$

Jimmy pays a $14.51 dinner charge with a $20 bill. How much change does he receive?

Simply subtract $14.51 from $20.

$$
\begin{array}{r}
\$20.00 \\
-\$14.51 \\
\hline
\$\ 5.49
\end{array}
$$

Multiplication of Whole Numbers

When two numbers are multiplied, the result is called the *product*. The first step in multiplying whole numbers is to line the numbers up, placing ones under ones, tens under tens, hundreds under hundreds and so on. Now, consider two possible cases:

Case 1. If the number on the bottom of your multiplication contains a single digit, multiply every digit in the number on top by this digit. Start on the right, and move to the left. If, at any time, the result of a multiplication is a number that contains more than one digit, write down the digit in the mulitiplied column, and carry the remaining digit to be added to the result of the multiplication in that column.

For example, suppose you need to multiply 542 by 3. Write the problem down as shown:

$$
\begin{array}{r}
542 \\
\times\ \ \ 3 \\
\hline
\end{array}
$$

Begin by multiplying 3 by 2, and write the result, which is 6, below the 3:

$$
\begin{array}{r}
542 \\
\times\ \ \ 3 \\
\hline
6
\end{array}
$$

Next, multiply the 3 on the bottom by the 4 on the top. The result is 12. Write the 2 from the 12 below the 4 in the problem, and 1, over to the next column:

```
  ¹542
×    3
 ‾‾26
```

Finally, multiply the 3 by the 5. The result of 15 should be added to the 1 that was carried from the previous column:

```
  ¹542
×    3
 1626
```

Case 2: If the number on the bottom contains more than one digit, begin as you did previously and multiply every digit on the top by the ones digit of the number on the bottom. Write the result in the usual spot. Then move over to the tens digit of the number on the bottom, and multiply each number on the top by this number. Write the result below your previous result, but position the ones digit of the result below the number you are multiplying by. Continue on to the hundreds digit, multiplying as usual, but positioning the ones digit of the result below the hundreds digit of the number on the bottom. Continue until you have multiplied the number on top by every digit on the bottom. Finish by adding together all the "partial products" you have written.

The following example illustrates the process discussed previously. To multiply 542 by 63, set up the problem as shown:

```
  542
× 63
```

Begin exactly as you did in the preceding example, multiplying the 542 by 3. After doing this, you should have written:

```
  542
×  63
 1626
```

Now, multiply the 542 by the 6 in the tens digit of the number on the bottom. Note that the result of this multiplication is 3,252. Also note how this number is positioned:

```
   542
×   63
  1626
 3252
```

Be very careful when multiplying to line up the numbers correctly. As the last step, add the 1,626 to the 3,252, as shown:

```
    542
×    63
  1626
+ 3252
 34,146
```

Multiply 234 by 16.

```
   234
×   16
  1404
+ 234
 3,744
```

Multiplication of Decimals

When we discussed addition and subtraction with decimals, we saw that the very first step in finding the answer is to correctly position the decimal point of the answer. When multiplying numbers with decimals, the procedure is almost exactly the opposite. Begin by ignoring the decimal points in the numbers you are multiplying, and figure out the answer as if the numbers involved were whole numbers. After you have done this, you can figure out where the decimal point in the answer goes.

To figure out where the decimal point in the answer goes, you need to do a little bit of counting. Begin by counting the total number of digits to the right of the decimal points in the two numbers you were multiplying. However many digits you count when you do this should also be the number of digits to the right of the decimal point in the answer.

A few examples make this procedure very clear. We previously solved the problem:

$$
\begin{array}{r}
542 \\
\times\ \ 63 \\
\hline
1626 \\
3252\ \ \\
\hline
34{,}146 \\
\end{array}
$$

Now, suppose that instead the problem had been:

$$
\begin{array}{r}
5.42 \\
\times\ 6.3 \\
\hline
\end{array}
$$

Note that the number on the top contains two digits to the right of the decimal point and that the number on the bottom contains one digit to the right of the decimal point. To start, multiply as you normally would, ignoring the decimal points:

$$
\begin{array}{r}
5.42 \\
\times\ \ \ 6.3 \\
\hline
1626 \\
+\ 3252\ \ \\
\hline
34146 \\
\end{array}
$$
Two digits to the right of the decimal point
One digit to the right of the decimal point

Decimal point needs to be positioned

Now, because we have a total of 2 + 1 = 3 digits to the right of the decimal point in the two numbers we are multiplying, we need to have three digits to the right of the decimal point in the product:

$$
\begin{array}{r}
5.42 \\
\times\ \ \ 6.3 \\
\hline
1626 \\
+\ 3252\ \ \\
\hline
34146 \\
\end{array}
$$
Two digits to the right of the decimal point
One digit to the right of the decimal point

Three digits to the right of the decimal point in the answer

That's all there is to it! What if the problem had been instead:

$$
\begin{array}{r}
5.42 \\
\times\ .63 \\
\hline
\end{array}
$$

In this case, we have a total of four digits to the right of the decimal point in the two numbers we are multiplying. Thus, the answer is not 34.146, but rather 3.4146.

Note that if you are multiplying an amount of money by a whole number, you can use the preceding process. Of course, when you do this, you have a total of two digits to the right of the decimal point in the two numbers you are multiplying, so the answer ends up looking like money, that is, it has two digits to the right of the decimal point.

Multiply 23.4 by 1.6.

> 23.4 *One digit to the right of the decimal point*
> ×   1.6 *One digit to the right of the decimal point*
> ‾‾‾‾‾‾
> 1404
> + 234
> ‾‾‾‾‾‾
> 37.44 *Two digits to the right of the decimal point in the answer*

John buys four calculators, each of which costs $3.51. What is the total cost of the four calculators?

> $3.51 *Two digits to the right of the decimal point*
> ×   4 *No digit to the right of the decimal point*
> ‾‾‾‾‾‾
> $14.04 *Two digits to the right of the decimal point in the answer*

Division of Whole Numbers

When one number is divided into another, the result is called the *quotient*. Division is probably the most complicated of the four fundamental arithmetic operations, but it becomes easier when you realize that the procedure for division consists of a series of four steps, repeated over and over again. The four steps are illustrated in the following sample problems.

Suppose, for example, you are asked to divide 7 into 245. Begin by writing the problem in the usual way:

$$7\overline{)245}$$

Now, for the first step, determine the number of times that 7 goes into 24. Because 7 goes into 24 three times (with something left over), begin by writing a 3 above the 4 in the division:

$$7\overline{)245}^{\,3}$$

As a second step, multiply the 3 by the 7 to obtain 21 and write this product below the 24:

$$\begin{array}{r} 3 \\ 7\overline{)245} \\ 21 \end{array}$$

The third step is to subtract the 21 from the 24. When you do this, you get 3, of course. This should be written below the 21, as shown:

$$\begin{array}{r} 3 \\ 7\overline{)245} \\ -21 \\ \hline 3 \end{array}$$

The final step in the four-step process is to "bring down" the next digit from the number we are dividing into. This next (and last) digit is 5, so bring it down next to the 3:

$$
\begin{array}{r}
3 \\
7\,)\overline{245} \\
-\,21 \\
\hline
35
\end{array}
$$

Now, the entire procedure starts over again. Divide 7 into 35. It goes in 5 times, so put a 5 next to the 3 in the solution.

$$
\begin{array}{r}
35 \\
7\,)\overline{245} \\
-\,21 \\
\hline
35
\end{array}
$$

When you multiply and subtract, note that you end up with 0. This means that you have finished, and the quotient (answer) is 35:

$$
\begin{array}{r}
35 \\
7\,)\overline{245} \\
-\,21 \\
\hline
35 \\
-\,35 \\
\hline
0
\end{array}
$$

The procedure for dividing by two digit numbers (or even larger numbers) is essentially the same, but involves a bit more computation. As an example, consider the following problem:

$$
23\,)\overline{11408}
$$

Note that 23 does not go into 11, so we have to start with 114. To determine how many times 23 goes into 114, you are going to have to estimate. Perhaps you might think that 23 is almost 25, and that it seems as if 25 would go into 114 four times. So, let's try 4. Write a 4 on top, and multiply, subtract, and bring down in the usual way:

$$
\begin{array}{r}
4 \\
23\,)\overline{11408} \\
-\,92 \\
\hline
220
\end{array}
$$

Continue, as before, by trying to estimate the number of times 23 goes into 220. If you try 9, things continue rather nicely:

$$
\begin{array}{r}
49 \\
23\,)\overline{11408} \\
-\,92 \\
\hline
220 \\
-\,207 \\
\hline
138
\end{array}
$$

As a final step, estimate that 23 goes into 138 six times:

```
        496
23 )11408
    − 92
     220
    − 207
      138
    − 138
        0
```

If at any step you make the incorrect estimate, simply modify your estimate and start over. For example, suppose that in the last step of the preceding example, you had guessed that 23 would go into 138 seven times. Look what would have happened:

```
        497
23 )11408
    − 92
     220
    − 207
      138
    − 161
```

Because 161 is larger than 138, it means that you have over estimated. Try again with a smaller number.

Divide 12 into 540.

```
       45
12 )540
   − 48
     60
   − 60
      0
```

Remember that division problems can always be checked by multiplying. In this case, because $12 \times 45 = 540$, we know we have the right answer.

Division with Decimals

Recall that when we added and subtracted with decimals, we began by positioning the decimal point for the answer, and then added or subtracted as usual. When you are dividing a whole number into a decimal number, the idea is similar; begin by putting a decimal point for the quotient (answer) directly above the decimal point in the number you are dividing into. Then divide as normal. So, for example, if you need to divide 4 into 142.4, begin as shown:

```
         .
4 )142.4
```
*Note the decimal po*int *positioned above the decimal po*int *in* 142.4

Now, divide in the usual way:

```
      35.6
4 )142.4
  − 12
    22
  − 20
    24
  − 24
     0
```

That's all that there is to it.

A dinner bill of $92.80 is shared equally between four friends. How much does each friend pay?

To find the answer, we need to divide $92.80 by 4.

```
        23.20
    4 ) 92.80
      − 8
        ‾‾
        12
      − 12
        ‾‾
        08
       − 8
         ‾‾
         00
        − 0
          ‾
          0
```

Arithmetic Word Problems

The Arithmetic sections of the AFOQT and ASTB might present word problems that involve arithmetic calculations. If you have learned how to do the computations discussed previously, the hardest part of these word problems is to determine which of the arithmetic operations is needed to solve the problem.

Basic One-Step and Two-Step Problems

Some of the word problems on the test involve only a single computation. Others are multiple-step problems in which several computations need to be performed. Examples of both types of problems are shown. Following these examples are some special types of problems that also appear on the test.

Brett earned $225.25 during his first week on a new job. During the second week, he earned $325.50, during the third week he earned $275.00, and during the fourth week he earned $285.75. How much did he earn over the course of the four weeks?

It should be obvious that, in this problem, all we need to do is add the weekly payments to find the total.

```
      $225.25
      $325.50
      $275.00
  +   $285.75
    $1,111.50
```

An office building is 540 feet high, including a 23 foot antenna tower on the roof. How tall is the building without the antenna tower?

It should be clear that, in this problem, we need to remove the 23 foot tower from the top of the building by subtracting. This is a one-step problem:

```
    540
  −  23
    517  feet
```

The building is 517 feet tall without the antenna tower.

Brett has a job that pays him $8.25 an hour. If during the first week he works 21 hours, and during the second week he works 19 hours, how much money has he earned over the course of the two weeks? This is an example of a two-step problem. One way to find the answer is to find how much he made each week by multiplying, and then to add the two weekly totals:

Week 1	Week 2
$8.25	$8.25
× 21	× 19
$173.25	$156.75

Because $173.25 + $156.75 = $330, Brett earned $330.

Perhaps you have noticed an easier way to solve the problem. If you begin by adding the number of hours he worked each week, you get 21 + 19 = 40 as a total. Then, you only need to multiply $8.25 by 40 to get the answer.

At a restaurant, the bill for dinner is $137.50. John contributes $20 to the bill, and then leaves. The rest of the bill is split evenly between the remaining five people. How much does each person contribute?

This is another two-step word problem. After John leaves, $137.50 - $20 = $117.50 remains to be paid. This has to be divided by the five people that remain.

$$
\begin{array}{r}
23.50 \\
5\overline{)117.50} \\
-10 \\
\overline{17} \\
-15 \\
\overline{25} \\
-25 \\
\overline{00} \\
-0 \\
\overline{0}
\end{array}
$$

Clearly, each person needs to pay $23.50.

Percent and Interest Problems

These tests also contain some problems that involve working with percents and interest. Typically, these problems involve finding percents of numbers. You need to remember to write the percent as a decimal. Several examples of this type of problem follow.

A family spends 26% of its monthly income on their mortgage. If their monthly income is $2,400, how much do they spend on their mortgage each month? This problem asks us to find 26% of $2,400. To do this, write 26% as .26, and then multiply.

$$
\begin{array}{r}
\$2,400 \\
\times \quad .26 \quad \textit{Two digits to the right of the decimal point} \\
\hline
14400 \\
+4800 \\
\hline
624.00 \quad \textit{Two digits to the right of the decimal point in the answer}
\end{array}
$$

Thus, the monthly expenditure for the mortgage is $624.00.

Bob invests $5,500 in an account that pays 9% annual interest. How much interest does he earn in one year? This is another one-step percent word problem. For this problem, we need to find 9% of $5,500. Begin by writing 9% as a decimal, which is .09. (Note carefully that 9% is equal to .09, not .9.) Then multiply to finish the problem:

$$
\begin{array}{r}
\$5,500 \\
\times \quad .09 \\
\hline
495.00
\end{array}
$$
*Two digits to the right of the decimal po*int
*Two digits to the right of the decimal po*int *in the answer*

He earns $495 in interest in one year.

Bob invests $5,500 in an account that pays 9% annual interest. How much money is in the account at the end of one year? Note that this problem is based on the preceding one, but includes an extra step. After determining how much interest is in the account at the end of the year, this amount needs to be added to the $5,500 to obtain $5,500 + $495 = $5,995.

Ratio and Proportion Problems

Another type of word problem that might appear on these tests involves ratios and proportions.

A ratio is a comparison of two numbers. For example, a school might say that its student-teacher ratio is eight to one. This means that, for every eight students at the school, there is one teacher. Another way to look at this ratio is that, for every one teacher, there are eight students.

You might have seen a ratio written with a colon between the two numbers, like 8:1. A ratio can also be written as a fraction, like $\frac{8}{1}$. When it comes to solving word problems involving ratios, it is usually best to write the ratios as fractions so that you can perform computations with them.

In the preceding ratio, we were comparing a number of people (students) to a number of people (teachers). When a ratio is used to compare two different kinds of quantities, it is called a *rate*. As an example, suppose that a car drives 300 miles in 5 hours. Then we can write the rate of the car as $\frac{300 \text{ miles}}{5 \text{ hours}}$. If we divide the number on the bottom into the number on the top, we get the number 60, and can then say that the rate of the car is $\frac{60 \text{ miles}}{1 \text{ hour}}$ or simply 60 *miles per hour*. Sixty miles per hour is also known as the speed of the car.

When we divide the number on the bottom of a ratio or a rate into the number on the top, the result is what is known as a *unit ratio* or a *unit rate*. Often, solving ratio problems hinges on computing a unit ratio or rate. The techniques of working with ratios and rates are illustrated in the following problems.

A supermarket customer bought a 15 ounce box of oatmeal for $3.45. What was the cost per ounce of oatmeal? The rate of cost to ounces is given in the problem as $\frac{\$3.45}{15 \text{ ounces}}$. To find the *unit cost,* we divide $3.45 by 15 ounces.

$$
\begin{array}{r}
.23 \\
15 \overline{)3.45} \\
-30 \\
\hline
45 \\
-45 \\
\hline
0
\end{array}
$$

Therefore, the cost is 23 cents per ounce.

A supermarket sells a 15 ounce box of oatmeal for $3.45. At the same rate, what would be the cost of a 26 ounce box of oatmeal? This type of problem is what is known as a proportion problem. In a proportion problem, you are given the rate at which two quantities vary, and asked to find the value of one of the quantities given the value of the other. A good way to approach a problem of this type is by first finding the unit rate and then multiplying. Note that in the preceding problem we found the unit rate of the oatmeal; it was 23 cents per ounce. The cost of 26 ounces, then, is 23 cents times 26:

$$
\begin{array}{r}
.23 \\
\times\ 26 \\
\hline
138 \\
+46 \\
\hline
5.98
\end{array}
$$

Thus, 26 ounces costs $5.98.

A bus travels at a constant rate of 45 miles per hour. How far can the bus go in 5½ hours? Previously, we saw that the rate of a vehicle is equal to its distance divided by its time. In the same way, the distance that the vehicle travels is equal to its rate multiplied by its time. You might remember from previous math classes that this formula is written $d = r \times t$, meaning distance = rate × time.

It is easier to solve this problem if we write 5½ as its decimal equivalent 5.5. Then, we simply need to multiply 45 by 5.5 to find the distance:

$$
\begin{array}{r}
45 \\
\times\ 5.5 \\
\hline
225 \\
+225 \\
\hline
247.5
\end{array}
$$

Thus, the car goes 247.5 miles in 5½ hours.

Measurement Problems

Some of the problems on the exams involve working with measurements and geometric shapes. Two concepts that you should be familiar with are *perimeter* and *area*.

The perimeter of a figure is the distance around it, that is, the sum of the lengths of its sides. Perimeter is measured in units of length, such as inches, feet, or meters. The area of a figure is the amount of surface contained within its boundaries. Area is measured in square units, such as square inches, square feet, or square meters.

Two important geometric figures that you should know how to find the perimeter and area of are the rectangle and the square.

A rectangle is a figure with four sides. The opposite sides are the same length. For example, the following figure depicts a rectangle with a measurement of four inches by three inches:

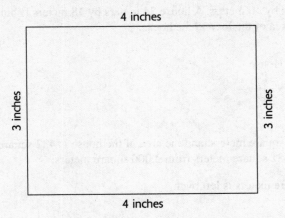

4 inches

3 inches

3 inches

4 inches

The perimeter of a rectangle is given by the formula $P = 2l + 2w$, which means that, to find the perimeter of a rectangle, you need to add together two lengths and two widths. If the rectangle is four inches by three inches, then its perimeter is $P = 3 + 3 + 4 + 4 = 14$ inches.

The area of a rectangle is given by the formula $A = l \times w$, which means that the area is the length times the width. In this case, the area would be 3 inches $\times$ 4 inches = 12 square inches. By the way, a square inch is simply a square that is an inch long on all 4 sides. If you look again at the preceding picture of the rectangle, you can see that it can be thought of as consisting of 12 squares that are each an inch on all sides (see the following figure). That is what is meant when we say that the area is 12 square inches.

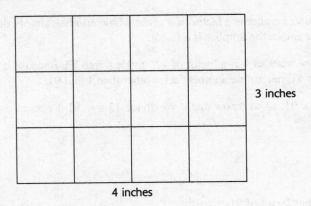

3 inches

4 inches

A square is a rectangle with 4 equal sides. In the case of a square, the formulas for the perimeter and the area of a rectangle take a simpler form. The perimeter of a square is $P = 4s$, where s is the length of the side, and the area is $A = s \times s$.

It also helps to know some common measurement conversions, such as 12 inches are in a foot, and 3 feet (or 36 inches) are in a yard. The following examples are based on the concepts discussed previously.

A small bag of fertilizer covers 20 square feet of lawn. How many bags are needed to cover a lawn that is 4 yards by 3 yards? The most direct way to handle this problem is to change the measurements of the lawn to feet because that is how the capacity of the bag of fertilizer is measured. A lawn that is 4 yards by 3 yards is 12 feet by 9 feet. Thus, its area is 12 feet $\times$ 9 feet = 108 square feet. Now, to determine the number of bags needed, we need to divide 20 into 108.

When we do this division, we get the answer 5.4 bags. Because you obviously cannot purchase 5.4 bags, you would need 6 bags to cover the lawn.

A lot of land measures 50 meters by 40 meters. A house 24 meters by 18 meters is built on the land. How much area is left over? Begin by finding the area of the lot and the house:

$$
\begin{array}{cc}
\text{Lot} & \text{House} \\
50 & 24 \\
\times\ \ 40 & \times\ \ 18 \\
\hline
2000 & \overline{432}
\end{array}
$$

Thus, the area of the lot is 2,000 square meters, and the area of the house is 432 square meters. To determine how much area is left, we need to subtract 432 square meters from 2,000 square meters:

$2,000 - 432 = 1,568$ square meters is left over.

Number Theory

Factors

Remember that earlier we defined *whole numbers* as the set of numbers 0, 1, 2, 3, 4, 5 and so on. We are now going to look at some of the properties of whole numbers, and then of the set of numbers called *integers*.

To begin, a *factor* of a given whole number is any number that can be used in a multiplication that results in the given whole number. For example, consider the whole number 24. Both 6 and 4 are factors of 24 because $6 \times 4 = 24$. Further, both 2 and 12 are factors of 24 because $2 \times 12 = 24$. Technically, both 1 and 24 are also factors of 24 because $1 \times 24 = 24$.

To determine whether a particular number is a factor of a given whole number, simply divide the number into the given whole number. If no remainder exists, the number is a factor.

Is 8 a factor of 72? To determine whether 8 is a factor of 72, divide 8 into 72. Because it goes in evenly (9 times), 8 is a factor of 72. If 13 is a factor of 91, determine another factor other than 1 and 91.

We are told that 13 is a factor of 91, so we know that if we divide 13 into 91 it goes in evenly. If we do this division, we get:

$$13 \overline{)91} \ \ ^{7}$$

Thus, $13 \times 7 = 91$, so 7 is another factor of 91.

Common Factors

A number that is a factor of two different whole numbers is called a *common factor*, or a *common divisor*, of those numbers. As the following examples show, two given whole numbers might have no common factors (other than, of course, 1), or they might have one or more. If two numbers have several common factors, the largest one is called the *greatest common factor*.

Find all the common factors and the greatest common factor of 36 and 48.

The factors of 36 are 1, 2, 3, 4, 6, 9, 12, 18, and 36.

The factors of 48 are 1, 2, 3, 4, 6, 8, 12, 16, 32, and 48.

The common factors of 36 and 48 are 1, 2, 3, 4, 6, and 12.

The greatest common factor is 12.

Find all the common factors of 35 and 66.

> The factors of 35 are 1, 5, 7, and 35.
>
> The factors of 66 are 1, 2, 3, 6, 11, 22, 33, and 66.
>
> The only common factor is 1.

Prime Numbers

Obviously, every number has at least two factors: the number itself and 1. Some other numbers have additional factors as well. For example, the number 14 not only has 1 and 14 as factors, but also 2 and 7 because $2 \times 7 = 14$.

Numbers that have no additional factors other than themselves and 1, are known as *prime numbers*. An example of a prime number is 13. While 1 and 13 divide evenly into 13, no other whole numbers divide evenly into 13.

By definition, the smallest prime number is 2. The first 10 prime numbers are:

> 2, 3, 5, 7, 11, 13, 17, 19, 23, 29

To determine if a number is prime or not, you need to find out whether any whole numbers (other than the number itself and 1) divide evenly into the number.

Which of the following numbers are prime: 33, 37, 39, 42, 43?

> 33 is not prime because $33 = 3 \times 11$.
>
> 37 is prime; it has no factors other than 1 and 37.
>
> 39 is not prime because $39 = 3 \times 13$.
>
> 42 is not prime because $42 = 2 \times 21$ or 6×7, and so on.
>
> 43 is prime; it has no factors other than 1 and 43.

A number that is not prime, is called a *composite* number. Any composite number can be *prime factored;* that is, it can be written as a product of prime numbers (excluding 1) in one and only one way. For example, 35 is a composite number, and can be prime factored as 5×7. The number 12 is also composite. Note that 2×6 is a factorization of 12, but is not the prime factorization because 6 is not prime. The prime factorization of 12 would be $2 \times 2 \times 3$. The quickest way to prime factor a number is two break the number up as a product of two smaller numbers, and then to break these two numbers up, until you are left with only prime numbers. The following example illustrates this process.

Prime factor the number 150.

By inspection, you can see that 150 can be factored as 15×10. This is not the prime factorization, however, as neither 15 nor 10 is prime. The number 15, however, can be further broken down as $15 = 3 \times 5$, and both 3 and 5 are prime. The number 10 can be further broken down as $10 = 2 \times 5$, and both 2 and 5 are prime. Therefore, the number 150 can be prime factored as $3 \times 5 \times 2 \times 5$. When prime factoring numbers, it is standard to rearrange the factors so that the numbers are in increasing order. Therefore, the prime factorization of 150 can best be expressed as $2 \times 3 \times 5 \times 5$.

What are the prime factors of 54?

You can begin by writing 54 as, for example, 2×27. The number 2 is prime, but 27 is not, so it can be further factored. Because 27 is 3×9, we get $54 = 2 \times 3 \times 9$. Now, 3 is prime, but 9 is not, so we need to factor the 9. The only way to do this is $9 = 3 \times 3$, so the prime factorization of 54 is $2 \times 3 \times 3 \times 3$. Thus, the prime factors of 54 are 2 and 3.

Multiples

A multiple of a given whole number is a number that results from the multiplication of the given whole number by another whole number factor. For example, the multiples of 7 are 7, 14, 21, 28, 35, 42, 49 and so on because $7 = 7 \times 1$, $14 = 7 \times 2$, $21 = 7 \times 3$ and so on.

A *common multiple* of two numbers is a number that is a multiple of both of the numbers. For example, 32 is a common multiple of 8 and 16 because it is a multiple of both 8 and 16. Should you ever need to find a common multiple of two numbers, one quick way to find one is to multiply the two numbers together. For example, a common multiple of 4 and 10 would be $4 \times 10 = 40$. Note, however, that 40 is not the smallest common multiple of 4 and 10 because 20 is also a common multiple.

The smallest common multiple of two numbers is called the *least common multiple,* abbreviated LCM. A quick way to find the LCM of two numbers is to write out the first several multiples of each number, and then find the smallest multiple that they have in common. The following examples show how to do this.

Find the first 8 multiples of 11.

To answer this question, we simply need to compute 11×1, 11×2, 11×3 and so on. The first 8 multiples would be 11, 22, 33, 44, 55, 66, 77 and 88.

Find the least common multiple of 3 and 8.

> The first several multiples of 3 are 3, 6, 9, 12, 15, 18, 21, 24 and 27.
> The first several multiples of 8 are 8, 16, 24 and 32.
> Clearly, the LCM is 24, which in this case is the same as the product of 3 and 8.

Find the LCM of 6 and 9.

> The first several multiples of 6 are 6, 12, 18, 24 and 30.
> The first several multiples of 9 are 9, 18, 27 and 36.
> Clearly, the LCM is 18, which in this case is less than $6 \times 9 = 54$.

Exponents

As we saw previously, the numbers used in multiplication are called factors. Whenever the same factor is repeated more than once, a special shorthand, called *exponential notation,* can be used to simplify the expression. In this notation, the repeated factor is written only once; above and to the right of this number is written another number that is called the *exponent,* or *power,* indicating the number of times the base is repeated.

For example, instead of writing 7×7, we can write 7^2. This expression is read "seven to the second power," or more simply, "seven squared," and it represents the fact that the seven is multiplied by itself two times. In the same way, $5 \times 5 \times 5 \times 5$ can be written as 5^4, which is read "five to the fourth power," or simply "five to the fourth."

Recall that previously, we prime factored the number 150 and obtained $2 \times 3 \times 5 \times 5$. It is more common (and a bit simpler) to write this prime factorization using exponential notation as $2 \times 3 \times 5^2$.

What is the value of 3^5? Based on the preceding definition, 3^5 represents $3 \times 3 \times 3 \times 3 \times 3 = 243$.

Simplify the expression $a \times a \times a \times a \times b \times b \times b \times b \times b \times b \times b$ by using exponential notation. Because we have four factors of a and seven factors of b, the expression is equal to $a^4 \times b^7$.

Prime factor the number 72, and write the prime factorization using exponential notation. Begin by prime factoring the number 72. One way to do this is as follows:

> $72 = 2 \times 36 = 2 \times 6 \times 6 = 2 \times 2 \times 3 \times 2 \times 3 = 2 \times 2 \times 2 \times 3 \times 3.$

Then, writing this using exponents, we get $2^3 \times 3^2$.

Square Roots

The *square root* of a given number is the number whose square is equal to the given number. For example, the square root of 25, is the number that yields 25 when multiplied by itself. Clearly, this number would be 5 because $5 \times 5 = 25$. The square root of 25 is denoted by the symbol $\sqrt{25}$.

The square roots of most numbers turn out to be messy, infinite nonrepeating decimal numbers. For example, $\sqrt{2}$ is equal to 1.414213562. . . . When such numbers appear on the test, you are able to leave them in what is known as *radical form;* that is, if the answer to a problem is $\sqrt{2}$, you can express the answer as $\sqrt{2}$, without worrying about its value.

Certain numbers, however, have nice whole-number square roots. Such numbers are called *perfect squares*. You should certainly be familiar with the square roots of the first 10 or so perfect squares. They are shown in the following table:

Perfect Square	Square Root
1	$\sqrt{1} = 1$
4	$\sqrt{4} = 2$
9	$\sqrt{9} = 3$
16	$\sqrt{16} = 4$
25	$\sqrt{25} = 5$
36	$\sqrt{36} = 6$
49	$\sqrt{49} = 7$
64	$\sqrt{64} = 8$
81	$\sqrt{81} = 9$
100	$\sqrt{100} = 10$

From time to time, you might be asked to find the *cube root* of a number. The cube root is defined in a way similar to that of the square root. For example, the cube root of eight is the number that when multiplied by itself three times, is equal to eight. Clearly, the cube root of eight would be two because $2 \times 2 \times 2 = 8$. A special notation also exists for the cube root. The cube root of eight is written as $\sqrt[3]{8}$. Therefore, $\sqrt[3]{8} = 2$.

Just as perfect squares have nice whole-number square roots, *perfect cubes* have whole-number cube roots. You don't really have to learn many of these, as they become large very quickly, but it is helpful to know the cube roots of the first five perfect cubes. The following table gives the values for these numbers.

Perfect Cube	Cube Root
1	$\sqrt[3]{1} = 1$
8	$\sqrt[3]{8} = 2$
27	$\sqrt[3]{27} = 3$
64	$\sqrt[3]{64} = 4$
125	$\sqrt[3]{125} = 5$

What is the value of $\sqrt{81} \times \sqrt{36}$? Because $\sqrt{81} = 9$ and $\sqrt{36} = 6$, $\sqrt{81} \times \sqrt{36} = 9 \times 6 = 54$

What is the value of $12\sqrt{49}$? To begin, you must know that $12\sqrt{49}$ is shorthand for $12 \times \sqrt{49}$. Because $\sqrt{49} = 7$, $12\sqrt{49} = 12 \times 7 = 84$.

The Order of Operations

Whenever a numerical expression contains more than one mathematical operation, the order in which the operations are performed can affect the answer. For example, consider the simple expression $2 + 3 \times 5$. On one hand, if the addition is performed first, the expression becomes $5 \times 5 = 25$. On the other hand, if the multiplication is performed first, the expression becomes $2 + 15 = 17$. To eliminate this ambiguity, mathematicians have established a procedure that makes the order in which the operations need to be performed specific. This procedure is called the *Order of Operations,* and is stated here:

The Order of Operations

1. Perform all operations in parentheses or any other grouping symbol.
2. Evaluate all exponents and roots.
3. Perform all multiplications and divisions in the order they appear in the expression, from left to right.
4. Perform all additions and subtractions in the order they appear in the expression, from left to right.

Note that the Order of Operations consists of four steps. A common acronym to help you remember these steps is PEMDAS: parentheses, exponents, multiplication and division, addition and subtraction. If you choose to memorize this acronym, be careful. The expression PEMDAS might make it appear as if the Order of Operations has six steps, but it actually has only four. In the third step, all multiplications and divisions are done in the order they appear. In the fourth step, all additions and subtractions are done in the order they appear. The following examples make this clear.

Evaluate the expression $18 - 6 \div 3 \times 7 + 4$.

Resist the temptation to begin by subtracting 6 from 18. Because this expression contains no parentheses and no roots, begin by starting on the left and performing all multiplications and divisions in the order they occur. This means that the division must be performed first. Because $6 \div 3 = 2$, we obtain:

$$18 - 6 \div 3 \times 7 + 4 = 18 - 2 \times 7 + 4$$

Next, we do the multiplication:

$$18 - 2 \times 7 + 4 = 18 - 14 + 4$$

Finally, we subtract, and then add:

$$18 - 14 + 4 = 4 + 4 = 8$$

Evaluate $14 - 2(1 + 5)$.

To begin, the operation in parentheses must be performed. This makes the expression $14 - 2(6)$. Now, remember that a number written next to another number in parentheses, such as $2(6)$, is a way of indicating multiplication. Because multiplication comes before subtraction in the Order of Operations, we multiply $2(6)$ to get 12. Finally, $14 - 12 = 2$.

Evaluate $5^3 - 3(8 - 2)^2$.

The first operation to perform is the one in parentheses, which gives us $5^3 - 3(6)^2$.

Next, evaluate the two exponents: $125 - 3(36)$. We now multiply, and then finish by subtracting: $125 - 108 = 17$.

Operations with Integers

When we include the negatives of the whole numbers along with the whole numbers, we obtain the set of numbers called the *integers*. Therefore, the integers are the set of numbers:

$$\ldots -4, -3, -2, -1, 0, 1, 2, 3, 4, \ldots$$

The ellipses to the left and right indicate that the numbers continue forever in both directions.

Up to this point, when we have talked about adding, subtracting, multiplying and dividing, we have always been working with positive numbers. However, on one of these tests, you are just as likely to have to compute with negative numbers as positive numbers. Therefore, let's take a look at how mathematical operations are performed on positive *and* negative numbers; that is, how mathematical operations are performed on *signed* numbers.

Adding Positive and Negative Numbers

Two different circumstances must be considered as we discuss how to add positive and negative numbers. The first circumstance is how to add two signed numbers with the same sign. If the numbers that you are adding have the same sign, simply add the numbers in the usual way. The sum, then, has the same sign as the numbers you have added. For example, $(+4) + (+7) = +11$. This, of course, is the usual positive number addition you are used to.

Consider $(-5) + (-9) = -14$.

In this problem, because the signs of the two numbers we are adding are the same, simply add them $(5 + 9 = 14)$. The result is negative because both numbers are negative. It might help to think of positive numbers as representing a gain, and negative numbers as representing a loss. In this case, $(-5) + (-9)$ represents a loss of 5 followed by a loss 9, which, of course, is a loss of 14.

Now, what if you have to add two numbers with different signs? Again, the rule is simple. Begin by ignoring the signs, and subtract the two numbers: the smaller from the larger. The sign of the answer is the same as the sign of the number with the larger size.

For example, to compute $(+9) + (-5)$, begin by computing $9 - 5 = 4$. Because 9 is bigger than 5, the answer is positive, or +4. You can think of the problem in this way: A gain of 9 followed by a loss of 5 is equivalent to a gain of 4.

On the other hand, to compute $(-9) + (+5)$, begin in the same way by computing $9 - 5 = 4$. This time, however, the larger number is negative, so the answer is −4. In other words, a loss of 9 followed by a gain of 5 is equivalent to a loss of 4.

Consider $(+6) + (-8) + (+12) + (-4)$.

Two ways can be used to evaluate this expression. One way is to simply perform the additions in order from left to right. To begin, $(+6) + (-8) = -2$. Then, $(-2) + (+12) = +10$. Finally, $(+10) + (-4) = +6$.

The other way to solve the problem, which might be a bit faster, is to add the positive numbers, then add the negative numbers, and then combine the result. In this case, $(+6) + (+12) = +18$; $(-8) + (-4) = -12$, and finally, $(+18) + (-12) = +6$.

Subtracting Positive and Negative Numbers

The easiest way to perform a subtraction on two signed numbers is to change the problem to an equivalent addition problem, that is, an addition problem with the same answer. To do this, you simply need to change the sign of the second number and add instead of subtract. For example, suppose you need to compute $(+7) - (-2)$. This problem has the same solution as the addition problem $(+7) + (+2)$ and is therefore equal to +9. Take a look at the following samples that help clarify this procedure:

Determine the value of $(-7) - (+2)$.

To evaluate this, we make it into an equivalent addition problem by changing the sign of the second number. Therefore, $(-7) - (+2) = (-7) + (-2) = -9$.

In the same way, we see that $(-7) - (-2) = (-7) + (+2) = -5$.

Find the value of $(-7) - (+4) - (-3) + (-1)$.

Begin by rewriting the problem with all subtractions expressed as additions:

$$(-7) - (+4) - (-3) + (-1) = (-7) + (-4) + (+3) + (-1)$$

Now, just add the four numbers in the usual way:

$$(-7) + (-4) + (+3) + (-1) = (-11) + (+3) + (-1) = -8 + (-1) = -9.$$

Multiplying and Dividing Positive and Negative Numbers

An easy way to multiply (or divide) signed numbers is to begin by ignoring the signs, and multiply (or divide) in the usual way. Then, to determine the sign of the answer, count up the number of negative signs in the original problem. If the number of negative signs is even, the answer is positive; if the number of negative signs is odd, the answer is negative. For example, $(-2) \times (+3) = -6$ because the original problem has one negative sign. However, $(-2) \times (-3) = +6$ because the original problem has two negative signs.

What about the problem $(-4) \times (-2) \times (-1) \times (+3)$? First of all, ignoring the signs and multiplying the four numbers, we get 24. Because the problem has a total of three negative signs, the answer must be negative. Therefore, the answer is -24.

Division works in exactly the same way. For example, $(-24) \div (+6) = -4$, but $(-24) \div (-6) = +4$.

Find the value of $\dfrac{(-6)(+10)}{(-2)(-5)}$.

The easiest way to proceed with this problem is to evaluate the number on the top and the number on the bottom separately, and then divide them. Because $(-6)(+10) = -60$, and $(-2)(-5) = +10$, we have $\dfrac{(-6)(+10)}{(-2)(-5)} = \dfrac{-60}{+10} = -6$.

Consider $(-5)(-2)(+4) - 6(-3) =$.

The multiplications in this problem must be done before the subtractions. Because:

$$(-5)(-2)(+4) = 40, \text{ and } 6(-3) = -18, \text{ we have:}$$

$$(-5)(-2)(+4) - 6(-3) = 40 - (-18) = 40 + 18 = 58.$$

Negative Numbers and Exponents

Be a little bit careful when evaluating negative numbers raised to powers. For example, if you are asked to find the value of $(-2)^8$, the answer is positive because we are technically multiplying eight -2s. For a similar reason, the value of $(-2)^9$ is negative.

Also, you must be careful to distinguish between an expression like $(-3)^2$ and one like -3^2. The expression $(-3)^2$ means -3×-3 and is equal to $+9$, but -3^2 means $-(3^2)$, which is equal to -9.

Evaluate $-2^4 - (-2)^2$.

Evaluating the exponents first, we get $-2^4 - (-2)^2 = -16 - (4) = -16 + -4 = -20$.

Find the value of $\dfrac{(-3)^3 + (-2)(-6)}{-5^2 + (-19)(-1)}$.

Again, let's determine the values of the top and bottom separately, and then divide. To begin, $(-3)^3 = -27$, and $(-2)(-6) = +12$, so the value on the top is $-27 + 12 = -15$. On the bottom, we have $-25 + 19 = -6$. Therefore:

$$\frac{(-3)^3 + (-2)(-6)}{-5^2 + (-19)(-1)} = \frac{-15}{-6} = \frac{15}{6} = 2.5$$

Operations with Fractions

In the "Arithmetic Reasoning" section, we discussed how to write a fraction as a decimal and vice versa. One thing that we did not discuss in that section was how to perform arithmetic operations on fractions. It is now time to review how to do this.

You probably remember learning a procedure called *reducing* or *simplifying* fractions. Simplifying a fraction refers to rewriting it in an equivalent form, with smaller numbers. As an easy example, consider the fraction $\frac{5}{10}$. This fraction can be simplified by dividing the top and bottom by the number 5. If we do this division, we get $\frac{5}{10} = \frac{5 \div 5}{10 \div 5} = \frac{1}{2}$. Thus, $\frac{5}{10}$ and $\frac{1}{2}$ have the same value, but $\frac{1}{2}$ is in simpler form.

In general, to simplify a fraction, you need to find a number that divides evenly into both the top and bottom, and then do this division. Sometimes, after you divide by one number, you might notice another number you can further divide by. As an example, suppose you wish to simplify $\frac{12}{18}$. The first thing that you might notice is that the top and bottom can be divided by 2. If you do this division, you get the fraction $\frac{6}{9}$. Now, this fraction can be further divided by 3, and if you do this division, you get the fraction $\frac{2}{3}$. Because no other numbers (except 1, of course) can divide evenly into the top and bottom, we have reduced the fraction to its *lowest terms*. If a problem on one of the tests has a fractional answer, you should always reduce the answer to its lowest terms.

Just as you can reduce a fraction to lower terms by dividing the top and bottom by the same number, you can raise a fraction to *higher terms* by multiplying the top and bottom by the same number. For example, consider the fraction $\frac{3}{4}$. If we multiply the top and bottom by 2, we get $\frac{6}{8}$. If we instead multiply the top and bottom by 5, we get $\frac{15}{20}$. The fractions $\frac{6}{8}$ and $\frac{15}{20}$ are two different ways to write $\frac{3}{4}$ in higher terms. As we see in the next section, it is often necessary to raise fractions to higher terms to add and subtract them.

Express the fraction $\frac{12}{15}$ in lowest terms.

It is easy to see that the number 3 can be divided evenly into both the numerator and the denominator. Performing this division, we get $\frac{12}{15} = \frac{12 \div 3}{15 \div 3} = \frac{4}{5}$, which is in lowest terms.

Rewrite the fraction $\frac{2}{3}$ as an equivalent fraction with a denominator of 21.

To change the denominator of 3 to 21, we need to multiply by 7. Because we need to perform the same operation to the numerator as well, we would get $\frac{2}{3} = \frac{2 \times 7}{3 \times 7} = \frac{14}{21}$.

Adding and Subtracting Fractions

You probably recall that the number on the top of a fraction is called the *numerator* and the number on the bottom of a fraction is called the *denominator*. If two fractions have the same denominator, they are said to have *common denominators*.

Adding or subtracting two fractions with common denominators is easy. Simply add the numerators and retain the common denominator. For example,

$$\frac{2}{9} + \frac{5}{9} = \frac{7}{9} \quad \text{and} \quad \frac{7}{8} - \frac{5}{8} = \frac{2}{8} = \frac{1}{4}$$

Note that, in the subtraction problem, we get a fraction that can be simplified, and we perform the simplification before finishing.

If you need to add or subtract two fractions that do not have the same denominator, you need to begin by raising them to higher terms so that they do have a common denominator. The first step in this process is determining a common denominator for the two fractions. For example, suppose that you are asked to add $\frac{3}{4} + \frac{1}{3}$. You need to find a common denominator for 4 and 3. Actually, an infinite number of common denominators exist for 4 and 3. Some of them would be 24, 36 and 48. While you can work with any of these denominators, it is easiest to work with the smallest one, which in this case is 12. This number is called the *least common denominator* of 4 and 3, and it is actually the same number as the least common multiple (LCM), which has already been discussed. Thus, the least common denominator can be found by using the same process we used to find the LCM previously.

When we know the least common denominator (LCD), we simply need to multiply the top and bottom of each fraction by the appropriate number to raise the denominators to the LCD. For example:

$$\frac{3}{4} + \frac{1}{3} = \frac{3}{3} \times \frac{3}{4} + \frac{4}{4} \times \frac{1}{3} = \frac{9}{12} + \frac{4}{12} = \frac{13}{12}$$

Note that the answer, $\frac{13}{12}$, is an improper fraction. Any improper fraction can also be written as a mixed number by dividing the denominator into the numerator, and writing the remainder as the numerator of a fraction with the original denominator. In this case, 12 goes into 13 one time with a remainder of one, so $\frac{13}{12} = 1\frac{1}{12}$, which is another way to write the answer to the question.

Note that this process can also be reversed. So, for example, the mixed number $2\frac{1}{5}$ can be written as an improper fraction. The denominator is the same, that is, 5, and the numerator is the denominator times the whole number plus the numerator; that is, $5 \times 2 + 1 = 11$. Therefore, $2\frac{1}{5} = \frac{11}{5}$. Often, when performing operations on mixed numbers, it is helpful to write them as improper fractions. The upcoming examples illustrate this.

Add $2\frac{3}{5} + 3\frac{1}{7}$.

You can proceed in two ways. You can write both mixed numbers as improper fractions and add, but it is quicker to just add the whole number part $(2 + 3 = 5)$ and the fractional part: $\frac{3}{5} + \frac{1}{7} = \frac{21}{35} + \frac{5}{35} = \frac{26}{35}$. The answer, then, is $5\frac{26}{35}$.

Find the value of $\frac{3}{7} - \frac{1}{2}$.

The LCD is 14. Thus, $\frac{3}{7} - \frac{1}{2} = \frac{6}{14} - \frac{7}{14} = \frac{-1}{14}$.

Multiplying and Dividing Fractions

Multiplying fractions is actually a bit easier than adding or subtracting them. When multiplying, you don't need to worry about common denominators: Just multiply the numerators, then multiply the denominators, and then simplify if possible. For example, $\frac{2}{3} \times \frac{4}{5} = \frac{2 \times 4}{3 \times 5} = \frac{8}{15}$. That's all you need to do!

To understand the procedure for dividing fractions, we first need to define a term. The *reciprocal* of a number is the number that is obtained by switching the numerator and the denominator of the number. For example, the reciprocal of $\frac{3}{8}$ is simply $\frac{8}{3}$. To find the reciprocal of a whole number, such as 7, visualize the 7 as the fraction $\frac{7}{1}$. The reciprocal, then, is $\frac{1}{7}$.

Now, the easiest way to divide two fractions is to change the division to a multiplication with the same answer. In fact, if you change the second fraction to its reciprocal and multiply, you get the correct answer! For example, $\frac{4}{5} \div \frac{3}{4} = \frac{4}{5} \times \frac{4}{3} = \frac{16}{15} = 1\frac{1}{15}$.

What is the value of $2\frac{2}{3} \times 1\frac{4}{5}$? Before we can multiply these mixed numbers, we need to write them as improper fractions:

$$2\frac{2}{3} \times 1\frac{4}{5} = \frac{8}{3} \times \frac{9}{5} = \frac{72}{15} = 4\frac{12}{15} = 4\frac{4}{5}$$

Evaluate $2\frac{2}{5} \div 6$.

Begin by writing the problem as $\frac{12}{5} \div \frac{6}{1}$. Then:

$$\frac{12}{5} \div \frac{6}{1} = \frac{12}{5} \times \frac{1}{6} = \frac{12}{30} = \frac{2}{5}$$

Algebraic Operations and Equations

Numerical Evaluation

Algebra is a generalization of arithmetic. In arithmetic, you learned how to perform mathematical operations (such as addition, subtraction, multiplication and division) on different types of numbers, such as whole numbers, decimals, percents and fractions. Algebra extends these concepts by considering how to perform mathematical operations on symbols standing for numbers and how to use these techniques to solve a variety of practical word problems.

In algebra, we refer to numbers that have a definite value as *constants*. For example, the numbers $17, -3, \frac{2}{3}, \sqrt{41}, 5.123$ and 12% are constants. Symbols standing for numbers are called *variables* because, until we specify further, they can take on any value. For example, in the expression $3x + 13y + 29$, the numbers 3, 13 and 29 are constants, and the symbols x and y are variables. As the following examples show, when we are given the values of all variables in an expression, we can find the value of the expression.

If $a = 4$ and $b = -3$, find the value of the expression $a^3 - b$.

When evaluating numerical expressions, it is crucial to remember the Order of Operations, and to pay careful attention to plus and minus signs. Begin by substituting the values of a and b in the given expression, and then carefully evaluate as in the previous section:

$$a^3 - b = (4)^3 - (-3) = 64 + 3 = 67$$

If $x = 3$, and $y = 2$, find the value of $\frac{24 - 2x}{-6y}$.

$$\frac{24 - 2x}{-6y} = \frac{24 - 2(3)}{-6(2)} = \frac{24 - 6}{-12} = \frac{18}{-12} = -\frac{3}{2}$$

The formula for the perimeter of a rectangle is $P = 2l + 2w$, where l represents the length of the rectangle and w represents the width. What is the perimeter of a rectangle with length 21 and width 15?

$$P = 2l + 2w = 2(21) + 2(15) = 42 + 30 = 72$$

Solving Equations

An *equation* is simply a mathematical expression that contains an equal sign. For example, $10 = 4 + 6$ is an equation, and is always true. Alternately, $10 = 5 + 4$ is also an equation, but it is always false.

An equation that contains a variable, such as $2x + 1 = 7$, might or might not be true depending on the value of x. *Solving an equation* refers to finding the value of the unknown that makes both sides of the equation equal. Note that the number three makes both sides of the equation equal. We therefore say that three *solves* the equation, or that three is the *solution* of the equation.

Some equations, like the preceding one, are easy to solve by just looking at them. Others are so complicated that we need an organized series of steps to solve them. In this section, we examine how to do this.

The principle for solving equations is, essentially, to rewrite the equation in simpler and simpler forms (without, of course, changing the solution), until the solution becomes obvious. The simplest equation of all, of course, would be an equation of the form $x = a$, where x is the variable and a is some number. Whenever you are given an equation that is more complicated than $x = a$, the idea is to change the equation so that it eventually looks like $x = a$, and you can read the answer right off.

Now, what can you do to change an equation? The answer is simple: almost anything you want as long as you do the same thing to both sides. To start, you can add or subtract the same number to or from both sides, multiply both sides by the same number, or divide both sides by the same number (as long as that number isn't zero). The following examples demonstrate this procedure with some very simple equations; after this, we will look at some more complicated ones.

Solve for x: $x + 7 = 20$.

Even though you can easily solve this equation in your head, pay attention to the procedure, as it will help you when we get to more complicated equations. Remember that the easiest possible type of equation is one of the form $x = a$. The equation that we have isn't quite like that; it has a +7 on the left side that we would like to get rid of. Now, how can we get rid of an addition of 7? Easy; we just subtract 7 from both sides:

$$\begin{aligned} x + 7 &= 20 \\ -7 &\quad -7 \\ \hline x &= 13 \end{aligned}$$

So, the solution to this equation is $x = 13$.

Solve for y: $9y = 72$.

In this equation, we have a 9 multiplying the y that we would like to get rid of. Now, how can we undo a multiplication by 9? Clearly, we need to divide both sides by 9:

$$\frac{9y}{9} = \frac{72}{9}$$

The solution is $y = 8$.

The equations in the two preceding examples are called one-step equations because they can be solved in one step. Some examples of equations that require more than one step to solve follow. The procedure is the same; keep doing the same thing to both sides of the equation until it looks like $x = a$.

Solve for t: $4t - 3 = 9$.

In this equation, we have a few things on the left hand side that we would like to get rid of. First of all, let's undo the subtraction of 3 by adding 3 to both sides.

$$
\begin{array}{rcr}
4t - 3 & = & 9 \\
+3 & & +3 \\
\hline
4t & & 12
\end{array}
$$

Now, we need to undo the multiplication by four, which can be done by dividing both sides by 4:

$$\frac{4t}{4} = \frac{12}{4}, \text{ or, } t = 3$$

Note that you can check your answer to any equation by substituting the answer back into the equation and making certain that both sides are equal. For example, we know that we did the preceding problem correctly because:

$$4(3) - 3 = 9$$
$$12 - 3 = 9$$
$$9 = 9$$

Solve for p: $15p = 3p + 24$.

This problem puts us in a situation that we have yet to encounter. The variable p appears on both sides of the equation, but we only want it on one side. To get this into the form we want, let's subtract $3p$ from both sides:

$$
\begin{array}{rcr}
15p & = & 3p + 24 \\
-3p & & -3p \\
\hline
12p & & 24
\end{array}
$$

Now, we have an equation that looks a bit better. It is easy to see that if we divide both sides by 12, we end up with the answer $p = 2$.

A few more examples for you to practice with follow. Before we get to them, it will be helpful if you refamiliarize yourself with a very important mathematical property called the *Distributive Property*.

Consider, for example, the expression $7(2 + 3)$. According to the Order of Operations, we should do the work in parentheses first, and therefore $7(2 + 3) = 7(5) = 35$. However, note that we get the same answer if we "distribute" the 7 to the 2 and the 3, and add afterward:

$$7(2 + 3) = 7(2) + 7(3) = 14 + 21 = 35$$

The Distributive Property tells us that we can always use this distribution as a way of evaluating an expression. Algebraically, the Distributive Property tells us that $a(b + c) = ab + ac$. The following examples incorporate the Distributive Property into the solving of equations.

Solve for c: $3(c - 5) = 9$.

Before we can get the c by itself on the left, we need to get it out of the parentheses, so let's distribute:

$$3c - 15 = 9$$

The rest is similar to what we have already done. Add 15 to both sides to get:

$$3c = 24$$

Now divide by 3 to get:

$c = 8$

Solve for q: $5q - 64 = -2(3q - 1)$.

As in the preceding example, we must begin by eliminating the parentheses, using the Distributive Property:

$5q - 64 = -6q + 2$

Now, add $6q$ to both sides:

$11q - 64 = +2$

Next, add 64 to both sides:

$11q = 66$.

Finally, dividing both sides by 11 gives us the answer: $q = 6$.

Solving Word Problems

Many problems that deal with practical applications of mathematics are expressed in words. To solve such problems, it is necessary to translate the words into an equation that can then be solved. The following table lists some common words and the mathematical symbols that they represent:

Words	Mathematical Representation
a equals 9, a is 9, a is the same as 9	$a = 9$
a plus 9, the *sum of a* and 9, *a added to 9, a increased by 9, a more than 9*	$a + 9$
9 *less than a, a minus 9, a decreased by 9*, the *difference of a and 9, a less 9*	$a - 9$
9 *times a*, the *product of 9* and *a*, 9 *multiplied by a*	$9a$ or $(9 \times a)$
The quotient of a and 9, a divided by 9, 9 divided into a	$a/9$
1/2 of *a* *50% of a*	$1/2 \times a$ $50\% \times a$

Now, when you are given a word problem to solve, begin by translating the words into an equation, and then solve the equation to find the solution.

If 5 increased by 4 times a number is 20, what is the number? Let's call the number x. Then, the problem statement tells us that:

$5 + 4x = 20$

Subtract 5 from both sides:

$4x = 16$

Divide by 4:

$x = 4$

Thus, the number is 4.

Brian needs $54 more to buy new hockey gloves. If new gloves cost $115, how much money does he already have to spend on the gloves?

Let m represent the amount of money that Brian has to spend on the gloves. Then, we have an easy equation: $m + 54 = 115$. If we subtract 54 from both sides, we get $m = 61$. Brian already has $61 to spend on the gloves.

Edgar bought a portable compact disc player for $69 and a number of discs for $14 each. If the total cost of his purchases (before tax) was $167, how many compact discs did he buy?

Let's start by letting d represent the number of discs he bought. Then, the cost of the player plus d discs at $14 each must add up to $167. Therefore, $14d + 69 = 167$.

Subtract 69 from both sides: $14d = 98$

Divide both sides by 14: $d = 7$

Edgar bought 7 discs.

Multiplication with Exponents

Consider the problem $x^3 \times x^5 = ?$ If you think about it, you realize that if we compute $x^3 \times x^5$, we end up with eight xs multiplied together. Therefore, $x^3 \times x^5 = x^8$. This indicates the general rule for multiplication of numbers with exponents: $x^n \times x^m = x^{m+n}$. In other words, to multiply two numbers with exponents, simply add the exponents and keep the common base.

This rule can be extended to other types of multiplication. For example, if you need to multiply $x(x + 3)$, we can use the distributive property to obtain:

$$x(x + 3) = x^2 + 3x$$

Now, how would you multiply something like $(x + 2)(x + 5)$? Basically, you need to take each of the terms in the first expression, that is, the x and the 2, and distribute them to both of the terms in the second expression. Doing this, you end up with:

$$(x + 2)(x + 5) = x^2 + 5x + 2x + 10 = x^2 + 7x + 10.$$

Multiply $2x(x^2 - 3x)$. Begin by distributing as you did previously:

$$2x(x^2 - 3x) = 2x(x^2) - 2x(3x)$$

Now, perform the indicated multiplications:

$$2x(x^2) - 2x(3x) = 2x^3 - 6x^2$$

Multiply $(2x + 7)(3x - 4)$.

As in the preceding example, begin by distributing the $2x$ and the 7 to the other terms:

$$(2x + 7)(3x - 4) = 2x(3x) - 2x(4) + 7(3x) - 7(4)$$

Now, perform the multiplications and combine terms where possible:

$$2x(3x) - 2x(4) + 7(3x) - 7(4) = 6x^2 - 8x + 21x - 28 = 6x^2 + 13x + 28$$

Factoring

Earlier in this chapter, we talked about factoring whole numbers; for example, 35 can be factored as $35 = 5 \times 7$. As you can see, the word *factoring* refers to taking a mathematical quantity and breaking it down into a product of other quantities.

Certain algebraic expressions can be factored, too. Earlier in this chapter, we saw how to perform two types of multiplication. In the first, we used the distributive property to perform multiplications such as $x(x + 3) = x^2 + 3x$. To use the correct vocabulary, the x at the front of this expression is called a *monomial* (one term), whereas the expression $x + 3$ is called a *binomial* (two terms). Thus, we have used the distributive property to help us multiply a monomial by a binomial. We also saw how to multiply two binomials, for example:

$$(2x + 7)(3x - 4) = 6x^2 + 13x - 28$$

The process of taking the results of these multiplications and breaking them back down into their component factors is also called factoring. It is not difficult to factor, but it does often require a bit of trial and error.

For example, if you are asked to multiply the expression $2x(x - 7)$, you would get:

$$2x^2 - 14x$$

If you were given $2x^2 - 14x$ and asked to factor it, you would basically need to undo the distribution process, and get the expression back to what it originally was.

To do this, begin by looking at the expression $2x^2 - 14x$, and try to find the largest common monomial factor, that is, the largest monomial that divides into both $2x^2$ and $14x$ evenly. Clearly, in this problem, the largest common factor is $2x$. You then place the $2x$ outside a set of parentheses. Finish by dividing the $2x$ into each of the two terms ($2x^2$ and $14x$), and write the resulting terms inside the parentheses. This leaves you with:

$$2x(x - 7)$$

We have successfully factored the expression.

Factor $2a^2b - 8ab$.

The largest common monomial factor in this expression is $2ab$. If we divide $2a^2b$ by $2ab$, we get a. If we divide $8ab$ by $2ab$, we get 4. Thus, putting the $2ab$ outside of the parentheses, and the a and 4 on the inside, we get $2ab(a - 4)$.

Note that it is easy to check whether you have factored correctly or not by multiplying the expression, and seeing if you get the original expression back.

It is also possible to factor certain *trinomial* (three term) expressions into two binomials. Consider a simple example: If you were asked to multiply $(x + 2)(x + 3)$, you would get $x^2 + 5x + 6$. Now, what if you were given the expression $x^2 + 5x + 6$ and asked to factor it back down to the two binomials it came from?

To begin, make two sets of parentheses, and note that you can position xs in the first position of each set because the first terms of each binomial multiply to give the x^2 in $x^2 + 5x + 6$. Therefore, to begin:

$$x^2 + 5x + 6 = (x \quad)(x \quad)$$

Because both signs in $x^2 + 5x + 6$ are positive, we can position plus signs within the parentheses:

$$x^2 + 5x + 6 = (x + \quad)(x + \quad)$$

Now, what are the last entries in each binomial? Well, we know that whatever we put in these spots must multiply to get 6, so the possibilities would be 1 and 6, or 2 and 3. The correct entries, however, must add up to 5 to get the correct middle term. Thus, it must be 2 and 3, and we get $x^2 + 5x + 6 = (x + 2)(x + 3)$. We can check the answer by multiplying:

$$(x + 2)(x + 3) = x^2 + 3x + 2x + 6 = x^2 + 5x + 6$$

As you can see, factoring a trinomial into two binomials requires a bit of trial and error. The following examples give you a bit more practice with this.

Factor $x^2 - 8x + 12$.

We begin as before, by making two sets of parentheses, and entering first terms of x in each:

$$x^2 - 8x + 12 = (x \quad\quad)(x \quad\quad)$$

Now, the two last entries must multiply to get +12, but add to get −8, so that we get the correct middle term. Proceed by trial and error, and it does not take long to determine that the two numbers that work are −2 and −6. The factorization is $x^2 - 8x + 12 = (x - 2)(x - 6)$.

Factor $x^2 - 49$.

This one might look at bit tricky, but actually it is rather easy. Begin, as before, by writing:

$$x^2 - 49 = (x \quad\quad)(x \quad\quad)$$

Now, the last two entries must multiply to get 49, and add to get 0, so that the middle term is, essentially, 0. Clearly, this works with +7 and −7. Thus, $x^2 - 49 = (x + 7)(x - 7)$.

Simplifying Algebraic Expressions

Earlier in this chapter, we talked about simplifying fractions. If, for example, the answer to a problem turns out to be $\frac{15}{20}$, it should be simplified to $\frac{3}{4}$. In the same way, certain algebraic expressions can be simplified as well. For example, consider the algebraic fraction $\frac{x^2 - 16}{3x + 12}$. To simplify this expression, begin by factoring the expressions on the top and on

the bottom: $\frac{x^2 - 16}{3x + 12} = \frac{(x + 4)(x - 4)}{3(x + 4)}$. Now, the common factor of $x + 4$ can be divided from the top and bottom,

giving us a simplified fraction of $\frac{x - 4}{3}$.

Mathematical operations can be performed on algebraic fractions in much the same way as they can be performed on fractions that contain only numbers. Consider this example:

Add $\frac{x + 1}{4x + 6} + \frac{x + 2}{4x + 6}$.

Because these two fractions have the same denominator, they can be added in the usual way:

$$\frac{x + 1}{4x + 6} + \frac{x + 2}{4x + 6} = \frac{x + 1 + x + 2}{4x + 6} = \frac{2x + 3}{4x + 6}$$

Now, finish by factoring the expression on the bottom and dividing:

$$\frac{x + 1}{4x + 6} + \frac{x + 2}{4x + 6} = \frac{x + 1 + x + 2}{4x + 6} = \frac{2x + 3}{4x + 6} = \frac{2x + 3}{2(2x + 3)} = \frac{1}{2}$$

Multiply $\frac{x^2 - 7x + 6}{x^2 - 1} \times \frac{x + 1}{x - 6}$.

Begin by factoring as much as possible, then multiply and cancel:

$$\frac{x^2 - 7x + 6}{x^2 - 1} \times \frac{x + 1}{x - 6} = \frac{(x - 6)(x - 1)}{(x - 1)(x + 1)} \times \frac{x + 1}{x - 6} = \frac{(x - 6)(x - 1)(x + 1)}{(x - 1)(x + 1)(x - 6)} = 1$$

Divide $\dfrac{a^2 - b^2}{5} \div \dfrac{a^2 + ab}{5a - 5}$.

Begin by changing this to a multiplication problem by reciprocating the second fraction. Then factor and cancel:

$$\frac{a^2 - b^2}{5} \div \frac{a^2 + ab}{5a - 5} = \frac{a^2 - b^2}{5} \times \frac{5a - 5}{a^2 + ab} = \frac{(a+b)(a-b)}{5} \times \frac{5(a-1)}{a(a+b)} = \frac{(a+b)(a-b)5(a-1)}{5a(a+b)} = \frac{(a-b)(a-1)}{a}$$

Geometry and Measurement

On the Mathematics Knowledge section of the AFOQT, you are asked some questions that require a basic knowledge of geometry. These facts are presented in the following section.

Angle Measurement

You measure angles in degrees, which you indicate with the symbol °. By definition, the amount of rotation needed to go completely around a circle one time is 360°.

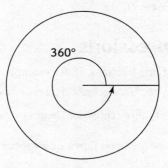

You can measure every angle by determining what fraction of a complete rotation around a circle it represents. For example, an angle that represents 1/4 of a rotation around a circle would have a measurement of 1/4 of 360° = 90°. The following diagram depicts a 90° angle. AB and AC are the sides of the angle, and the point A is the vertex.

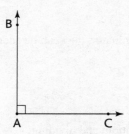

Angles that measure less than 90° are called *acute* angles, and angles that measure more than 90° are called *obtuse* angles. The following diagram depicts an acute angle of 60° as well as an obtuse angle of 120°.

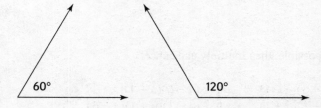

Note that an angle with the size of 1/2 a revolution around the circle has a measure of 180°. In other words, a straight line can be thought of as an angle of 180°.

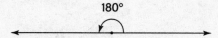

Two angles whose measures add up to 90° are called *complementary* angles, and two angles whose measures add up to 180° are called *supplementary* angles. In the following diagram, angles 1 and 2 are complementary, and angles 3 and 4 are supplementary. As the diagram shows, whenever a straight angle is partitioned into two angles, the angles are supplementary.

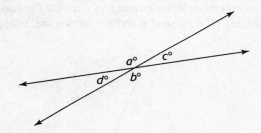

Another very important fact about angles relates to what are known as *vertical* angles. As the following diagram shows, when two lines intersect, four angles are formed. In this situation, the angles that are across from each other are called *vertical* angles. All vertical angles are equal, so $a° = b°$, and $c° = d°$.

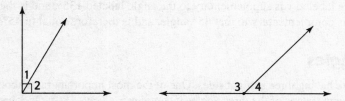

In the following diagram, what is the value of a?

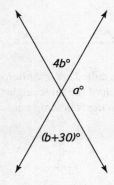

Begin by noting that the angles labeled $4b$ and $b + 30$ are vertical angles, and therefore have the same measure. In this case, we can set the two angles equal and solve the resulting equation for b:

$4b = b + 30$

$3b = 30$

$b = 10$

Now, if $b = 10$, then $4b = 40$. Because the angle labeled $a°$ is supplementary to this angle, a must be equal to 140°.

In the following diagram, what is the value of x?

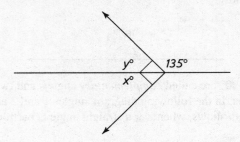

Begin by noting that the angle labeled y is supplementary to the angle labeled 135°, and is therefore equal to 45°. Next, note that the angle labeled x is complementary to that 45° angle, and is therefore equal to 45°.

Properties of Triangles

A triangle is a geometric figure having three straight sides. One of the most important facts about a triangle is that, regardless of its shape, the sum of the measures of the three angles it contains is always 180°. Of course, then, if you know the measures of two of the angles of a triangle, you can determine the measure of the third angle by adding the two angles you are given, and subtracting from 180.

Some triangles have special properties that you should know about. To begin, an *isosceles* triangle is a triangle that has two sides of the same length. In an isosceles triangle, the two angles opposite the equal sides have the same measurement. For example, in the following figure, $AB = BC$, and therefore the two angles opposite these sides, labeled $x°$, have the same measure.

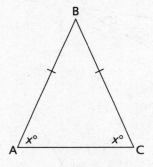

A triangle that has all three sides the same length is called an *equilateral* triangle. In an equilateral triangle, all three angles also have the same measure. Because the sum of the three angles must be 180°, each angle in an equilateral triangle must measure 180° ÷ 3 = 60°. Therefore, in the following equilateral triangle, all three angles are 60°.

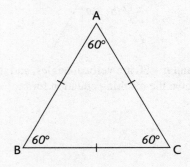

Another extremely important triangle property relates to what are known as *right* triangles, that is, triangles containing a right angle. In such triangles, the side opposite the right angle is called the *hypotenuse,* and must be the longest side of the triangle. The other two sides of the triangle are called its legs. Therefore, in the following right triangle, the side labeled *c* is the hypotenuse, and sides *a* and *b* are the legs.

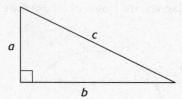

The three sides of a right triangle are related by a formula known as the Pythagorean theorem. The Pythagorean theorem states that the square of the hypotenuse is equal to the sum of the squares of the legs of the triangle, or, using the notation in the preceding diagram, $a^2 + b^2 = c^2$.

The importance of this result is that it enables you, given the lengths of two of the sides of a right triangle, to find the length of the third side.

In triangle XYZ, angle X is twice as big as angle Y, and angle Z is equal to angle Y. What is the measure of angle X? Because the measure of angle X is twice as big as angle Y, we can say that the measure of angle X is equal to $2Y$. Because it must be true that $X + Y + Z = 180$, we can write:

$2Y + Y + Y = 180$

$4Y = 180$

$Y = 45$

If the measure of angle Y is 45°, the measure of angle X, which is twice as big, must be 90°.

In the following triangle, what is the length of a?

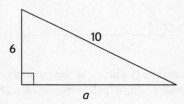

The triangle is a right triangle, so we can use the Pythagorean theorem to find the length of the missing side. Note that the hypotenuse is 10, one of the legs is 6, and we are looking for the length of the other leg. Therefore:

$a^2 + 6^2 = 10^2$

$a^2 + 36 = 100$

$a^2 = 64$

$a = \sqrt{64}$

$a = 8$

Properties of Circles

A circle is a closed figure, consisting of all the points that are the same distance from a fixed point called the *center* of the circle. A line segment from the center of the circle to any point on the circle is called a *radius* of the circle. A line segment from one point on a circle, through the center of the circle, to another point on the circle is called a *diameter* of the circle. As you can see in the following diagram, the length of a diameter of a circle is always twice the length of a radius of a circle.

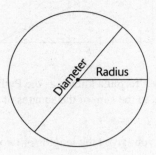

Perimeter and Area

To find the perimeter of a triangle, you simply need to add together the lengths of the three sides. The area of a triangle is given by the formula Area = 1/2 *bh,* where *b* represents the length of the base of the triangle, and *h* represents the height of the triangle. The height of a triangle is defined as the length of a line segment drawn from a *vertex* (corner) of the triangle to the base, so that it hits the base at a right angle.

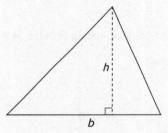

Formulas for the perimeter (which is more commonly known as the *circumference*) and the area of circles are based on the length of the radius, and include the symbol π (pi), which represents a number that is approximately equal to 3.14.

The circumference of a circle is given by the formula $C = 2\pi r$, where *r* is the radius of the circle. The area of the circle is given by the formula $A = \pi r^2$. Unless you are told otherwise, when answering problems involving the circumference or area of a circle, you can leave the answer in terms of π, as in the following problem.

What is the circumference of a circle whose area is 36π? The area of a circle is πr^2, so you have $\pi r^2 = 36\pi$. This means that $r^2 = 36$, so $r = 6$.

Now, the circumference of a circle is $2\pi r$, so the circumference in this case would be $2\pi(6) = 12\pi$.

What is the area of the shaded part of the following rectangle?

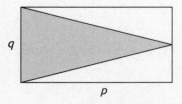

The shaded area is a triangle, so we can use the formula $A = \frac{1}{2}bh$ to find its area. The width of the rectangle, labeled q, is also the base of the triangle. You can see that the length of the rectangle, labeled p, is equal to the height of the triangle. Therefore, the area of the shaded region is $\frac{1}{2}pq$.

Coordinates and Slope

Points in a plane can be located by means of a reference system called the coordinate system. Two number lines are drawn at right angles to each other, and the point where the lines cross is considered to have a value of zero for both lines also known as the origin. Then, positive and negative numbers are positioned on the lines.

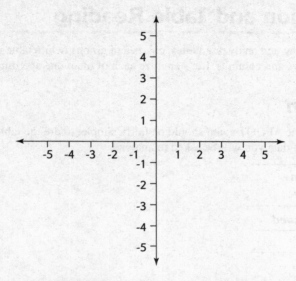

The horizontal line is called the *x-axis,* and the points on this axis are called *x-coordinates.* The vertical line is called the *y-axis,* and the points on this axis are called *y-coordinates.* Points on the plane are identified by first writing a number that represents where they lie in reference to the *x*-axis, and then writing a number that expresses where they lie in reference to the *y*-axis. These numbers are called the coordinates of the point. The coordinates of a variety of points are shown in the following diagram:

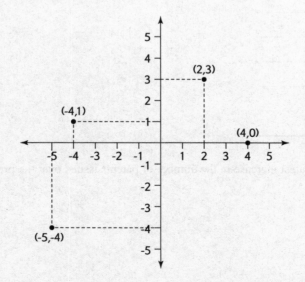

Any two points on a plane determine a line. One of the important characteristics of a line is its steepness, or *slope*. The slope of a line can be determined from the coordinates of the two points that determine the line. If the coordinates of the two points are (x_1, y_1) and (x_2, y_2), the formula for the slope is $\frac{y_2 - y_1}{x_2 - x_1}$. In other words, to find the slope of a line, find two points on the line and divide the difference of the y-coordinates by the difference of the x-coordinates.

Find the slope of the line that goes through the points (3, −2) and (9, 5).

The slope of the line can be computed as $\frac{y_2 - y_1}{x_2 - x_1} = \frac{5 - (-2)}{9 - 3} = \frac{5 + 2}{6} = \frac{7}{6}$.

Data Interpretation and Table Reading

Data interpretation involves reading and analyzing tables, charts and graphs, while table reading tests your ability to select appropriate material by rows and columns. Let's analyze each of them one at a time.

Data Interpretation

The questions on this section of the AFOQT exam should be fairly simple, as are the table reading questions. Following are some examples of the types of data you will be asked to analyze.

Patents Issued for Inventions, 1790–1900

Period	Patents Issued
1790–1800	309
1801–10	1,093
1811–20	1,930
1821–30	3,086
1831–40	5,519
1841–50	5,933
1851–60	23,065
1861–70	79,459
1871–80	125,438
1881–90	207,514
1891–1900	220,608

1. In what period was the greatest increase in the number of patents issued over the previous period?

   A. 1790–1800
   B. 1801–10
   C. 1831–40
   D. 1841–50
   E. 1851–60

The correct answer is **E**. Do you understand why that is correct? If you analyze each of the answers, you should be able to determine the correct answer. Choice **A** is incorrect because you have no information before 1790–1800. You cannot, therefore, determine the increase from the previous period. Choice **B** shows an increase of about three times the previous period. (You don't always have to perform mathematics in these tables or graphs. You can often determine the answer just by looking at the choices.) Choice **C** also is incorrect. The growth from the previous period is less than double. Choice **D** does not indicate much growth at all from the previous period. And choice **E**, the correct answer, is almost four times the previous period.

Let's answer another question based on this table.

2. In what period was there the least amount of growth from the previous period?

    A. 1801–10
    B. 1811–20
    C. 1821–30
    D. 1831–40
    E. 1841–50

Again, let's analyze each answer. To find the answers, subtract the previous period from the current period. We are only going to estimate here.

    A. From 1790–1800 to the next period, about 700 more patents were issued. (1,093 − 309 = 784)
    B. From 1801–10 to the next period, just over 800 more patents were issued. (1,930 − 1,093 = 837).
    C. From 1811–20 to the next period, over 1,100 more patents were issued. (3,086 − 1,930 = 1,156)
    D. From 1821–30 to the next period, about 2,400 more patents were issued. (5,519 − 3,086 = 2,433)
    E. From 1831–40 to the next period, about 400 more patents were issued. (5,933 − 5,519 = 414)

The correct answer, therefore, is **E**.

Line graphs and bar graphs are essentially comparisons. In a line graph, you are asked to read and analyze the information based on different styles or widths of lines. The information is present on the horizontal and vertical axes. A bar graph is not as accurate as a table, but it gives you a quick, visual comparison of the data.

The following is an example of another type of question you will encounter.

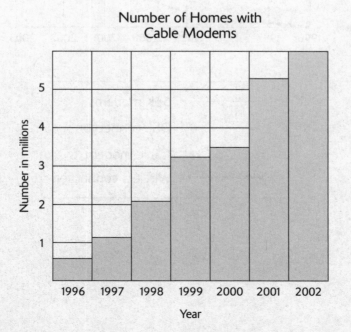

Number of Homes with Cable Modems

3. In what year was there the greatest amount of growth over the previous year?

    A. 1997
    B. 1998
    C. 2000
    D. 2001
    E. 2002

A quick look at the graph shows that the answer is **D**, and that the greatest amount of growth was from 2000 to 2001. You can see that visually by the bars. At the same time, by looking along the left, you can also see that about 3.2 million homes had cable modems in 2000 and 5.2 million homes had cable modems in 2001. This is an increase of 2 million. None of the other bars indicate that type of growth.

Let's look at one other type of graph—a line graph.

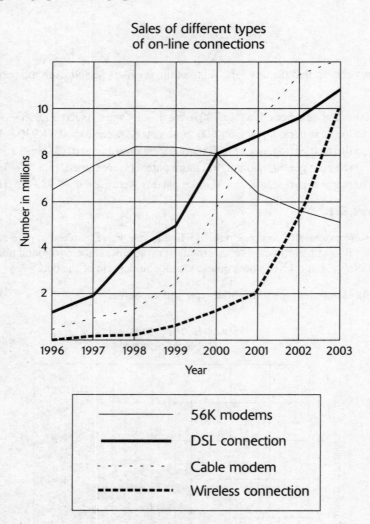

Sales of different types
of on-line connections

4. In what year were the most 56K modems installed?

    A. 1996
    B. 1997
    C. 1998
    D. 1999
    E. 2000

If you follow the thin line that indicates 56K modems on the scale, and then trace it across the graph, starting at about 6.8 million, you'll see that sales peaked in 1998 with a little over 8 million sold. The correct answer is **C**.

Answering these types of questions involves some arithmetic and requires strong reading skills. You have to know what the question is asking, and you have to be aware of what is being illustrated graphically. When you find the bars, numbers or lines that you are asked to deal with, you can then do the math.

Table Reading

The second type of question that appears on the AFOQT is table reading. This portion of the test is designed to measure your ability to read tables quickly and accurately. Like the earlier material, it involves less mathematics.

Tables normally present you with columns of information, and the data corresponds to the rows and columns. There are always units such as numbers, years, dollars and even people. You have to compare the items on both the X and Y axes to find the answers. Let's look at a typical table.

Player	At Bats	Runs	Hits	Walks	Strike Outs	Average	Annual Salary (millions $)
Johnson rf	4	0	1	0	0	.255	$2.7
Smith 3b	3	0	0	0	1	.231	$5.6
Hernando cf	3	0	0	1	1	.255	$6.0
Lubitz 1b	4	0	1	0	1	.291	$8.8
MacDonald lf	3	3	2	1	0	.294	$5.5
Philips dh	4	0	0	0	1	.246	$8.0
Auerhaan 2b	4	0	1	0	0	.306	$2.0
Augustine c	3	0	0	1	0	.275	$3.3
Borger ss	3	1	1	0	1	.248	$4.1
Totals	31	4	6	3	5		$46.0

5. Which player had the most hits?

    A. Johnson
    B. Lubitz
    C. MacDonald
    D. Auerhaan
    E. Borger

Find the Hits column along the top and match it to the player along the left side. The correct answer is MacDonald, with 2 hits—choice **C**. All the other players given as choices had only one hit.

A second form of table reading question might appear on the tests. In these questions you are presented with a table of numbers, with X values running along the top and Y values running along the side. You will be asked to select the answer that occurs where the two axes intersect.

		-4	-3	-2	-1	0	+1	+2	+3	+4
					X-Values					
	+4	16	18	20	22	24	27	29	31	33
	+3	17	19	21	23	25	26	28	30	32
	+2	18	20	22	24	26	28	30	32	34
Y-Values	+1	19	21	23	25	27	29	30	33	35
	0	20	22	24	27	29	31	33	35	36
	-1	22	23	25	28	30	32	34	36	37
	-2	24	25	26	29	31	33	36	37	38
	-3	26	27	28	30	32	34	37	39	40
	-4	28	29	30	31	33	36	38	40	42

For each question, determine the number that can be found at the intersection of the row and column.

This is how the questions will appear. Try the first one, and let's analyze it.

     X   **Y**

6.   −1   +2

    A. 22
    B. 23
    C. 24
    D. 25
    E. 26

To find the answer, locate the X values along the top and find −1. Then trace down the column until you find +2 in the Y-value row. Where they intersect, you'll find the number 24. Choice **C** is the correct answer.

Now that you have an idea of the types of questions you'll encounter, take the time to answer all the following practice questions. If you have any problems with them, go back and reread this chapter. Make sure you read the questions carefully so that you don't misinterpret what is being asked of you, and as a result, misread the tables or charts.

Practice Questions

Answer questions 1 and 2 based on the following table showing the number of games won by each of five teams in each month of a seven-month season.

Number of Games Won

	Team				
	1	**2**	**3**	**4**	**5**
April	11	10	10	12	16
May	12	12	17	15	11
June	15	13	13	14	13
July	10	17	13	14	10
August	11	12	14	12	15
Sept.	14	11	12	11	16
Oct.	14	16	12	13	17

Month (label for rows)

1. How many games did team 4 win in the first three months of the season?

   A. 38
   B. 40
   C. 41
   D. 43
   E. 44

2. In the month of August, team 5 won how many more games than team 1?

   A. 4
   B. 5
   C. 6
   D. 11
   E. 15

Answer questions 3 and 4 based on the following table of earned interest.

Interest Earned in One Year

	Principal in Dollars					
	1000	**1100**	**1200**	**1300**	**1400**	**1500**
$1\frac{1}{4}$	12.50	13.75	15.00	16.25	17.50	18.75
$1\frac{3}{4}$	17.50	19.25	21.00	22.75	24.50	26.25
$2\frac{1}{4}$	22.50	24.75	27.00	29.25	31.50	33.75
$2\frac{3}{4}$	27.50	30.25	33.00	35.75	38.50	41.25
$3\frac{1}{4}$	32.50	35.75	39.00	42.25	45.50	48.75
$3\frac{3}{4}$	37.50	41.25	45.00	48.75	52.50	56.25
$4\frac{1}{4}$	42.50	46.75	51.00	55.25	59.50	63.75

Interest Rate in Percent (label for rows)

3. If Lauren invested $1,400 at 2 1/4% and Evan invested $1,200 at 3 1/4%, what would be the combined earnings of Lauren and Evan in one year?

    A. $57.50

    B. $63.00

    C. $70.50

    D. $80.00

    E. $82.50

4. How much more interest is earned on $1,500 invested at 2 1/4% than on $1,000 invested at 2 3/4%?

    A. $6.25

    B. $6.50

    C. $6.75

    D. $7.00

    E. $7.25

Answer questions 5 and 6 based on the following circle graph showing the breakdown of elementary school students by grade level.

Percent of Students by Grade Based on a Total of 750 Students

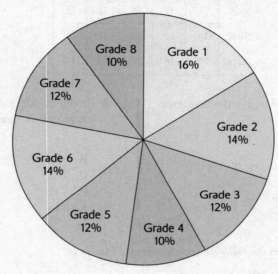

5. How many students are in grade 5?

    A. 12

    B. 63

    C. 87

    D. 90

    E. 150

6. The total number of students in grades 1 and 3 is the same as the total number of students in which of the following grades?

    A. 2 and 7

    B. 4, 7 and 8

    C. 4, 5 and 7

    D. 2 and 6

    E. 5 and 6

Answer questions 7 and 8 based on the following bar graph showing the distances covered by the drivers of the ABC Taxi Company in a one-week period.

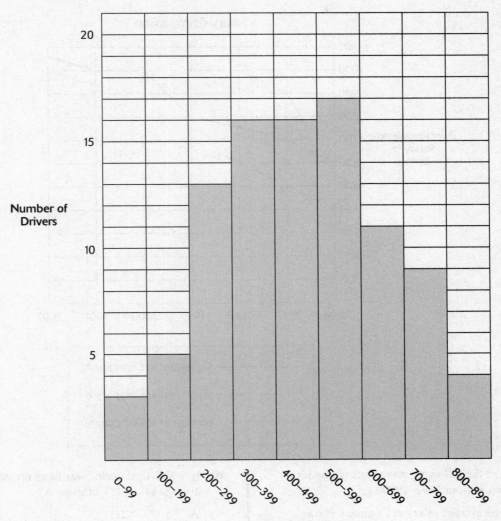

Number of Drivers

Number of Miles

7. What is the total number of drivers?

   A. 17
   B. 45
   C. 63
   D. 94
   E. 99

8. How many drivers drove at least 700 miles?

   A. 4
   B. 5
   C. 9
   D. 11
   E. 13

Answer questions 9 and 10 based on the following line graph showing average weekly salaries at three different companies.

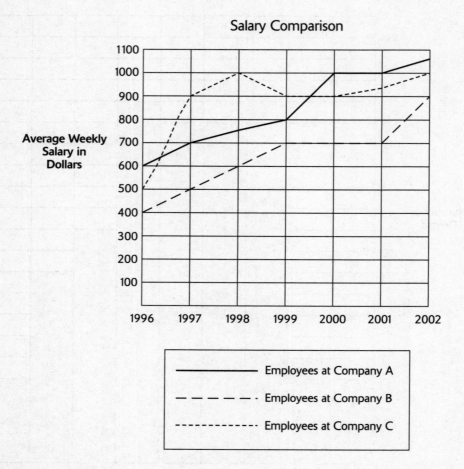

Salary Comparison

9. Which of the following statements is true for the time period from 1997–1999?

   A. The average salary at Company C was less than at Company A.
   B. The average salary at Company B was greater than at Company A.
   C. The average salary at Company B was greater than at Company C.
   D. The average salary at Company C was greater than at Company B.
   E. The average salary at Company A was greater than at Company C.

10. In which time period was there no increase in the average salary at Company A?

    A. 1999–2000
    B. 1999–2001
    C. 2000–2001
    D. 2000–2002
    E. 2001–2002

Answers and Explanations

1. **C.** The number of games won by team 4 in April, May and June: 12 + 15 + 14 = 41.

2. **A.** In August, team 5 won 15 games and team 1 won 11 games. 15 – 11 = 4.

3. **C.** If Lauren invested $1,400 at 2 1/4%, she would earn $31.50. If Evan invested $1,200 at 3 1/4%, he would earn $39.00. $31.50 + $39.00 = $70.50.

4. **A.** The interest earned on $1,500 at 2 1/4% is $33.75. The interest earned on $1,000 at 2 3/4% is $27.50. $33.75 – $27.50 = $6.25.

5. **D.** The school has 750 students and 12% of them are in grade 5. 12% of 750 = .12 × 750 = 90.

6. **D.** Sixteen percent of the students are in grade 1, and 12% of the students are in grade 3. Therefore, 16% + 12% = 28% of the students are in grades 1 and 3. For choice **A** we need to add the percentages for grades 2 and 7: 14% + 12% = 26%. For choice **B** we need to add the percentages for grades 4, 7 and 8: 10% + 12% + 10% = 32%. For choice **C** we need to add the percentages for grades 4, 5 and 7: 10% + 12% + 12% = 34%. For choice **D** we need to add the percentages for grades 2 and 6: 14% + 14% = 28%. This is the correct answer.

7. **D.** The number of drivers who drove 0–99 miles is 3. The number of drivers who drove 100–199 miles is 5. The number of drivers who drove 200–299 miles is 13, and so on. 3 + 5 + 13 + 16 + 16 + 17 + 11 + 9 + 4 = 94.

8. **E.** At least 700 miles means 700 or more miles. 9 + 4 = 13.

9. **D.** In the time period from 1997–1999, the line representing the average salary at Company C is higher on the graph than the lines representing either of the other 2 companies. Therefore, the average salary at Company C was greater than at Company B and choice **D** is the correct answer.

10. **C.** No increase in average salary is indicated when the line in the line graph is horizontal. For Company A this occurs from 2000–2001.

Scale Reading

The "Scale Reading" test is Part 9 of the Air Force Officer Qualifying Test (AFOQT). It is a test of your ability to read scales, dials, and meters. You are given a variety of scales with various points indicated on them by numbered arrows. You are to estimate the numerical value indicated by each arrow, and then choose your answer. Look at the following sample items from the official AFOQT handbook.

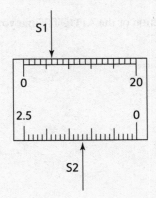

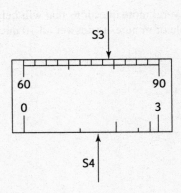

S1

    A.   6.00
    B.   5.00
    C.   4.25
    D.   2.25
    E.   1.25

S3

    A.   81.75
    B.   79.50
    C.   78.75
    D.   77.60
    E.   67.50

S2

    A.   13.0
    B.   12.0
    C.   10.2
    D.   1.30
    E.   1.20

S4

    A.   1.75
    B.   1.65
    C.   1.50
    D.   0.75
    E.   0.65

In S1 there are five subdivisions of four steps each between 0 and 20. The arrow points between the long subdivision markers that represent 4 and 8. Because it points to the marker that is one step to the right of subdivision marker 4, it points to 5.00. This is choice **B** in sample item S1.

In S2 the scale runs from right to left. There are five subdivisions of five steps each, so each step represents .1, and the arrow points to the marker representing 1.20. This is choice **E** in sample item S2.

In S3 the arrow points between two markers. You must estimate the fractional part of the step as accurately as possible. Because the arrow points halfway between the markers representing 77.5 and 80.0, it points to 78.75. This is choice **C** in sample item S3.

In S4 each step represents .5, but the steps are of unequal width with each step being two-thirds as wide as the preceding one. Therefore, the scale is compressed as the values increase. The arrow is pointing to a position halfway between the marker representing .5 and 1.0, but because of the compression of the scale, the value of this point must be less than 0.75. Actually it is 0.65, which is choice **E** in sample item S4.

All that's required of you is to read the scales and determine which selection is the correct one. You have 10 minutes in which to answer 40 questions. As with all tests, the more you practice, the better you become. Keep in mind, also, that your score is based on the number of correct answers. Because you do not lose any points for incorrect answers, answer all the questions, whether you think you know the answer or not.

Following are several more questions that will help you review for this section of the AFOQT. Time yourself. It should only take a couple of minutes to answer all 10 questions.

Practice Questions

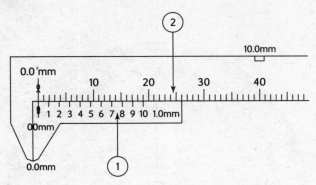

1.

A. 7.5mm
B. 7.8mm
C. 8.5mm
D. 17.5mm
E. 107.5mm

2.

A. 240mm
B. 245mm
C. 24mm
D. 24.5mm
E. 25.5mm

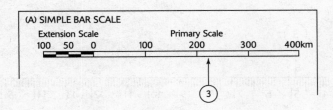

3.

A. 200km
B. 225km
C. 250km
D. 300km
E. 375km

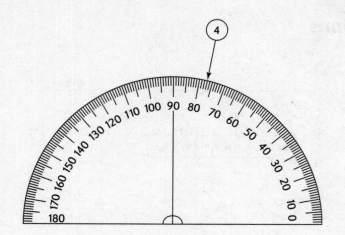

4.

    A.   80.5

    B.   80.4

    C.   77.0

    D.   75.7

    E.   75.2

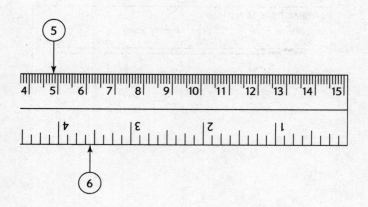

5.

    A.   4.70cm

    B.   4.80cm

    C.   4.85cm

    D.   5.02cm

    E.   5.02cm

6.

    A.   3.45

    B.   3.50

    C.   3.60

    D.   3.85

    E.   3.95

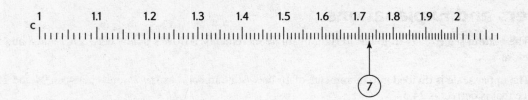

7.

A. 172
B. 173
C. 17.3
D. 1.73
E. .173

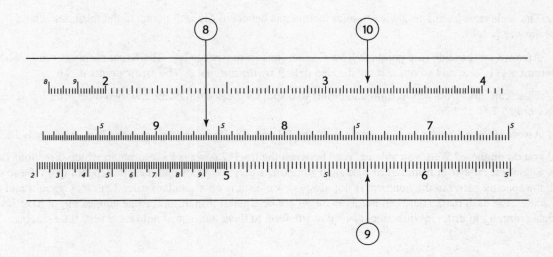

8.

A. 9.40
B. 8.52
C. 8.6
D. 5.10
E. 5.00

9.

A. 5.2
B. 5.7
C. 52.0
D. 55.2
E. 57.0

10.

A. 322
B. 47.60
C. 32.20
D. 8.40
E. 3.24

Answers and Explanations

1. A. The bottom scale reads from left to right in single increments. Arrow 1 points between 7 and 8 and is therefore 7.5.

2. D. The upper scale is divided into increments of 10 between numbers. Arrow 2 points between 24 and 25. The only choice that is correct is 24.5.

3. B. On the bar scale, the arrow is closer to the 200 mark, and the only choice would be 225.

4. C. The numbers run from right to left with 10 increments between numbers. Arrow 4 points to 77 on the scale. Make sure you always notice in which direction the numbers run.

5. C. On the centimeter scale, arrow 5 points to a number just between 4.8 and 4.9. The only choice is 4.85.

6. C. On the inches scale, each minor tick represents an eighth of an inch, and between them, although not marked, would be 1/16 inches. The arrow points to between 3⅛ and 3⅝. Therefore, you would have to say the answer was 3 9/16 or 3.5625, or 3.6, based on the choices given.

7. D. The scale runs from 1 to 2 with smaller increments between. Arrow 7 points to the third tick after 1.7. Thus the answer is 1.73.

8. C. Arrow 8 on the slide rule points to Row C1 that runs from right to left. The larger numbers run in whole increments (1, 2, 3, and so on) and are divided in half by the number 5. The arrow points to 8.6.

9. B. This scale runs from left to right and points to a spot on the bottom of the row two ticks after 5.5. Thus the answer is 5.7.

10. E. Arrow 10 points to the very top scale between 3.2 and 3.3. Based on the choices given, it can only be 3.24.

How did you do on these? Were you able to "read between the lines"? Always look to see in which directions the numbers run. Sometimes they run from left to right, and sometimes they run from right to left, depending on the scale. In addition, the spacing between the numbers is not always even, as it is on a standard ruler. On many gauges and other types of scales, the hash marks between numbers might not be equal. Furthermore, some gauges might have several different scales running in different directions. Just pay attention to them and you should have very little trouble.

Mechanics Review

This review covers all the basic concepts you need to know to score well on all three of the military flight aptitude tests.

Mechanics

In this section, we cover the different ways the three tests (AFOQT, AFAST, and ASTB) present questions on mechanics information. The content is basically the same, however, for each of the three tests. The difference is in approach and the number of question choices.

Part 7 of the AFOQT, called *Mechanical Comprehension,* gives you five choices from which to choose the correct answer—A through E. It includes both text questions and questions accompanied by an illustration. There are a total of 20 questions.

The AFAST section of the exam, called *Mechanical Functions Test,* also has 20 questions, but there are only three choices for each question—A, B, and C. In addition, each question is accompanied by an illustration, and you must choose the correct answer based on that illustration.

Finally, the ASTB section of the exam, called *Mechanical Comprehension Test,* has 30 questions, with two choices—A and B. These questions are also accompanied by illustrations.

These three tests are designed to measure your ability to learn and reason with mechanical terms. You should have some basic concept of mechanics to score well on this test. The following are sample practice questions utilizing the specific formats from each exam to give you familiarity with both the question types and the material. We suggest that you answer all the questions in this section, regardless of the specific test you plan to take. It will help you evaluate your knowledge of mechanics and give you a direction to help you in your studying for the final exam.

Practice Questions

AFOQT Questions

In questions 1 and 2, you should neglect air resistance to select the correct choice.

1. A ball in freefall will have

   A. increasing speed and increasing acceleration.
   B. increasing speed and decreasing acceleration.
   C. increasing speed and constant acceleration.
   D. decreasing speed and increasing acceleration.
   E. constant speed and constant acceleration.

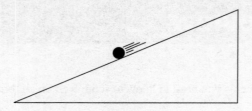

2. A ball rolling down the slope of a steep hill will have

    A.   increasing speed and increasing acceleration.
    B.   increasing speed and decreasing acceleration.
    C.   increasing speed and constant acceleration.
    D.   decreasing speed and increasing acceleration.
    E.   constant speed and constant acceleration.

Questions 3 and 4 are based on the following illustration:

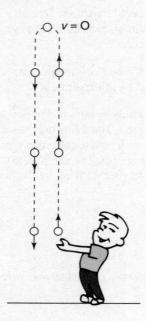

3. A ball thrown straight up will come to a full stop at the top of its path where the acceleration at that moment equals

    A. 9.8 m/s^2.
    B.   zero.
    C.   less than 9.8 m/s^2.
    D.   more than 9.8 m/s^2.
    E.   cannot be determined.

4. After the ball is thrown up and comes to full stop and starts falling down, its speed after 1 second of fall is

    A.   4.9 m/s.

    B.   9.8 m/s.

    C.   19.6 m/s.

    D.   1 m/s.

    E.   32 m/s.

5. A gun is aimed at an orange hanging down from a tree and fired. The incoming bullet is assumed to be at the same height above the ground as the center of the orange. The bullet hits the orange and the orange falls to the ground. The orange's elapsed time to the ground is determined by

    A.   the height of the orange above ground.

    B.   the speed of the bullet.

    C.   whether the bullet penetrates the orange or is embedded in the orange.

    D.   the mass of the orange.

    E.   the mass of the bullet.

Questions 6 and 7 are based on the following figure:

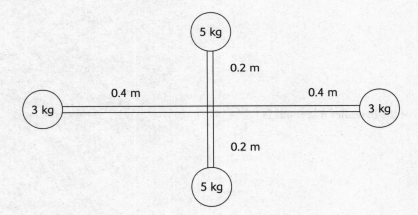

6. The rods joining the four masses shown in the preceding figure have negligible weight. Assuming that the four masses are point masses (that is, their masses are assumed concentrated at their centers of gravity), the moment of inertia of the system is

    A.   16 kg.m^2.

    B.   34 kg.m^2.

    C.   13.6 kg.m^2.

    D.   1.36 kg.m^2.

    E.   0.136 kg.m^2.

7. If the preceding system rotates with an angular velocity ω of 8 radians/second, what is the rotational kinetic energy of the system?

    A.   4.352 J

    B.   43.52 J

    C.   435.2 J

    D.   4352 J

    E.   0.435 J

Questions 8–10 are related to a ball thrown up the inclined plane as shown with an initial velocity v_o of 10 m/s. Two seconds later the ball velocity is 4 m/s.

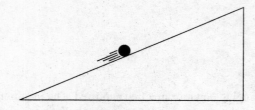

8. The acceleration a of the ball is

   A. -9.8 m/s^2.
   B. 0.
   C. -3 m/s^2.
   D. -6 m/s^2.
   E. 6.8 m/s^2.

9. The maximum distance s the ball travels up the plane from the bottom is

   A. 20 m.
   B. 12.66 m.
   C. 13.66 m.
   D. 16.66 m.
   E. 18.66 m.

10. The velocity v_f of the ball after 3 seconds is

   A. 1 m/s.
   B. 2 m/s.
   C. 3 m/s.
   D. 4 m/s.
   E. 5 m/s.

AFAST Questions

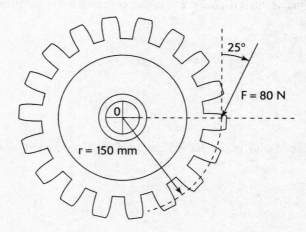

11. The force F in the diagram is applied to the gear of radius r and has a magnitude of 80 N. The resulting moment of F about the center point O is

   A. 1.368 N-m.
   B. 10.87 N-m.

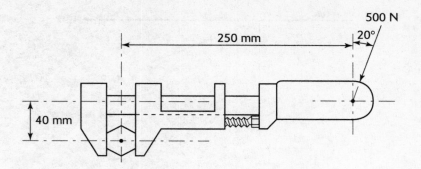

12. The moment M of the 500 N force on the handle of the monkey wrench about the center point of the bolt is

    A.   83.92 N-m.

    B.   110.61 N-m.

ASTB Questions

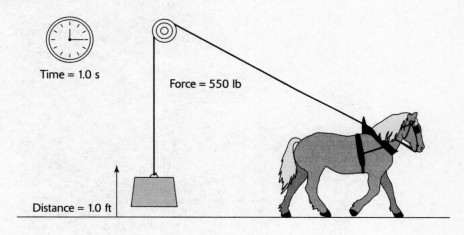

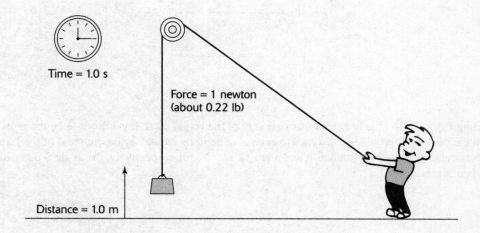

13. In the preceding figure, who is exerting more power? the horse or the man?

    A.   The horse.

    B.   The man.

    C.   Both exert the same power.

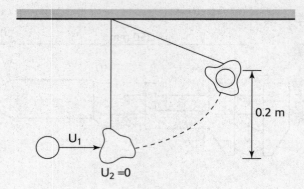

14. A 5-kg wad of clay is tied to the end of a string as shown in the figure. A 300-gm copper ball moving horizontally at velocity u_1 is embedded into the clay and causes the combination of clay and ball to rise to a height of 0.2 m. The initial velocity u_1 of the ball is nearly

   A. 6.3 m/s.
   B. 7.3 m/s.
   C. 8.3 m/s.

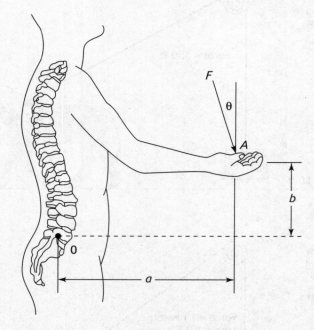

15. The preceding figure shows the lower lumbar region O of the spinal cord. It is known to be the most susceptible part to damage because it provides resistance to excessive bending caused by the moment of the force F about O. If in a particular loading the distances b and a are 12 and 30 cm, respectively, the angle θ that causes the maximum bending strain is

   A. 21.8°
   B. 23.57°
   C. 66.42°

Answers and Explanations

1. **C.** The acceleration is constant at 9.8 m/s^2, but the speed increases with time.

2. **B.** The acceleration a equals g or 9.8 m/s^2 for a straight downfall, but decreases to zero on the level surface at the bottom of the slope.

3. **A.** Acceleration a = g = 9.8 m/s^2 because the ball is under the influence of gravity throughout its path.

4. **B.** The average speed is one half of the initial speed (which is zero) and the final speed after one second (which is 9.8 m/s).

5. **A.** No matter how fast the bullet is, the travel time depends on the height of the orange and the acceleration of gravity regardless of the mass of the orange and bullet. The speed of the bullet determines the horizontal distance of impact of the falling orange when it reaches the ground.

6. **D.** Moment of inertia I = 2[3(0.4)^2 + 5(0.2)^2] = 1.36 kg.m^2.

7. **B.** The rotational kinetic energy E$_k$ = 0.5 Iω^2 = 0.5 (1.36) (8)^2 = 43.52 J.

8. **C.** a = [4 − 10]/2 = −3 m/s^2.

9. **D.** The time t it takes the ball to stop at its maximum point of travel is 10/3 = 3.33 s. As a result s = v$_o$t + 0.5at^2 = 16.66 m.

10. **A.** v$_f$ = v$_o$ + at. Hence v$_f$ = 10 − 3(3) = 1 m/s.

11. **B.** Taking moments about O we obtain net moment M = (0.15)(80 cos 25°) = 10.87 N.m.

12. **B.** Taking moments about the center of the bolt we obtain M = 500 (0.25) cos 20° − 500 (0.04) sin 20° = 110.61 N.m.

13. **A.** It takes 746 watts (or 746 newton.m/s) to equal I horsepower (or 550 ft.lb/s). The horse exerts 550 ft.lb/s or 1 horsepower while the man exerts 1 newton.m/s or 1 Joule/s, which is 1 watt.

14. **C.** Conservation of energy requires that the initial kinetic energy of the ball is converted to potential energy of the ball-clay combination, that is, 0.5 (0.3)u1^2 = (5 + 0.3)(9.8)(0.2) or u1 = 8.32 m/s.

15. **A.** Moment about A is maximum when the force vector F is perpendicular to distance from A to B where B is the point on the hand where F is applied. Thus θ = tan^{-1}(h/b) = tan^{-1} (12/30) = 21.8°.

Instrument Comprehension

Two basic parts make up the instrument comprehension tests that appear in both the Air Force Officer Qualifying Test (AFOQT) and the Alternate Flight Aptitude Selection Test (AFAST): the artificial horizon (sometimes known as an attitude indicator) and the compass. Both sets of questions are similar, except the AFOQT has 20 questions (with 4 choices each) to be answered in 6 minutes, and the AFAST has 15 questions (with 5 choices each) to be answered in 5 minutes.

The key to scoring well in this specific part of either test is to fully understand what you're looking at and being able to match the correct airplane with the illustrations of both the artificial horizon and the compass.

The Compass

Let's start with the compass because it should be easy for most people. After all, you have probably used a compass some time in your life, whether it was as a child, a teenager or an adult. Four basic directions appear on the compass: north, east, south and west. These are known as the *cardinal points*. In addition, *intercardinal points* appear between the cardinal points. These are northeast (45°), southeast (135°), southwest (225°) and northwest (315°). As you can see from this typical compass, all the points are measured in degrees (°).

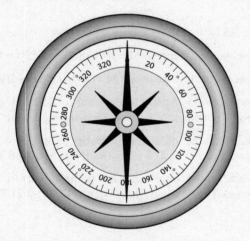

This illustration shows the basic cardinal and intercardinal points, but the compass has a total of 360°. The points that fall between the cardinal and intercardinal points are the *combination points*. However, the tests focus primarily on the cardinal and intercardinal points.

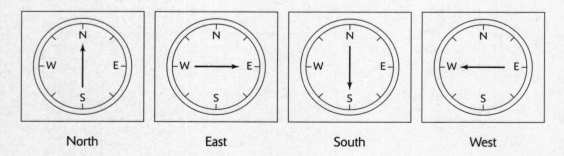

| North | East | South | West |

This is an illustration of the four cardinal points as they would appear on the compass.

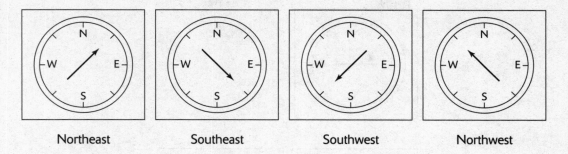

Northeast   Southeast   Southwest   Northwest

This is an illustration of the four intercardinal points as they would appear on the compass.

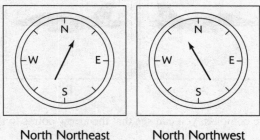

North Northeast   North Northwest

This is an illustration of combination points. You can see that the directional names are combined, so if the arrow appears between north and northeast, the direction would be north northeast. The following is an illustration of what the various degrees are including cardinal points, intercardinal points, and combination points.

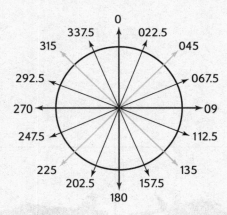

Before we get too involved in other details about the question types, let's look at an example using two planes. Which of the two would be flying in the direction indicated by the compass? **Refer to the chart of aircraft flying positions on page 145.**

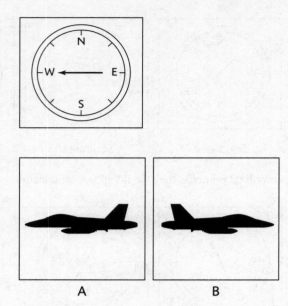

The correct answer is A. Based on the compass, you can see that the arrow points to the west. Plane B is flying east.

In both tests, you are asked to determine which of the four or five airplanes is *most nearly* flying in the direction indicated. Keep in mind that you are always looking north, and therefore east is to the right of the page, south is at the bottom and west is always to your left. The pictures might not always be exact, but you are usually able to start by eliminating those airplanes flying in the wrong direction, such as in the following question.

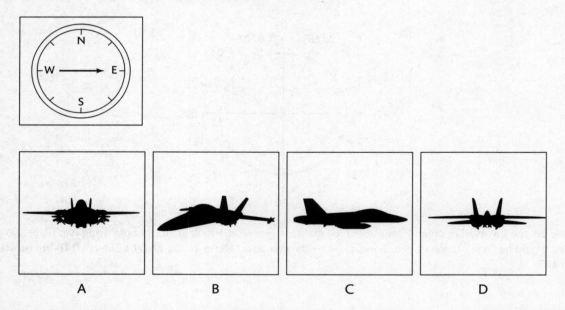

The correct answer is C. The compass points to the right, the east, and all the other planes are flying in other directions.

The Attitude Indicator

The attitude indicator indicates whether you are climbing, diving or flying level. It also indicates whether you are banking to the right, to the left or not banking at all. Combined with the compass, you can get an exact indication of where and how the plane is flying.

For example, the heavy black line is representative of an artificial horizon. On a point in the center for the Attitude Indicator is a representative of an artificial horizon. On a point in the center for the Attitude Indicator is a representation of the aircraft. This artificial aircraft indicator will always remain level to the pilot as the artificial horizon line moves relative to the artificial aircraft. As the aircraft dives, the artificial horizon will move down from the aritificial aircraft indicator. As, the aircraft banks the artificial horizon line will cross through the artificial aircraft indicator in a diagonal direction. If the aircraft is diving or climbing and banking in any direction; the artificial horizon will be at a diagonal relative to the aircraft indicator.

In addition, a small arrowhead indicates the degree of banking to the left or right. If it remains in the middle, no banking is indicated. If the plane is banking to the left, the arrowhead points to the right of zero. If the plane is banking to the right, the arrowhead points to the left of zero.

The following are some typical examples of how the attitude indicator looks.

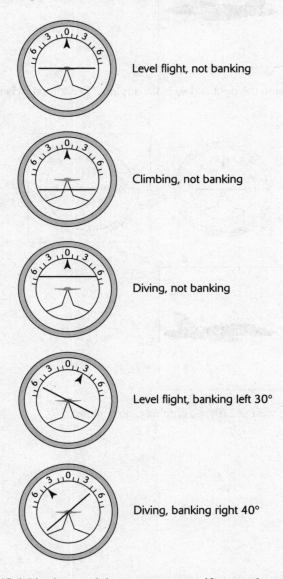

Level flight, not banking

Climbing, not banking

Diving, not banking

Level flight, banking left 30°

Diving, banking right 40°

Now, let's combine both the artificial horizon and the compass to see if you understand what you've just read.

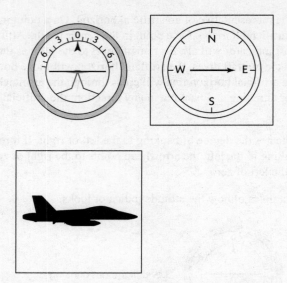

You can see that the arrow is pointing to the right and so is the airplane. In addition, it is in level flight with no banking and heading east at 090°.

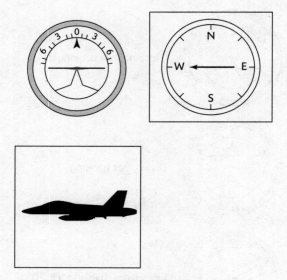

In this illustration, the plane is flying west at 270°, no climbing, no banking.

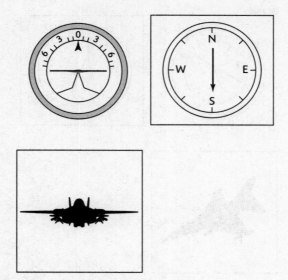

This plane is neither banking nor climbing, and it is flying south at 180°.

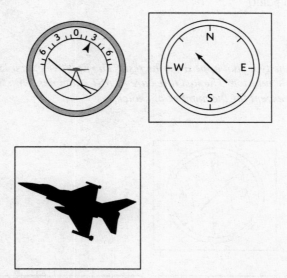

In this illustration, the plane is climbing, banking left and heading 315° northwest.

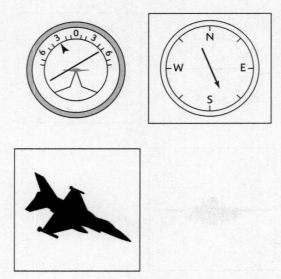

The plane is diving. It is also banking to the right and heading south southeast (because the arrow is pointing between a cardinal point and an intercardinal point).

Practice Questions

It's time to try some questions of the type that appear on the tests. The first five examples are typical of those on the AFOQT, with four choices for each question. The last three are AFAST examples, with five choices each. As you can see, these questions are the same, except for the number of choices.

1.

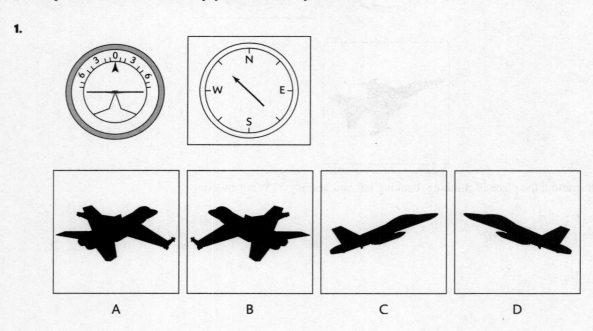

A   B   C   D

2.

 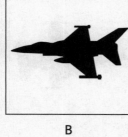

 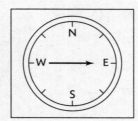 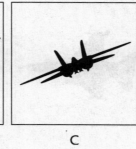 

A   B   C   D

3.

 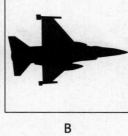

A   B   C   D

4.

 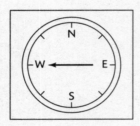  

A   B   C   D

5.

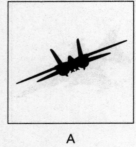 

A   B   C   D

6.

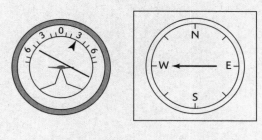

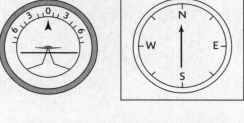

A · · · · · · B · · · · · · C · · · · · · D · · · · · · E

7.

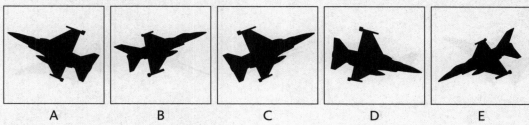

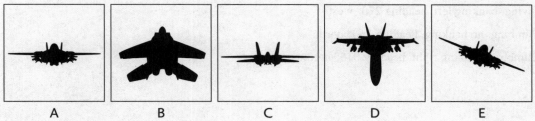

A · · · · · · B · · · · · · C · · · · · · D · · · · · · E

8.

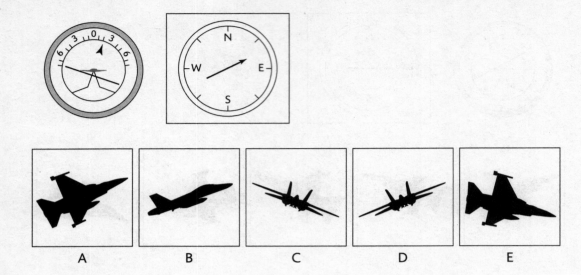

A   B   C   D   E

Answers and Explanations

1. **B.** Level flight, no banking, heading 315° northwest.

2. **C.** Level flight, banking left, heading 360° north.

3. **B.** Level flight, banking 30° left, heading 090° east.

4. **C.** Level flight, banking right, heading 270° west.

5. **B.** Level flight, banking left, heading 270° west.

6. **E.** Diving, banking left, heading 270° west.

7. **B.** Climbing, no banking, heading 360° north.

8. **A.** Climbing, banking right, heading 075° northeast.

Science Review

Life Sciences

The General Sciences test appears in the Air Force Officers Qualifying Test (AFOQT) and is designed to test your general knowledge of science, including life science, physical science, earth science and space science. You probably studied most of these concepts in high school, so this chapter merely serves as a brief review. You don't have to know everything in this chapter, but it's worth reading through quickly and then answering the questions at the end.

Life Sciences

The Cellular Basis of Life

Cells make up all living organisms. Some organisms consist of a single cell, while others are composed of multiple cells organized into tissues and organs.

All cells share two basic features:

- A plasma membrane (the outer boundary of the cell)
- Cytoplasm (a semi-liquid substance that composes the foundation of the cell)

Cells can be classified as either prokaryotic or eukaryotic:

- Prokaryotic cells are relatively simple cells, such as those of bacteria.
- Eukaryotic cells are more complex and contain many internal bodies (organelles) that carry out specialized functions.

The main components of eukaryotic cells include the following:

- The nucleus contains DNA.
- Mitochondria is where the cell produces energy.
- Chloroplasts are where plant cells make food (sugar); animal cells do not contain chloroplasts.
- Ribosomes are where the cell makes proteins.

Movement Through the Plasma Membrane

For cells to exchange materials with the external environment, substances must be able to move through the plasma membrane (the "skin" of a cell). Materials pass through the plasma membrane in one of the following four ways:

- Diffusion: The passive movement of molecules from a region of higher concentration to a region of lower concentration.
- Osmosis: A special type of diffusion that involves the movement of water into and out of the cell.
- Facilitated diffusion: Diffusion of molecules across the cell membrane with the help of special proteins in the cell membrane.
- Active transport: Molecules move across the cell membrane from a region of lower concentration to a region of higher concentration with the help of special proteins in the cell membrane; active transport requires the cell to expend energy.

Photosynthesis

Plants make their own food from simple molecules such as carbon dioxide and water in a process known as photosynthesis. This process requires energy, which the plant obtains from sunlight and captures by way of specialized pigments (chlorophyll) in the chloroplasts of its cells. As a byproduct of photosynthesis, oxygen is released into the atmosphere. This process can be summarized with the following equation:

$$\text{carbon dioxide} + \text{water} \rightarrow \text{glucose (sugar)} + \text{oxygen} + \text{water}$$

Plants absorb light in the red and blue wavelengths for use in photosynthesis. Chlorophyll molecules reflect green light, which is why most plants' leaves appear green.

Cellular Respiration and Fermentation

Animals, plants and microorganisms obtain the energy they need through the process of cellular respiration. In cellular respiration, the cell breaks down carbohydrates (such as glucose) to produce water and carbon dioxide. Energy is released during this process and is stored in the form of adenosine triphosphate (ATP). When a cell needs energy, the bonds in ATP molecules are broken down, and the cell uses the stored energy in metabolism. This process of cellular respiration, which requires the presence of oxygen, can be summarized by the following equation:

$$\text{glucose} + \text{oxygen} \rightarrow \text{water} + \text{carbon dioxide} + \text{energy (ATP)}$$

When no oxygen is present, the cells of some organisms (for example, yeast) carry out a form of anaerobic respiration (respiration without oxygen) known as fermentation. The products of fermentation are carbon dioxide and ethanol.

Cell Division

One distinguishing feature of living organisms is that their cells can divide and reproduce exact copies of themselves. Cell division, combined with cell expansion, allows for the growth and development of organisms.

Cell division occurs in two ways: mitosis and meiosis.

Mitosis

Most of the cells in the body of an organism undergo mitosis. When a cell undergoes mitosis, it produces two exact copies of itself. Before the cell divides, it goes through a synthesis phase during which the DNA (genetic information of a cell) molecules duplicate in each chromosome. Because the DNA duplicates before cell division, the two cells produced during mitosis (daughter cells) each have a complete set of chromosomes containing all the necessary DNA that was present in the original cell (parent cell). After the chromosomes divide, the cytoplasm of the cell divides into two new cells. Thus, the end result of mitosis is an equal separation and distribution of the chromosomes from one parent cell into two new daughter cells.

Meiosis

Specialized cells in the body of an organism (germ cells or sex cells) undergo a unique type of cell division that produces four daughter cells from each parent cell. These daughter cells, each containing half the number of chromosomes as the parent cell, function as gametes (eggs and sperm). Most plant and animal cells have two sets of chromosomes. In human cells, 46 chromosomes are organized into 23 pairs. For sexual reproduction to occur, gametes from two individuals must unite to form a new individual (embryo). For this to occur successfully, while maintaining the normal number of chromosomes in each individual, the germ cells giving rise to the gametes must undergo meiosis. In humans, meiosis produces egg cells and sperm cells that contain 23 chromosomes each—one member of each chromosome pair. When the gametes unite at fertilization, the normal chromosome number (46 in humans) is reestablished in the resulting zygote. The end result of meiosis is the production of four genetically distinct daughter cells from each parent cell.

Genetics

Genetics is the study of how genes control characteristics or traits in living organisms. Genes are portions of DNA molecules that determine the characteristics of an individual. Through the processes of meiosis (which produces eggs and sperm) and reproduction (when eggs and sperm unite to form a zygote), genes are transmitted from parents to offspring.

Genes can take on various forms called alleles. For example, in humans two alleles control earlobe type. One allele codes for earlobes that are attached, while the other allele codes for earlobes that hang free. The alleles inherited from each of their parents determine the type of earlobes a person has.

The following terms summarize the most important genetic concepts:

- Genotype: All the genes present in an individual.
- Phenotype: The expression of the genes in an individual.
- Homozygote: An individual in which both alleles for a given gene are the same.
- Heterozygote: An individual in which the two alleles for a given gene are different.
- Dominant allele: When two alleles are present together in an individual, the allele that is expressed is dominant; it is usually represented by a capital letter.
- Recessive allele: An allele that is masked (not expressed) when present together with a dominant allele in an individual; it is usually represented by a lowercase letter.

Principles of Evolution

Evolution is defined as the change in one or more characteristics of a population of organisms over time. The process of evolution can be summarized using the following principles:

- A large amount of genetic variation is present among living organisms.
- Organisms must compete with each other for a limited supply of natural resources.
- Those individuals that are best able to survive and reproduce are selected through a process called natural selection.

Two essential points underlie natural selection:

- The genetic variation that occurs among individuals is random.
- Traits that allow an individual to survive and reproduce are passed on to the individual's offspring.

Therefore, individuals that are better adapted to their environment are more likely to reproduce and pass on their genes to the next generation. The ability of some individuals to survive and reproduce to a greater degree than other individuals is known as differential reproductive fitness, or survival of the fittest.

As the most reproductively fit individuals contribute a higher percentage of alleles to the next generation, the population gradually evolves.

Other factors that contribute to evolution include:

- Mutations: These give rise to new alleles that didn't previously exist in the population. Mutations might be harmful and selected against, or they might be beneficial and selected for.
- Migration: Movement of individuals into or out of a population, which results in gene flow between two or more populations.
- Random genetic drift: Occurs when a small group of individuals leaves a population and establishes a new population in a geographically isolated region. These individuals might become reproductively isolated from the original population and develop into a separate species.

Several pieces of evidence strongly support evolution:

- The fossil record: Illustrates evidence of a descent of modern organisms from common ancestors.
- Comparative anatomy: Has shown similar structures on many organisms. For example, the forelimbs of such diverse animals as humans, porpoises, cats, birds and bats are strikingly similar, even though the forelimbs are used for very different purposes (lifting, swimming, flying and so on). Also, many organisms have structures that they don't use. In humans, these vestigial structures include the appendix, the fused tail vertebrae and wisdom teeth.

The following figure illustrates the forelimbs of a human and two other animals showing the similarities in construction. These anatomical similarities are considered evidence for evolution.

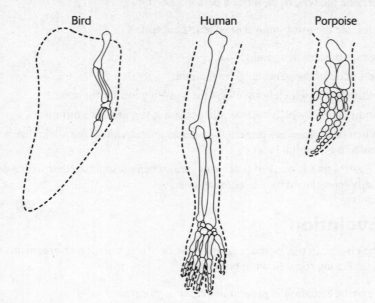

Bird   Human   Porpoise

- Embryology offers additional evidence for evolution. The embryos of fish, reptiles, chickens, rabbits and humans share many similarities. For example, all have gill slits, a two-chambered heart and a tail with muscles. In the later stages of embryo development, the organisms appear less and less similar.

- Biochemical studies have shown similarities among all living organisms. For example, DNA and RNA serve as the basis for inheritance in all living organisms, and the structure of the genetic code is virtually identical in all living organisms.

The Origin and Evolution of Life

Scientists believe that the universe originated about 15 billion years ago with a huge explosion known as the Big Bang. The gases and dust from the explosion produced the earliest stars, and over a period of years, the stars exploded and their debris formed other stars and planets. The solar system is thought to have formed this way 4 to 5 billion years ago. During the next billion years, the Earth cooled, forming a hardened outer crust, and the first living organisms appeared approximately 3.5 billion years ago.

Scientists believe that the first cells lived within the organic environment of the Earth and used organic compounds to obtain energy. However, the organisms would soon use up the organic materials if they were the only source of nutrition and energy. The evolution of a pigment system that could capture energy from the sun and store it in chemical bonds was essential for the evolution of living things. The first organisms to possess these pigments were photosynthetic bacteria, ancestors of modern cyanobacteria. Oxygen, which is produced as a byproduct of photosynthesis, enriched the atmosphere.

Approximately 1.5 billion years ago, in an oxygen-rich environment, the first eukaryotic cells came into being. One theory explaining the development of eukaryotic cells suggests that bacteria were engulfed by larger cells. The bacteria remained in the larger cells and performed specific functions, such as energy production or photosynthesis. This could explain the origin of mitochondria (an energy-producing organelle in a cell) and chloroplasts (the sites of photosynthesis in plant cells). The cells were then able to carry out more complex metabolic functions and eventually came to be the dominant life forms.

For billions of years, the only life on Earth existed in the nutrient-rich environments of the oceans, lakes and rivers. About 600 million years ago, as the atmosphere became rich in oxygen, living organisms began to colonize land. The first multicellular organisms were probably marine invertebrates (animals that lack a spine), followed by wormlike animals with stiff rods in their backs. These organisms, now called chordates, were the ancestors of the amphibians, reptiles, birds and mammals.

Human Evolution

Fossils and fragments of jaws suggest to scientists that the ancestors of monkeys, apes and humans began their evolution approximately 50 million years ago. Additional evidence comes from studies of biochemistry and changes that occur in the DNA of cells.

Scientific evidence indicates that the following species led to modern humans:

- Austrolopithecus: The first hominids (human-like organisms). Members of this group displayed a critical step in human evolution: the ability to walk upright on two feet. Their brains were small in comparison with humans, and they had long, monkey-like arms. Members of this group eventually died out about 1 million years ago.
- Homo habilis: Scientists have found fossils dating back to 2 million years ago that have brain capacities much larger than any Australopithecus fossil. On the basis of brain size, these fossils are called Homo habilis. Homo habilis is regarded as the first human. Members of this species were able to make tools, build shelters and make protective clothing. They also walked upright on two feet.
- Homo erectus: The first hominid to leave Africa for Europe and Asia. Members of this species were about the same size as modern humans and were fully adapted for upright walking. Their brains were much larger than those of their ancestors, and scientists believe that they developed the concept of language.

The earliest fossils of Homo sapiens date to about 200,000 years ago. Scientists classify modern humans in this species. The evolution from Homo erectus to Homo sapiens is thought to have taken place in Africa. Fossil evidence shows a gradual change in 200,000 years, but no new species have emerged.

Classification of Life (Taxonomy)

The Earth is home to more than 300,000 species of plants and over 1 million species of animals. Taxonomists classify organisms in a way that reflects their relationships with each other. All living organisms are named according to an international system in which the organism is given a two-part name. The first name reflects the genus in which the organism is classified, while the second name is the species. For example, humans are assigned the name Homo sapiens.

A group of organisms that can mate with each other under natural conditions and produce fertile offspring is known as a species. Individuals of different species usually do not mate. If they are forced to mate, their offspring are usually sterile and cannot produce offspring of their own. For example, a horse (Equus caballus) can mate with a donkey (Equus assinus); however, the offspring (a mule) is sterile and cannot reproduce.

The standard classification scheme provides a mechanism for bringing together various species into progressively larger groups, as follows:

- Genus: Consists of one or more related species
- Family: Consists of similar genera
- Order: Consists of families with similar characteristics
- Class: Consists of orders with similar characteristics
- Phylum (or Division): Consists of related classes (The term division is used for classifying plants and fungi, while phylum is used for classifying animals and animal-like organisms.)
- Kingdom: Consists of related divisions or phyla
- Domain: The broadest level of classification

The classification scheme that is currently most widely accepted recognizes three domains: domain Archaea, domain Eubacteria and domain Eukarya. Domain Eukarya is subdivided into four kingdoms: Protista, Fungi, Plantae and Animalia.

The following illustration shows hypothetical relationships among organisms.

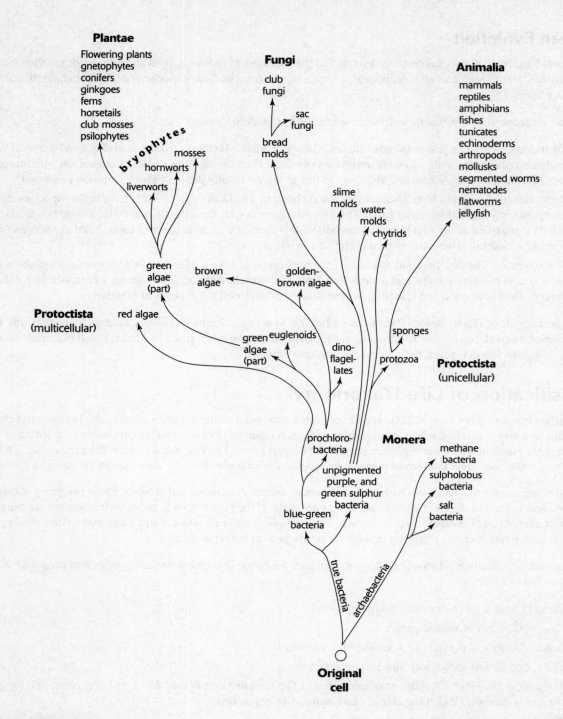

Plantae

Flowering plants
gnetophytes
conifers
ginkgoes
ferns
horsetails
club mosses
psilophytes

bryophytes

mosses
hornworts
liverworts

green algae (part)

brown algae

red algae

Protoctista
(multicellular)

green algae (part)

euglenoids

Fungi

club fungi

sac fungi

bread molds

slime molds

water molds

chytrids

golden-brown algae

dino-flagel-lates

sponges

protozoa

Animalia

mammals
reptiles
amphibians
fishes
tunicates
echinoderms
arthropods
mollusks
segmented worms
nematodes
flatworms
jellyfish

Protoctista
(unicellular)

prochloro-bacteria

unpigmented purple, and green sulphur bacteria

blue-green bacteria

Monera

methane bacteria

sulpholobus bacteria

salt bacteria

true bacteria

archaebacteria

Original cell

Domain Archaea

Members of the domain Archaea are primitive bacteria, most of which are prokaryotic anaerobic organisms that use methane production in their energy metabolism. They are primarily found in marshes and swamps.

Domain Eubacteria

Members of the eubacteria are prokaryotic organisms. You can find them in nearly all environments on Earth, including soil, water and air. Most species of eubacteria are heterotrophic—they acquire their food from organic matter. Many are saprobic—they feed on dead and decaying organic matter. Some are parasitic—living within a host organism and causing disease. Several species of eubacteria are autotrophic—they have the ability to synthesize their own food. Most of the autotrophic eubacteria use pigments to absorb light energy and make food through the process of photosynthesis. Some autotrophic bacteria are chemosynthetic—they use chemical reactions as a source of energy from which they synthesize their own food.

Unfortunately, many eubacteria are pathogenic, causing diseases in plants, animals and humans, including such diseases as tuberculosis, gonorrhea, syphilis, pneumonia and food poisoning.

The cyanobacteria are photosynthetic members of the eubacteria. They are important components of the plankton found in oceans, and they contribute a significant amount of oxygen to the atmosphere. Scientists believe the cyanobacteria were among the first photosynthetic organisms to colonize the Earth's surface.

Domain Eukarya

Members of the domain Eukarya are all eukaryotic organisms. They include members of the kingdoms Protista, Fungi, Plantae and Animalia.

Kingdom Protista

Members of the kingdom Protista are a highly varied group of organisms, including protozoa, slime molds and algae. Many species are autotrophs, creating their own food, while others are heterotrophs, feeding on organic matter.

- Protozoa: Protozoa are subdivided into four phyla based on their method of locomotion:
  - ❑ Mastigophora: Organisms that move about by using one or more whip-like flagella. Some species live within the bodies of animals, such as the wood-digesting organisms found in the intestines of termites. Other species contain photosynthetic pigments and are often found as components of plankton.
  - ❑ Sarcodina: The amoebas and their relatives. They each consist of a single cell that lacks a definite shape, and they typically feed on small particles of organic matter, which they engulf.
  - ❑ Ciliophora: Organisms that move by means of cilia, such as the common paramecium.
  - ❑ Sporozoa: Organisms in this phylum are all parasites.
- Slime molds: Slime molds have certain properties that resemble fungi, as well as protozoa-like properties. True slime molds consist of a single, flat, large, multinucleate cell, while cellular slime molds consist of amoeba-like cells that live independently but unite with other cellular slime mold cells to form a single, large, flat, multinucleate organism.
- Algae: The term algae refers to a large number of photosynthetic organisms that range from single-celled forms to complex, multicellular organisms that resemble plants. Algal species occur in bodies of both fresh and salt water. Algae are subdivided into several divisions, based in part on the pigments they possess.
  - ❑ Red algae: These are almost exclusively marine organisms (seaweeds) and include both single-celled and multicellular species.
  - ❑ Golden-brown algae (dinoflagellates): These are single-celled organisms that are surrounded by thick plates that give them an armored appearance.
  - ❑ Golden algae (diatoms): These are single-celled organisms with cell walls containing silica (glass). In the ocean, diatoms carry out photosynthesis and serve as an important food source at the base of food chains.
  - ❑ Brown algae: These are primarily multicellular marine organisms (seaweeds), and include the rock-weeds and kelps.
  - ❑ Green algae: These include both single-celled forms and complex, multicellular organisms. They share many characteristics with plants and are thought to be the ancestors of higher plants.

Kingdom Fungi

Fungi, together with eubacteria and some protists, are the major decomposers of organic matter on Earth. Most fungi digest nonliving organic matter such as wood, leaves and dead animals. However, some fungi are parasitic, living off other living organisms. Parasitic fungi cause many diseases affecting plants, animals and humans. Other fungi are economically important, including species used to flavor cheeses. One species, Penicillium notatum, is the original source of the antibiotic penicillin.

The method by which they obtain nutrients distinguishes fungi from the other kingdoms. Fungi secrete enzymes into the environment that break down organic matter, and then they absorb the nutrients through their cell membranes. This process is referred to as extracellular digestion.

Kingdom Plantae

Plants are multicellular eukaryotic organisms with the ability to produce their own food through the process of photosynthesis. They are divided into two main groups:

- Nonvascular plants: These are plants that do not have specialized tissues for transporting water and nutrients. Nonvascular plants include the mosses, liverworts and hornworts. Because these plants lack conducting tissues, they cannot grow very large and cannot retain water for extended periods of time. This is why they are typically found only in moist areas. They also must rely on the presence of water for fertilization to occur.
- Vascular plants: These are plants that contain specialized structures for transporting water and nutrients. The vascular plants encompass several divisions of plants. They are characterized by the presence of two types of specialized tissue, the xylem and the phloem. Xylem conducts water and minerals upward through the plant, while phloem transports sugars from the leaves, where they are made during photosynthesis, to other parts of the plant body. The vascular tissue also serves as a means of support in the plant, so vascular plants are capable of maintaining a much larger size than nonvascular plants.

The different types of vascular plants are as follows:

- Seedless vascular plants: Among the seedless vascular plants are the ferns and fern allies (whisk ferns, club mosses, spike mosses and horsetails). These plants reproduce by producing spores on the surfaces of their leaves or in specialized cone-shaped structures.
- Vascular plants with unprotected seeds: The vascular plants that produce unprotected (naked) seeds are known as gymnosperms. Their seeds are not enclosed within tissues of the female parent. Included in the gymnosperms are pines, firs, spruces, redwoods, cypress, yews, cycads, ginkgo and ephedra.

   Mature trees produce male and female cones. The male cones produce pollen grains, which contain sperm, while the female cones produce two or three egg cells that develop within ovules located on the surfaces of the cone scales.
- Vascular plants with protected seeds: The angiosperms are the most highly developed and complex of the vascular plants. They are the flowering plants, of which more than a quarter of a million species have been identified. The seeds of angiosperms develop within protective tissues of the female parent.

Angiosperms deserve more discussion. The flower of the angiosperm consists of four rings of modified leaves:

- Sepals: These comprise the outer ring of modified leaves that enclose and protect the developing flower bud. In some species the sepals are small and green, while in others they become colored and resemble petals.
- Petals: These comprise the next ring of modified leaves found in the flower. Flower petals are usually colorful and serve to attract pollinators.
- Stamens (male reproductive structures): These comprise the third ring of modified leaves. Each stamen consists of a stalk called the filament with a bulbous structure at the end called the anther, in which pollen grains are produced.
- Pistil (female reproductive structure): These consist of a tubular structure called the style, with a sticky surface at the top for catching pollen called the stigma, and an enlarged region (ovary) at the base. Within the ovary, an embryo sac develops that consists of eight nuclei.

During pollination, pollen grains land on the stigma of a female flower where they germinate and form a pollen tube. The pollen tube grows down the style and into an opening in the ovary. When the pollen tube reaches the ovary, two sperm cells are released. One sperm cell unites with the egg cell in the embryo sac to form a diploid zygote, while the second sperm unites with two other nuclei to form a triploid endosperm. The remaining nuclei in the embryo sac degenerate.

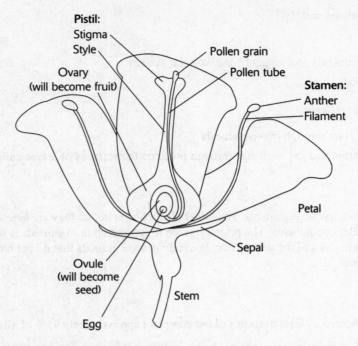

Pistil:
Stigma
Style
Ovary
(will become fruit)
Pollen grain
Pollen tube
Stamen:
Anther
Filament
Petal
Sepal
Ovule
(will become seed)
Stem
Egg

The zygote develops into an embryo surrounded by the endosperm, which serves as nutritive tissue for the developing embryo. The ovary tissue expands, forming a fruit, which serves as a protective covering for the developing seed. The protective fruit tissue also serves as an important dispersal mechanism:

- Fleshy fruits are often eaten by animals, and the seeds travel inside the animals to other locations where they are dispersed when the animals defecate.
- Some fruits have barbs or hooks on the outer fruit that attach to the fur of animals and are dispersed in that manner.
- Some fruits become dry when they mature. Some of these split open quite forcefully, ejecting their seeds great distances, while other dry fruits have thin paper tissue attached to them that serve as wings for dispersal by wind.

Structure and Function of Higher Plants

Higher plants have four types of tissues:

- Vascular tissues: These include xylem, which conducts water and minerals from the roots upward throughout the plant, and phloem, which transports dissolved foods in all directions throughout the plant.
- Dermal tissues: Dermal tissues cover the outside of the plant and consist primarily of epidermal cells (equivalent to the skin cells of humans). These tissues protect the plant from injury and water loss.
- Ground tissues: These tissues are located between the vascular tissues and dermal tissues and are responsible for storing carbohydrates that the plant produces.
- Meristematic tissues: Meristematic tissues are found in regions where the plant is actively growing (where cell division is occurring). Primary meristematic tissues are found in the root tips and shoot tips and are responsible for growth in length. Secondary (lateral) meristematic tissues are found only in woody plants and are responsible for growth in width.

Plant Organs

The three organs found in plants are the roots, the stems and the leaves. Flowers are modified leaves.

The main functions of the roots are:

- Anchoring the plant in the soil
- Taking in water and minerals from the soil

The main functions of the stems are:

- Supporting the plant
- Transporting water, minerals and sugars by the vascular system
- Storing water and food

The main functions of the leaves are:

- Making food for the plant through photosynthesis
- Allowing for evaporation and gas exchange through pores on the surfaces of leaves called stomata

Kingdom Animalia

Animals are multicellular eukaryotic organisms. They differ from plants in that they are heterotrophic: They take in food and digest it into smaller components. The primary mode of reproduction in animals is sexual. Two major groups of animals exist: the invertebrates and the vertebrates. Invertebrates are animals that do not have a spine, while vertebrates are animals with spines.

Invertebrates

The invertebrates are represented by numerous phyla and comprise approximately 95% of all animal species.

- Phylum Porifera includes a number of simple animals commonly referred to as sponges.
- Phylum Cnidaria includes hydras, jellyfish, sea corals and sea anemones.
- Phylum Platyhelminthes includes the flatworms, such as planaria and tapeworms.
- Phylum Aschelminthes (also known as Nematoda) includes the nematodes, or roundworms, many of which are microscopic.
- Phylum Annelida includes the segmented worms, such as earthworms and leeches.
- Phylum Mollusca includes soft-bodied animals, such as the snail, clam, squid, oyster and octopus. Some members secrete a hard shell.
- Phylum Arthropoda includes spiders, ticks, centipedes, lobsters and insects.
- Phylum Echinodermata includes sea stars, brittle stars, sea urchins and sea cucumbers. These animals have spiny skin that helps protect them from predators. All echinoderms have an internal support system called an endoskeleton and a large body cavity containing a set of canals called a water vascular system.
- Phylum Chordata includes both invertebrate members and vertebrate members.

Vertebrates

Members of the phylum Chordata that have spines are classified in the subphylum Vertebrata. More than 40,000 living species of vertebrates exist, divided into several classes encompassing the fishes, amphibians, reptiles, birds and mammals.

- Fishes are aquatic animals with a streamlined shape and a functional tail that allows them to move rapidly through water. Fishes exchange gases with their environment through gills, although a few species have lungs that supplement gas exchange.
- Amphibians are animals that live both on land and in water. They include the frogs, toads and salamanders. Amphibians live on land and breathe air; however, they are also able to exchange gases through their skin and the inner lining of their mouth. Amphibians remain in moist environments to avoid dehydration and lay their eggs in water because the eggs would quickly dry out on land. Young amphibians (for example, tadpoles) live in the water, while the adults live on land.
- Reptiles include lizards, snakes, crocodiles, alligators and turtles. Reptiles have a dry, scaly skin that retards water loss, and the structure of their limbs provides better support for moving quickly on land. Their lungs have a greater surface area than those of amphibians, allowing them to inhale greater quantities of air. The circulatory

system in reptiles includes a three-chambered heart that separates oxygen-rich blood from oxygen-poor blood. Reproduction in reptiles occurs on land.

- Birds have many structures that make them adapted to flight. For example, the body is streamlined to minimize air resistance, they have feathers, and their bones are light and hollow. Feathers also serve to insulate against loss of body heat and water. Birds are homeothermic, meaning they are able to maintain a constant body temperature. The rapid pumping of their four-chambered heart and a high blood flow rate contribute to this characteristic.

- Mammals are animals that have hair and nourish their young with milk that they produce through mammary glands. The presence of body hair or fur helps maintain a constant body temperature in these homeothermic animals. Several types of mammals exist:

  ❑ Monotremes are egg-laying mammals that produce milk. The duck-billed platypus and the spiny anteater are monotremes.

  ❑ Marsupials are mammals whose embryos develop within the mother's uterus for a short period of time before birth. After birth, the immature babies crawl into the mother's abdominal pouch where they complete their development. Kangaroos, opossums and koala bears are marsupials.

  ❑ Placental mammals include rabbits, deer, dogs, cats, whales, monkeys and humans. These mammals have a placenta—a connection between the embryo and the mother's uterine wall that allows the embryo to obtain nutrients from the mother. Embryos are attached to the placenta and complete their development within their mother's uterus.

All mammals have a highly developed nervous system, and many have developed acute senses of smell, hearing, sight, taste or touch. Mammals rely on memory and learning to guide their activities. They are considered the most successful group of animals on Earth today.

Anatomy and Physiology

The Human Digestive System

All the elements and compounds that a living organism takes in are considered nutrients. Animals, including humans, are heterotrophic organisms, and their nutrients consist of preformed organic molecules. These organic molecules usually must be processed into more simple forms by digestion before cells can take them in.

The nutrients used by animals include:

- Carbohydrates: These are the basic source of energy for all animals. Glucose is the carbohydrate most often used as an energy source; it is metabolized during cellular respiration to provide energy in the form of adenosine triphosphate (ATP). Other useful carbohydrates include maltose, lactose, sucrose and starch.

- Lipids: These are used to form cellular membranes, the sheaths surrounding nerve fibers, and certain hormones. One type of lipid, fat, is a useful energy source.

- Nucleic acids: These are used to make DNA and RNA. They are obtained from ingesting plant and animal tissues.

- Proteins: These form the framework of the animal body and are major components of membranes, muscles, ligaments, tendons and enzymes. Twenty different amino acids make up proteins. While the body can make some amino acids, others must be supplied by diet.

- Minerals: These are required by animals in small amounts and include phosphorous, sulfur, potassium, magnesium and zinc. Animals usually obtain these minerals when they consume plants.

- Vitamins: These are organic compounds essential in trace amounts for animal health. Some vitamins are water soluble (break down easily in water), while others are fat soluble (break down easily in fats).

Human digestion is a complex process that consists of breaking down large organic masses into smaller particles that the body can use as fuel. The major organs or structures that coordinate digestion in humans include the mouth, esophagus, stomach, small intestine and large intestine.

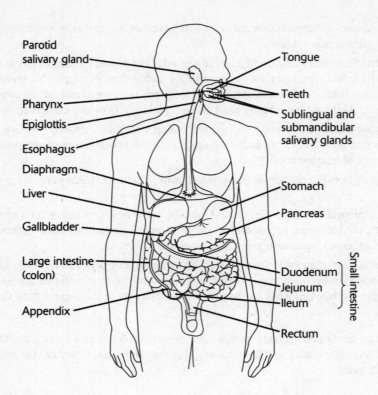

Parotid salivary gland

Tongue

Teeth

Pharynx

Sublingual and submandibular salivary glands

Epiglottis

Esophagus

Diaphragm

Stomach

Liver

Pancreas

Gallbladder

Large intestine (colon)

Duodenum

Jejunum

Ileum

Small intestine

Appendix

Rectum

Human Respiratory System

The human respiratory system consists of a complex set of organs and tissues that capture oxygen from the environment and transport the oxygen to the lungs. The organs and tissues that comprise the human respiratory system include the following:

- Nose: The human respiratory system begins with the nose, where air is conditioned by warming and moistening. Hairs trap dust particles and purify the air.

- Pharynx: Air passes from the nose into the pharynx (throat). From the pharynx, two tubes called Eustachian tubes open to the middle ear to equalize pressure. The pharynx also contains tonsils and adenoids, which trap and filter microorganisms.

- Trachea: From the pharynx, air passes into the trachea (windpipe). The opening to the trachea is a slit-like structure called the glottis. A thin flap of tissue called the epiglottis folds over the opening during swallowing and prevents food from entering the trachea. At the upper end of the trachea, several folds of cartilage form the larynx, or voice box. In the larynx, flap-like tissues called vocal cords vibrate when a person exhales and produce sounds. At its lower end, the trachea branches into two large bronchi. These tubes branch into smaller bronchioles, which terminate into sacs called alveoli.

- Lungs: Human lungs are composed of approximately 300 million alveoli, which are cup-shaped sacs surrounded by a capillary network. Red blood cells pass through the capillaries, and oxygen enters and binds to the hemoglobin. In addition, carbon dioxide contained in the red blood cells leaves the capillaries and enters the alveoli.

Human Circulatory System

The function of the human circulatory system is to transport blood and oxygen from the lungs to various tissues of the body. The components of the human circulatory system include the following:

- Heart: The human heart is about the size of a clenched fist. It contains four chambers: two atria and two ventricles. Oxygen-poor blood enters the right atrium through a major vein called the vena cava. The blood passes into the right ventricle and is pumped through the pulmonary artery to the lungs for gas exchange. Oxygen-rich blood returns to the left atrium via the pulmonary vein. The oxygen-rich blood flows into the left ventricle from which it is pumped through a major artery, the aorta. Coronary arteries supply the heart muscle with blood. The heart is controlled by nerves that originate on the right side in the upper region of the atrium at a node called the pacemaker.

- Blood: The fluid portion of the blood, the plasma, is a straw-colored liquid composed primarily of water. Nutrients, hormones, clotting proteins and waste products are transported in the plasma. Red blood cells and white blood cells are also suspended in the plasma.

- Red blood cells: Also called erythrocytes, red blood cells are disk-shaped cells produced in the bone marrow. They do not have a nucleus and are filled with hemoglobin. Hemoglobin is a red-pigmented protein that binds loosely to oxygen and carbon dioxide and transports these substances throughout the body. Red blood cells usually have immune-stimulating antigens on their surfaces.

- White blood cells: Also called leukocytes, white blood cells are generally larger than red blood cells and contain nuclei. They are also produced in the bone marrow and have various functions in the body. Certain white blood cells, called lymphocytes, are part of the immune system. Other cells, called neutrophils and monocytes, function primarily as phagocytes; they attack and engulf invading microorganisms.

- Platelets: Platelets are small, disk-shaped blood fragments produced in the bone marrow. They lack nuclei and are much smaller than red blood cells. They serve as the starting material for blood clotting.

- Lymphatic system: The lymphatic system is an extension of the circulatory system consisting of:
  - ❑ Lymph: A watery fluid derived from plasma that has seeped out of capillaries.
  - ❑ Lymphatic vessels: Capillaries that return fluids to the circulatory system.
  - ❑ Lymph nodes: Hundreds of tiny, capsule-like bodies located in the neck, armpits and groin; the lymph nodes filter the lymph and digest foreign particles.
  - ❑ Spleen: Composed primarily of lymph-node tissue, it is the site where red blood cells are destroyed.

Human Excretory System

The human excretory system removes waste from the body through the kidneys. The human kidneys are bean-shaped organs located on either side of the spine at about the level of the stomach and liver. Blood enters the kidneys through renal arteries and leaves through renal veins. Tubes (ureters) carry waste products from the kidneys to the urinary bladder for storage or release. The product of the kidneys is urine, a watery solution of waste products, salts, organic compounds, uric acid and urea. Uric acid results from the breakdown of nucleic acids and urea results from the breakdown of amino acids in the liver. Both of these nitrogen-rich compounds can be poisonous to the body and must be removed in the urine.

Human Endocrine System

The human body has two levels of coordination: nervous coordination and chemical coordination. Chemical coordination is centered on a system of glands known as endocrine glands, which secrete hormones that help coordinate the major body systems. These glands are situated throughout the body and include the following:

- Pituitary gland: The pituitary gland is located at the base of the human brain.
- Thyroid gland: The thyroid gland lies against the pharynx at the base of the neck.
- Adrenal glands: The adrenal glands are two pyramid-shaped glands lying atop the kidneys.
- Pancreas: The pancreas is located just behind the stomach. It produces two hormones: insulin and glucagon.
- Ovaries: The ovaries in females function as endocrine glands; they secrete estrogens, which encourage the development of secondary female characteristics.
- Testes: The testes in males also function as endocrine glands; they secrete androgens (including testosterone), which promote secondary male characteristics.

Human Nervous System

Nervous coordination enables the body to rapidly respond to external or internal stimuli. The human nervous system is divided into the central nervous system (the brain and spinal cord) and the peripheral nervous system (the nerves extending to and from the central nervous system).

Central Nervous System

The spinal cord extends from the base of the brain to the end of the spine. Three membranes called meninges surround the spinal cord and protect it. The neurons of the spinal cord serve as a coordinating center and a connecting system between the peripheral nervous system and the brain.

The brain is the organizing and processing center of the central nervous system. It is the site of consciousness, sensation, memory and intelligence. The brain receives impulses from the spinal cord and from 12 pairs of cranial nerves coming from and extending to the other senses and organs. The brain can also initiate activities without external stimuli. Three major regions of the brain are recognized:

- Hindbrain: The hindbrain consists of the following three regions:
  - ❑ Medulla: The swelling at the tip of the brain; serves as a passageway for nerves extending to and from the brain.
  - ❑ Cerebellum: Lies adjacent to the medulla; coordinates muscle contractions.
  - ❑ Pons: The swelling between the medulla and the midbrain; acts as a bridge between various regions of the brain.
- Midbrain: The midbrain lies between the hindbrain and forebrain. It consists of a collection of crossing nerve tracts and a group of fibers that arouse the forebrain when something unusual happens.
- Forebrain: The forebrain consists of the following regions:
  - ❑ Cerebrum: The site of such activities as speech, vision, movement, hearing, smell, learning, memory, logic, creativity and emotion.
  - ❑ Thalamus: Serves as an integration point for sensory impulses.
  - ❑ Hypothalamus: Synthesizes hormones for storage in the pituitary gland and serves as the control center for hunger, thirst, body temperature and blood pressure.
  - ❑ Limbic system: A collection of structures that ring the edge of the brain and serve as centers of emotion.

Peripheral Nervous System

The peripheral nervous system is a collection of nerves that connect the brain and spinal cord to other parts of the body and the external environment. It includes the following:

- Sensory somatic system: Carries impulses from the external environment and the senses; it permits humans to be aware of the outside environment and react to it voluntarily.
- Autonomic nervous system: Works on an involuntary basis; it is divided into two regions:
  - ❑ Sympathetic nervous system: Prepares the body for emergencies; impulses propagated by the sympathetic nervous system cause the heartbeat to increase, the arteries to constrict and the pupils to dilate.
  - ❑ Parasympathetic nervous system: Allows the body to return to its normal state following an emergency, and is also responsible for helping digestion and preparing the body for sleep.

Human Reproduction

Reproduction is an essential process for the survival of a species. Human reproduction takes place by the coordination of the male and female reproductive systems. In humans, both males and females have evolved specialized organs and tissues that produce haploid cells by meiosis, the sperm and the egg. These cells fuse to form a zygote that eventually develops into a growing fetus. A network of hormones is secreted that controls both the male and female reproductive systems and assists in the growth and development of the fetus, as well as the birthing process.

Male Reproductive System

The male reproductive system is composed of the following structures:

- Testes (or testicles): Two egg-shaped organs located in a pouch outside the body called the scrotum.
- Seminiferous tubules: Coiled passageways within the testes where sperm cells are produced.

- Penis: The organ responsible for carrying the sperm cells to the female reproductive tract; within the penis, the sperm are carried in a tube called the urethra.
- Semen: Composed of secretions from the prostate gland, seminal vesicles, and Cowper's glands, plus the sperm cells.

Female Reproductive System

The organs of the female reproductive system include the following structures:

- Ovaries: Two oval organs lying within the pelvic cavity.
- Fallopian tubes: Tubes leading from the ovaries that the eggs enter after they are released from the ovaries following meiosis; the site of fertilization of the egg by the sperm.
- Uterus: A muscular organ in the pelvic cavity to which the eggs travel through the Fallopian tubes.
- Endrometrium: The inner lining of the uterus; it thickens with blood and tissue in anticipation of a fertilized egg cell. If fertilization fails to occur, the endometrium degenerates and is shed in the process of menstruation.
- Cervix: The opening at the lower end of the uterus.
- Vagina: The tube leading from the cervix to the outside of the body; the vagina receives the penis and the semen.

The sperm cells in the semen pass through the cervix and uterus into the Fallopian tubes, where fertilization takes place. Fertilization brings together 23 chromosomes from the male (sperm) and 23 chromosomes from the female (egg), resulting in the formation of a fertilized egg cell (called a zygote) with 46 chromosomes—the number present in normal human cells.

Ecology

Ecology is the discipline of biology concerned primarily with the interaction between organisms and their environments. Many levels of organization exist among living organisms, including the following:

- Population: A population is a group of individuals belonging to one species living in a defined area.
- Community: A community consists of the various plant and animal species living in a defined area. Within a community, each population of organisms has a habitat (the physical location where an organism lives) and a niche (the role that organism plays in the community).
- Ecosystem: An ecosystem includes all the organisms living together in a community, interacting with each other and with nonliving factors (water, light, soil and so on).

Organisms living together in an ecosystem interact with each other in various ways, including the following:

- Mutualism: The relationship between two organisms is mutually beneficial, such as the relationship between fungi and cyanobacteria in lichens.
- Commensalism: The relationship benefits one organism but does not affect the other organism, such as the bacteria living in the guts of humans.
- Parasitism: The relationship benefits one organism, while the other is harmed. The microorganisms that cause human diseases are parasites.
- Predation: This occurs when one organism feeds on another organism. In this type of relationship, one organism benefits and the other is harmed (as in parasitism).

One of the major factors responsible for sustaining an ecosystem is the flow of energy within it. Energy is transferred from one organism to another in an ecosystem through food chains. Food chains are composed of the following:

- Producers: Photosynthesizing organisms (plants, algae) that trap the energy from the sun to make their own food
- Primary consumers: Organisms that feed directly on producers (herbivores)
- Secondary consumers: Organisms that feed on primary consumers (carnivores)
- Decomposers: Organisms (fungi, slime molds, bacteria) that break down dead organisms and recycle the nutrients back into the environment

Many food chains interact to form a food web.

The food pyramid illustrates the availability of food in an ecosystem at successive levels (trophic levels) of a food chain. The number of producers, which are always at the base of the pyramid, is high, and the number of consumers at the top of the pyramid is always low. The difference in numbers of individuals at each trophic level occurs because only a small percentage of the food energy available at one level can be passed on to the next. This is because much of the energy is used up during metabolism in the organisms at each level. The following figure shows a hypothetical food pyramid.

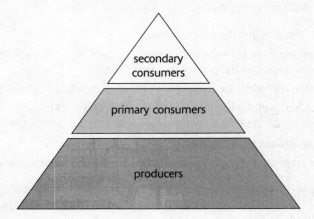

Another mechanism for sustaining an ecosystem is the recycling of nutrients and minerals. Carbon, nitrogen and phosphorus are examples of substances that are recycled through ecosystems. Much of the carbon is recycled through respiration; however, the majority is recycled through decomposition. Nitrogen, which is vital for the synthesis of proteins and nucleic acids, is released to the atmosphere as waste products by bacteria.

All life is confined to a five-mile vertical space around the surface of the Earth, called the biosphere. The biosphere is composed of the living organisms and the physical environment that blankets the Earth. The physical environment includes the rocky material of the Earth's surface, the water on or near the Earth's surface, and the blanket of gases surrounding the Earth.

The biosphere is divided into subunits called biomes. Each biome is characterized by the climatic conditions present, which determine which species can live there. Examples of biomes include deserts, tropical forests, temperate forests, prairies, tundra and taiga (the southern edge of the tundra).

Chemistry

Matter and Atomic Structure

Matter is defined as anything with a definite mass that takes up volume. The three common states of matter are solids, liquids and gases. Matter can be made of simple things like diamond, water or neon, or it can be made of very complex things like heat resistant shields on the Space Shuttle, blood plasma or anesthesiology gases. Several distinctions exist between solids, liquids and gases, and they can be summarized as follows:

- Solids have a defined mass, volume and shape.
- Liquids have a defined mass and volume, but not a defined shape.
- Gases have a defined mass, but not a defined volume or shape. (They expand to fill any container.)

All the matter you see and use is made of a few fundamental particles called protons, neutrons and electrons. These subatomic particles make up atoms. Atoms are specific collections of protons and neutrons surrounded by electrons. Each of these subatomic particles is different by mass and charge.

Protons and neutrons are located at the center of the atom and make up a region called the nucleus. Outside the nucleus are the electrons, which make up the electron cloud. The current model of an atom is fairly complex. The electrons are not randomly arranged in the electron cloud, but occupy locations called orbitals. These orbitals can be arranged in shells around the nucleus of the atom.

With these three particles, atoms can be made, and from these atoms, every solid, liquid and gas in the universe is formed. Conceivably, an infinite number of combinations of subatomic particles could exist, but not all combinations are stable. In fact, only 112 elements have been found or created. An element is a material that cannot be chemically broken down into something simpler. Elements are made of atoms and, as noted, atoms are made of electrons, protons and neutrons.

The Periodic Table

To save time and space, elements have been assigned a one- or two-letter designation called an atomic or elemental symbol. Always capitalize the first letter and, if there is a second letter, always write it in lower case. Without this rule, some chemical formulas might be misinterpreted. (Co is the symbol for cobalt, but CO is the symbol for a compound containing one carbon atom and one oxygen atom.) A list of all atomic symbols is given in the periodic table.

Key (for the first few cells):
- Atomic number
- Elemental symbol
- Atomic mass

1A	2A	3B	4B	5B	6B	7B	8B	8B	8B	1B	2B	3A	4A	5A	6A	7A	8A
1 H 1.00794																	2 He 4.00260
3 Li 6.941	4 Be 9.01218											5 B 10.811	6 C 12.011	7 N 14.0067	8 O 15.9994	9 F 18.99840	10 Ne 20.1797
11 Na 22.98977	12 Mg 24.305											13 Al 26.9815	14 Si 28.0855	15 P 30.97376	16 S 32.066	17 Cl 35.4527	18 Ar 39.948
19 K 39.0983	20 Ca 40.07838	21 Sc 44.9556	22 Ti 47.88	23 V 50.9415	24 Cr 51.994	25 Mn 54.938	26 Fe 55.847	27 Co 58.9332	28 Ni 58.6934	29 Cu 63.546	30 Zn 65.39	31 Ga 69.723	32 Ge 72.61	33 As 74.9216	34 Se 78.96	35 Br 79.904	36 Kr 93.80
37 Rb 85.4678	38 Sr 87.62	39 Y 88.9059	40 Zr 91.224	41 Nb 92.9064	42 Mo 95.94	43 Tc (98)	44 Ru 101.07	45 Rh 102.9055	46 Pd 105.42	47 Ag 107.868	48 Cd 112.41	49 In 114.82	50 Sn 118.710	51 Sb 121.757	52 Te 127.60	53 I 126.9045	54 Xe 131.29
55 Cs 132.9045	56 Ba 137.33	57 La 138.9055	72 Hf 178.49	73 Ta 180.9479	74 W 183.85	75 Re 186.207	76 Os 190.2	77 Ir 192.22	78 Pt 195.08	79 Au 196.966	80 Hg 200.59	81 Ti 204.383	82 Pb 207.2	83 Bi 208.98	84 Po (209)	85 At (210)	86 Rn (222)
87 Fr (223)	88 Ra 226.0254	89 Ac (227)	104 Rf (261)	105 Ha (263)	106 Sg (263)	107 Ns (265)	108 Hs (265)	109 Mt (266)	110 – (269)	111 – (272)	112 – (277)						

58 Ce 140.12	59 Pr 140.9077	60 Nd 144.24	61 Pm (145)	62 Sm 150.36	63 Eu 151.965	64 Gd 157.25	65 Tb 158.9253	66 Dy 162.50	67 Ho 164.9303	68 Er 167.26	69 Tm 168.9342	70 Yb 173.04	71 Lu 174.967
90 Th 232.0381	91 Pa 231.0359	92 U 238.029	93 Np 237.0482	94 Pu (244)	95 Am (243)	96 Cm (247)	97 Bk (247)	98 Cf (251)	99 Es (252)	100 Fm (257)	101 Md (258)	102 No (259)	103 Lr (260)

Though it might appear to have an unusual shape, the periodic table is an incredibly useful document. Reading left to right across the periodic table, the elements are arranged in order of the number of protons in their nucleus. (The number of protons in a nucleus is called an element's atomic number.) Thus, the element hydrogen is listed first because atoms of hydrogen have only one proton in the nucleus. The element helium has two protons in the nucleus, so it is listed second. The atomic number of iron (Fe) is 26, so it has 26 protons in its nucleus and is listed just after manganese (Mn, atomic number 25) and just before cobalt (Co, atomic number 27). The atomic number is a very important concept in chemistry. Not only does every iron atom have 26 protons in its nucleus, but any atom that has 26 protons in its nucleus must be an iron atom. The atomic number is the defining characteristic of an atom. All atoms of the same element must have the same number of protons, but can have differing numbers of neutrons and electrons.

If the number of electrons is the same as the atomic number (number of protons), then the atom is neutral because the number of negative and positive charges from the electrons and protons, respectively, is the same. If there are fewer electrons than protons, a cation (pronounced CAT-ion) results, which has a positive charge. Metals usually form cations (for example, Ag forms Ag^+). If there is an excess of electrons compared to the number of protons, a negative charge arises on the atom resulting in an anion (pronounced AN-ion). Nonmetals usually form anions (for example, N forms N^{3-}). An atom, or group of atoms, with a charge is called an ion.

Elements that have the same number of protons, but different numbers of neutrons, are called isotopes. An example of an element with two isotopes is copper. All copper atoms contain 29 protons; however, 69% of copper atoms contain 34 neutrons and 31% contain 36 neutrons. The two types of copper atoms have different masses because they have a different number of neutrons; however, they are both copper atoms.

This difference in atomic composition is reflected by the atomic mass (or atomic weight) of an element. In the periodic table, it is the number found underneath each atomic symbol. By definition, the atomic mass is the average mass of all the naturally occurring isotopes of an element.

Another piece of useful information found within the periodic table is the number of electrons found in the outer shell of an atom. These electrons are known as the valence electrons and are responsible for holding atoms together when making a compound. Each column in the periodic table is called a group, and each group of atoms has a similar configuration of electrons. Taking a look at the first column of the periodic table (1A), you find H, Li, Na, K, Rb, Cs and Fr. Each of these elements has only one electron in its outer shell; group 2A elements have two electrons in their outer shell; group 8A elements have 8 electrons in their outer shell.

Atoms, Molecules, and Compounds

From the periodic table, you can see that there are many elements. Think for a moment, though, about the matter around you. The number of different materials, colors, odors, tastes and tactile sensations is almost limitless. How can 112 different elements make up the billions of different materials that we perceive everyday?

Most of the materials you see are not made of just one type of element. Most of the materials are made of compounds. Compounds are substances with two or more different atoms of an element bound together. Examples of compounds are water (H_2O), sulfuric acid (battery acid, H_2SO_4), sodium hydrogen carbonate (baking soda, $NaHCO_3$), sucrose (table sugar, $C_{12}H_{22}O_{11}$) and sodium chloride (table salt, NaCl). Each of these substances is made of more than one kind of element. If those elements are nonmetals (for example, H_2O, H_2SO_4 and $C_{12}H_{22}O_{11}$), they are classified as molecules. Molecules are collections of nonmetals that are tightly bound together. In the case where a metal and a nonmetal are bound together (for example, NaCl or Na_2CO_3), they are classified as formula units.

Some elements also occur in molecular form, and examples include oxygen (O_2), hydrogen (H_2), nitrogen (N_2) and fluorine (F_2). Thus, when chemists speak of elemental hydrogen, they actually refer to two hydrogen atoms bound together, which is different than just two atoms of hydrogen.

A compound has different properties than the elements that make it up. Thus, hydrogen is a gas at room temperature and is quite flammable, oxygen is a gas at room temperature that supports combustion, but water (made from hydrogen and oxygen) is a liquid at room temperature and doesn't burn or support combustion. Because water has different properties than the elements that comprise it, water is a compound of hydrogen and oxygen and not simply a mixture.

Chemical Equations and Reactions

To describe the chemical changes that are occurring around and inside of you, chemists have developed a shorthand notation in which the symbols for elements and compounds are written showing the chemical change. An example of a chemical equation is the combustion of propane (C_3H_8) with elemental oxygen (O_2) to form carbon dioxide (CO_2) and water (H_2O).

$$C_3H_8 + O_2 \rightarrow CO_2 + H_2O$$

The equation is written with the reactants on the left and the products of the reaction on the right. The arrow shows that a reaction is taking place. While this shows the transformation of propane and oxygen into two different compounds, the equation is not quite complete. Because of the Law of Mass Conservation, matter cannot be created or destroyed, and the same kind and number of atoms must be on each side of the reaction arrow. Thus, to correctly write the preceding equation, coefficients in front of each chemical species must be added.

$$C_3H_8 + 5\,O_2 \rightarrow 3\,CO_2 + 4\,H_2O$$

Thus, one molecule of propane reacts with five molecules of oxygen to form three molecules of carbon dioxide and four molecules of water. Information about the state of the reactant or product is written after each chemical formula to indicate whether that substance is a gas (g or $\uparrow$), liquid (l), solid (s or $\downarrow$) or dissolved in water (aq).

$$C_3H_8\,(g) + 5\,O_2\,(g) \rightarrow 3\,CO_2\,(g) + 4\,H_2O\,(l)$$

Many different types of chemical reactions exist; however, you can classify some of them according to one of the four basic reaction types: synthesis, decomposition, single replacement or double replacement.

Acids, Bases, and Solutions

An acid is a compound that increases the quantity of hydrogen ions (H^+) in an aqueous solution. A base is a compound that decreases the H^+ concentration by increasing hydroxide (OH^-) concentration. The pH scale is a measure of how much acid is in a solution. Solutions with low pH's (0–7) are considered acidic, solutions with a pH of exactly 7 are neutral (neither acidic nor basic), and solutions with a high pH (7–14) are considered basic.

Because acids and bases are all around you, it is a good idea to know some of the more common compounds that constitute acids and bases. Examples of common acids are the following:

- Acetic acid ($HC_2H_3O_2$): Vinegar is a 5% solution of acetic acid.
- Carbonic acid (H_2CO_3): This is found in carbonated beverages, resulting from CO_2 dissolving in water.
- Citric acid ($H_3C_6H_5O_7$): This is found in citrus fruits and is responsible for their tangy flavor.
- Hydrochloric acid (HCl): This is found in the gastric juices of humans.
- Nitric acid (HNO_3): This is used in fertilizer production.
- Phosphoric acid (H_3PO_4): This is used in colas to prevent bacterial growth, and is also used in fertilizer production.
- Sulfuric acid (H_2SO_4): This is the most industrially produced compound in the world and is also used in car batteries.

Examples of common bases are the following:

- Ammonia (NH_3): This is used as a general cleanser and in fertilizers.
- Lime (CaO): This is used to raise the pH of soil for farming.
- Lye (NaOH): This is used in the manufacture of soap.
- Milk of magnesia ($Mg(OH)_2$): This is used as an antacid.
- Sodium carbonate (Na_2CO_3): This is used in paper manufacturing and water softening.

Pure water is neutral and therefore is neither acidic nor basic. When acids and bases react, they form water and salt as the products. For example:

$$NaOH(aq) + HCl(aq) \rightarrow H_2O(l) + NaCl(aq)$$

The sodium hydroxide (base) reacts with hydrochloric acid to form water and sodium chloride (salt).

A solution is a homogeneous mixture that is composed of a solvent (the material in greater proportion) and a solute (the material dissolved in the solvent). Salt water is an example in which water is the solvent, and sodium chloride (NaCl) is the solute.

Measurements

Knowing the chemical properties of various elements and compounds is obviously essential to understanding chemistry, but of nearly equal importance is being able to measure quantities of chemicals. To systematically quantify such properties as mass, length, temperature and the quantity of material, the Systeme Internationale d'Unites (SI units) was developed. The following table lists common SI units.

Common SI Units of Measurement in Chemistry

Property	Unit	Abbreviation
Mass	kilogram	kg
Length	meter	m
Temperature	kelvin	K
Amount of material	mole	mol

To express very large or very small numbers, another concept is used, metric system prefixes. The following table lists common prefixes encountered in chemistry.

Common Metric Prefixes

Prefix Name	Prefix Abbreviation	Meaning
giga-	G	1 billion (1,000,000,000)
mega-	M	1 million (1,000,000)
kilo-	k	1 thousand (1,000)
hecta-	h	100
deka-	da	10
deci-	d	0.1
centi-	c	0.01
milli-	m	1 thousandth (0.001)
micro-	μ	1 millionth (0.000 001)
nano-	n	1 billionth (0.000 000 001)

With these two concepts, it is possible to express very large or very small quantities in a uniform way that other scientists can understand. Thus, if you have 1,000,000 grams, it can be reported as 1 megagram or 1 Mg. If the length of a piece of material is 0.000 05 meters, it can be reported as 0.05 mm or 50 μm.

No SI unit exists for volume. Because volume has units of length cubed, officially, scientists should use cubic meters (m^3) to express volume. In practice, this is rarely done, so a unit called the liter was established. See the following table for common conversions for mass, length and volume.

Common Conversions for Mass, Length and Volume

Mass Conversions	Length Conversions	Volume Conversions
1 pound = 453.59 g	1 inch = 2.54 cm	1 m^3 = 264.17 gallons
1 kg = 1,000 g	1 km = 0.6214 miles	1 dm^3 = 1 liter (1 L)
1 g = 1,000 mg	1 m = 100 cm	1 cm^3 = 1 mL
	1 m = 1,000 mm	1 L = 1,000 mL
	1 km = 1,000 m	

Though the SI unit of temperature is the kelvin, it is more common to measure temperature in the Celsius scale (this used to be called the centigrade scale) or in Fahrenheit. The formulas to convert from one scale to another follow:

To convert from Celsius (°C) to kelvin (K): K = 273 + °C

To convert from Celsius (°C) to Fahrenheit (°F): °F = (1.8×°C) + 32

To convert from Fahrenheit (°F) to Celsius (°C): °C = (°F − 32)÷1.8

The unit most useful to chemists is the mole because it defines how much material is present. By definition, one mole of anything is $6.022 \cdot 10^{23}$ of those things. This is an unfathomable number because it is so large. (For example, a mole of pennies would stretch to the sun and back 38 billion times stacked side by side!) The reason this is useful for chemists is because dealing with individual atoms means dealing with masses so small that no balance in the world is able to measure them. Due to the way mass and moles are defined, the atomic weight of any atom is equivalent to 1 mole of that element. Thus, 55.847 grams of element 26 (iron, Fe) is $6.022 \cdot 10^{23}$ Fe atoms. For oxygen (atomic number 8), only 15.9994 grams contain 1 mole ($6.022 \cdot 10^{23}$) of oxygen atoms.

Energy

In addition to mass conservation, energy is conserved, too. Energy can be either a reactant or a product of a reaction. The two main types of energy are kinetic and potential. Kinetic energy is the energy of motion. The faster something is moving, the higher the kinetic energy. Kinetic energy often expresses itself in terms of temperature; materials that are hot generally have atoms that are moving more quickly than the atoms of materials that are cold. Potential energy is energy that is stored. (It has the potential to do work.) This type of energy is dependent on the distance an object is from the ground or, more importantly for chemists, the types of chemical bonds that are present. When bonds form, energy is released; when bonds break, energy is absorbed.

Radioactivity

The energy stored in the nucleus of an atom is also a type of potential energy. This energy is used in nuclear power plants, radiation therapy medical treatments, and even to build powerful bombs. This energy releases when an unstable nucleus decomposes into a more stable nucleus. Often times, this nuclear change results in the emission of a gamma ray (a high-energy light particle), or it might even emit a neutron, a beta particle (an electron) or an alpha particle (two neutrons and two protons).

It is impossible to determine exactly which atom will emit radiation, but scientists can measure an average decay time. The most useful measurement is the half-life. The half-life of a material is the time it takes for 50% of it to decay into another material. The half-life of the uranium isotope with a mass number of 235 (U-235, the isotope used in building the first nuclear bomb) is 700 million years; if you had 100 grams of U-235, in 700 million years (one half-life) only 50 grams would be left. After 1.4 billion years (two half-lives), only 25 grams of U-235 would be left. After 2.1 billion years (three half-lives), only 12.5 grams of U-235 would remain. After each half-life period, 50% of the remaining material converts to a new material.

Metals

A quick look at the periodic table indicates that the vast majority of elements are metals. Because of this, many elements share common properties. The metals are all:

- Solid at room temperature (Mercury—Hg—is an exception because it is a liquid.)
- Malleable, which means that you can hammer them into thin sheets
- Ductile, which means that you can draw them into thin wires
- Sectile, which means that you can cut them into thin sheets
- Good conductors of heat and electricity
- Shiny
- Silvery in color (except for copper and gold)

Most metals are found combined with oxygen or sulfur in nature; however, the coinage metals (copper, silver and gold) can occur in their native (that is, elemental) state.

Metals can also form alloys, which are solid mixtures of two or more metals. An amalgam is a mixture of mercury with some other metal and can be a solid or liquid, depending on the amount of mercury.

Physics

Motion

Motion occurs when an object or body is moved from one place to the next. Three types of motion exist: translational, rotational and vibrational. Translational (or linear) motion involves motion in a straight line, rotational motion happens when motion occurs about an axis, and vibrational motion is motion about a fixed point.

Translational Motion

Two factors characterize the motion of an object in a straight line: a change in position or displacement of the object over a period of time and movement with respect to a reference point. The motion of an object can be described quantitatively by making references to its speed, velocity and acceleration.

Speed and Velocity

The speed of an object is a measure of how fast it is moving and can be calculated using the following equation:

$$\text{Speed} = \frac{\text{Distance traveled}}{\text{Time taken}}$$

Like speed, velocity describes how fast an object is moving. Unlike speed, velocity specifies the direction of motion as well. In this respect, speed is said to be a scalar quantity, while velocity is described as a vector quantity. The mathematical representation of the velocity of an object is given by the following equation:

$$\text{Velocity} = \frac{\text{Displacement}}{\text{Time}}$$

When the velocity of an object changes with time, the object is said to be accelerating. In general, an increase in velocity is called acceleration, and a decrease in velocity is called deceleration. Both can be calculated using the following equation:

$$\text{Acceleration} = \frac{\text{Change in velocity}}{\text{Time}}$$

Acceleration, like velocity, is a vector quantity. Acceleration is positive when acceleration occurs in the same direction in which the object is moving (acceleration), and negative when acceleration occurs in a direction opposite to that in which the object is moving (deceleration).

Graphical Analysis of Motion

You can analyze the motion of an object by using two types of graphs: position-time graphs and velocity-time graphs.

- A position-time graph shows how the displacement or position of a moving object changes with time. As a result, the velocity of such an object is equal to the slope of the graph.

- A velocity-time graph illustrates how the velocity of an object changes over time. Hence, you can determine the acceleration of an object from the slope of a velocity-time graph. In addition to acceleration, you can use a velocity-time graph to determine the distance covered by an object that is undergoing acceleration. You can derive the distance traveled by an object in motion from the area under the graph.

Motion in One Dimension

Motion occurs in one dimension when an object or body moves along either the x or y coordinate. Motion along the x coordinate is often referred to as linear motion, while motion along the y coordinate is referred to as motion in a vertical plane, or free fall. In many instances, the acceleration of an object along either coordinate is constant or is such that the acceleration can be considered constant. When this occurs, motion can be quantified using a series of equations called the equations of kinematics.

Equations of Kinematics

The equations of kinematics consist of four main equations that are the result of the mathematical manipulation of the equations used to calculate velocity and acceleration. These equations involve five variables:

x = displacement

a = acceleration

v = final velocity

v_0 = initial velocity

t = time

The equations are:

$$v = v_0 + at$$

$$x = \frac{1}{2}(v_0 + v)t$$

$$x = v_0t + \frac{1}{2}at^2$$

$$v^2 = v_0^2 + 2ax$$

Each of the equations of kinematics contains four of these five variables. Therefore, if you know three of them, you can calculate the fourth variable by transposing the relevant equation.

Motion in a Vertical Plane

All objects above the Earth undergo vertical motion with an acceleration of about 9.81m/s^2. This *vertical motion* is called *free fall* and is the result of the force of gravity. Because all objects above the Earth have the same acceleration, the motion of an object undergoing vertical motion can be quantified using the equations of kinematics.

When using the equations of kinematics to describe the motion of an object in free fall, the acceleration due to gravity, g, is substituted for a, and x is substituted for y. In addition, you can consider the vector quantities v and y as positive when they are directed downward and negative when directed upward.

When an object is thrown upward it undergoes uniform deceleration, as a result of gravity, until it comes to rest. The object then begins to fall, during which time it is uniformly accelerated by the force of gravity. If air resistance is neglected, the time required for the object to rise is the same as the time required for the object to fall.

Newton's Laws of Motion

A force is defined as a push or pull and can result in the motion of an object at rest, or a change in the velocity of an object in motion. At any particular time, multiple forces can act on an object. How these multiple forces affect the motion of the object is governed by a collection of laws called Newton's laws of motion. The laws of motion are as follows:

- First law of motion: An object that has no net or unbalanced force acting on it remains at rest or moves with a constant velocity in a straight line.
- Second law of motion: The acceleration of an object is directly proportional to the net force acting on it and inversely proportional to its mass.
- Third law of motion: When one object exerts a force on a second object, the second object exerts a force on the first that is equal in magnitude but opposite in direction.

Weight and Mass

The weight (W) of an object is the force exerted on it by the force of gravity and, like all forces, is measured in newtons. The force of gravity acts on an object whether it is falling, resting on the ground or being lifted, and results in a downward acceleration of 9.81 m/s^2. The weight of an object can be calculated using the equation: $W = mg$.

W is the weight of the object, m is the mass of the object, and g is the acceleration due to gravity.

From the weight equation, it is obvious that the mass of an object is not the same as its weight. The weight of an object depends on the acceleration due to gravity, and thus varies from place to place. On the other hand, mass is a measure of the amount of matter contained within an object and is independent of gravity. Hence, an astronaut weighs less on the moon, where the acceleration due to gravity is about 1.6 m/s^2, but his or her mass is the same as it is on Earth.

Frictional Force

Friction is the force that opposes the motion between two surfaces that are in contact. The two types of friction are static and kinetic. Static friction is the force that opposes motion of an object at rest, while kinetic friction is the opposing force between surfaces in relative motion. Kinetic friction is always less than static friction.

Energy and Work

The mass of an object not only measures the amount of matter it contains, but also the amount of energy. The energy of an object can be divided into two main types: potential and kinetic. Potential energy is the energy possessed by an object due to its position and is often called stored energy. Kinetic energy is the energy possessed by an object because of its motion.

Both the kinetic and potential energy of an object change when work is done by or on the object. Therefore, work is defined as the transfer of energy to an object when the object moves due to the application of a force. The work done on an object can be calculated using the formula $W = F \times d$.

W is work measured in joules, F is force measured in newtons, and d is distance measured in meters.

Gravitational Potential Energy

Energy is defined as the capacity to do work. When you raise an object, such as a hammer, above the Earth, you do work against gravity. The work that you do against gravity is the gravitational potential energy, and you can calculate it by using the following equation: $PE = mgh$.

PE is the potential energy in joules, m is the mass of the object in kilograms, g is the acceleration due to gravity, and h is the height above the ground.

As the object falls, it is accelerated by the force of gravity, and the object loses gravitational potential energy. According to the law of conservation of energy, energy can neither be created nor destroyed but can be converted from one form to another. Thus, any decrease in the gravitational potential energy of the object is accompanied by a corresponding increase in the object's kinetic energy. You can calculate the kinetic energy of a moving body by using the following equation: $KE = \frac{1}{2}mv^2$. KE is the kinetic energy of the object, m is its mass, and v is its velocity.

The conversion of energy from one form to another is generally carried out by a number of practical devices. Such devices include the following:

- Generators: Convert mechanical energy into electrical energy
- Motors: Convert electrical energy into mechanical energy
- Batteries: Convert chemical, thermal, nuclear or solar energy into electrical energy
- Photocells or photovoltaic cells: Convert light energy into electrical energy

The rate at which any device converts energy from one form to another is called the power and is defined by the following formula: $P = \frac{W}{t}$. P is power in watts, W is work in joules, and t is time in seconds.

Fluids

A fluid is any substance that offers little resistance to changes in its shape when pressure is applied to it. Of the three states of matter, only gases and liquids are considered fluids. Of all the properties that characterize fluids, one of the most important is their capability to exert pressure.

Pressure

Pressure is defined as the force exerted per unit area and is mathematically represented by the following equation: $P = \frac{F}{A}$. P is pressure in pascals, F is force in newtons, and A is area in square meters.

You can explain the capability of fluids to exert pressure by the kinetic molecular theory, which states that the particles that make up fluids are in continuous, random motion, as illustrated in the following figure. These particles undergo collisions with the walls of their container or any surface with which they make contact. Each time a particle makes contact, it exerts a force, and it is this force that is referred to as pressure.

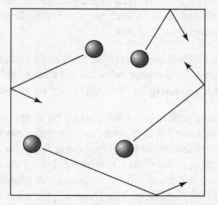

Molecular motion and collisions
of particles in a fluid

When dealing with fluids in motion or at rest, three governing principles are essential: Archimedes', Pascal's and Bernoulli's principles.

Archimedes' Principle

According to Archimedes' principle, an object immersed in a fluid is buoyed up by a force equal to the weight of the fluid that the object displaces. The magnitude of the buoyant force is given by the following equation: $F = \rho Vg$. F is the buoyant force in newtons, ρ is density of the fluid, V is volume of the fluid displaced, and g is acceleration due to gravity. It can be proven that the volume of an object immersed in a fluid is the same as the volume of the fluid that it displaces.

An object immersed in a fluid sinks or floats depending on the relative value of its weight and the buoyant force exerted on it by the fluid. An object sinks if the buoyant force is less than the weight of the object. If the buoyant force equals the weight of the object, the object floats at any depth in the liquid; if the buoyant force is greater than the weight of the object, the object floats with part of its volume above the surface.

Pascal's Principle

Pascal's principle states that any pressure applied to a confined fluid, at any point, is transmitted undiminished throughout the fluid. Pascal's principle led to the development of hydrostatics, in which machines, such as the hydraulic lift, use pistons to multiply forces applied to fluids at rest. Pascal's principle is represented by the following equation: $\frac{F_1}{A_1} = \frac{F_2}{A_2}$. F_1 and F_2 are the forces on pistons 1 and 2 respectively, and A_1 and A_2 are their respective areas.

Bernoulli's Principle

According to this principle, as the velocity of a fluid increases, the pressure exerted by that fluid decreases. This principle underlies the study of hydrodynamics, which is the study of the effects of fluids in motion. Most aircraft get part of their lift by taking advantage of this principle.

Sound Waves

Sound waves consist of a series of pressure variations that are transmitted through matter. These pressure variations are of two types: compressions and rarefactions. Compressions are areas of high pressure and rarefactions are areas of low pressure. The compressions and rarefactions associated with sound waves are produced when a vibrating source causes air molecules to collide and, in so doing, transmit the pressure variations away from the source of the sound. As such, sound cannot travel through a vacuum because no particles are present for motion and collision to occur.

The speed at which sound travels in air depends on the temperature of the air. At sea level and room temperature, the speed of sound is about 343 m/s. In addition to gases, sound can also travel through solids and liquids. In general, the speed of sound is greater in solids and liquids than in gases.

When sound waves encounter hard surfaces, they undergo reflections called echoes. The time required for an echo to return to its source can be used to determine the distance between the source and the reflecting surface. The use of echoes to determine distance is used by bats to navigate their night flights, as well as by ships equipped with sonar.

The number of compressions or rarefactions generated in one second by sound waves is called the frequency or pitch of the sound. However, if the source of the sound is in motion, an observer detecting the sound perceives sound of higher or lower frequencies. If the source of the sound is moving away from the observer, the observer detects sound waves of decreasing frequencies. Conversely, if the source is moving toward the observer, the observer detects sound waves of increasing frequencies. This apparent change in the frequency of sound due to movement on the part of the sound source or an observer is called the Doppler effect. The Doppler effect has many practical applications, such as its use in radar detectors and ultrasound.

Electricity

Electricity involves the flow of electrical energy from a source, such as a battery or generator, to a load, such as a lamp or motor. A load is any device that transforms electrical energy into other forms of energy. For example, a lamp transforms electrical energy into light and heat energy, while a motor transforms electrical energy into mechanical energy.

Electrical energy is transported in the form of an electric current, consisting of the flow of negatively charged electrons. This flow of electrons occurs in a closed conducting path, called an electrical circuit, in which conducting metal wires provide the pathway for the flow of electrons from the source of the electrical energy to the various loads within the circuit. A substance that allows for the flow of an electric current is called a conductor and a substance that does not is called an insulator.

For an electric current to flow in a conductor, a potential difference or voltage must exist between its ends. The greater the voltage is, the greater the current is, and vice versa. All substances, insulators or conductors, offer some form of resistance to the flow of an electric current. The amount of resistance depends on the length of the material, the area of the material, an intrinsic property called resistivity and the temperature. The magnitude of the current flowing in a conductor can be calculated using the following equation: $I = \dfrac{V}{R}$. I is current in amperes, V is voltage in volts, and R is resistance in ohms.

Earth Science

Geology

The Earth is a relatively solid planet revolving around the sun. It is approximately 8,000 miles in diameter. It is not a uniform sphere but is comprised of several different layers: core, mantle, asthenosphere (plastic mantle) and crust.

We live on the thinnest layer, the crust. The nature of Earth's interior structure has been inferred from seismic (earthquake) activity and studies. The following illustration shows the upper level of the Earth.

The Earth's Crust and Interior

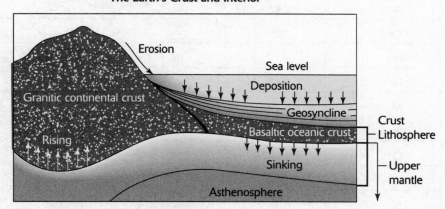

The crust (our home) is, itself, not uniform. The continental portion of the crust is mostly granitic rock. The portions of the crust underlying the oceans are comprised mostly of basaltic rock. Both segments of the crust are broken into large tectonic plates that move over the plastic asthenosphere.

This activity is known as plate tectonics and helps explain many patterns of major crustal activity, including earthquake zones, volcanic zones, mountain building, sea-floor spreading and ocean trench zones.

The Earth's crust is stable only over a relatively short period of geologic time. Minor earthquakes occur constantly throughout the crust, volcanoes are active, and the ocean bottoms are constantly in flux.

The rocks of the Earth themselves are constantly changing. Rocks are comprised of a mixture of minerals (inorganic crystalline substances with definite chemical compositions and unique physical properties). The most common minerals on Earth's crust are feldspar, quartz, mica, pyroxene and olivine, but many others exist as well. These myriad minerals are recombined into various rock types due to crustal activity.

The major rock types are named based on their origin: igneous rock, sedimentary rock and metamorphic rock. Each type has specific structures that allow geologists to identify it. Igneous rocks are crystalline; sedimentary rocks are comprised of cemented rock fragments and can contain fossils; metamorphic rocks are usually foliated (minerals aligned into bands).

The Earth's crust is in contact with other layers, the atmosphere and hydrosphere. There's a vast exchange of energy where these disparate structures meet (interfaces). The result of this energy exchange is erosion, weathering and deposition. The crustal material above sea level is constantly worn down, but it is constantly replaced as tectonic activity adds new material. Thus, the Earth's crust is in a dynamic equilibrium.

Meteorology

The Earth's gaseous envelope, our atmosphere, provides a means to absorb, refract, and reflect the energy reaching us from the sun (insolation). In the process of these activities, the atmosphere maintains a dynamic equilibrium of energy flow that gives us weather and climate. Weather is the day-to-day condition of the atmosphere; climate is the long-term condition in a given area.

The Earth's atmosphere is a layered structure of mainly two gases, nitrogen (78%) and oxygen (21%), with many other gases (1%) mixed in. Though they make up less than 1% of the air, these other gases are important in meteorological events; they include carbon dioxide, water vapor, sulfur dioxide, argon and ozone.

The following table shows what elements make up various parts of the Earth and its atmosphere.

Percentage by Volume				
Element	Symbol	Crust	Hydrosphere	Troposphere
Aluminum	Al	0.47	—	—
Calcium	Ca	1.03	—	—
Hydrogen	H	—	66	—
Iron	Fe	0.43	—	—
Magnesium	Mg	0.29	—	—
Nitrogen	N	—	—	78
Oxygen	O	93.77	33	21
Potassium	K	1.83	—	—
Silicon	Si	0.86	—	—
Sodium	Na	1.32	—	—
Others		—	1	1

The layer of the atmosphere we live in is called the troposphere, and it is here that the phenomenon called weather occurs. Weather variables include temperature of the air, barometric pressure (the air's weight), wind speed and direction, humidity (the air's moisture content), cloud cover and precipitation. The measurement of these weather elements requires the use of specialized instruments such as thermometers, barometers, wind vanes, anemometers, hydrometers and rain gauges.

Climate and seasonal variations are caused by the complex interactions of latitude, altitude, water proximity and change in the Earth's relative axial tilt with respect to the sun. The complexity of these events is one reason climate change and even seasonal changes are not easy to predict.

Much of the energy needed to power the Earth's weather and climate is the result of the water cycle that converts insolation into useable force in the Earth's transparent air.

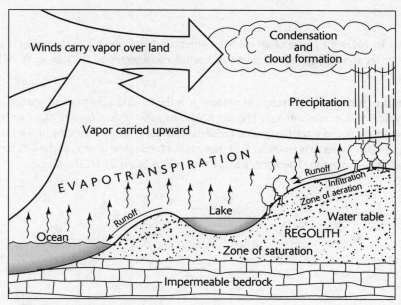

The water cycle

Oceanography

The Earth's surface (71%) is covered by a relatively thin layer of water. Most of this water contains dissolved salts and resides in four major ocean basins. The rest of the water is found frozen in ice caps at both poles, in seas, lakes, rivers and in porous rocks in the crust.

The four oceans, in size order largest to smallest, are the Pacific, Atlantic, Indian and Arctic. They are largely responsible for maintaining the relatively stable environment that allowed our world to evolve as it has. The tilt of the Earth's axis, its spherical shape and its rotation all work to cause uneven heating of the Earth's oceans. This variation in thermal distribution, coupled with the Coriolis effect (deflection due to rotation), gives rise to ocean currents. The ocean waters absorb and release insolation, thus regulating weather and climate. The oceans' currents also influence atmospheric circulation. They are the source of life on Earth. The oceans' currents shape coastlines.

The ocean basins (land under the oceans) are mostly stable areas of fine-grained basaltic rock. There are, however, sites on the ocean floor where scientists have studied considerable crustal and seismic activity. These locations are responsible for much of the plate tectonic activity, including sea-floor spreading, rise of mid-oceanic ridges, sea floor trenching and continental plate movement.

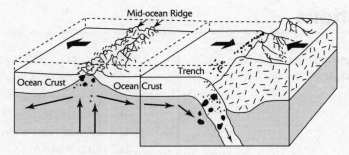

Ocean Basin Reformation

Astronomy

The science of astronomy involves the study of all celestial objects (objects in space) including planet Earth. It was approximately only 400 years ago that the actual nature of Earth's relationship to the vast array of heavenly bodies was observed.

Earth is part of a heliocentric (sun-centered) system of planets. It is the third of nine planets that are all moving in elliptical paths (orbits) around a typical yellow star, our sun. The sun holds our solar system together by its enormous gravitational effect. Its tremendous energy output of electromagnetic radiation provides energy for many of the Earth's activities. Like the other planets, the Earth spins on its axis (rotates) as it moves counterclockwise around the sun (revolution). The Earth also has a satellite that orbits it, the moon. The Earth's axis of rotation is tilted 23 1/2 degrees.

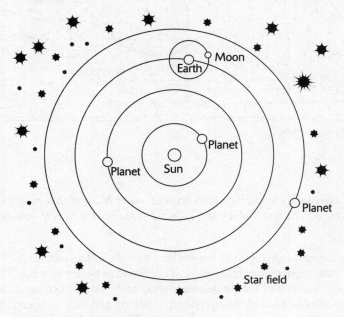

Heliocentric model

The two major motions of the Earth, rotation and revolution, coupled with the Earth's tilt, result in a number of important and familiar effects. Day and night, as well as variations in daylight periods, are due to the rotation and the tilt of the Earth's axis. The year and seasons are due to revolution and axial tilt. Variation in incoming solar radiation (insolation) that powers many of the Earth's processes is due to all three factors.

Practice Questions

1. How much power is developed by a machine that does 300 joules of work in 10 seconds?

   A. 30 W
   B. 2500 W
   C. 240 W
   D. 260 W

2. The process by which green plants manufacture food in the form of glucose is:

   A. photosynthesis
   B. photorespiration
   C. cellular respiration
   D. fermentation

3. A reproductive cell containing 30 chromosomes produces _____ cells with _____ chromosomes during meiosis.

A. 2, 30
B. 2, 15
C. 4, 30
D. 4, 15

4. An object is in free-fall near the surface of the Earth. What is the velocity before impact if it takes 5 seconds to hit the ground? Assume g to be 10 m/s^2.

A. 5 m/s
B. 2 m/s
C. 50 m/s
D. 125 m/s

5. Which of the following represents the correct order of structures through which food travels in the human digestive system?

A. mouth ___ duodenum ___ esophagus ___ stomach ___ large intestine
B. mouth ___ pancreas ___ stomach ___ small intestine ___ large intestine
C. mouth ___ esophagus ___ stomach ___ large intestine ___ small intestine
D. mouth ___ esophagus ___ stomach ___ small intestine ___ large intestine

6. Interactions between the organisms in communities and their physical environment form _____.

A. food chains
B. food webs
C. populations
D. ecosystems

7. Which of the following compounds forms a basic solution?

A. battery acid
B. water
C. lye
D. vinegar

8. Which statement is true?

A. Minerals are comprised of rocks.
B. Minerals are formed during erosion.
C. Rocks are made of minerals.
D. All minerals have the same chemical makeup.

9. If the temperature is 25°C, what is the temperature in °F?

A. 25°F
B. 298°F
C. 0°F
D. 77°F

10. Oxygen-poor blood enters the human heart through the _____, is pumped to the lungs where it receives oxygen, and returns to the heart through the _____.

A. right atrium, left atrium
B. left atrium, right atrium
C. left ventricle, right ventricle
D. pulmonary artery, vena cava

11. What is the acceleration of a car whose velocity changes from 60 m/s to 45 m/s in 5 seconds?

A. 3.0 m/s^2
B. 53 m/s^2
C. 15 m/s^2
D. 9.8 m/s^2

12. Which phrase best describes the environment of the Earth?

A. a steady, unchanging star
B. a dynamic equilibrium
C. regular, predictable catastrophes
D. a constant energy imbalance

13. Which of the following structure-function pairs is mismatched?

A. ribosome—protein synthesis
B. mitochondrion—cellular respiration
C. chloroplast—photosynthesis
D. nucleus—ATP production

14. Life on Earth is found on the Earth's:

A. core
B. mantle
C. asthenosphere
D. crust

Answers and Explanations

1. **A.** The solution requires direct substitution into the equation $P = W/t$.

2. **A.** Choices **B**, **C**, and **D** are all forms of cellular respiration, which is the process by which organisms break down glucose to obtain energy.

3. **D.** Meiosis leads to the production of four haploid daughter cells from one diploid parent cell.

4. **C.** The answer is obtained by direct substitution into one of the equations of kinematics: $v = v_0 + gt$. Because the object falls from rest, v_0 is equal to 0 m/s, and the equation is reduced to $v = gt$.

5. **D.** Movement of food in the human digestive system begins in the mouth where it is chewed and moisturized to form a bolus. It then moves down the esophagus to the stomach where it is combined with gastric juices and churned into a soupy liquid called chyme. From the stomach, it moves into the small intestine where much of digestion and absorption occurs. Any substances that are not digested or absorbed move into the large intestine, which processes the residue into feces for elimination from the body.

6. **D.** An ecosystem is formed through the interaction of the living organisms in communities and their physical environment (rocks, soil, light, air and water). Food chains, **A**, and food webs, **B**, describe the transfer of energy among organisms in an ecosystem. A population, **C**, is a group of individuals of the same species occupying a defined area.

7. **C.** Lye is sodium hydroxide, and any compound that increases the hydroxide concentration is considered a base. Battery acid (sulfuric acid) and vinegar (acetic acid) are acidic. Water is neutral (neither acidic nor basic).

8. **C.** Rocks are made of minerals. All the other answer choices are false.

9. **D.** Using the formula °F = [1.8×(°C)] + 32, you can see that the answer is 77°F. For choice **B**, 273 was added to 25, which gives the temperature in kelvin.

10. **A.** The pathway for blood through the human heart starts when oxygen-poor blood enters the right atrium through a major vein called the vena cava. The blood passes through the tricuspid valve into the right ventricle and is then pumped through the pulmonary artery to the lungs for gas exchange. Oxygen-rich blood returns to the left atrium of the heart through the pulmonary vein. It then flows through the bicuspid (mitral) valve into the left ventricle, from which it is pumped through a major artery called the aorta.

11. **A.** The first step in solving the problem is to determine the change in velocity, which is simply the difference between the final and initial velocity. Dividing the difference by the time gives the acceleration of the car. In this case, the difference in velocity is negative and is an indication that the car is decelerating.

12. **B.** The Earth's environment is constantly changing, but at any given time the Earth's environment is stable enough to support life and endure changes without major crust, atmospheric or hydrospheric disruption.

13. **D.** The nucleus contains the genetic information for an organism in the form of DNA. ATP is produced by cellular respiration, which takes place in the mitochondria and the cytoplasm.

14. **D.** Life on Earth requires liquid water, atmospheric gases and nutrients from the solid Earth. These are all found on or near the surface of the crust.

Spatial Relations Review

Both the AFOQT and the ASTB tests include subtests that measure your ability to visualize and understand the physical world around you. This chapter gives you a chance to review the spatial-intelligence areas you need to be familiar with in order to score well on these tests.

Block Counting

In this portion of the AFOQT test, you are asked 20 questions on block counting—testing your ability to analyze a three-dimensional collection of blocks to determine how many pieces are touched by certain indicated blocks. It is a form of spatial relations, and, although it might seem complicated and confusing at first glance, it should be relatively simple to solve these puzzles. In fact, because you have only three minutes to complete these 20 questions on the test, you can assume that the questions are not that difficult.

Not much can be explained about this type of question without looking at illustrations. With this first set of blocks, keep in mind that all the blocks are of equal size. We are going to demonstrate the art of visualization by building a puzzle block by block. When we are done, you will understand what the entire puzzle consists of.

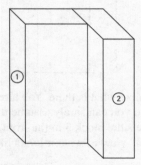

How many other blocks are touching block 1? In this first problem, visualize how the blocks touch in this way: The side of bock 1 touches the side of block 2. Normally this would be a multiple-choice question, and you would have five choices (**A–E**). However, this is a step-by-step learning process, so for these examples, we dispense with the choices.

Now we add another block. How many blocks is block 1 touching?

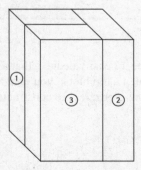

It should be easy to visualize where block 1 touches block 2, as in the earlier example, and it also touches block 3. So your answer would be 2.

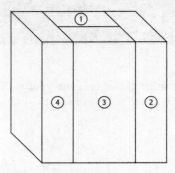

We now add a fourth block. Block 1 now touches blocks 2, 3 and 4. So your answer to the number of blocks that block 1 touches is now 3.

Finally, we add a block to the top of the pile.

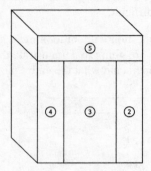

You can no longer see block 1, but have to visualize what is there. You already know that block 1 touches blocks 2, 3 and 4, and you know where block 1 is located, so you can safely assume that part of block 5 is touching the top of block 1. Thus, block 1 is touching block 2 on the side, block 3 in the front, block 4 on the side and block 5 on the top. The following is a top transparent and "exploded" view of what it looks like.

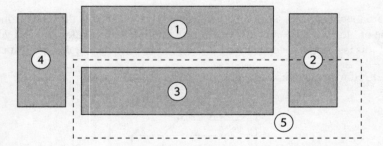

The good news is that unless you can actually see, or easily deduce, that a block exists, you do not have to assume it is there. Therefore, in the illustration where we added a top block, you could not normally assume that block 1 exists. We only did it this way to give you an idea of how these puzzles are constructed.

Try the following one.

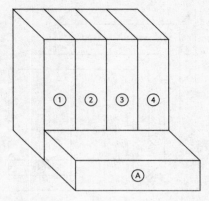

How many blocks is block 2 touching? It touches blocks 1 and 3 on the sides, and block A on the front edge. The answer is 3. How many blocks is block A touching? It touches blocks 1, 2, 3 and 4, so the answer is 4.

Again, we add another block.

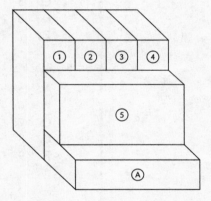

How many blocks is block A touching? It touches blocks 1, 2, 3, 4 and 5. The answer is 5.

How many blocks is block 4 touching? It touches block 3 on the side, block A and block 5. The answer is 3.

As a multiple-choice question, you might see the following:

How many blocks is block 2 touching?

    A.   1
    B.   2
    C.   3
    D.   4
    E.   5

The correct answer is 4. Do you see why this is correct? It touches blocks 1 and 3 on the sides, and in front it touches blocks 5 and A.

The following are sample questions of the sort that you will find on this part of the test.

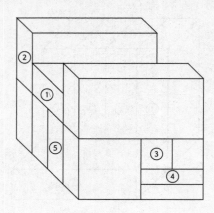

1. Block 1

 A. 3
 B. 4
 C. 5
 D. 6
 E. 7

2. Block 2

 A. 3
 B. 4
 C. 5
 D. 6
 E. 7

3. Block 3

 A. 7
 B. 8
 C. 9
 D. 10
 E. 11

4. Block 4

 A. 3
 B. 4
 C. 5
 D. 6
 E. 7

5. Block 5

 A. 5
 B. 6
 C. 7
 D. 8
 E. 9

Answers: 1. **D.**, 2. **B.**, 3. **C.**, 4. **E.**, 5. **B.**

How did you do? Can you visualize these answers? An analysis might help if you are having trouble. To make it easier to understand, *all* the blocks are numbered. You will notice a total of 11 blocks.

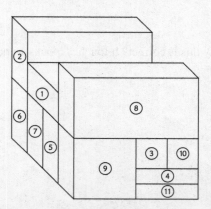

1. Block 1 touches blocks 2 and 8, 5 and 7, and the edges of 3 and 10. These last two are harder to see, but you have to visualize them passing under block 1. The answer is 6.

2. Block 2 touches blocks 6 and 1 as well as the edges of blocks 3 and 10. The answer is 4.

3. Block 3 touches blocks 4, 8, 9 and 10, which you can easily see. But it also touches the right sides of blocks 5, 6 and 7, as well as the bottom of block 1 and one edge of block 2. The answer is 9.

4. Block 4 touches the right edges of blocks 5, 6, 7 and 9, as well as the edges of blocks 3 and 10, and (of course) the side of block 11. The answer is 7.

5. Block 5 touches blocks 7 and 9, the side of block 1, and the edges of blocks 4 and 11. It also touches the side of block 3. The answer is 6.

Hopefully, these explanations make it somewhat easier to visualize where the blocks fit in with each other. Try the next series. With any luck, they will be pretty easy. It might be helpful to shade the boxes with your pencil.

Practice Questions

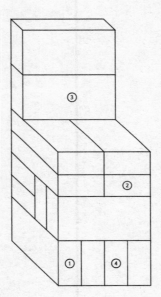

1. Block 1

  A. 1
  B. 2
  C. 3
  D. 4
  E. 5

2. Block 2

  A. 3
  B. 4
  C. 5
  D. 6
  E. 7

3. Block 3

  A. 1
  B. 2
  C. 3
  D. 4
  E. 5

4. Block 4

  A. 3
  B. 4
  C. 5
  D. 6
  E. 7

Answers and Explanations

1. D.

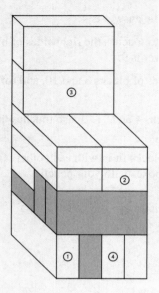

3. C.

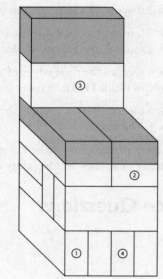

2. C.

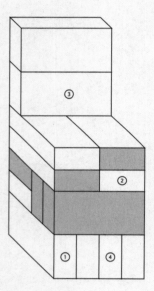

4. C.

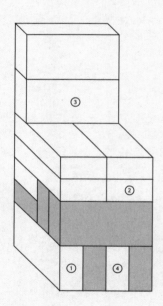

Rotated Blocks

This is one of the more challenging parts of the AFOQT exam. It measures your ability to visualize an object and then manipulate that object in space (in your mind) so that you can choose the appropriate form of that object.

If you approach the problems like the typical multiple-choice questions that they are, you will be able to work faster. The test has 15 questions that must be answered in 12 minutes—less than a minute per question. If you have a good visual and three-dimensional sense, these should be fairly easy. Keep in mind that of the five choices, only one is correct. It is likely to be rotated to another viewpoint—top, bottom, left, right, and at various angles.

To solve these problems, start by looking at the object and seeing if you can quickly identify the correct match among the choices. Let's start with a simple example.

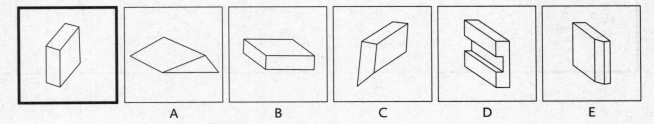

It should be clear that choice **B** is correct. The object given is a rectangle. Choice **A** is a triangle, choices **C** and **E** have slanted sides or edges, and choice **D** has a channel cut out in the middle. Therefore, only choice **B** is correct.

Try one more.

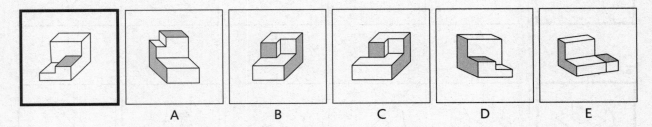

This is a little trickier. Choice **B** is correct. Choices **A** and **E** are completely different shapes, and choices **C** and **D** are somewhat opposite forms of the object. Again, only choice **B** is correct. It is just turned in a different direction.

Practice Questions

1.

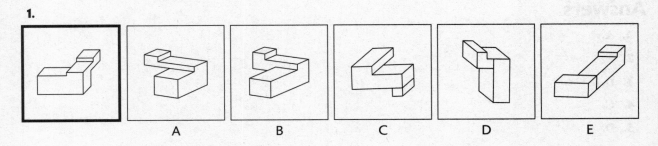

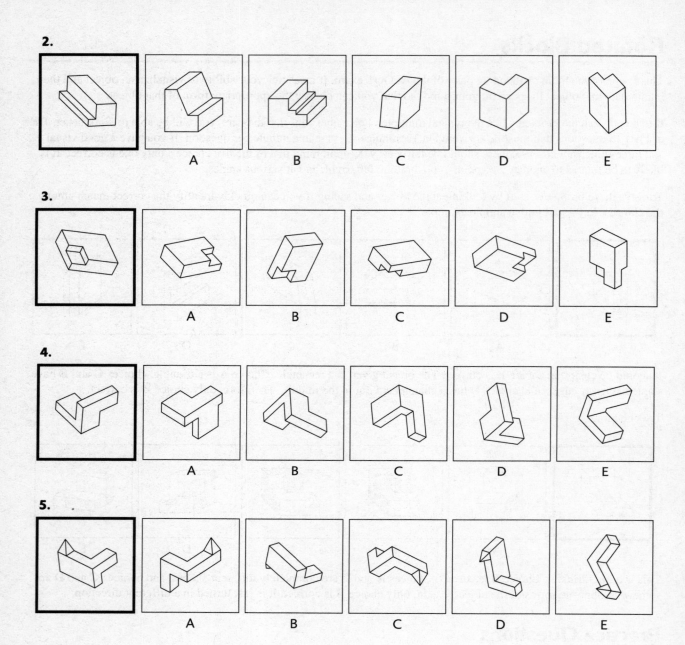

2. A B C D E

3. A B C D E

4. A B C D E

5. A B C D E

Answers

1. A.

2. E.

3. D.

4. C.

5. D.

How did you do? For some people this test is very easy, but for others it's a struggle. Do the best you can on the test—you have only 12 minutes, so jump to those that you can answer quickly, and then return to the unanswered questions. If you skip questions, however, don't forget to skip the appropriate boxes on your answer page.

Hidden Figures

The Hidden Figures section measures your ability to see a simple figure within a complex drawing. In this section you will see a series of lettered figures, A, B, C, D and E followed by several numbered drawings. You are to determine which lettered figure is contained within each of the numbered drawings.

A few things to note:

- Each numbered drawing contains only one of the lettered figures.
- The correct figure in each drawing is always the same size and in the same position as it appears in the preceding lettered figure.

Sometimes you will be able to spot the figure in the drawing immediately, and sometimes it will require some effort. The drawing might have overlapping figures and create optical illusions. If you can spot the figure quickly, mark that answer on your answer key. However, it's not always easy to spot the hidden figures. It requires trial and error, and even the process of elimination.

Let's take a look at a couple of samples before we go too far along. Following is a list of the figures that you will be looking for.

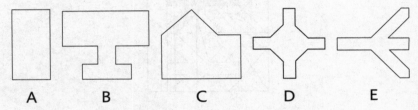

Now look at the following drawing and select the letter of the figure that you find in this drawing.

1.

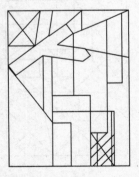

How long did it take you to find the hidden figure? You should have chosen **A**. See the following figure for an explanation.

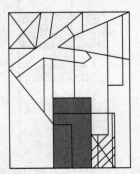

Using the same set of figures, solve the next one

2.

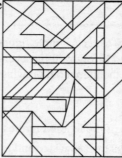

This one should have been fairly easy to spot. The correct answer is **E** (see the following figure). Although at least four figures are similar to the correct answer, only one of them is a complete figure. The others are partial figures. This is where you have to learn to read between the lines.

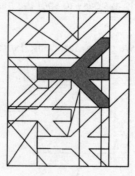

Try one more.

3.

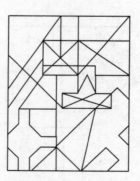

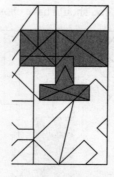

At the bottom left is part of figure D. At the bottom right is part of figure B, but turned at an angle. Even if it was completely in the box, it wouldn't be correct because it's not in the same position as choice **B**.

As we said earlier, sometimes you have to search a little harder to find the figure. It might require you to use the process of elimination. We'll take you through the steps to locate the correct answer using the process of elimination.

This next problem features a slightly different set of figures. Remember to look carefully at each one because the figures might differ only slightly from the previous set.

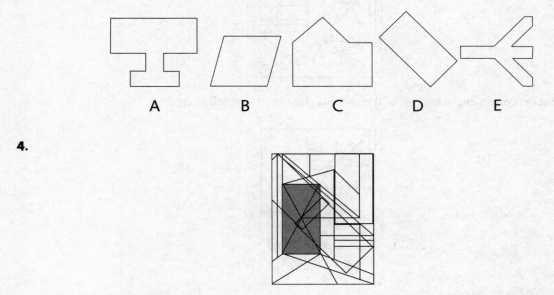

A   B   C   D   E

4.

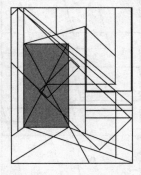

Although you might have already spotted the correct answer, we'll try to eliminate the other choices. First, we can see several rectangles throughout, and more important, we can't find any of the other figures. Choice **D** seems correct, but let's double check.

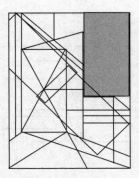

Note that although we have a rectangle, figure D, is at an angle. So we can eliminate this rectangle.

Try another one.

It's the same problem as in the preceding example—it's not at an angle.

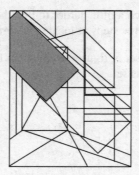

This rectangle is at the correct angle, but part of it is missing. That leaves the following.

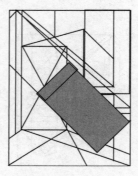

Choice **D** is correct, and this is the correct figure.

5.

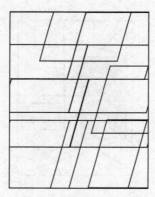

This is choice **B**, although with all the angles, you could possibly choose **D.** However, you can eliminate that one. A variety of possible choices follow, but they are all incorrect.

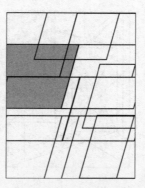

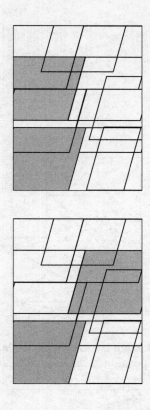

And now the correct one!

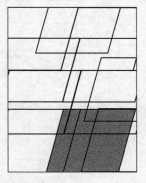

Were you able to find the correct answer? These two problems were fairly easy. We used them to illustrate how to go about eliminating those choices that are almost correct. But of course, ALMOST doesn't count. The next one is a little more complex and requires you to be more creative.

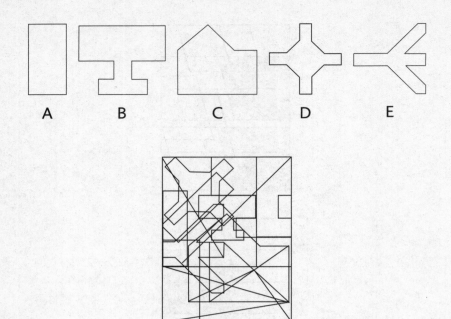

A   B   C   D   E

6.

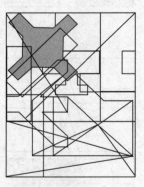

In the following solution, choice **D** is apparent, but it is turned at an angle, so it is incorrect. Remember that the correct figures are both the same size and in the same position as the lettered figures.

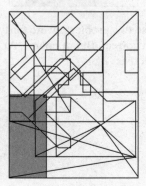

In the following, choice **A** is there, but it is too small.

The same is true about choice **B**.

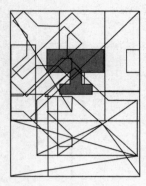

In choice **E**, only part of the figure appears.

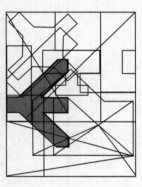

And finally, the correct answer is **C**.

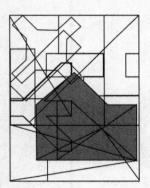

Practice Questions

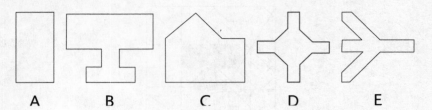

A   B   C   D   E

1.

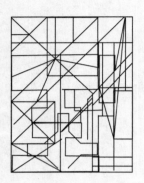

4.

2.

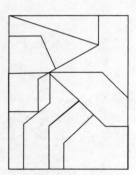

5.

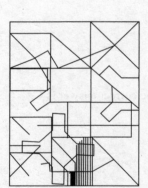

3.

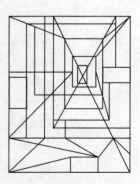

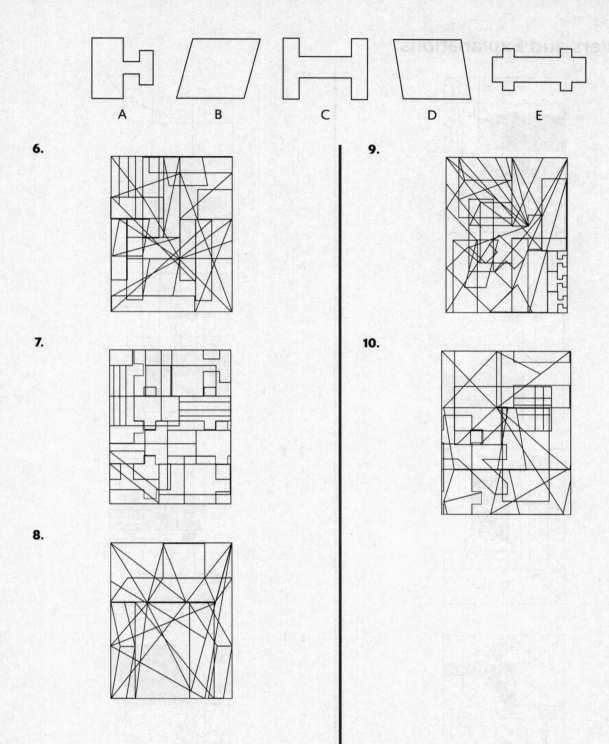

A   B   C   D   E

6.

7.

8.

9.

10.

Answers and Explanations

1. B.

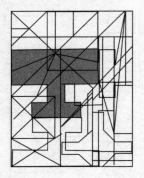

2. C.

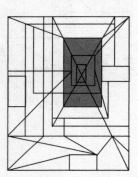

3. A.

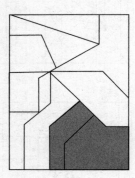

4. E.

5. D.

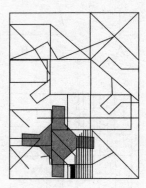

6. C.

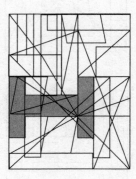

7. E.

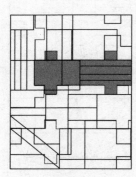

8. B.

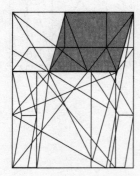

9. A.

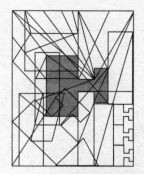

10. D.

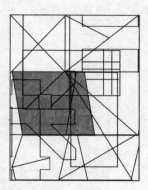

Spatial Apperception

The Spatial Apperception Test (SAT) portion of the ASTB is designed to measure your ability to perceive spatial relationships from differing orientations. This portion of the test was added in the early 1950s when the test was revised. Studies indicated that spatial orientation was significant in the prediction of success in flight training. While the other portions of the test are important, this section of the ASTB probably requires the most attention.

On the test you are presented with a picture of a ship on water, and you are asked to select the position of an aircraft in relation to that ship. You are presented with five individual pictures of airplanes in flight, and you are asked to choose the one that best represents the answer. The planes might be banking, climbing, diving, flying at an angle to land, in level flight, flying out to sea, flying along the coastland and so on. You are considered to be looking at the ship from the middle of your windscreen.

You should look for a couple of things as you answer the questions. The first thing you should look for is the position of the horizon, which indicates whether the plane is climbing, diving or in level flight. If the horizon is above the middle of the picture, the plane is diving. If it is below the middle, it is climbing. See the following illustration.

In the first panel, the plane is diving, and in the second, the plane is climbing.

The next thing to look for is the angle of the horizon.

In the first picture, the angle of the horizon indicates that the plane is banking right, and the second picture indicates that the plane is banking left. The level of the horizon also indicates that the plane, in both instances, is diving.

What would the following illustration indicate about the plane's movement?

The horizon is in the middle of the picture, and everything else is level. Thus, the plane is in level flight and not banking.

The third item to look for is the position of the coastline. Is it on the right or left side of the aircraft? This adds another dimension to the questions. Is the plane flying at an angle to the coastline?

According to the illustration, the first plane is flying diagonally to the coastline, which is on its left. In the second illustration, the coastline is on the right, and again the plane is flying at a diagonal to the coastline. Don't be tempted to think the plane is banking because the land is at an angle. The position of the horizon is what indicates whether the plane is banking or not.

Following is a chart of the different aircraft and their flying positions. You may remove this page and use it for each of the appropriate tests in this book.

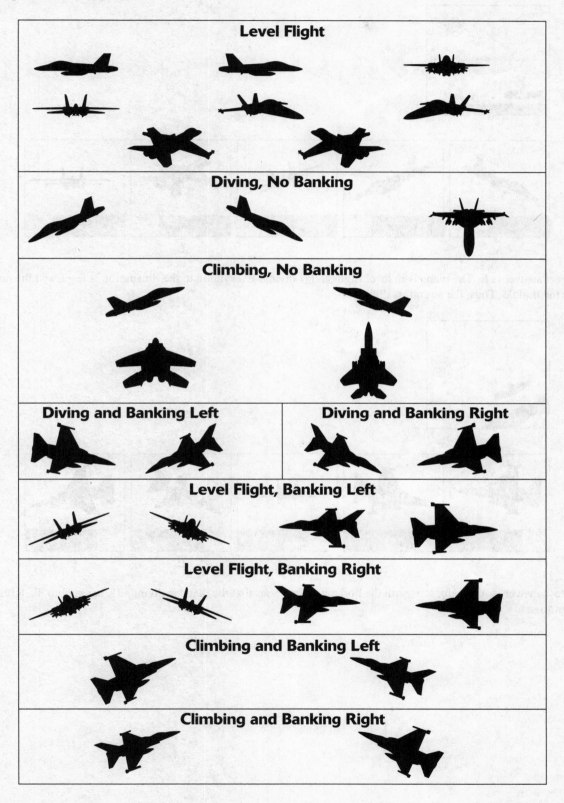

Let's try a few actual problems.

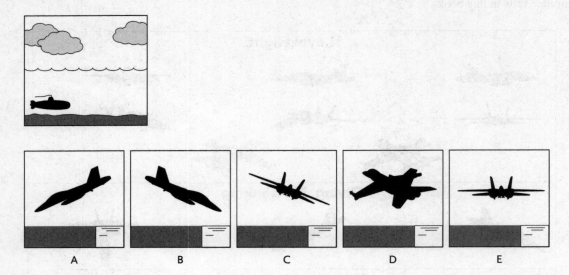

The correct answer is **E**. The plane is in level flight and is diving. Everything in the illustration is level, and the horizon is above the middle. Thus, the aircraft is diving.

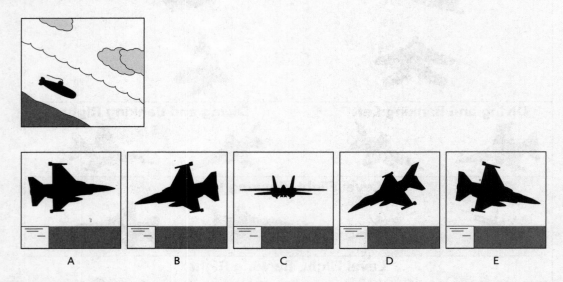

The correct answer is **A**. Again, start with the horizon. It indicates that the plane is diving; it's banking to the left and flying out to sea.

Practice Questions

1.

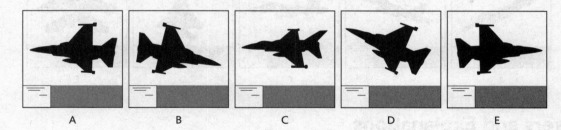

A   B   C   D   E

2.

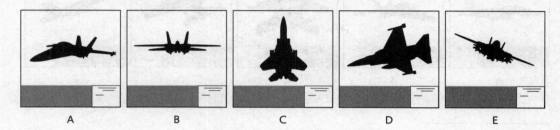

A   B   C   D   E

3.

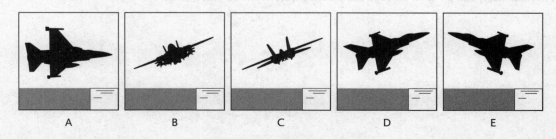

A   B   C   D   E

4.

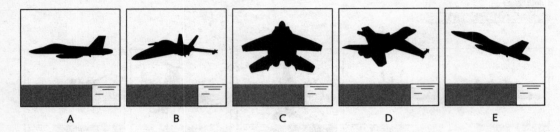

     A   B   C   D   E

5.

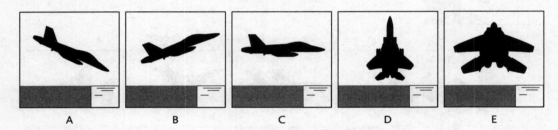

     A   B   C   D   E

Answers and Explanations

  1. B. The plane is level, not banking and flying out to sea.

  2. A. The plane's flight is level and flying out to sea.

  3. A. The plane's flight is level, it is banking left and flying out to sea.

  4. D. The plane's flight is level, not banking and heading 45° along the coastline on the right.

  5. C. The plane is not diving, not banking and the coastline is on the right.

If you missed any of these questions, read this section again, study the illustrations of the aircraft so that you can recognize them immediately, and go back through the practice questions one more time.

Electrical Maze

The purpose of the Electrical Maze problems (AFOQT) is to test your ability to choose a correct path from among several choices. The test itself has 20 mazes, and you have 10 minutes in which to answer all the questions. This entails having a quick eye for mazes and the ability to trace the lines to a logical end, while quickly eliminating other paths. The best way to learn how to solve these problems is to actually work on them.

First, take a look at the following:

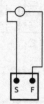

This is a typical box, and each maze has five of them. Your job is to find the line that leads from the starting point (S) to the finishing point (F) while passing through the circle at the top. Some of the lines lead to other boxes. Some of the lines are dead ends. Some just return to themselves. The preceding illustration is a very simplistic rendering of what you will be looking at on this portion of the test, but as you can see, the line runs from S, through the circle at the top, and back to F.

Look at the following illustration. Only one box has the line from the S, through the circle, and back to the F in the same box. Dots on the line show the *only* places where turns or direction changes can be made between lines. If lines meet or cross where there is *no dot,* turns or direction changes *cannot be made.*

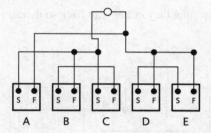

The correct answer is **A.** Let's look at the incorrect answers first, so we can eliminate them. In the second box, choice **B**, the S connects to the F in the third box, choice **C**. This automatically eliminates both choices. In the fourth box, choice **D**, the S connects to the S in the fifth box, choice **E**. Again, this eliminates both of them as correct choices. You should have been able to eliminate those four boxes, which leaves choice **A**. Keep in mind that with 20 questions on the test and only 10 minutes in which to answer them, you have only 30 seconds for each question. Therefore, the faster you can eliminate boxes, the faster you can narrow down the choices and choose the correct answer.

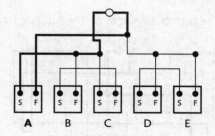

Try another one.

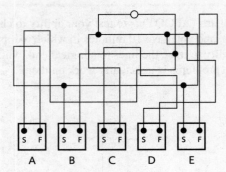

The correct answer is **B**. How quickly did you find the answer? The correct solution follows.

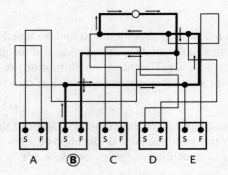

If you follow any of the other lines, you see that they either lead back to themselves, to other boxes or just end at another line.

Try one more.

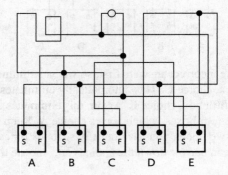

This is one that takes you round about. The correct answer is **A**. The solution follows.

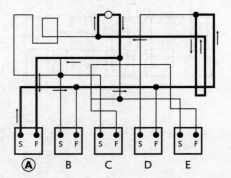

If you follow some of the other lines in other boxes, you see why you cannot solve the maze with any answer but **A**. For example, if you follow the S line from box B and turn right, you end up at the S in box C. If you turn left, you end up at the circle, but it does not take you back to the box. In box C, the S line also takes you through the circle, but the F line connects only with the F line in box E. Remember that you cannot make turns, even if lines are crossing, except at the dots on the lines. In box D, both lines end up taking you to the same line, and nothing leads back to the F dot.

Practice Questions

1.

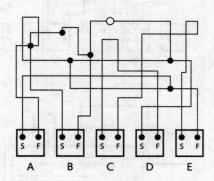

2.

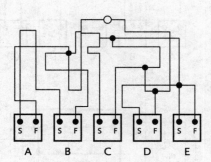

3.

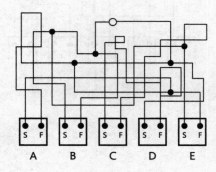

4.

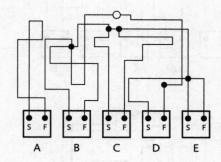

5.

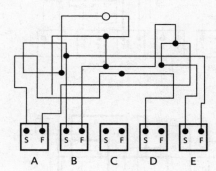

6.

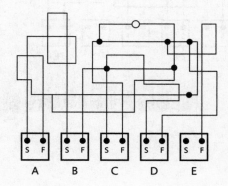

Answers and Explanations

1. B.

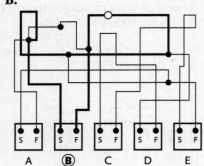

2. C.

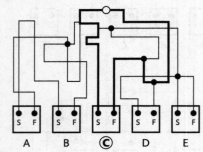

3. E.

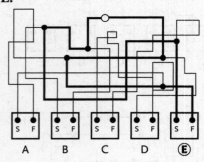

4. D.

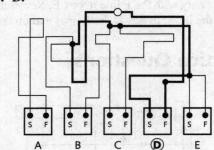

5. E.

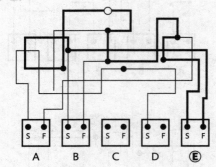

6. C.

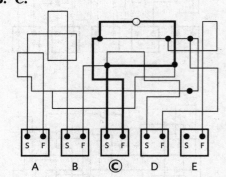

Aviation Review

To do well in any of the aviation sections of these tests, you should have some basic knowledge of how airplanes and helicopters fly. We recommend that you take the time to visit an airport and spend some time speaking with pilots and getting some basic information about how to fly a plane. It might even be worth hiring a pilot for a few hours to take you up so you get the basic concepts. Even better, go through this book, note down any questions with which you had problems and then ask the pilots for help. A hands-on demonstration will assure that you will never forget the material.

Complex Movement

The Complex Movement test (AFAST) measures your ability to judge distance and motion. You are given five pairs of symbols that represent both distance and direction. You have to select the appropriate symbols that represent the distance and direction. You have to move a dot from outside a circle into the center of that circle.

Let's start by analyzing each of the components of these questions. The first is the circle and the dot.

The whole object of this exercise, as stated previously, is to move the dot into the middle of the circle. From this illustration you should see that if you move the dot to the left, you are able to center it. However, another aspect of this example is HOW FAR TO MOVE IT.

You are given a key that gives you three distances, each somewhat approximate, but in 1/8 inch increments (enlarged in this book so that you can see it better). You have to determine whether the dot should be moved 1/8 inch, 2/8 inches or 3/8 inches horizontaly and/or vertically.

$$\odot \quad \bullet \qquad = \frac{1}{8} \text{ inch}$$

$$\odot \qquad \bullet \qquad = \frac{2}{8} \text{ inch}$$

$$\odot \qquad\qquad \bullet = \frac{3}{8} \text{ inch}$$

Try the following example.

It looks like the dot should be moved 1/8 inch to the left and 3/8 inches up. Try another one.

In this one, you must move the dot 3/8 inche to the right and 2/8 inch down.

The next part of the exercise is to determine which symbol, of the five that you are given, best represents the movement needed to align the dot in the middle of the circle. You are given the key to all the symbols on the test pages, but it's important to memorize them to save time. You have only 5 minutes to answer 30 questions, so the more time you save by memorizing the codes, the better you will do.

The symbols are as follows:

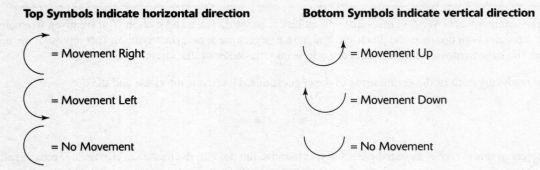

Top Symbols indicate horizontal direction	Bottom Symbols indicate vertical direction
= Movement Right	= Movement Up
= Movement Left	= Movement Down
= No Movement	= No Movement

The distance is indicated by the thickness of the arrows as follows:

— $\frac{1}{8}$ inch

— $\frac{2}{8}$ inch

— $\frac{3}{8}$ inch

To utilize this properly, first determine the distances to be moved, and then find the appropriate arrows. Let's look at a couple of samples.

The movement in the preceding figure should be 2/8 inches to the left and 2/8 inches down. This is represented as follows — notice the direction and thickness of the arrows:

This is another one:

The movement is to the left 3/8 inches with no up or down movement. This is represented as follows:

Remember that no arrow indication means no movement. The top arrow signifies movement to the left; the width of the arrow indicates a movement of 3/8 inches. Again, the bottom symbol indicates no up or down movement.

Remember to look at the KEYS: These show the meaning of the symbols in the test. A DIRECTION KEY shows the meaning of the TOP ROW OF SYMBOLS for movement RIGHT or LEFT (horizontal movement), and the BOTTOM ROW OF SYMBOLS for movement UP or DOWN (vertical movement). Notice that each includes a symbol for no movement. The DISTANCE KEY shows the three line widths in which the arrows can be drawn. The thinnest line width represents movement of approximately 1/8 inch. The medium-width line represents approximately 2/8 inches, and the thickest line represents approximately 3/8 inches.

Before getting to actual practice questions, see if you can quickly figure out what these arrows mean:

1.

2.

3.

4.

5.

6.

7.

8.

9.

10.

Answers:

1. Move right 1/8 inch.

2. Move right 3/8 inches.

3. Move up 3/8 inches.

4. Move down 2/8 inches.

5. Move left 2/8 inches.

6. No left or right movement.

7. Move down 3/8 inches.

8. Move left 1/8 inch.

9. Move right 2/8 inches.

10. No up or down movement.

Now let's look at the test format. The following is the type of key you will see on the test.

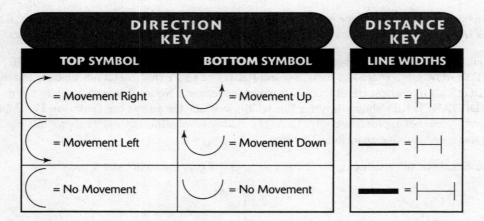

You can see that everything is spelled out. However, you should have this memorized and use it only for reference—just in case. Let's look at a sample test question.

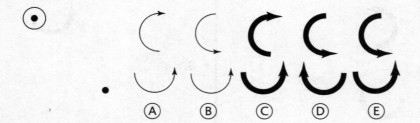

The dot should be moved 3/8 inches to the left and 3/8 inches up to center it.

If you look at choice **A**, it shows a movement of 1/8 inch to the right and 1/8 inch up. However, when you look at the dot, you can quickly eliminate any answer that indicates movement to the right because the dot must move left. This automatically eliminates choices **A** and **C**. You can also eliminate any symbols that indicate a downward movement, such as choice **D**. That leaves only choices **B** and **E** from which to choose. They look the same EXCEPT for the width of the lines. Choice **B** is thinner, and this indicates a movement of 1/8 inch, so you can eliminate choice **B**—this leaves choice **E** as the correct answer.

With enough practice, you should be able to get this type of question immediately. See if you can spot the correct answers to the following practice questions as quickly as possible. We've included the standard directions that you'll find on the AFAST.

Practice Questions

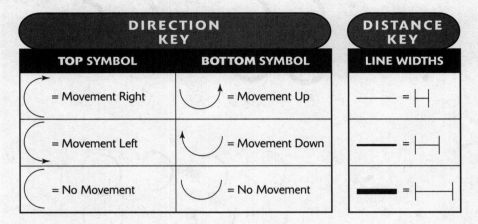

DIRECTION KEY		DISTANCE KEY
TOP SYMBOL	**BOTTOM SYMBOL**	**LINE WIDTHS**
= Movement Right	= Movement Up	=
= Movement Left	= Movement Down	=
= No Movement	= No Movement	=

1.

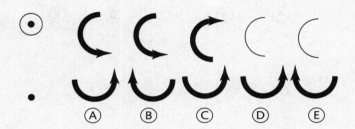

2.

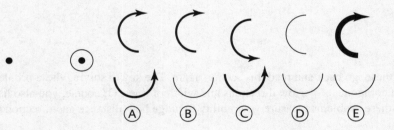

3.

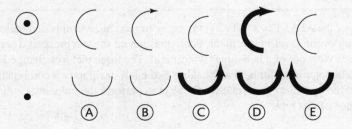

4.

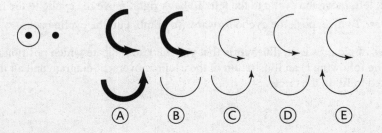

5.

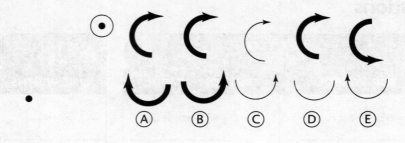

6.

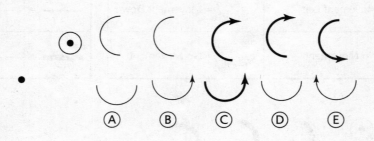

Answers

1. D.
2. E.
3. C.
4. D.
5. B.
6. C.

If you had trouble with these, go back and read this section again. The key to solving these problems is to break them down into their smallest components—arrow directions and width of lines. Of course, you also have to be able to estimate distances because these problems measure your ability to judge both distance and direction of movement.

Cyclic Orientation

The Cyclic Orientation portion of the AFAST is a test of your ability to recognize simple changes in helicopter position and to indicate the corresponding cyclic (stick) movement. Each question on the test presents a series of three sequential pictures that represents the pilot's view out of a helicopter windshield. The three pictures change FROM TOP TO BOTTOM showing a view from a helicopter in a climb, dive, banking to the left or right, or a combination of these maneuvers. You are required to determine which position the cyclic would be in to perform the maneuver indicated by the picture. The AFAST test contains 15 questions of this type.

For items in this test, the cyclic is moved as follows:

- **For banks:** To bank left, move the cyclic to the left. To bank right, move the cyclic to the right.
- **For climbs and dives:** To dive, push the cyclic forward. To climb, pull the cyclic back.

Accompanying each series of pictures is an illustration that you mark to indicate which position the cyclic should be in to answer the question. The following is an illustration of the cyclic movement diagram and an indication of what each circle means. You are asked to fill in the circle.

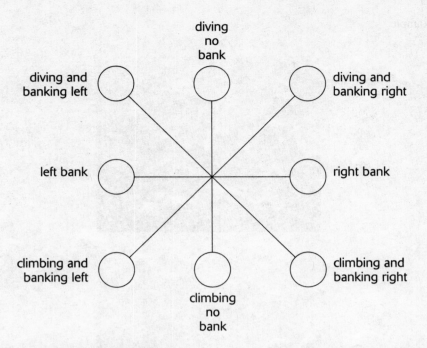

It is sometimes helpful to hold a picture in front of you and move it in different directions, keeping in mind that YOU are the one who is moving (that is, in the helicopter). The view is not moving. Move the picture and hold it. Which way would you have moved to see the picture in the position in which it's being held and viewed? That's the way the helicopter has moved.

Let's look at one example.

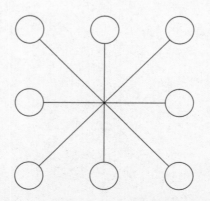

You should be able to look at these pictures and see that the helicopter is climbing and banking to the right. The horizon is getting higher, so the helicopter is climbing. The ships and planes below appear to moving to the left. If they're moving to the left, the helicopter is banking right. Therefore, fill in the diagram as follows.

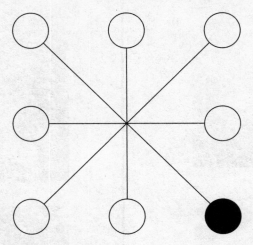

Try the practice questions on your own. Keep in mind the direction that the objects in front of you appear to be moving in each picture. Remember that the pictures should be read from top to bottom. The answers and explanations follow the questions.

Practice Questions

1.

2.

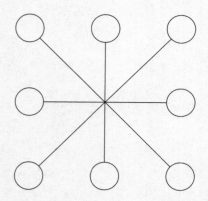

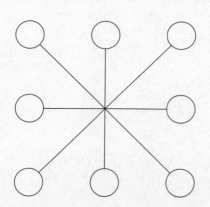

3.

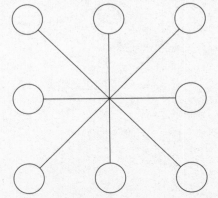

4.

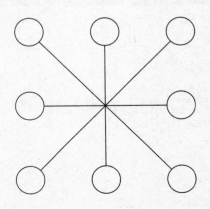

5.

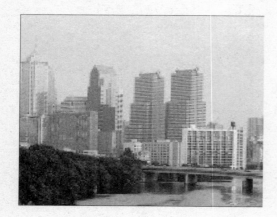

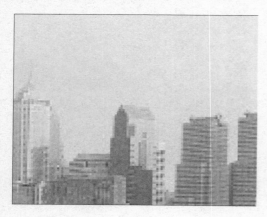

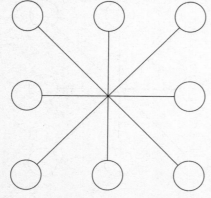

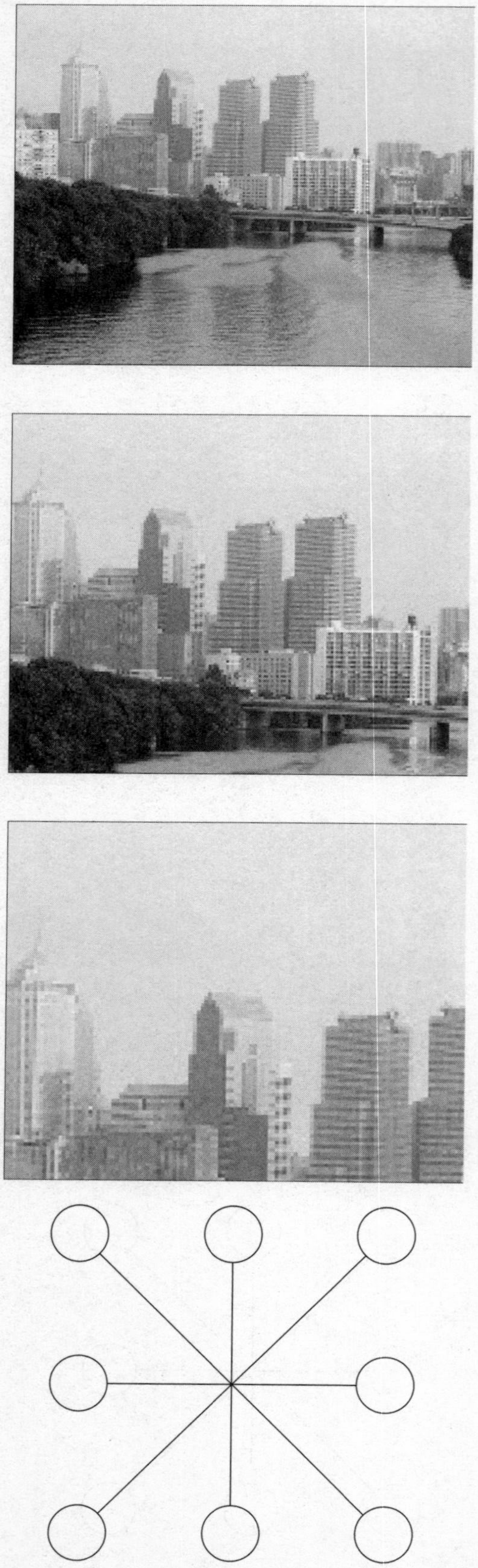

6.

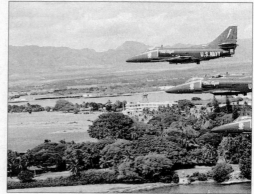

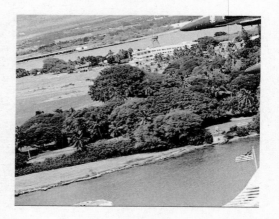

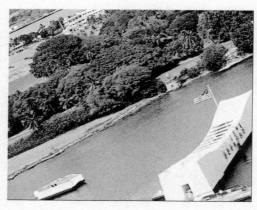

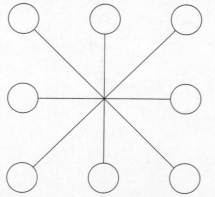

Answers and Explanations

1. Diving and banking left

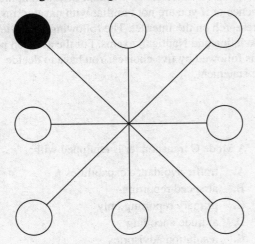

2. Diving and banking left

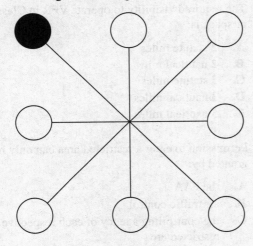

3. Diving, no banking

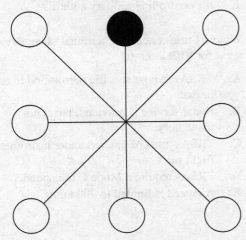

4. Banking left

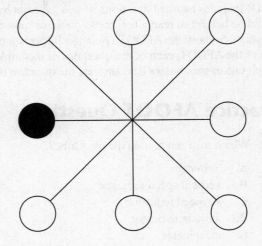

5. Climbing, no banking

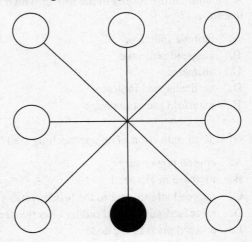

6. Diving and banking right

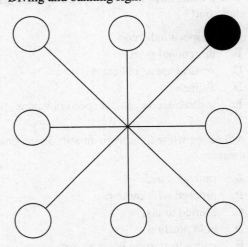

Aviation and Nautical Information

On both the AFOQT and the ASTB you will find tests that assess your basic knowledge of aviation. In addition, the ASTB includes nautical questions. If you have not had flying experience or if you are not familiar with naval terms, it would be helpful to read a few books on these subjects or do some research on the Internet. The following are review questions for both the AFOQT (Aviation Information) and ASTB (Aviation and Nautical) exams. For the aviation portion of the AFOQT, each of the questions or incomplete statements is followed by five choices. You have to decide which one of the choices best answers the question or completes the statement.

Practice AFOQT Questions

1. Which instrument uses the pitot tube?

   A. altimeter
   B. vertical speed indicator
   C. airspeed indicator
   D. attitude indicator
   E. tachometer

2. A vacuum failure results in the loss of which instrument?

   A. attitude indicator
   B. airspeed indicator
   C. altimeter
   D. vertical speed indicator
   E. manifold pressure gauge

3. What is an indication of an approaching stall?

   A. engine power surge
   B. increase in airspeed
   C. reduced aileron and rudder effectiveness
   D. increased aileron and rudder effectiveness
   E. upward pitch in the nose

4. Which instrument is NOT affected by a clogged static port?

   A. airspeed indicator
   B. directional gyro
   C. vertical speed indicator
   D. altimeter
   E. instantaneous vertical speed indicator

5. A flashing white light to an aircraft on the ground means:

   A. runway unsafe
   B. proceed with caution
   C. cleared to taxi
   D. hold position
   E. return to starting point on airport

6. A Mode C transponder is equipped with:

   A. traffic avoidance capabilities
   B. airspeed reporting
   C. primary reporting only
   D. altitude encoding
   E. resolution advisories

7. The required visibility to operate VFR in Class D airspace is:

   A. 2 statute miles
   B. 2 nautical miles
   C. 3 statute miles
   D. 3 nautical miles
   E. 5 nautical miles

8. Permission to enter a restricted area can only be granted by:

   A. the FAA
   B. air traffic control
   C. the controlling agency of each respective restricted area
   D. flight service
   E. the controlling military authority

9. Which is true concerning terminal radar service areas for VFR aircraft?

   A. TRSAs require specific permission to enter or exit.
   B. Radar service is provided, but is not mandatory.
   C. TRSAs must be entered under instrument flight rules.
   D. TRSAs require a Mode C transponder.
   E. Airspeed is limited to 200 knots.

10. What is a requirement for entering an air defense identification zone?

   A. automatic directional finder

   B. strobe lights

   C. filed DVFR or IFR flight plan

   D. VOR indicator

   E. global positioning system receiver

11. If a tornado touches down over water, it is called a:

   A. funnel cloud

   B. squall storm

   C. gust front

   D. waterspout

   E. towering cumulus

12. A thunderstorm requires which of the following?

   A. stable air

   B. downward force

   C. dry air

   D. unstable air

   E. low moisture levels

13. Standard temperature and pressure values at mean sea level are:

   A. 15° F and 29.92" Hg

   B. 15° C and 1013" Hg

   C. 59° C and 29.99" Hg

   D. 59° F and 29.92 millibars

   E. 15° C and 29.92" Hg

14. An above glide path indication from a pulsating approach slope indicator is:

   A. a pulsating red light

   B. a pulsating white light

   C. a pulsating green light

   D. a steady white light

   E. alternating red and white lights

15. A heliport's rotating beacon is identified by:

   A. two quick white flashes followed by a green light

   B. a green light followed by a white light

   C. a yellow light followed by a white light

   D. a yellow, green and white light

   E. a red light followed by a white light

16. Higher induced drag on the outside wing of an aircraft in a turn causes:

   A. adverse yaw

   B. overbanking tendency

   C. torque

   D. asymmetrical thrust

   E. P factor

17. A stopway can be used for which of the following?

   A. taxiing

   B. takeoff

   C. parking

   D. run up

   E. none of the above

18. Which of the following airspaces is uncontrolled?

   A. Class G

   B. Class A

   C. Class B

   D. Class C

   E. Class D

19. What airspace are student pilots restricted from operating in without specific permission from an authorized instructor pilot?

   A. Class A

   B. Class B

   C. Class C

   D. Class D

   E. Class E

20. The basic empty weight of an airplane includes which of the following?

   A. weight of passengers

   B. weight of cargo

   C. maximum fuel capacity

   D. unusable fuel

   E. undrainable oil

Practice ASTB Questions

1. The direction away from the wind is called:

   A. windward
   B. downwind
   C. upwind
   D. leeward
   E. none of the above

2. The upper edge of a boat's side is called:

   A. the gunwale
   B. the chine
   C. the transom
   D. freeboard
   E. draft

3. Lines of latitude:

   A. are east and west circle lines running parallel to the equator at 0°, measuring distance north and south at 90°
   B. are north and south circle lines pointing true north, measuring distance east and west
   C. run east and west
   D. run north and south
   E. none of the above

4. Lines of longitude:

   A. run east and west
   B. run north and south
   C. are north and south circle lines
   D. are east and west circle lines
   E. none of the above

5. The minimum vertical distance from the surface of the water to the gunwale is called:

   A. draft
   B. chine line
   C. freeboard
   D. waterline
   E. lubber's line

6. Longitude and latitude are use to determine a ship's:

   A. speed
   B. position
   C. direction
   D. time
   E. depth

7. A ship is at a latitude of 15°N and a longitude of 60°E. Its location is in the:

   A. Caribbean Sea
   B. Gulf of Mexico
   C. Arabian Sea
   D. North Atlantic
   E. Mediterranean Sea

8. Which of the following are considered aids to navigation?

   1. buoys
   2. lighthouses
   3. shorelines
   4. mountain peaks
   5. lorans

   A. 1, 2 and 5
   B. 3 and 4
   C. 5 only
   D. 2, 3 and 4
   E. 1 only

9. At sea, time zones are measured in:

   A. bands of longitude 15° in width
   B. bands of longitude 30° in width
   C. bands of latitude 15° in width
   D. bands of latitude 30° in width
   E. Greenwich Mean Time

10. A fathom is:

    A. a measurement of depth in 10-foot increments
    B. 100 feet
    C. a large fish thought to be extinct
    D. a measurement of depth in 6-foot increments
    E. 12 feet

Answers to Aviation Questions

1. C. The airspeed indicator is the only instrument that uses the pitot tube. The pitot tube allows the airspeed indicator to measure dynamic pressure versus static pressure through the static port.

2. A. A vacuum failure results in a loss of the attitude indicator. It is the only listed instrument that is a gyroscopic gauge, which is operated through the vacuum system.

3. C. As an aircraft approaches a stall, the ailerons and rudder lose effectiveness. This is due to reduced airflow over the flight controls, causing the pilot to have increased inputs resulting in small aircraft movements.

4. B. A directional gyro is not affected by a clogged static port. The directional gyro is the only listed instrument that is not a part of the pitot-static system.

5. E. A flashing white light gun signal from a control tower is an indication to taxi back to the starting point on the airport. A flashing white signal is only given to aircraft on the ground.

6. D. A Mode C transponder is one that provides altitude encoding to the interrogating radar. This helps controllers provide vertical and horizontal separation between participating aircraft.

7. C. The required visibility to operate under visual flight rules in Class D airspace is 3 statute miles. Aircraft cannot operate under VFR when visibility is below this value.

8. C. Restricted airspace is monitored by the agency that controls each restricted airspace. The proper government publications should be consulted to determine the times of use for restricted airspace.

9. B. Terminal radar service areas do not fit into any of the U.S. airspace classes. As a result, radar services are provided only to participating aircraft and are not mandatory for all VFR aircraft.

10. C. To enter or exit an air defense identification zone, an aircraft must have a two-way radio, a Mode C transponder and a filed DVFR or IFR flight plan.

11. D. A tornado that touches down over water is a waterspout. It has all the same qualities as a tornado except that it is over water instead of land.

12. D. Unstable air, a lifting force, and high moisture levels are the requirements for thunderstorm development.

13. E. Standard temperature and pressure values are set at 15° C and 29.92" Hg at sea level. These values decrease as your height above sea level increases.

14. B. An approach slope indicator (PLASI) indicates that an aircraft is above glide path with a pulsating white light.

15. D. A heliport's beacon alternates between green, yellow and white lights.

16. A. Adverse yaw is caused by the greater induced drag on the outside wing in a turn. This causes the airplane to yaw toward the outside of the turn. This is counteracted through use of the rudder.

17. E. A stopway/blast pad cannot be used for any normal aircraft operations. It can only be used as an emergency overrun for landing aircraft.

18. A. Class G airspace is the only U.S. airspace that is uncontrolled. All other U.S. airspaces are considered controlled airspace.

19. B. Student pilots cannot enter or exit Class B airspace unless they have received flight instruction on entering and exiting the airspace from an authorized instructor.

20. D. The basic empty weight of an aircraft includes the weight of the airplane and equipment, unusable fuel and full oil, and normal operating fluids.

Answers to Nautical Questions

1. **D.** Leeward is away from the wind.

2. **A.** The gunwales are the upper edges of a ship.

3. **A.** Lines of latitude measure distances north and south.

4. **C.** Lines of longitude run north and south; they measure distances east and west.

5. **C.** The distance between the gunwale and the surface of the water is called freeboard.

6. **B.** Longitude and latitude are used to determine a ship's position.

7. **C.** A ship with these coordinates is located in the Arabian Sea.

8. **A.** Objects not established for the sole purpose of assisting a navigator in fixing a position are not considered aids to navigation.

9. **A.** Time zones are measured in bands of longitude 15° in width.

10. **D.** A fathom equals 6 feet.

Helicopter Knowledge

A helicopter creates lift in a unique way. It has a rotary wing, compared to the fixed wing on a regular airplane. Where a fixed wing aircraft has to be moving to produce lift by the *plane* or angle of attack on the wing, a helicopter achieves it by manipulating the main rotor blades, changing the angle at which they meet the air and subsequently the angle of attack. The drawback with this setup is the need for torque control with a tail rotor, which bleeds power from the engine every time it's used. That becomes a factor when you start getting into advanced maneuvers.

Helicopters are highly sensitive to input and very responsive. Slight pressures are required to master the finer techniques in hovering and landing.

Most helicopters have no appreciable form of adjustable trim. For example, if you pitch down when leveling off from a climb, the aircraft will continue descending unless you make an opposite cyclic input from the neutral position. Once you've leveled out, you need another input to take out that correction. This characteristic applies to forward, backward and sideways flight, and on a smaller scale in a hover.

Performance in any mode will be more responsive to input in a helicopter, rather than in a fixed wing aircraft. Whereas a fixed wing may become sluggish and hard to control at slow airspeeds a chopper may get only slightly less stable when slowing down. When it's hovering, however, it is completely stable.

The reduction of power also requires attention. The main rotor blades are the only means of creating lift, so if you drop the collective completely there's nothing holding you up, even though the throttle is wide open. All helicopter pilots are taught to glide the helicopter with little or no power to the ground.

Winds and turbulence also play a large role in how you control and master the dynamics. The helicopter should take off in the direction of the wind, the same as a fixed wing plane.

One of the things that remain constant in fixed and non-fixed wing aircraft is that in a turn you lose altitude and go nose down without correction.

We've presented some questions for you to practice your knowledge of helicopters and helicopter flight. However, before taking the actual test, we would recommend renting some time to go with an experienced helicopter pilot for an hour or two. Then you will have a better understanding of the unique flight characteristics of helicopters.

Practice Questions

1. When landing behind a large aircraft, the helicopter pilot should avoid wake turbulence by staying

    A. above the large aircraft final approach path and landing beyond the large aircraft touchdown point
    B. below the large aircraft approach path and beyond the large aircraft touchdown point
    C. above the large aircraft final approach path and landing prior to the large aircraft touchdown point
    D. below the large aircraft final approach path and prior to the large aircraft touchdown point
    E. as close to the same final approach path and touchdown point of the large aircraft as possible

2. The wind condition that requires the most caution when avoiding wake turbulence on landing is

    A. a light quartering tailwind
    B. a light quartering headwind
    C. a strong headwind
    D. a strong tailwind
    E. no wind

3. While in cruise level flight, low-frequency vibrations (100–400 cycles per minute) are usually associated with

    A. the engine
    B. the tail rotor
    C. the cooling fan
    D. the main rotor
    E. the navigation equipment

4. Medium-frequency vibrations would be associated with a defect in

    A. the main rotor
    B. the cooling fan
    C. the engine
    D. the tail rotor
    E. the navigation equipment

5. During surface taxi, the collective pitch is used to control

    A. forward movement
    B. altitude
    C. rate of speed
    D. heading
    E. drift

6. If possible, when departing from a defined area, what type of takeoff is preferred?

    A. a running takeoff
    B. a takeoff from a hover
    C. a vertical takeoff
    D. a normal takeoff from the surface
    E. either **A** or **C**

7. High airspeeds, especially in turbulent air, should be avoided because of the possibility of

   A. an abrupt pitch up
   B. tail rotor vibration
   C. retreating blade stall
   D. midfrequency vibration
   E. low-frequency vibration

8. When operating at high forward airspeeds, retreating blade stalls are more likely to occur under which conditions?

   A. low gross weight
   B. low density altitude
   C. high RPM
   D. steep turns
   E. hover flight

9. Under what conditions should a pilot consider using a running takeoff?

   A. during strong cross winds
   B. a takeoff with high density altitude
   C. no wind
   D. taking off in a confined area
   E. when the helicopter is not loaded to max gross weight

10. The most effective method of scanning for other aircraft for collision avoidance during daylight hours is to use

    A. off-center viewing to scan small sectors
    B. spaced concentration at the 12, 3, 6 and 9 o'clock positions
    C. a series of short regular eye movements to search each 10-degree sector
    D. continuous sweeping from right to left
    E. continuous sweeping from left to right

Answers and Explanations

1. **A.** When landing behind a large aircraft, stay at or above the large aircraft's final approach path and beyond its touchdown point. Vortices generated by the large aircraft sink, so it is important to fly above the flight path and beyond the touchdown point.

2. **A.** Light tailwinds can move the vortices of a preceding aircraft forward into the anticipated touchdown zone of another. Although tailwinds can be dangerous, strong winds might help diffuse wake turbulence vortices.

3. **D.** Low-frequency vibrations are always associated with the main rotor.

4. **D.** Medium-frequency vibrations are associated with a defect in the tail rotor.

5. **C.** The collective pitch controls the rate of speed during surface taxi. The higher the collective pitch the faster the taxi speed.

6. **D.** A normal takeoff from a hover should be made from a confirmed area.

7. **C.** A tendency for the retreating blade to stall in forward flight is a major factor in limiting a helicopter's forward airspeed. When operating at high airspeed, stalls are more likely to occur under conditions of high gross weight, low RPM, high density altitude, steep or abrupt turns, and/or turbulent flight.

8. **D.** Again, an important fact to remember when operating at high airspeed is that stalls are more likely to occur under conditions of high gross weight, low RPM, high density altitude, steep or abrupt turns, and/or turbulent flight.

9. **B.** A running takeoff should be utilized when gross weight OR density altitude prevent a sustained hover at normal hovering altitude. This is often referred to as a high-density altitude takeoff.

10. **C.** See and avoid is the pilot's responsibility in VFR conditions. Effective scanning is accomplished with a series of short, regularly spaced eye movements that bring successive areas of the sky into the central visual field. Each movement should not exceed 10 degrees, and each area should be observed for at least one second to enable detection. Keep in mind that any aircraft which appears to have no relative motion and stays in one scan quadrant is likely to be on a collision course.

Both the "Background Information" and "Self-Description" tests appear on the AFAST exam. There are no right or wrong answers. Instead, these are questions that are designed to give a quick snapshot of your background and who you are.

Background Information

The questions here are very simple. There are only 25 questions, and they are all multiple choice. They ask about your age, where you were born, your parents, siblings, school and work experience. All you have to do is select the answer that most applies to you. The following is a sample question.

1. How old are you?

   A. under 21 years old

   B. 21–24 years old

   C. 25–29 years old

   D. 30–34 years old

   E. 35+ years old

This should be fairly simple to understand. There might be a few questions that do not pertain to you, and you can skip them. The instructions should be clear and understandable.

Self-Description

This section of the AFAST contains 75 questions, and you have 25 minutes in which to answer them. These questions are also multiple choice but take different formats. Here are samples of the types of questions you'll encounter.

Section A (20 Questions)

There are two types of questions in this section. The first asks which of the choices most accurately describes you, and the second asks which of the choices least accurately describes you. There are 10 pairs of questions.

1. Which of the following MOST accurately describes you?

   A. happy

   B. joyful

   C. smiling

   D. content

   E. disappointed

2. Which of the following LEAST accurately describes you?

   A. happy

   B. joyful

   C. smiling

   D. content

   E. disappointed

Section B (20 Questions)

These are simple yes or no questions.

1. Do you usually like to meet new people?

   Y. Yes.

   N. No.

2. Are you usually able to control your temper?

   Y. Yes.

   N. No.

Section C (20 Questions)

These are career-oriented questions. They help provide information as to where your interests lie, even though you're applying for a flight program with the military. It's a guide to where you might eventually be placed.

1. Police officer

   L. like

   D. dislike

2. School teacher

   L. like

   D. dislike

Section D (9 Questions)

The following are examples of another form of question to evaluate your preferences.

1. **A.** I like to work on projects by myself.

   B. I prefer working in groups.

2. **A.** I look forward to meeting new people.

   B. I prefer my own group of friends.

Section E (6 Questions)

In this section, you are presented with a statement that might be somewhat controversial. You are asked to take a position that ranges from a strong agreement to a strong disagreement.

1. All it takes is to be diligent at a job, and you will succeed.

   A. strongly agree

   B. tend to agree

   C. tend to disagree

   D. strongly disagree

2. Open communication is the key to a successful relationship.

    A.   strongly agree

    B.   tend to agree

    C.   tend to disagree

    D.   strongly disagree

The questions require some thought, but keep in mind that there are no right or wrong answers. Don't try to outguess the questions because the tests are constructed to double check your answers and to provide balance to your answers.

PART II

FULL-LENGTH PRACTICE TESTS

This part includes test questions, answer keys, and explanations for each of the following military flight aptitude tests:

- Air Force Officer Qualifying Test (AFOQT)
- Army Alternate Flight Aptitude Selection Test (AFAST)
- Navy and Marine Corps Aviation Selection Test Battery (ASTB)

Answer Sheet for AFOQT Practice Test

Part 1 Verbal Analogies

1 Ⓐ Ⓑ Ⓒ Ⓓ Ⓔ
2 Ⓐ Ⓑ Ⓒ Ⓓ Ⓔ
3 Ⓐ Ⓑ Ⓒ Ⓓ Ⓔ
4 Ⓐ Ⓑ Ⓒ Ⓓ Ⓔ
5 Ⓐ Ⓑ Ⓒ Ⓓ Ⓔ
6 Ⓐ Ⓑ Ⓒ Ⓓ Ⓔ
7 Ⓐ Ⓑ Ⓒ Ⓓ Ⓔ
8 Ⓐ Ⓑ Ⓒ Ⓓ Ⓔ
9 Ⓐ Ⓑ Ⓒ Ⓓ Ⓔ
10 Ⓐ Ⓑ Ⓒ Ⓓ Ⓔ
11 Ⓐ Ⓑ Ⓒ Ⓓ Ⓔ
12 Ⓐ Ⓑ Ⓒ Ⓓ Ⓔ
13 Ⓐ Ⓑ Ⓒ Ⓓ Ⓔ
14 Ⓐ Ⓑ Ⓒ Ⓓ Ⓔ
15 Ⓐ Ⓑ Ⓒ Ⓓ Ⓔ

16 Ⓐ Ⓑ Ⓒ Ⓓ Ⓔ
17 Ⓐ Ⓑ Ⓒ Ⓓ Ⓔ
18 Ⓐ Ⓑ Ⓒ Ⓓ Ⓔ
19 Ⓐ Ⓑ Ⓒ Ⓓ Ⓔ
20 Ⓐ Ⓑ Ⓒ Ⓓ Ⓔ
21 Ⓐ Ⓑ Ⓒ Ⓓ Ⓔ
22 Ⓐ Ⓑ Ⓒ Ⓓ Ⓔ
23 Ⓐ Ⓑ Ⓒ Ⓓ Ⓔ
24 Ⓐ Ⓑ Ⓒ Ⓓ Ⓔ
25 Ⓐ Ⓑ Ⓒ Ⓓ Ⓔ

Part 2 Arithmetic Reasoning

1 Ⓐ Ⓑ Ⓒ Ⓓ Ⓔ
2 Ⓐ Ⓑ Ⓒ Ⓓ Ⓔ
3 Ⓐ Ⓑ Ⓒ Ⓓ Ⓔ
4 Ⓐ Ⓑ Ⓒ Ⓓ Ⓔ
5 Ⓐ Ⓑ Ⓒ Ⓓ Ⓔ
6 Ⓐ Ⓑ Ⓒ Ⓓ Ⓔ
7 Ⓐ Ⓑ Ⓒ Ⓓ Ⓔ
8 Ⓐ Ⓑ Ⓒ Ⓓ Ⓔ
9 Ⓐ Ⓑ Ⓒ Ⓓ Ⓔ
10 Ⓐ Ⓑ Ⓒ Ⓓ Ⓔ
11 Ⓐ Ⓑ Ⓒ Ⓓ Ⓔ
12 Ⓐ Ⓑ Ⓒ Ⓓ Ⓔ
13 Ⓐ Ⓑ Ⓒ Ⓓ Ⓔ
14 Ⓐ Ⓑ Ⓒ Ⓓ Ⓔ
15 Ⓐ Ⓑ Ⓒ Ⓓ Ⓔ

16 Ⓐ Ⓑ Ⓒ Ⓓ Ⓔ
17 Ⓐ Ⓑ Ⓒ Ⓓ Ⓔ
18 Ⓐ Ⓑ Ⓒ Ⓓ Ⓔ
19 Ⓐ Ⓑ Ⓒ Ⓓ Ⓔ
20 Ⓐ Ⓑ Ⓒ Ⓓ Ⓔ
21 Ⓐ Ⓑ Ⓒ Ⓓ Ⓔ
22 Ⓐ Ⓑ Ⓒ Ⓓ Ⓔ
23 Ⓐ Ⓑ Ⓒ Ⓓ Ⓔ
24 Ⓐ Ⓑ Ⓒ Ⓓ Ⓔ
25 Ⓐ Ⓑ Ⓒ Ⓓ Ⓔ

Part 3 Reading Comprehension

1 Ⓐ Ⓑ Ⓒ Ⓓ Ⓔ
2 Ⓐ Ⓑ Ⓒ Ⓓ Ⓔ
3 Ⓐ Ⓑ Ⓒ Ⓓ Ⓔ
4 Ⓐ Ⓑ Ⓒ Ⓓ Ⓔ
5 Ⓐ Ⓑ Ⓒ Ⓓ Ⓔ
6 Ⓐ Ⓑ Ⓒ Ⓓ Ⓔ
7 Ⓐ Ⓑ Ⓒ Ⓓ Ⓔ
8 Ⓐ Ⓑ Ⓒ Ⓓ Ⓔ
9 Ⓐ Ⓑ Ⓒ Ⓓ Ⓔ
10 Ⓐ Ⓑ Ⓒ Ⓓ Ⓔ
11 Ⓐ Ⓑ Ⓒ Ⓓ Ⓔ
12 Ⓐ Ⓑ Ⓒ Ⓓ Ⓔ
13 Ⓐ Ⓑ Ⓒ Ⓓ Ⓔ
14 Ⓐ Ⓑ Ⓒ Ⓓ Ⓔ
15 Ⓐ Ⓑ Ⓒ Ⓓ Ⓔ

16 Ⓐ Ⓑ Ⓒ Ⓓ Ⓔ
17 Ⓐ Ⓑ Ⓒ Ⓓ Ⓔ
18 Ⓐ Ⓑ Ⓒ Ⓓ Ⓔ
19 Ⓐ Ⓑ Ⓒ Ⓓ Ⓔ
20 Ⓐ Ⓑ Ⓒ Ⓓ Ⓔ
21 Ⓐ Ⓑ Ⓒ Ⓓ Ⓔ
22 Ⓐ Ⓑ Ⓒ Ⓓ Ⓔ
23 Ⓐ Ⓑ Ⓒ Ⓓ Ⓔ
24 Ⓐ Ⓑ Ⓒ Ⓓ Ⓔ
25 Ⓐ Ⓑ Ⓒ Ⓓ Ⓔ

Part 4 Data Interpretation

1 Ⓐ Ⓑ Ⓒ Ⓓ Ⓔ
2 Ⓐ Ⓑ Ⓒ Ⓓ Ⓔ
3 Ⓐ Ⓑ Ⓒ Ⓓ Ⓔ
4 Ⓐ Ⓑ Ⓒ Ⓓ Ⓔ
5 Ⓐ Ⓑ Ⓒ Ⓓ Ⓔ
6 Ⓐ Ⓑ Ⓒ Ⓓ Ⓔ
7 Ⓐ Ⓑ Ⓒ Ⓓ Ⓔ
8 Ⓐ Ⓑ Ⓒ Ⓓ Ⓔ
9 Ⓐ Ⓑ Ⓒ Ⓓ Ⓔ
10 Ⓐ Ⓑ Ⓒ Ⓓ Ⓔ
11 Ⓐ Ⓑ Ⓒ Ⓓ Ⓔ
12 Ⓐ Ⓑ Ⓒ Ⓓ Ⓔ
13 Ⓐ Ⓑ Ⓒ Ⓓ Ⓔ
14 Ⓐ Ⓑ Ⓒ Ⓓ Ⓔ
15 Ⓐ Ⓑ Ⓒ Ⓓ Ⓔ

16 Ⓐ Ⓑ Ⓒ Ⓓ Ⓔ
17 Ⓐ Ⓑ Ⓒ Ⓓ Ⓔ
18 Ⓐ Ⓑ Ⓒ Ⓓ Ⓔ
19 Ⓐ Ⓑ Ⓒ Ⓓ Ⓔ
20 Ⓐ Ⓑ Ⓒ Ⓓ Ⓔ
21 Ⓐ Ⓑ Ⓒ Ⓓ Ⓔ
22 Ⓐ Ⓑ Ⓒ Ⓓ Ⓔ
23 Ⓐ Ⓑ Ⓒ Ⓓ Ⓔ
24 Ⓐ Ⓑ Ⓒ Ⓓ Ⓔ
25 Ⓐ Ⓑ Ⓒ Ⓓ Ⓔ

Part 5 Word Knowledge

1 Ⓐ Ⓑ Ⓒ Ⓓ Ⓔ
2 Ⓐ Ⓑ Ⓒ Ⓓ Ⓔ
3 Ⓐ Ⓑ Ⓒ Ⓓ Ⓔ
4 Ⓐ Ⓑ Ⓒ Ⓓ Ⓔ
5 Ⓐ Ⓑ Ⓒ Ⓓ Ⓔ
6 Ⓐ Ⓑ Ⓒ Ⓓ Ⓔ
7 Ⓐ Ⓑ Ⓒ Ⓓ Ⓔ
8 Ⓐ Ⓑ Ⓒ Ⓓ Ⓔ
9 Ⓐ Ⓑ Ⓒ Ⓓ Ⓔ
10 Ⓐ Ⓑ Ⓒ Ⓓ Ⓔ
11 Ⓐ Ⓑ Ⓒ Ⓓ Ⓔ
12 Ⓐ Ⓑ Ⓒ Ⓓ Ⓔ
13 Ⓐ Ⓑ Ⓒ Ⓓ Ⓔ
14 Ⓐ Ⓑ Ⓒ Ⓓ Ⓔ
15 Ⓐ Ⓑ Ⓒ Ⓓ Ⓔ

16 Ⓐ Ⓑ Ⓒ Ⓓ Ⓔ
17 Ⓐ Ⓑ Ⓒ Ⓓ Ⓔ
18 Ⓐ Ⓑ Ⓒ Ⓓ Ⓔ
19 Ⓐ Ⓑ Ⓒ Ⓓ Ⓔ
20 Ⓐ Ⓑ Ⓒ Ⓓ Ⓔ
21 Ⓐ Ⓑ Ⓒ Ⓓ Ⓔ
22 Ⓐ Ⓑ Ⓒ Ⓓ Ⓔ
23 Ⓐ Ⓑ Ⓒ Ⓓ Ⓔ
24 Ⓐ Ⓑ Ⓒ Ⓓ Ⓔ
25 Ⓐ Ⓑ Ⓒ Ⓓ Ⓔ

Part 6 Mathematics Knowledge

1 Ⓐ Ⓑ Ⓒ Ⓓ Ⓔ
2 Ⓐ Ⓑ Ⓒ Ⓓ Ⓔ
3 Ⓐ Ⓑ Ⓒ Ⓓ Ⓔ
4 Ⓐ Ⓑ Ⓒ Ⓓ Ⓔ
5 Ⓐ Ⓑ Ⓒ Ⓓ Ⓔ
6 Ⓐ Ⓑ Ⓒ Ⓓ Ⓔ
7 Ⓐ Ⓑ Ⓒ Ⓓ Ⓔ
8 Ⓐ Ⓑ Ⓒ Ⓓ Ⓔ
9 Ⓐ Ⓑ Ⓒ Ⓓ Ⓔ
10 Ⓐ Ⓑ Ⓒ Ⓓ Ⓔ
11 Ⓐ Ⓑ Ⓒ Ⓓ Ⓔ
12 Ⓐ Ⓑ Ⓒ Ⓓ Ⓔ
13 Ⓐ Ⓑ Ⓒ Ⓓ Ⓔ
14 Ⓐ Ⓑ Ⓒ Ⓓ Ⓔ
15 Ⓐ Ⓑ Ⓒ Ⓓ Ⓔ

16 Ⓐ Ⓑ Ⓒ Ⓓ Ⓔ
17 Ⓐ Ⓑ Ⓒ Ⓓ Ⓔ
18 Ⓐ Ⓑ Ⓒ Ⓓ Ⓔ
19 Ⓐ Ⓑ Ⓒ Ⓓ Ⓔ
20 Ⓐ Ⓑ Ⓒ Ⓓ Ⓔ
21 Ⓐ Ⓑ Ⓒ Ⓓ Ⓔ
22 Ⓐ Ⓑ Ⓒ Ⓓ Ⓔ
23 Ⓐ Ⓑ Ⓒ Ⓓ Ⓔ
24 Ⓐ Ⓑ Ⓒ Ⓓ Ⓔ
25 Ⓐ Ⓑ Ⓒ Ⓓ Ⓔ

Answer Sheet for AFOQT Practice Test

Part 7 Mechanical Comprehension

1 Ⓐ Ⓑ Ⓒ Ⓓ Ⓔ	11 Ⓐ Ⓑ Ⓒ Ⓓ Ⓔ
2 Ⓐ Ⓑ Ⓒ Ⓓ Ⓔ	12 Ⓐ Ⓑ Ⓒ Ⓓ Ⓔ
3 Ⓐ Ⓑ Ⓒ Ⓓ Ⓔ	13 Ⓐ Ⓑ Ⓒ Ⓓ Ⓔ
4 Ⓐ Ⓑ Ⓒ Ⓓ Ⓔ	14 Ⓐ Ⓑ Ⓒ Ⓓ Ⓔ
5 Ⓐ Ⓑ Ⓒ Ⓓ Ⓔ	15 Ⓐ Ⓑ Ⓒ Ⓓ Ⓔ
6 Ⓐ Ⓑ Ⓒ Ⓓ Ⓔ	16 Ⓐ Ⓑ Ⓒ Ⓓ Ⓔ
7 Ⓐ Ⓑ Ⓒ Ⓓ Ⓔ	17 Ⓐ Ⓑ Ⓒ Ⓓ Ⓔ
8 Ⓐ Ⓑ Ⓒ Ⓓ Ⓔ	18 Ⓐ Ⓑ Ⓒ Ⓓ Ⓔ
9 Ⓐ Ⓑ Ⓒ Ⓓ Ⓔ	19 Ⓐ Ⓑ Ⓒ Ⓓ Ⓔ
10 Ⓐ Ⓑ Ⓒ Ⓓ Ⓔ	20 Ⓐ Ⓑ Ⓒ Ⓓ Ⓔ

Part 8 Electrical Maze

1 Ⓐ Ⓑ Ⓒ Ⓓ Ⓔ	11 Ⓐ Ⓑ Ⓒ Ⓓ Ⓔ
2 Ⓐ Ⓑ Ⓒ Ⓓ Ⓔ	12 Ⓐ Ⓑ Ⓒ Ⓓ Ⓔ
3 Ⓐ Ⓑ Ⓒ Ⓓ Ⓔ	13 Ⓐ Ⓑ Ⓒ Ⓓ Ⓔ
4 Ⓐ Ⓑ Ⓒ Ⓓ Ⓔ	14 Ⓐ Ⓑ Ⓒ Ⓓ Ⓔ
5 Ⓐ Ⓑ Ⓒ Ⓓ Ⓔ	15 Ⓐ Ⓑ Ⓒ Ⓓ Ⓔ
6 Ⓐ Ⓑ Ⓒ Ⓓ Ⓔ	16 Ⓐ Ⓑ Ⓒ Ⓓ Ⓔ
7 Ⓐ Ⓑ Ⓒ Ⓓ Ⓔ	17 Ⓐ Ⓑ Ⓒ Ⓓ Ⓔ
8 Ⓐ Ⓑ Ⓒ Ⓓ Ⓔ	18 Ⓐ Ⓑ Ⓒ Ⓓ Ⓔ
9 Ⓐ Ⓑ Ⓒ Ⓓ Ⓔ	19 Ⓐ Ⓑ Ⓒ Ⓓ Ⓔ
10 Ⓐ Ⓑ Ⓒ Ⓓ Ⓔ	20 Ⓐ Ⓑ Ⓒ Ⓓ Ⓔ

Part 9 Scale Reading

1 Ⓐ Ⓑ Ⓒ Ⓓ Ⓔ	11 Ⓐ Ⓑ Ⓒ Ⓓ Ⓔ	21 Ⓐ Ⓑ Ⓒ Ⓓ Ⓔ	31 Ⓐ Ⓑ Ⓒ Ⓓ Ⓔ
2 Ⓐ Ⓑ Ⓒ Ⓓ Ⓔ	12 Ⓐ Ⓑ Ⓒ Ⓓ Ⓔ	22 Ⓐ Ⓑ Ⓒ Ⓓ Ⓔ	32 Ⓐ Ⓑ Ⓒ Ⓓ Ⓔ
3 Ⓐ Ⓑ Ⓒ Ⓓ Ⓔ	13 Ⓐ Ⓑ Ⓒ Ⓓ Ⓔ	23 Ⓐ Ⓑ Ⓒ Ⓓ Ⓔ	33 Ⓐ Ⓑ Ⓒ Ⓓ Ⓔ
4 Ⓐ Ⓑ Ⓒ Ⓓ Ⓔ	14 Ⓐ Ⓑ Ⓒ Ⓓ Ⓔ	24 Ⓐ Ⓑ Ⓒ Ⓓ Ⓔ	34 Ⓐ Ⓑ Ⓒ Ⓓ Ⓔ
5 Ⓐ Ⓑ Ⓒ Ⓓ Ⓔ	15 Ⓐ Ⓑ Ⓒ Ⓓ Ⓔ	25 Ⓐ Ⓑ Ⓒ Ⓓ Ⓔ	35 Ⓐ Ⓑ Ⓒ Ⓓ Ⓔ
6 Ⓐ Ⓑ Ⓒ Ⓓ Ⓔ	16 Ⓐ Ⓑ Ⓒ Ⓓ Ⓔ	26 Ⓐ Ⓑ Ⓒ Ⓓ Ⓔ	36 Ⓐ Ⓑ Ⓒ Ⓓ Ⓔ
7 Ⓐ Ⓑ Ⓒ Ⓓ Ⓔ	17 Ⓐ Ⓑ Ⓒ Ⓓ Ⓔ	27 Ⓐ Ⓑ Ⓒ Ⓓ Ⓔ	37 Ⓐ Ⓑ Ⓒ Ⓓ Ⓔ
8 Ⓐ Ⓑ Ⓒ Ⓓ Ⓔ	18 Ⓐ Ⓑ Ⓒ Ⓓ Ⓔ	28 Ⓐ Ⓑ Ⓒ Ⓓ Ⓔ	38 Ⓐ Ⓑ Ⓒ Ⓓ Ⓔ
9 Ⓐ Ⓑ Ⓒ Ⓓ Ⓔ	19 Ⓐ Ⓑ Ⓒ Ⓓ Ⓔ	29 Ⓐ Ⓑ Ⓒ Ⓓ Ⓔ	39 Ⓐ Ⓑ Ⓒ Ⓓ Ⓔ
10 Ⓐ Ⓑ Ⓒ Ⓓ Ⓔ	20 Ⓐ Ⓑ Ⓒ Ⓓ Ⓔ	30 Ⓐ Ⓑ Ⓒ Ⓓ Ⓔ	40 Ⓐ Ⓑ Ⓒ Ⓓ Ⓔ

Part 10 Instrument Comprehension

1 Ⓐ Ⓑ Ⓒ Ⓓ Ⓔ	11 Ⓐ Ⓑ Ⓒ Ⓓ Ⓔ
2 Ⓐ Ⓑ Ⓒ Ⓓ Ⓔ	12 Ⓐ Ⓑ Ⓒ Ⓓ Ⓔ
3 Ⓐ Ⓑ Ⓒ Ⓓ Ⓔ	13 Ⓐ Ⓑ Ⓒ Ⓓ Ⓔ
4 Ⓐ Ⓑ Ⓒ Ⓓ Ⓔ	14 Ⓐ Ⓑ Ⓒ Ⓓ Ⓔ
5 Ⓐ Ⓑ Ⓒ Ⓓ Ⓔ	15 Ⓐ Ⓑ Ⓒ Ⓓ Ⓔ
6 Ⓐ Ⓑ Ⓒ Ⓓ Ⓔ	16 Ⓐ Ⓑ Ⓒ Ⓓ Ⓔ
7 Ⓐ Ⓑ Ⓒ Ⓓ Ⓔ	17 Ⓐ Ⓑ Ⓒ Ⓓ Ⓔ
8 Ⓐ Ⓑ Ⓒ Ⓓ Ⓔ	18 Ⓐ Ⓑ Ⓒ Ⓓ Ⓔ
9 Ⓐ Ⓑ Ⓒ Ⓓ Ⓔ	19 Ⓐ Ⓑ Ⓒ Ⓓ Ⓔ
10 Ⓐ Ⓑ Ⓒ Ⓓ Ⓔ	20 Ⓐ Ⓑ Ⓒ Ⓓ Ⓔ

Part 11 Block Counting

1 Ⓐ Ⓑ Ⓒ Ⓓ Ⓔ	11 Ⓐ Ⓑ Ⓒ Ⓓ Ⓔ
2 Ⓐ Ⓑ Ⓒ Ⓓ Ⓔ	12 Ⓐ Ⓑ Ⓒ Ⓓ Ⓔ
3 Ⓐ Ⓑ Ⓒ Ⓓ Ⓔ	13 Ⓐ Ⓑ Ⓒ Ⓓ Ⓔ
4 Ⓐ Ⓑ Ⓒ Ⓓ Ⓔ	14 Ⓐ Ⓑ Ⓒ Ⓓ Ⓔ
5 Ⓐ Ⓑ Ⓒ Ⓓ Ⓔ	15 Ⓐ Ⓑ Ⓒ Ⓓ Ⓔ
6 Ⓐ Ⓑ Ⓒ Ⓓ Ⓔ	16 Ⓐ Ⓑ Ⓒ Ⓓ Ⓔ
7 Ⓐ Ⓑ Ⓒ Ⓓ Ⓔ	17 Ⓐ Ⓑ Ⓒ Ⓓ Ⓔ
8 Ⓐ Ⓑ Ⓒ Ⓓ Ⓔ	18 Ⓐ Ⓑ Ⓒ Ⓓ Ⓔ
9 Ⓐ Ⓑ Ⓒ Ⓓ Ⓔ	19 Ⓐ Ⓑ Ⓒ Ⓓ Ⓔ
10 Ⓐ Ⓑ Ⓒ Ⓓ Ⓔ	20 Ⓐ Ⓑ Ⓒ Ⓓ Ⓔ

Part 12 Table Reading

1 Ⓐ Ⓑ Ⓒ Ⓓ Ⓔ	11 Ⓐ Ⓑ Ⓒ Ⓓ Ⓔ	21 Ⓐ Ⓑ Ⓒ Ⓓ Ⓔ	31 Ⓐ Ⓑ Ⓒ Ⓓ Ⓔ
2 Ⓐ Ⓑ Ⓒ Ⓓ Ⓔ	12 Ⓐ Ⓑ Ⓒ Ⓓ Ⓔ	22 Ⓐ Ⓑ Ⓒ Ⓓ Ⓔ	32 Ⓐ Ⓑ Ⓒ Ⓓ Ⓔ
3 Ⓐ Ⓑ Ⓒ Ⓓ Ⓔ	13 Ⓐ Ⓑ Ⓒ Ⓓ Ⓔ	23 Ⓐ Ⓑ Ⓒ Ⓓ Ⓔ	33 Ⓐ Ⓑ Ⓒ Ⓓ Ⓔ
4 Ⓐ Ⓑ Ⓒ Ⓓ Ⓔ	14 Ⓐ Ⓑ Ⓒ Ⓓ Ⓔ	24 Ⓐ Ⓑ Ⓒ Ⓓ Ⓔ	34 Ⓐ Ⓑ Ⓒ Ⓓ Ⓔ
5 Ⓐ Ⓑ Ⓒ Ⓓ Ⓔ	15 Ⓐ Ⓑ Ⓒ Ⓓ Ⓔ	25 Ⓐ Ⓑ Ⓒ Ⓓ Ⓔ	35 Ⓐ Ⓑ Ⓒ Ⓓ Ⓔ
6 Ⓐ Ⓑ Ⓒ Ⓓ Ⓔ	16 Ⓐ Ⓑ Ⓒ Ⓓ Ⓔ	26 Ⓐ Ⓑ Ⓒ Ⓓ Ⓔ	36 Ⓐ Ⓑ Ⓒ Ⓓ Ⓔ
7 Ⓐ Ⓑ Ⓒ Ⓓ Ⓔ	17 Ⓐ Ⓑ Ⓒ Ⓓ Ⓔ	27 Ⓐ Ⓑ Ⓒ Ⓓ Ⓔ	37 Ⓐ Ⓑ Ⓒ Ⓓ Ⓔ
8 Ⓐ Ⓑ Ⓒ Ⓓ Ⓔ	18 Ⓐ Ⓑ Ⓒ Ⓓ Ⓔ	28 Ⓐ Ⓑ Ⓒ Ⓓ Ⓔ	38 Ⓐ Ⓑ Ⓒ Ⓓ Ⓔ
9 Ⓐ Ⓑ Ⓒ Ⓓ Ⓔ	19 Ⓐ Ⓑ Ⓒ Ⓓ Ⓔ	29 Ⓐ Ⓑ Ⓒ Ⓓ Ⓔ	39 Ⓐ Ⓑ Ⓒ Ⓓ Ⓔ
10 Ⓐ Ⓑ Ⓒ Ⓓ Ⓔ	20 Ⓐ Ⓑ Ⓒ Ⓓ Ⓔ	30 Ⓐ Ⓑ Ⓒ Ⓓ Ⓔ	40 Ⓐ Ⓑ Ⓒ Ⓓ Ⓔ

CUT HERE

Answer Sheet for AFOQT Practice Test

Part 13 Aviation Information

1 Ⓐ Ⓑ Ⓒ Ⓓ Ⓔ		11 Ⓐ Ⓑ Ⓒ Ⓓ Ⓔ
2 Ⓐ Ⓑ Ⓒ Ⓓ Ⓔ		12 Ⓐ Ⓑ Ⓒ Ⓓ Ⓔ
3 Ⓐ Ⓑ Ⓒ Ⓓ Ⓔ		13 Ⓐ Ⓑ Ⓒ Ⓓ Ⓔ
4 Ⓐ Ⓑ Ⓒ Ⓓ Ⓔ		14 Ⓐ Ⓑ Ⓒ Ⓓ Ⓔ
5 Ⓐ Ⓑ Ⓒ Ⓓ Ⓔ		15 Ⓐ Ⓑ Ⓒ Ⓓ Ⓔ
6 Ⓐ Ⓑ Ⓒ Ⓓ Ⓔ		16 Ⓐ Ⓑ Ⓒ Ⓓ Ⓔ
7 Ⓐ Ⓑ Ⓒ Ⓓ Ⓔ		17 Ⓐ Ⓑ Ⓒ Ⓓ Ⓔ
8 Ⓐ Ⓑ Ⓒ Ⓓ Ⓔ		18 Ⓐ Ⓑ Ⓒ Ⓓ Ⓔ
9 Ⓐ Ⓑ Ⓒ Ⓓ Ⓔ		19 Ⓐ Ⓑ Ⓒ Ⓓ Ⓔ
10 Ⓐ Ⓑ Ⓒ Ⓓ Ⓔ		20 Ⓐ Ⓑ Ⓒ Ⓓ Ⓔ

Part 14 Rotated Blocks

1 Ⓐ Ⓑ Ⓒ Ⓓ Ⓔ	6 Ⓐ Ⓑ Ⓒ Ⓓ Ⓔ	11 Ⓐ Ⓑ Ⓒ Ⓓ Ⓔ
2 Ⓐ Ⓑ Ⓒ Ⓓ Ⓔ	7 Ⓐ Ⓑ Ⓒ Ⓓ Ⓔ	12 Ⓐ Ⓑ Ⓒ Ⓓ Ⓔ
3 Ⓐ Ⓑ Ⓒ Ⓓ Ⓔ	8 Ⓐ Ⓑ Ⓒ Ⓓ Ⓔ	13 Ⓐ Ⓑ Ⓒ Ⓓ Ⓔ
4 Ⓐ Ⓑ Ⓒ Ⓓ Ⓔ	9 Ⓐ Ⓑ Ⓒ Ⓓ Ⓔ	14 Ⓐ Ⓑ Ⓒ Ⓓ Ⓔ
5 Ⓐ Ⓑ Ⓒ Ⓓ Ⓔ	10 Ⓐ Ⓑ Ⓒ Ⓓ Ⓔ	15 Ⓐ Ⓑ Ⓒ Ⓓ Ⓔ

Part 15 General Science

1 Ⓐ Ⓑ Ⓒ Ⓓ Ⓔ		11 Ⓐ Ⓑ Ⓒ Ⓓ Ⓔ
2 Ⓐ Ⓑ Ⓒ Ⓓ Ⓔ		12 Ⓐ Ⓑ Ⓒ Ⓓ Ⓔ
3 Ⓐ Ⓑ Ⓒ Ⓓ Ⓔ		13 Ⓐ Ⓑ Ⓒ Ⓓ Ⓔ
4 Ⓐ Ⓑ Ⓒ Ⓓ Ⓔ		14 Ⓐ Ⓑ Ⓒ Ⓓ Ⓔ
5 Ⓐ Ⓑ Ⓒ Ⓓ Ⓔ		15 Ⓐ Ⓑ Ⓒ Ⓓ Ⓔ
6 Ⓐ Ⓑ Ⓒ Ⓓ Ⓔ		16 Ⓐ Ⓑ Ⓒ Ⓓ Ⓔ
7 Ⓐ Ⓑ Ⓒ Ⓓ Ⓔ		17 Ⓐ Ⓑ Ⓒ Ⓓ Ⓔ
8 Ⓐ Ⓑ Ⓒ Ⓓ Ⓔ		18 Ⓐ Ⓑ Ⓒ Ⓓ Ⓔ
9 Ⓐ Ⓑ Ⓒ Ⓓ Ⓔ		19 Ⓐ Ⓑ Ⓒ Ⓓ Ⓔ
10 Ⓐ Ⓑ Ⓒ Ⓓ Ⓔ		20 Ⓐ Ⓑ Ⓒ Ⓓ Ⓔ

Part 16 Hidden Figures

1 Ⓐ Ⓑ Ⓒ Ⓓ Ⓔ	6 Ⓐ Ⓑ Ⓒ Ⓓ Ⓔ	11 Ⓐ Ⓑ Ⓒ Ⓓ Ⓔ
2 Ⓐ Ⓑ Ⓒ Ⓓ Ⓔ	7 Ⓐ Ⓑ Ⓒ Ⓓ Ⓔ	12 Ⓐ Ⓑ Ⓒ Ⓓ Ⓔ
3 Ⓐ Ⓑ Ⓒ Ⓓ Ⓔ	8 Ⓐ Ⓑ Ⓒ Ⓓ Ⓔ	13 Ⓐ Ⓑ Ⓒ Ⓓ Ⓔ
4 Ⓐ Ⓑ Ⓒ Ⓓ Ⓔ	9 Ⓐ Ⓑ Ⓒ Ⓓ Ⓔ	14 Ⓐ Ⓑ Ⓒ Ⓓ Ⓔ
5 Ⓐ Ⓑ Ⓒ Ⓓ Ⓔ	10 Ⓐ Ⓑ Ⓒ Ⓓ Ⓔ	15 Ⓐ Ⓑ Ⓒ Ⓓ Ⓔ

AFOQT Practice Test

Part 1: Verbal Analogies

Time: 8 Minutes

25 Questions

Directions: This part of the test measures your ability to reason and see relationships between words. Choose the answer that best completes the analogy developed at the beginning of each question.

1. SANCTUARY is to REFUGE as

  A. FINGER is to HAND
  B. IMPRISONMENT is to PUNISHMENT
  C. BANJO is to COUNTRY
  D. BALLOON is to HELIUM
  E. SADNESS is to BLUES

2. BATHING is to CLEANLINESS as

  A. MEDICINE is to HARM
  B. SCHOOLING is to EDUCATION
  C. SPITE is to KINDNESS
  D. UTENSIL is to CHEF
  E. SEW is to CLOTHING

3. SMILING is to HAPPINESS as

  A. EXERCISE is to RUNNING
  B. MOTORCYCLE is to TRAVEL
  C. MILK is to BREAKFAST
  D. SCOWLING is to DISPLEASURE
  E. SHOUTING is to POWER

4. HANDS is to CLOCK as

  A. PIANO is to MUSIC
  B. JUSTICE is to COURT
  C. LEGS is to BODY
  D. ANNOYED is to FURIOUS
  E. CARNIVORE is to TIGER

5. QUARTER is to DOLLAR as

  A. BOREDOM is to YAWN
  B. WEEK is to MONTH
  C. MONEY is to POUND
  D. CRANE is to LIFT
  E. FLOWER is to PETALS

6. DANCER is to ENSEMBLE as

  A. YOGURT is to MILK
  B. STUDENT is to CLASS
  C. MOUNTAIN is to PRECIPICE
  D. FLOCK is to SHEEP
  E. DOODLE is to NOTEBOOK

7. ANARCHIST is to DISORDER as

  A. YAWN is to BOREDOM
  B. MONTH is to YEAR
  C. GOOD is to BEST
  D. PACIFIST is to PEACE
  E. CONSTELLATION is to STARS

8. DOCTOR is to HEALING as

  A. PRISON is to GUARD
  B. DINOSAURS is to PALEONTOLOGIST
  C. AUTHOR is to WRITING
  D. CLAP is to HANDS
  E. PLANETS is to UNIVERSE

GO ON TO THE NEXT PAGE

9. POLICE is to LAW as

- **A.** LION is to DEN
- **B.** BRUSH is to HAIR
- **C.** CONDUCTOR is to ORCHESTRA
- **D.** BOOK is to LIBRARY
- **E.** CLERGY is to RELIGION

10. COOL is to FRIGID as

- **A.** SPEAKER is to ASSEMBLY
- **B.** BUG is to COLD
- **C.** WATER is to BUCKET
- **D.** DISLIKE is to DETEST
- **E.** STUNT is to GROWTH

11. CRUMB is to LOAF as

- **A.** PAINTER is to CANVAS
- **B.** PUDDLE is to OCEAN
- **C.** SOUND is to MICROPHONE
- **D.** PRIDE is to FALL
- **E.** FEATHER is to QUILL

12. BREEZE is to GALE as

- **A.** EYES is to FACE
- **B.** MALEVOLENT is to CHARITABLE
- **C.** HOSTILE is to ENEMY
- **D.** SNOWFLAKE is to BLIZZARD
- **E.** PUNGENT is to SMELL

13. CROISSANT is to PASTRY as

- **A.** SCHOOL is to FISH
- **B.** TREE is to PEACH
- **C.** HAIKU is to POEM
- **D.** KNIFE is to CUT
- **E.** VENISON is to DEER

14. ROMANCE is to NOVEL as

- **A.** BOON is to BLESSING
- **B.** RAP is to MUSIC
- **C.** CREDO is to IMMORAL
- **D.** FRICTION is to SANDPAPER
- **E.** DETERMINED is to HESITANT

15. TANKER is to SHIP as

- **A.** INSECT is to ANT
- **B.** MATRIARCH is to MOTHER
- **C.** MINIVAN is to AUTOMOBILE
- **D.** COW is to VEAL
- **E.** DEGREE is to COLLEGE

16. WHALE is to OCEAN as

- **A.** CONGREGATION is to CROWD
- **B.** POUND is to DOGCATCHER
- **C.** CHURCH is to STEEPLE
- **D.** COURT is to TENNIS
- **E.** BEE is to HIVE

17. ACTOR is to STAGE as

- **A.** PATIENT is to DOCTOR
- **B.** OUTSIDE is to BENCH
- **C.** GARAGE is to CAR
- **D.** TEACHER is to CLASSROOM
- **E.** METER is to ELECTRIC

18. TYRANT is to CRUELTY as

- **A.** DRAWL is to SPEAKER
- **B.** COMPILE is to DISASSEMBLE
- **C.** ACCOLADE is to AWARD
- **D.** SYCOPHANT is to FLATTERY
- **E.** WAX is to CANDLE

19. SLOTH is to LAZINESS as

- **A.** GENTEEL is to VULGAR
- **B.** INSOMNIAC is to SLEEPLESSNESS
- **C.** HACKNEYED is to UNIQUE
- **D.** ACCEDE is to RESPECT
- **E.** CRYPT is to TOMB

20. HALLOWED is to SACRED as

- **A.** SOLDIER is to ARMY
- **B.** GAMUT is to PROVINCIAL
- **C.** LIBEL is to PRAISE
- **D.** NOMADIC is to WANDERING
- **E.** OBLIVIOUS is to KEEN

21. SANCTIMONIOUS is to SMUG as

   A.   ALTRUISTIC is to GREEDY
   B.   LUGUBRIOUS is to MELANCHOLY
   C.   GRANDIOSE is to MINISCULE
   D.   RETICENT is to TALKATIVE
   E.   EXACERBATE is to AMELIORATE

22. PRISTINE is to UNSPOILED as

   A.   TAINTED is to CONTAMINATED
   B.   EASE is to TAXING
   C.   ARID is to DELUGED
   D.   CHAMPIONED is to ABASED
   E.   ANIMUS is to KINDNESS

23. BIRTH is to LIFE as

   A.   RODENT is to SKUNK
   B.   GENTRY is to NOBILITY
   C.   PROLIFERATE is to CEASE
   D.   WINCE is to JOY
   E.   EXPOSURE is to INFECTION

24. MEDITATION is to RELAXATION as

   A.   ORDER is to CHAOS
   B.   SYMPTOMS is to BACTERIA
   C.   HONE is to WHET
   D.   SATIATION is to SATISFACTION
   E.   DEXTERITY is to ACCOMPLISHMENT

25. ISOLATION is to LONELINESS as

   A.   SHORTEN is to NIP
   B.   QUIET is to TACIT
   C.   PROMOTION is to ADVANCEMENT
   D.   MONOTONY is to HOMOGENOUS
   E.   RUSTIC is to CITY

GO ON TO THE NEXT PAGE

Part 2: Arithmetic Reasoning

Time: 29 Minutes

25 Questions

Directions: This section of the AFOQT test measures your mathematical reasoning, or your ability to arrive at solutions to problems. Each problem is followed by five possible answers. Select the answer that is most nearly correct.

1. If 400 people can be seated in 8 subway cars, how many people can be seated in 5 subway cars?

   A. 200
   B. 250
   C. 300
   D. 350
   E. 400

2. An employee earns $8.25 an hour. In 30 hours, what earnings are made?

   A. $240.00
   B. $247.50
   C. $250.00
   D. $255.75
   E. $257.00

3. A bread recipe calls for $3\frac{1}{4}$ cups of flour. If you only have $2\frac{1}{8}$ cups, how much more flour is needed?

   A. $1\frac{1}{8}$

   B. $1\frac{1}{4}$

   C. $1\frac{3}{8}$

   D. $1\frac{3}{4}$

   E. 2

4. How many omelets can be made from 2 dozen eggs if an omelet contains 3 eggs?

   A. 1
   B. 3
   C. 6
   D. 8
   E. 11

5. Two runners finish a race in 80 seconds, another runner finishes the race in 72 seconds, and the final runner finishes in 68 seconds. The average of these times is:

   A. 73 seconds
   B. 74 seconds
   C. 75 seconds
   D. 76 seconds
   E. 77 seconds

6. Seventy-two freshmen are in the band. If freshmen make up $\frac{1}{3}$ of the entire band, the total number of students in the band is:

   A. 24
   B. 72
   C. 144
   D. 203
   E. 216

7. Dana receives $30 for her birthday and $15 for cleaning the garage. If she spends $16 on a CD, how much money does she have left?

   A. $29
   B. $27
   C. $14
   D. $1
   E. $0.45

8. A television is on sale for 20% off. If the sale price is $800, what is the original price?

   A. $160
   B. $640
   C. $960
   D. $1,000
   E. $1,160

9. Jackie earns $9.50 an hour plus 3% commission on all sales made. If her total sales during a 30-hour work week are $500, how much does she earn?

A. $15
B. $250
C. $275
D. $285
E. $300

10. The area of one circle is 4 times as large as a smaller circle with a radius of 3 inches. The radius of the larger circle is:

A. 12 inches
B. 9 inches
C. 8 inches
D. 6 inches
E. 4 inches

11. You use a $20 bill to buy a magazine for $3.95. What change do you get back?

A. $16.05
B. $16.95
C. $17.05
D. $17.95
E. $18.05

12. Standing by a pole, a boy $3\frac{1}{2}$ feet tall casts a 6-foot shadow. The pole casts a 24-foot shadow. How tall is the pole?

A. 14 feet
B. 18 feet
C. 28 feet
D. 41 feet
E. 43 feet

13. Rae earns $8.40 an hour plus an overtime rate equal to $1\frac{1}{2}$ times her regular pay for each hour worked beyond 40 hours. What are her total earnings for a 45-hour work week?

A. $336
B. $370
C. $399
D. $567
E. $599

14. A sweater originally priced at $40 is on sale for $30. What percent is the discount?

A. 25%
B. 33%
C. 70%
D. 75%
E. 80%

15. A cardboard box has a length of 3 feet, a height of $2\frac{1}{2}$ feet and a depth of 2 feet. If the length and depth are doubled, by what percent does the volume of the box change?

A. 200%
B. 300%
C. 400%
D. 600%
E. 800%

16. Mr. Harrison earns a weekly salary of $300 plus 10% commission on all sales. If he sold $8,350 last week, what were his total earnings?

A. $835
B. $865
C. $1,135
D. $1,835
E. $1,925

17. Luis collects 300 stamps one week, 420 stamps the next week and 180 stamps the last week. He can trade the stamps for collector coins. If 25 stamps earns him one coin, how many coins can Luis collect?

A. 27
B. 36
C. 50
D. 900
E. 925

18. On a map, 1 centimeter represents 4 miles. A distance of 10 miles would be how far on the map?

A. $1\frac{3}{4}$ cm
B. 2 cm
C. $2\frac{1}{2}$ cm
D. 4 cm
E. $4\frac{1}{2}$ cm

GO ON TO THE NEXT PAGE

19. Davis donates $\frac{4}{13}$ of his paycheck to his favorite charity. If he donates $26.80, what is the amount of his paycheck?

- **A.** $8.25
- **B.** $82.50
- **C.** $87.10
- **D.** $137.50
- **E.** $348.40

20. Rachel runs $\frac{1}{2}$ mile in 4 minutes. At this rate, how many miles can she run in 15 minutes?

- **A.** $1\frac{7}{8}$
- **B.** 4
- **C.** 30
- **D.** 60
- **E.** 75

21. Tiling costs $2.89 per square foot. What is the cost to tile a kitchen whose dimensions are 4 yards by 5 yards?

- **A.** $57.80
- **B.** $173.40
- **C.** $289.00
- **D.** $520.20
- **E.** $640.40

22. One-eighth of a bookstore's magazines are sold on a Friday. If $\frac{1}{4}$ of the remaining magazines are sold the next day, what fractional part of the magazines remains at the end of the second day?

- **A.** $\frac{1}{64}$
- **B.** $\frac{1}{32}$
- **C.** $\frac{1}{8}$
- **D.** $\frac{7}{32}$
- **E.** $\frac{21}{32}$

23. Roxanne deposits $300 into a savings account earning $5\frac{1}{4}$ % annually. What is her balance after one year?

- **A.** $15.75
- **B.** $315
- **C.** $315.25
- **D.** $315.75
- **E.** $375.15

24. One phone plan charges a $20 monthly fee and $0.08 per minute on every phone call made. Another phone plan charges a $12 monthly fee and $0.12 per minute for each call. After how many minutes would the charge be the same for both plans?

- **A.** 60 minutes
- **B.** 90 minutes
- **C.** 120 minutes
- **D.** 200 minutes
- **E.** 320 minutes

25. The length of a rectangle is three times its width. If the perimeter of the rectangle is 48, what is its area?

- **A.** 108
- **B.** 96
- **C.** 54
- **D.** 48
- **E.** 32

Part 3: Reading Comprehension

Time: 18 Minutes

25 Questions

Directions: This test is designed to measure your ability to read and understand paragraphs. For each paragraph and question, select the answer that best completes the statement or answers the question based on the passage. Do not bring in outside information.

1. In January 2002, a person buys a car that comes with a three-year or 36,000-mile free replacement guarantee on the engine and transmission. In June 2005, the car has 34,300 miles on it. The transmission fails.

   According to the situation described in the paragraph, the car dealer will

   A. put in a new transmission
   B. give the person a new car
   C. not fix the transmission free
   D. not replace the car's engine
   E. replace the engine free

2. A sonnet is a specific type of poem. It has 14 lines. The lines must rhyme in a set pattern. Sometimes, the last 6 lines of a sonnet contrast with the first 8 lines. Many sonnets are love poems.

   To be a sonnet, a poem must

   A. be a love poem
   B. present a contrast
   C. have fewer than 14 lines
   D. rhyme in a specific way
   E. have 6 lines that rhyme with the 14 lines

3. When many people want to buy a product, the price will probably go up. In the summer, Americans travel more than they do at other times of year. They might take planes or trains, and many families drive to their vacation spots.

   From the information in the paragraph, you can conclude that

   A. gasoline prices rise in the summer
   B. gasoline prices rise in the winter
   C. gasoline prices go down in the summer
   D. gasoline prices do not change in any season
   E. gasoline prices are lower for planes

4. When you send a document to someone by electronic means, you are faxing it. The word FAX comes from the word FACSIMILE. Earlier ways of making facsimiles included photocopying and photographing. The oldest facsimiles were handwritten versions of original texts.

   The word FACSIMILE means

   A. an electronic copy
   B. an exact copy
   C. any document
   D. a photocopy
   E. a photograph

5. The United States Supreme Court is the highest court in the nation. Its nine judges review cases from other courts. They decide if these courts have ruled in a way that agrees with the United States Constitution. They cannot make new laws. Their decision is based on a majority vote of the nine judges.

   The main idea of this paragraph is that

   A. the United States Constitution is the basis for our laws
   B. the Supreme Court is the highest court in the United States
   C. the Supreme Court cannot make new laws
   D. the Supreme Court's decisions are based on a majority vote
   E. the Supreme Court has nine judges

GO ON TO THE NEXT PAGE

6. Most cars today have automatic transmissions, but it is useful to know how to shift gears in a car with a standard transmission. Press the clutch pedal in with your left foot. Then use the shift lever to choose the proper gear. Release the clutch pedal while gently applying pressure to the gas pedal.

The last thing to do when shifting gears is to

   A. step on the gas
   B. release the clutch
   C. use the shift lever
   D. press down on the clutch
   E. know how to use the clutch

7. Recycling household waste is very important. Space for landfills where garbage is dumped is becoming scarce. Putting waste in the oceans causes pollution. Recycling is a way for cities to make money by selling recyclable items, and recycling helps to saves natural resources.

The author's purpose in this passage is to

   A. explain what recycling is
   B. tell a story
   C. show a contrast
   D. argue for recycling
   E. show how to recycle

8. Jackrabbits are not rabbits but members of the hare family. Hares are larger than rabbits, and they have longer ears. Newborn rabbits are naked and helpless, but infant hares are covered with fur and aware of their surroundings.

Hares and rabbits are contrasted by describing all the following except

   A. their size
   B. the length of their ears
   C. what color they are
   D. newborn rabbits and hares
   E. infant hares

9. Superman originated as a character in a comic book in the 1930s. Then a radio program called *The Adventures of Superman* was created. Later, Superman became part of going to the movies. Short episodes were shown each week in theaters in addition to a feature film. When television became part of American life, it too had a weekly program about Superman. In the 1980s, several full-length films about Superman appeared.

From this passage, you can conclude that

   A. Superman is a great hero
   B. Superman has been popular for a long time
   C. Superman has often appeared in films
   D. Superman began in comic books
   E. Superman films are popular

10. People might think of pizza as a snack food, but it is nutritious. The crust, made of a kind of bread, provides carbohydrates. The tomatoes contain vitamin C and provide fiber. The cheese is a good source of calcium, which is needed for healthy bones.

Pizza is healthful because it

   A. includes a good source of calcium
   B. tastes good
   C. is a snack food
   D. can be ordered in a restaurant
   E. can be baked at home

11. The space shuttle is coming in for a landing. Over a loudspeaker, the waiting spectators hear, "STS 42 is now over Brandenburg, making its turn for the coast." They quickly stand, look up and turn their eyes skyward. They hear the sonic boom and stare at the sky even more closely. There it is! First it is only a speck. Then the crowd applauds and cheers as they see it approaching Earth.

The spectators who watch the shuttle land feel

   A. fear
   B. anger
   C. happiness
   D. concern
   E. excitement

12. When people are in a group, they might not react to an emergency the same way they would if they were alone. One reason might be that each person thinks someone else has already done something. Or, hearing no one else speak; a person might feel that nothing needs to be done. A third possibility is that the person does not want to draw attention to him or herself.

This passage explains

   A. the differences between individuals and people in groups
   B. the effects of being part of a group
   C. the causes for behavior in a group
   D. how people react to an emergency
   E. why people do nothing unless asked

13. In 1963, Martin Luther King, Jr. led a protest march in Birmingham, Alabama. Because he did not have a permit to hold the march, he was arrested. Then eight clergymen wrote a letter that was published in the local newspaper. The letter opposed protest marches as a way to end racial problems. While King was in jail, he wrote a reply to that letter. It has been reprinted many times since then under the title "Letter from Birmingham Jail."

King wrote the letter

A. before the protest march
B. when he was arrested
C. while he was thinking about racial problems
D. after he read the clergymen's letter
E. to become famous

14. King was arrested because

A. the clergymen wrote a letter
B. he did not have a permit to hold the march
C. Birmingham had racial problems
D. he was put in jail
E. he wrote a letter

15. People sometimes say they will return back to a place they have visited. But because RETURN means the same thing as GO BACK TO, the expression RETURN BACK is REDUNDANT.

The word REDUNDANT could be used to describe which one of the following phrases?

A. cooperate together
B. walk slowly
C. review again
D. add information
E. speak loudly

16. In the early 1900s, horticulturalist George Washington Carver developed more than 325 products from the peanut. Peanut meatloaf and chocolate-covered peanuts were just two of the food items that Carver developed. However, most interestingly, Carver also engineered many unusual peanut products. For example, he formulated beauty products from peanuts such as hand lotion, shaving cream and shampoo.

The best title for this selection is

A. Carver and Peanut Food Products
B. Carver's Many Peanut Products

C. Carver's Beauty Products from the Peanut
D. The Life of George Washington Carver
E. Carver's Unusual Products

17. College professors often present pedantic lectures. Yawning, sleepy students in many classrooms emphasize this fact.

In this context, the word PEDANTIC means

A. dull
B. exciting
C. childish
D. inspiring
E. sleepy

18. To the untrained eye, differentiating between an alligator and a crocodile is a difficult task. However, one main difference exists between these two reptiles. Alligators tend to have wide, rounded snouts, while crocodiles have longer, more pointed noses.

Which of the following is implied by the preceding passage?

A. One can never tell the difference between a crocodile and an alligator.
B. No discernible physical differences exist between crocodiles and alligators.
C. Most people can differentiate between crocodiles and alligators if they know about the reptiles' differing snout structures.
D. Only experts can distinguish between crocodiles and alligators.
E. Crocodiles have more deadly teeth than other animals.

19. Mineral forms of carbon vary greatly. For example, both diamonds and graphite are forms of carbon. However, graphite is very weak and soft, while diamonds are the hardest gemstones known to man.

This passage is mainly about

A. diamonds
B. graphite
C. the similarities between diamonds and graphite
D. the difference between carbon and diamonds
E. the varying mineral forms of carbon

GO ON TO THE NEXT PAGE

Questions 20 and 21 relate to the following passage.

Many environmentalists believe that natural gas is the answer to decreasing pollution produced by other traditional forms of energy. Although natural gas comes from the earth's crust like oil, it burns cleaner than oil does.

As a result, environmentalists and manufacturers put a great emphasis on developing more vehicles that operate on natural gas rather than regular fuel. Proponents of natural gas vehicles state that such vehicles emit up to 95% less pollution than standard gasoline or diesel vehicles.

20. The principal reason for using natural gas vehicles is that they

    A. are more attractive than their gasoline and diesel counterparts

    B. emit less pollution and are safer for the environment

    C. are less expensive to operate than traditional vehicles

    D. are mandated by law

    E. are not a traditional form of energy

21. One might conclude from the preceding selection that

    A. a great emphasis is put on producing natural gas vehicles to reduce pollution

    B. traditional vehicles that operate on gasoline or diesel fuel produce very little pollution

    C. the difference in emissions between regular vehicles and natural gas vehicles is unimportant

    D. natural gas is a pollutant and should not be used to fuel vehicles

    E. natural gas is less expensive than gasoline or diesel fuel

Questions 22 and 23 relate to the following passage.

Because of their reputation from myth and legend for sucking blood from animals and humans, vampire bats are viewed as heinous creatures. However, someday these greatly feared but little known animals might save lives.

Scientists have discovered that vampire bats do not suck blood from other animals. Rather, they make tiny cuts in the skin of such animals as cows. Interestingly, the bats' saliva contains a substance that aids in blood clotting. Thus, this substance might eventually be used to prevent heart attacks and strokes.

22. In this context, the word HEINOUS means

    A. playful

    B. friendly

    C. busy

    D. monstrous

    E. helpful

23. The author apparently feels that

    A. vampire bats are dangerous to humans

    B. vampire bats are harmful to cows

    C. vampire bats have potential in the medical field

    D. vampire bats are friendly creatures

    E. vampire bats live up to their legends

24. Tsunamis are large waves caused by earthquakes or underwater landslides. The word TSUNAMI is a Japanese word meaning HARBOR WAVE, used to describe these events because of the destructive effects that they have on coastal Japanese communities.

What is the best title for this selection?

    A. What Is a Tsunami?

    B. Japanese Natural Disasters

    C. Japanese Words and Their Meanings

    D. Effects of a Tsunami

    E. Harbor Waves in Japan

25. Pyromaniacs are very rarely the setters of most criminal fires. Most people who set fires do so for insurance fraud, although others often set fires for revenge and terrorism. Very few people actually start fires because they receive strong psychological gratification from the act.

A PYROMANIAC can best be described as

    A. a person who never sets fires

    B. a person who is afraid of fire

    C. a person who sets fires and receives strong psychological gratification from the act

    D. a person who sets fires to obtain revenge

    E. a person who needs insurance money

Part 4: Data Interpretation

Time: 24 Minutes

25 Questions

Directions: This section of the test measures one's ability to interpret data from tables and graphs. Each question is followed by four or five possible answers. Select the answer that best answers the question based on the table or chart.

Answer questions 1–3 based on the following graphs.

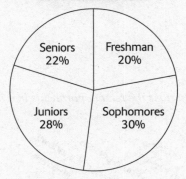

Grade-levels at Smithfield High School (5000 students total)

Seniors 22% | Freshman 20% | Juniors 28% | Sophomores 30%

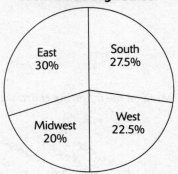

Geographical locations of colleges chosen by college-bound seniors at Smithfield High School

East 30% | South 27.5% | Midwest 20% | West 22.5%

1. How many students are sophomores at Smithfield High School?

   A. 1,100
   B. 1,200
   C. 1,300
   D. 1,400
   E. 1,500

2. If 80% of the high school seniors are college bound, what is the total number of students represented by the graph on the right?

   A. 176
   B. 270
   C. 880
   D. 1,100
   E. 4,000

3. If 80% of the high school seniors are college bound, how many are planning to attend colleges in the east?

   A. 150
   B. 194
   C. 264
   D. 326
   E. 458

Answer questions 4–7 based on the following circle graph, which shows monthly household expenditures as a percent of the total monthly budget.

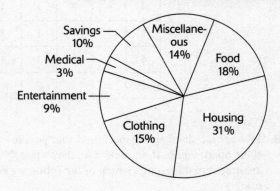

Monthly household expenditures as percent of total monthly budget

Savings 10% | Miscellaneous 14% | Food 18% | Medical 3% | Entertainment 9% | Housing 31% | Clothing 15%

4. If clothing expenses are $192, what is the total monthly budget?

   A. $1,500
   B. $1,280
   C. $1,800
   D. $1,920
   E. $2,880

GO ON TO THE NEXT PAGE

5. On which of the following groups of items is the most money spent?

 A. housing and medical
 B. food and clothing
 C. medical, entertainment and savings
 D. clothing and miscellaneous
 E. food, medical and entertainment

6. If the total monthly budget is increased to $1,500, how much more money will be spent on food than put away for savings?

 A. $80
 B. $120
 C. $150
 D. $270
 E. $280

7. If $125 is spent on entertainment, how much money will be spent on food?

 A. $125
 B. $175
 C. $200
 D. $225
 E. $250

Answer questions 8–11 based on the following chart, which describes the rental apartments in a building.

Apartment number	Number of rooms	Number of bedrooms	Number of bathrooms	Number of closets	Eat-in kitchen	Maximum persons	Number of windows	Monthly rent
1	5	2	1	4	No	4	7	$520
2	5	3	2	6	Yes	5	7	$600
3	3	1	1	3	Yes	2	4	$460
4	4	2	1	4	Yes	4	5	$480
5	2	1	1	2	No	2	3	$400
6	4	2	1	4	Yes	4	5	$480
7	5	2	2	4	Yes	4	7	$560

8. Five people share apartment 2, and four people share apartment 6. If, in each case, they share the apartment rental evenly, which of the following is true?

 A. A renter in apartment 2 spends $24 a month more than a renter in apartment 6.
 B. A renter in apartment 2 spends $24 a month less than a renter in apartment 6.
 C. A renter in apartment 2 spends $30 a month more than a renter in apartment 6.
 D. A renter in apartment 2 spends $30 a month less than a renter in apartment 6.
 E. A renter in apartment 2 spends the same each month as a renter in apartment 6.

9. If a family of four needs an apartment with two bathrooms, what is the least amount of money they could pay each month for rent in this building?

 A. $400
 B. $460
 C. $480
 D. $560
 E. $600

10. If a window cleaner is hired to clean all the windows in the building and he charges $7.50 per window, what will he earn?

- **A.** $266
- **B.** $285
- **C.** $292
- **D.** $304
- **E.** $320

11. If each monthly rental is raised 5%, which apartment will cost $546?

- **A.** apartment 5
- **B.** apartment 4
- **C.** apartment 3
- **D.** apartment 2
- **E.** apartment 1

Questions 12 and 13 are based on the following table.

Tabulation of factory accidents by week																
Week																
	1	2	3	4	5	6	7	8	9	10	11	12	13	14	15	16
Number of accidents	1	3	2	4	0	4	0	2	5	1	1	1	0	2	2	1

12. How many total accidents occurred at the factory?

- **A.** 5
- **B.** 29
- **C.** 33
- **D.** 45
- **E.** 54

13. Which number of accidents was most likely to occur in any randomly chosen week?

- **A.** 0
- **B.** 1
- **C.** 2
- **D.** 3
- **E.** 4

GO ON TO THE NEXT PAGE

Questions 14–17 are based on the following bar graphs, which show the heights of male and female job applicants. All heights have been calculated to the nearest inch.

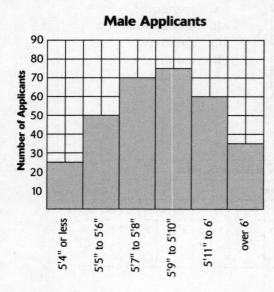

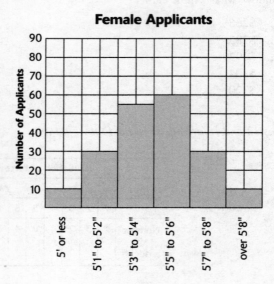

14. How many male applicants are at least 5'9" tall?

A. 60
B. 70
C. 75
D. 170
E. 200

15. How many more women are there than men in the 5'5" to 5'6" range?

A. 10
B. 20
C. 40
D. 50
E. 60

16. If 40% of the male applicants are accepted, how many are rejected?

A. 126
B. 132
C. 180
D. 189
E. 198

17. Twenty-five females are added to the applicant pool, and their heights are as follows: 8 in the 5'3" to 5'4" range, 10 in the 5'7" to 5'8" range, and 7 in the 5'1" to 5'2" range. Which of the following statements will now be true?

A. There are more females in the 5'1" to 5'2" range than in the 5'7" to 5'8" range.

B. There are more females in the 5'7" to 5'8" range than in the 5'5" to 5'6" range.

C. There is the same number of females in the 5'7" to 5'8" range as in the 5'1" to 5'2" range.

D. There are more females in the 5'3" to 5'4" range than in the 5'5" to 5'6" range.

E. There are fewer females in the 5'5" to 5'6" range than in the over 5'8" range.

Questions 18–21 are based on the following line graph, which shows calorie consumption.

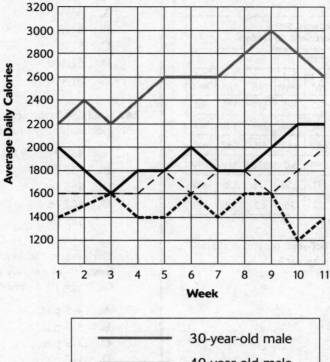

30-year-old male
40-year-old male
50-year-old male
60-year-old male

18. In which period did the 40-year-old males exhibit the greatest increase in average daily calories consumed?

   A. weeks 2–4
   B. weeks 3–5
   C. weeks 6–8
   D. weeks 7–9
   E. weeks 8–10

19. The number of calories consumed by the 30-year-old male in week 9 was how many times the number of calories consumed by the 40-year-old male in the same week?

   A. 1/2
   B. 2/3
   C. 1 1/2
   D. 1 2/3
   E. 1 3/4

20. What is the approximate number of daily calories consumed by the 50-year-old male over the 11-week period?

   A. 1,500
   B. 1,600
   C. 1,700
   D. 1,800
   E. 1,900

21. In which week was there the greatest difference between the number of calories consumed by the 40-year-old male and the 60-year-old male?

   A. week 10
   B. week 8
   C. week 6
   D. week 3
   E. week 1

GO ON TO THE NEXT PAGE

Answer questions 22–25 based on the following table, which shows average daily sales.

Mason Department Store Store Totals by Department (in Dollars)							
Time Period							
	10-11 AM	11-12 AM	12-1 PM	1-2 PM	2-3 PM	3-4 PM	4-5 PM
Shoes	48	92	130	125	149	173	88
Children's wear	43	234	181	208	219	301	187
Women's wear	182	207	452	457	415	687	412
Menswear	49	187	250	517	528	411	299
Housewares	128	212	111	250	175	328	310
Notions	28	46	50	75	62	43	110

22. What is the difference between the greatest and least hourly sales in menswear?

- **A.** $250
- **B.** $479
- **C.** $528
- **D.** $505
- **E.** $577

23. What were Mason Department Store's total sales after 4 p.m.?

- **A.** $88
- **B.** $412
- **C.** $799
- **D.** $1,100
- **E.** $1,406

24. Rounded to the nearest cent, what were the average hourly sales in the notions department?

- **A.** $53.28
- **B.** $56.34
- **C.** $59.14
- **D.** $62.18
- **E.** $65.09

25. The sales in children's wear during the period from 10–11 a.m. are equal to the sales in notions for which time period?

- **A.** 4–5 p.m.
- **B.** 3–4 p.m.
- **C.** 2–3 p.m.
- **D.** 1–2 p.m.
- **E.** 12–1 p.m.

Part 5: Word Knowledge

Time: 5 Minutes

25 Questions

Directions: This part of the test measures verbal comprehension involving your ability to understand written language. For each question choose the answer that means the same as the capitalized word.

1. DISTRAUGHT

    A. fatal
    B. deeply agitated
    C. greedy
    D. rudely sarcastic
    E. angry

2. FUROR

    A. despair
    B. sorrow
    C. frustration
    D. anger
    E. happiness

3. TRIVIAL

    A. boring
    B. unoriginal
    C. extreme
    D. unimportant
    E. laughable

4. VERBOSE

    A. stout
    B. ungrammatical
    C. delicate
    D. sympathetic
    E. wordy

5. VOGUE

    A. fashion
    B. impression
    C. elegance
    D. decoration
    E. fancy

6. ASSAIL

    A. appoint
    B. attack

    C. disappoint
    D. substitute
    E. pretend

7. RUSE

    A. trick
    B. pause
    C. fault
    D. pattern
    E. error

8. PRUDENCE

    A. motive
    B. hatred
    C. caution
    D. distinction
    E. carefree

9. LISTLESS

    A. discouraging
    B. indifferent
    C. attentive
    D. careful
    E. awake

10. SUPERFICIAL

    A. buried
    B. overhead
    C. extreme
    D. external
    E. important

11. FEASIBLE

    A. expensive
    B. foolish
    C. imaginative
    D. possible
    E. incapable

GO ON TO THE NEXT PAGE

201

12. SQUELCH

    A. offend

    B. silence

    C. embarrass

    D. expel

    E. hire

13. ANTITHESIS

    A. result

    B. source

    C. opposite

    D. approximation

    E. nearly

14. DESTITUTE

    A. poverty stricken

    B. mistreated

    C. saddened

    D. uneducated

    E. overworked

15. BELLIGERENT

    A. unstable

    B. wealthy

    C. warlike

    D. productive

    E. docile

16. RECLUSE

    A. naturalist

    B. hermit

    C. retiree

    D. ex-convict

    E. veteran

17. SADDLED

    A. committed

    B. burdened

    C. hopeful

    D. bored

    E. encouraged

18. ROSTRUM

    A. speaker's platform

    B. backstage area

    C. telephone

    D. reserved section

    E. main office

19. INANE

    A. selfish

    B. detailed

    C. personal

    D. unusual

    E. silly

20. PESSIMISTIC

    A. fearful

    B. strange

    C. gloomy

    D. disturbed

    E. disquieting

21. NATAL

    A. by name

    B. of marriage

    C. of birth

    D. by size

    E. seaworthy

22. RIGOROUS

    A. useful

    B. demanding

    C. confusing

    D. laughable

    E. unpleasant

23. IDEOLOGY

    A. philosophy

    B. government

    C. goal

    D. heritage

    E. purpose

24. LACKADAISICAL

    A. delicate

    B. needy

    C. lifeless

    D. honest

    E. faulty

25. ABORIGINES

    A. volcanic ashes

    B. native inhabitants

    C. cave paintings

    D. specialized cells

    E. artistic designs

Part 6: Mathematics Knowledge

Time: 22 Minutes

25 Questions

Directions: This section of the test measures your ability to use learned mathematical relationships. Each problem is followed by five possible answers. Select the answer that is most nearly correct.

1. If $a = \frac{5}{2}$, then $\frac{1}{a}$

   A. 2

   B. 5

   C. $\frac{2}{5}$

   D. $\frac{5}{2}$

   E. 7

2. Twelve is 15% of what number?

   A. .0125

   B. 1.8

   C. 18

   D. 36

   E. 80

3. Evaluate $3x + 7$ when $x = -3$.

   A. −2

   B. 10

   C. 16

   D. 21

   E. 30

4. Find the diagonal of a square whose area is 36.

   A. 6

   B. $6\sqrt{2}$

   C. 9

   D. $9\sqrt{2}$

   E. $\sqrt{9}$

5. If $a + b = 6$, what is the value of $3a + 3b$?

   A. 9

   B. 12

   C. 18

   D. 24

   E. 36

6. Find the length of the radius in the following figure.

   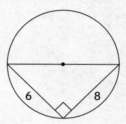

   A. 3

   B. 4

   C. 5

   D. 10

   E. 12

7. $(3 - 1) \times 7 - 12 \div 2 =$

   A. 1

   B. −2

   C. 4

   D. 8

   E. 12

8. The greatest common factor of 24 and 36 is

   A. 6

   B. 12

   C. 36

   D. 60

   E. 72

9. Solve for m: $3m - 12 = -6$.

   A. −6

   B. 0

   C. 2

   D. 4

   E. 6

GO ON TO THE NEXT PAGE

10. If $7p + 5q = -3$, find q when $p = 1$.

    A. -1

    B. -2

    C. $-8/7$

    D. $-2/7$

    E. $2/7$

11. The slope of the line shown is

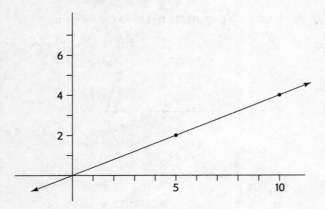

    A. $-\dfrac{2}{5}$

    B. $-\dfrac{5}{2}$

    C. $\dfrac{2}{5}$

    D. $\dfrac{5}{2}$

    E. 5

12. Simplify $\dfrac{9x^2 y^3 z - 12xy^2 z^2}{3yz}$.

    A. $3xy^2z - 4xyz$

    B. $3x^2y^2 - 12xyz$

    C. $3x^2y^2 - 4xyz$

    D. $3y^2 - 4xy^2z^2$

    E. $3y - 3xyz$

13. The value of x is

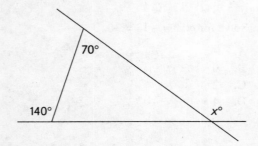

    A. $70°$

    B. $110°$

    C. $140°$

    D. $180°$

    E. $210°$

14. In a standard deck of playing cards, a king of hearts is drawn and not replaced. What is the probability of drawing another king from the deck?

    A. $\dfrac{1}{4}$

    B. $\dfrac{1}{13}$

    C. $\dfrac{1}{17}$

    D. $\dfrac{3}{52}$

    E. $\dfrac{4}{52}$

15. How many minutes are there in one week?

    A. $10,080$

    B. $1,440$

    C. 420

    D. 168

    E. 24

16. If $2^{b+3} = \dfrac{1}{8}$, $b =$

    A. -6

    B. -3

    C. 0

    D. 2

    E. 4

17. The angles of a triangle are in the ratio 3:4:5. What is the measure of the smallest angle?

    A. $15°$

    B. $30°$

    C. $45°$

    D. $75°$

    E. $90°$

18. Subtract $(2x^3 - 3x + 1) - (x^2 - 3x - 2)$.

    A. $2x^2 + x + 1$

    B. $2x^3 - x^2 - 6x - 1$

    C. $x^3 - 6x + 1$

    D. $x^2 + 3$

    E. $2x^3 - x^2 + 3$

19. If the area of a square is 400, what is the length of its side?

    A. 20

    B. 40

    C. 100

    D. 200

    E. 400

20. Seven more than 3 times a number is equal to 70. Find the number.

    A. 10

    B. 17

    C. 21

    D. 30

    E. 210

21. Which expression represents the volume of a cylinder whose height is equivalent to the length of the radius?

    A. πr^2

    B. πr^3

    C. $(\pi r)^2$

    D. $(\pi r)^3$

    E. $2\pi r^2$

22. How many distinct prime factors are there in 120?

    A. 2

    B. 3

    C. 4

    D. 5

    E. 12

23. What percent of $\frac{3}{4}$ is $\frac{1}{8}$?

    A. $9\frac{3}{8}\%$

    B. 12%

    C. $16\frac{2}{3}\%$

    D. 20%

    E. 25%

24. What is the area of the figure shown?

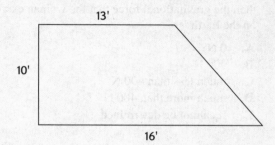

    A. 130 ft^2

    B. 145 ft^2

    C. 154 ft^2

    D. 160 ft^2

    E. 175 ft^2

25. If x is a positive integer, solve $x^2 + 6x = 16$.

    A. 2

    B. 4

    C. 8

    D. 10

    E. 12

GO ON TO THE NEXT PAGE

Part 7: Mechanical Comprehension

Time: 22 Minutes

20 Questions

Directions: This part of the test measures your ability to learn and reason with mechanical terms. Choose the answer that best completes the statement. Also included in this part of the test are diagrams of mechanical devices. Following each diagram are several questions or incomplete statements. Study the diagram carefully and select the choice that best answers the question or completes the statement.

1. If the Earth exerts a force of 400 N on a woman, then the gravitational force that the woman exerts on the Earth is

   A. 0 N
   B. 400 N
   C. much less than 400 N
   D. much more than 400 N
   E. It cannot be determined.

2. People driving up a mountain would find that their mass would _____ and their weight would _____.

   A. increase, decrease
   B. decrease, increase
   C. decrease, remain the same
   D. remain the same, decrease
   E. remain the same, remain the same

3. In order for Jean to drive her station wagon at constant speed around a curve without accelerating, she must

   A. maintain a constant speed
   B. speed up gradually
   C. slow down gradually
   D. It is impossible to maintain her speed without accelerating.
   E. decelerate

4. The angular velocity of the second hand of a clock is _____ rad/s.

   A. .105
   B. 9.53
   C. 6.28
   D. .159
   E. 60

5. If Jean runs with a constant velocity of −5 m/s, then her speed is _____ m/s.

   A. 5
   B. −5
   C. 0
   D. It is impossible to have a negative velocity.
   E. Her speed cannot be determined.

6. An object can accelerate by

   A. changing the direction of its velocity but not the magnitude
   B. changing the magnitude of the velocity but not the direction
   C. changing speed
   D. any of the above
   E. changing initial velocity

7. A foul ball hit vertically upward with an initial speed of 46.8 m/s will take _____ s to reach the top of its trajectory.

   A. 9.56
   B. 5.82
   C. 4.78
   D. .21
   E. 1.46

8. Anne walks 8 m to the right, then 24 m to the left and finally 48 m to the right. If she completes this in 160 s, then her average velocity is _____ m.

   A. .6
   B. .5
   C. .2
   D. .3
   E. 2

9. A wheel with a moment of inertia of .3 kg.m^2 is rotating with an initial angular velocity of 4 rad/s. The magnitude of the torque needed to increase the angular velocity to 6.5 rad/s in 4 s is _____ N.m.

A. 1.5
B. 3
C. .188
D. .788
E. .625

10. A 60 N weight is lifted by the lever arrangement shown in the figure. If the weight of the lever is negligible, the ideal mechanical advantage (F$_o$/F$_i$) and the input force F$_i$ required to achieve equilibrium are

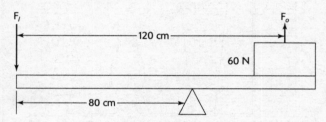

A. 3, 30 N
B. 2, 30 N
C. 2, 120 N
D. 3, 1 N
E. 0, 0 N

11. The magnitude of the force necessary to change the momentum of a particle from 10 kg m/s to 50 kg m/s in 12 s is _____ N.

A. 3.33
B. 4.16
C. 4
D. 720
E. 480

12. An 80 kg man jumps with a velocity of 3 m/s off the bow of a 120 kg boat initially at rest. Ignoring the friction of the water on the boat, the velocity v of the boat after the man jumps will be _____ m/s.

A. −1
B. −1.5
C. −2
D. −3
E. −4

13. A 10 kg mass attached to a spring oscillates with a period of 3.14 s. The force constant of the spring k is

A. 40
B. 20
C. 4
D. 2
E. 31.4

14. A 5 kg block starts downward from rest at the top of a 40 m long frictionless inclined plane. If the block starts at a height h of 10 m above the ground, its speed v as it hits the ground is _____ m/s, and the force on the block while sliding is _____ N.

A. 19.6, 1.225
B. 19.6, 12.25
C. 14, 12.25
D. 14, 1.225
E. 0, 0

15. A car is traveling forward at a speed of 108 km/hour and has a box in the trunk where the coefficient of friction with the bed μ equals 0.3. What is the shortest time in which the car can be brought to a stop without any shift in the box?

A. 0 s
B. 11.17 s
C. 9.23 s
D. 10.19 s
E. 324 s

GO ON TO THE NEXT PAGE

Consider the following diagram where a uniform steel rod of length L = 3 m and mass m = 12 kg is pivoted at the frictionless point A. The rod is released from a position of 60° above the horizontal plane and strikes point B at the top of the spring when the rod reaches the horizontal position AB. The spring constant is k = 100 kN/m, and the mass moment of inertia of the rod is I = mL²/3. Study the diagram carefully, and select from the choices in the next three questions.

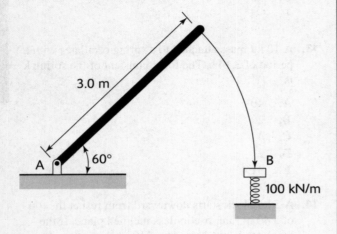

3.0 m

A 60°

B

100 kN/m

16. What is the velocity of the rod when it strikes the spring?

   A. 8.74 m/s
   B. 6.95 m/s
   C. 5.97 m/s
   D. 4 m/s
   E. .866 m/s

17. How far will the rod bounce after striking the spring at point B?

   A. 1.06 m
   B. 1.56 m
   C. 2.60 m
   D. 3.06 m
   E. 4.56 m

18. If the rod drops from an arbitrary position and reaches the spring with an angular velocity of 5 rad/s, what is the maximum compression of the spring in this case?

   A. .095 m
   B. .225 m
   C. .326 m
   D. .816 m
   E. 1.908 m

19. The four partitioned compartments A, B, C and D shown in the figure are filled to the same height. After the partition walls are suddenly removed, the liquid level adjusts itself so that

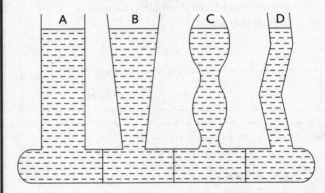

   A. the liquid rises in A and drops in B, C and D
   B. the liquid rises in B and drops in A, C and D
   C. the liquid rises in C and drops in A, B and D
   D. the liquid rises in D and drops in A, B and C
   E. the liquid level stays the same

20. The most common gear drive system is shown in which of the following?

A.

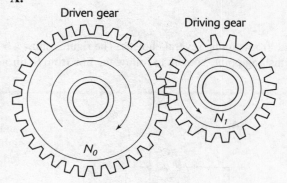

Driven gear

Driving gear

N_0

N_1

B.

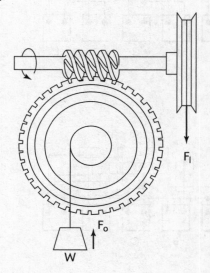

F_l

F_o

W

C.

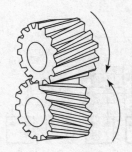

D.

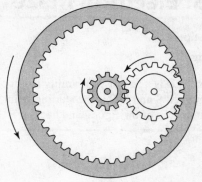

E.

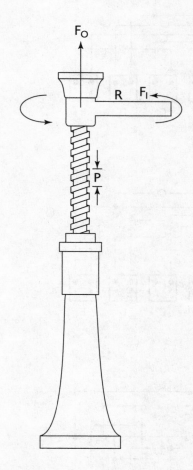

F_O

R

F_l

P

GO ON TO THE NEXT PAGE

Part 8: Electrical Maze

Time: 10 Minutes

20 Questions

Directions: This is a test of your ability to choose a correct path from among several choices. The figures show a box with dots marked S and F. S is the starting point, and F is the finishing point. You are to follow the line from S, through the circle at the top of the figure, and back to F.

1.

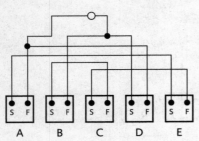

2.

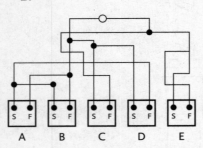

3.

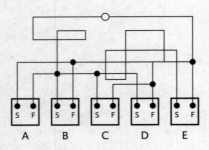

4.

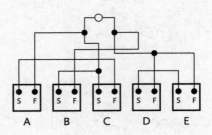

5.

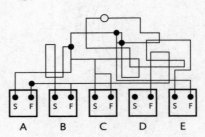

6.

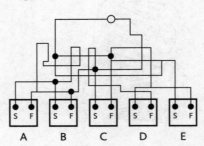

7.

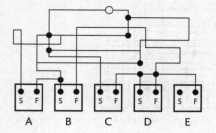

8.

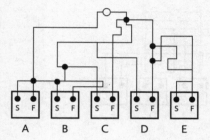

9.

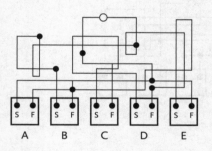

10.

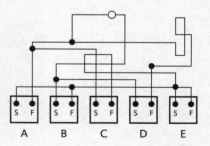

11.

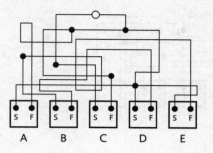

12.

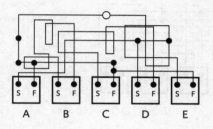

13.

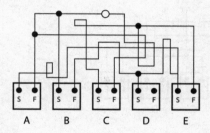

14.

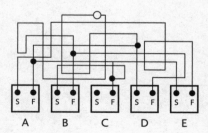

GO ON TO THE NEXT PAGE

15.

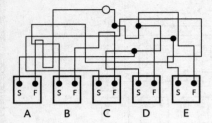

16.

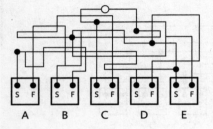

17.

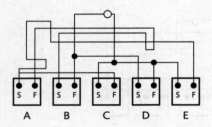

18.

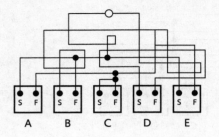

19.

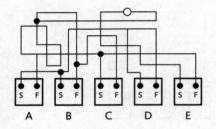

20.

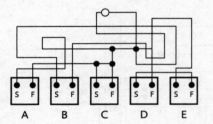

Part 9: Scale Reading

Time: 10 Minutes

40 Questions

Directions: The questions in this part are designed to test your ability to read scales, meters, and dials. Determine the numerical value indicated by the arrows in the figures then mark your answer sheet appropriately.

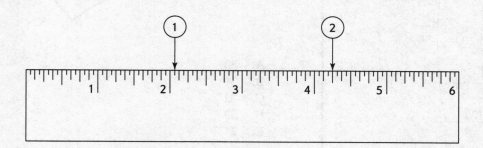

1.

   A. 2.0
   B. 2.02
   C. 2.0625
   D. 2.125
   E. 2.25

2.

   A. 4.50
   B. 4.40
   C. 4.25
   D. 4.20
   E. 4.02

3.

   A. 1.1
   B. 1.0
   C. 0.1
   D. −0.1
   E. −1

4.

   A. 3.01
   B. 2.10
   C. 2.3
   D. 3.3
   E. 2.35

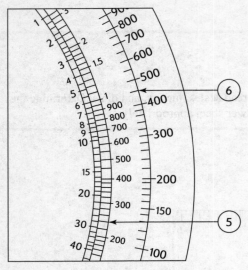

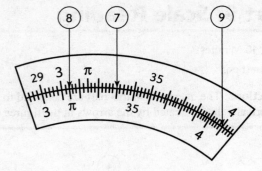

5.

    A. 320
    B. 280
    C. 240
    D. 32
    E. 28

6.

    A. 400
    B. 450
    C. 425
    D. 550
    E. 575

7.

    A. 30
    B. 31
    C. 32
    D. 33
    E. 34

8.

    A. 3.1
    B. 3.14
    C. 3.175
    D. 3.2
    E. 3.21

9.

    A. 4.1
    B. 40.1
    C. 41
    D. 34.9
    E. −4

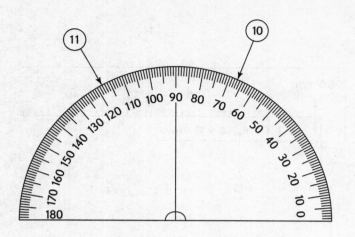

10.

    A. 65.2
    B. 67
    C. 60.6
    D. 70.3
    E. 73.0

11.

    A. 120.3
    B. 123.0
    C. 115.2
    D. 118.0
    E. 119.0

12.

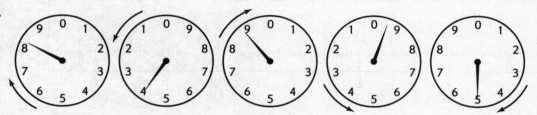

    A. 93904
    B. 93895
    C. 94905
    D. 84895
    E. 83905

13.

    A. 55132
    B. 56132
    C. 65132
    D. 65142
    E. 66143

GO ON TO THE NEXT PAGE

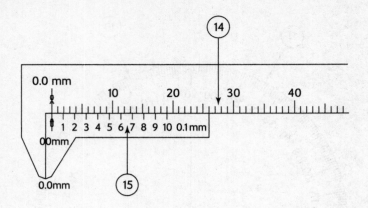

14.

- A. 20.7
- B. 20.75
- C. 27.00
- D. 27.05
- E. 27.50

15.

- A. 6.5
- B. 6.7
- C. 7.0
- D. 7.3
- E. 66

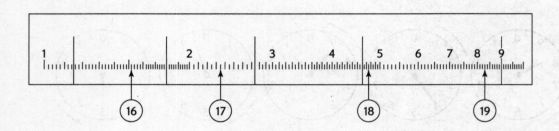

16.

- A. 1.14
- B. 1.50
- C. 1.52
- D. 1.55
- E. 1.60

18.

- A. 4.650
- B. 4.670
- C. 4.675
- D. 4.700
- E. 4.750

17.

- A. 2.30
- B. 2.32
- C. 2.35
- D. 2.40
- E. 2.60

19.

- A. 8.30
- B. 8.35
- C. 8.40
- D. 9.70
- E. 9.75

Part 10: Instrument Comprehension

Time: 6 Minutes

20 Questions

Directions: This test measures your ability to determine the position of an airplane in flight from reading instruments showing its compass heading, its amount of climb or dive, and its degree of bank to right or left. Each item in this test consists of two dials and four silhouettes of airplanes in flight. Your task is to determine which of the four airplanes is most nearly in the same position indicated by the two dials. You are always looking north at the same altitude for each plane. East is always to the right as you look at the page. **A chart of aircraft flying positions can be found on page 145.**

1.

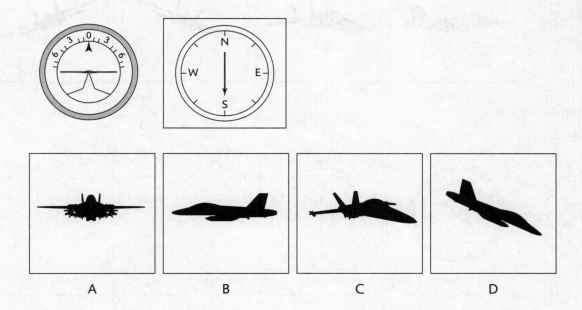

A   B   C   D

2.

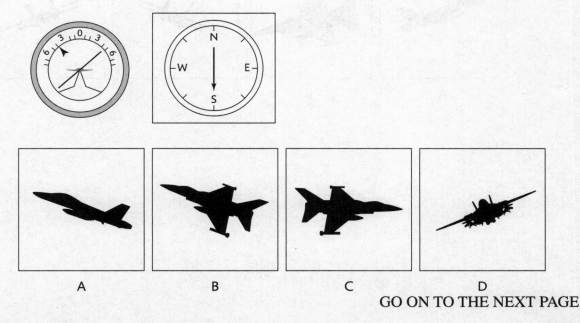

A   B   C   D

GO ON TO THE NEXT PAGE

3.

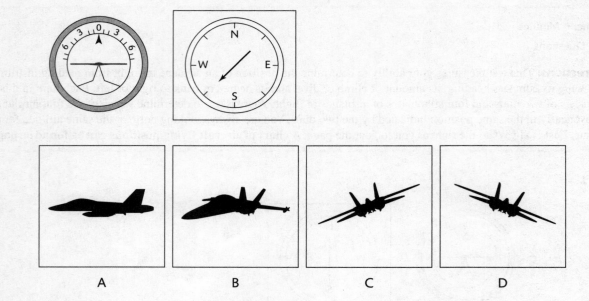

4.

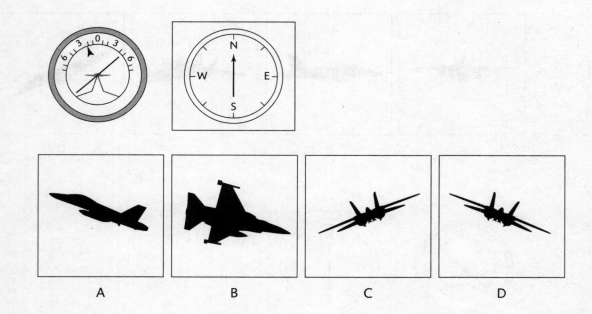

5.

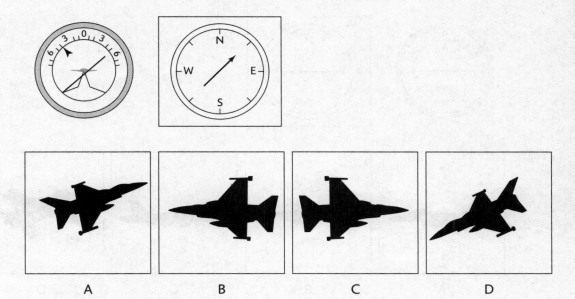

A   B   C   D

6.

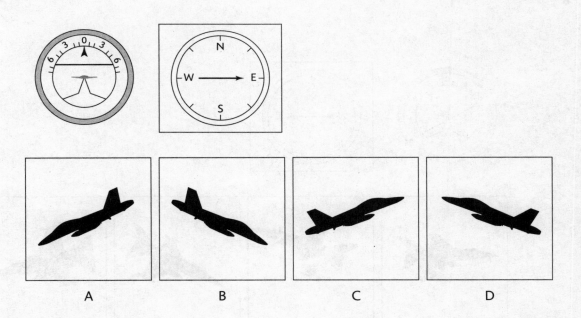

A   B   C   D

GO ON TO THE NEXT PAGE

7.

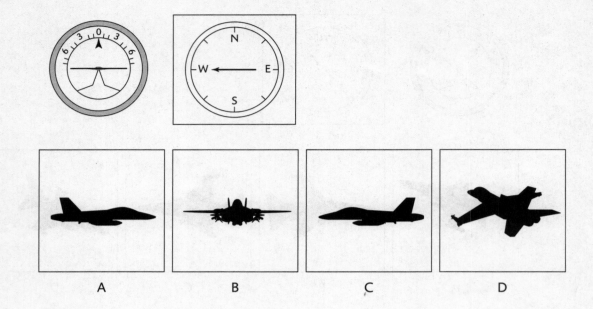

8.

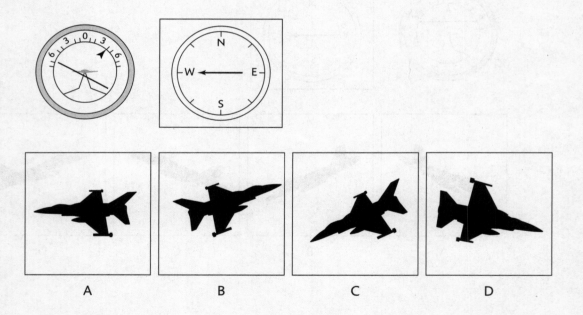

9.

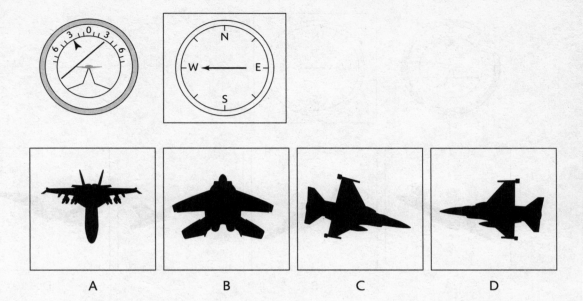

10.

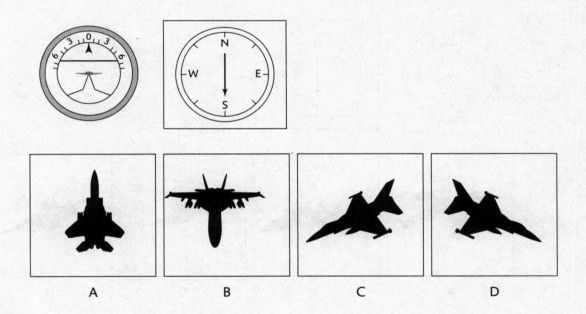

GO ON TO THE NEXT PAGE

11.

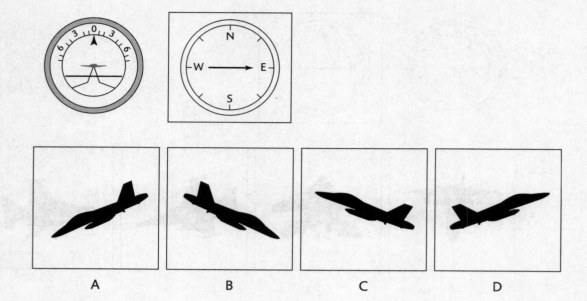

12.

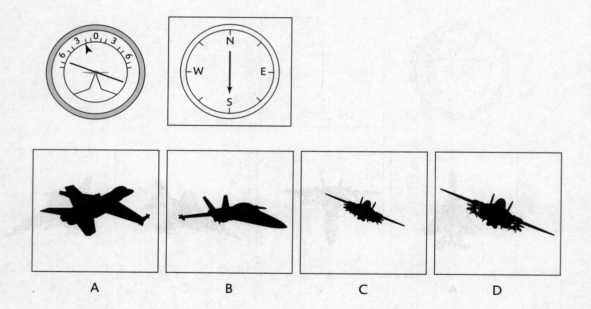

13.

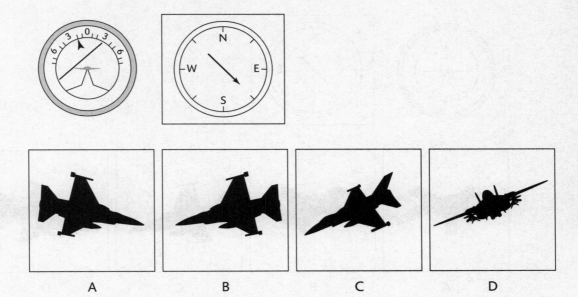

A   B   C   D

14.

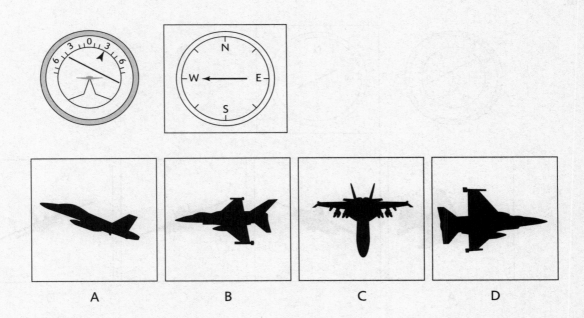

A   B   C   D

GO ON TO THE NEXT PAGE

15.

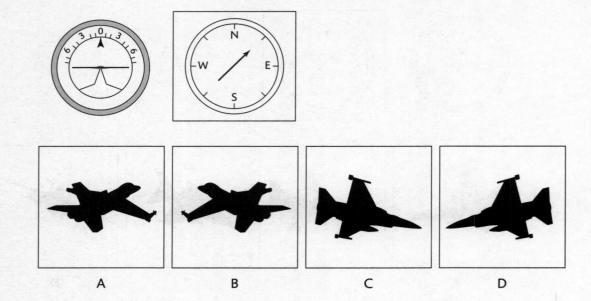

16.

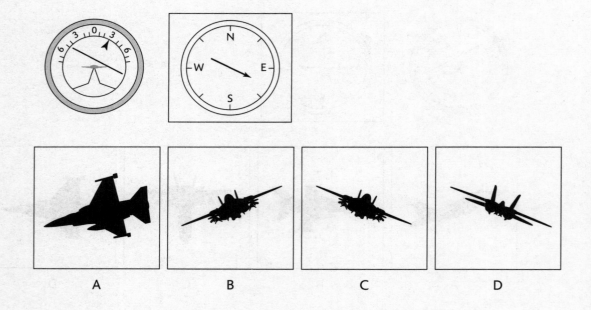

17.

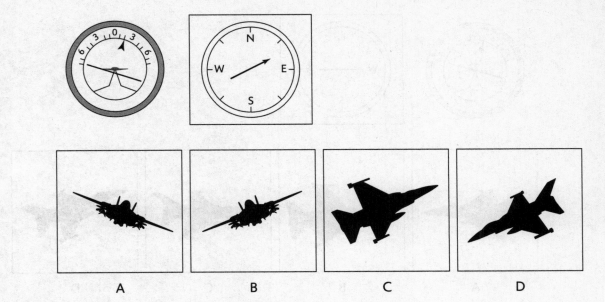

A   B   C   D

18.

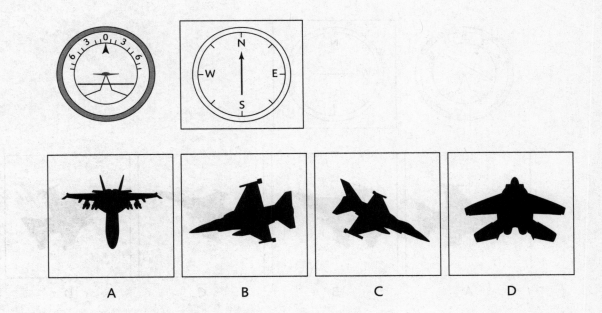

A   B   C   D

GO ON TO THE NEXT PAGE

19.

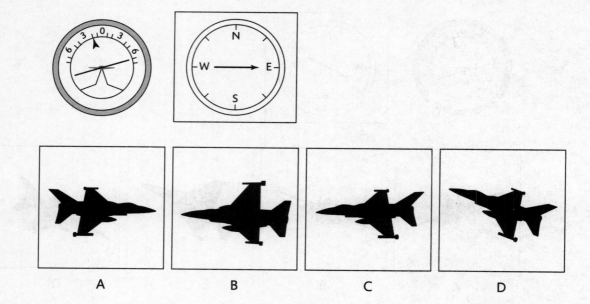

A   B   C   D

20.

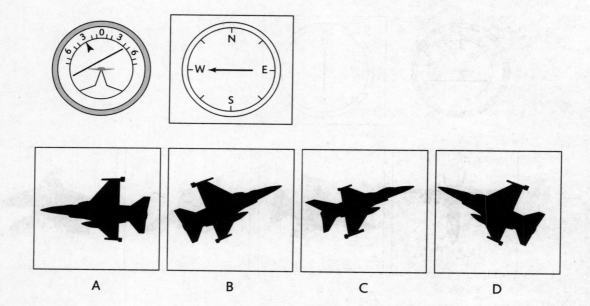

A   B   C   D

Part 11: Block Counting

Time: 3 Minutes

20 Questions

Directions: This is a test of your ability to "see into" a three-dimensional pile of blocks and determine how many pieces are touched by certain numbered blocks. All the blocks in each pile are the same size and shape.

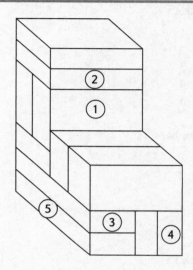

1. Block 1

   A. 1
   B. 2
   C. 3
   D. 4
   E. 5

2. Block 2

   A. 1
   B. 2
   C. 3
   D. 4
   E. 5

3. Block 3

   A. 5
   B. 6
   C. 7
   D. 8
   E. 9

4. Block 4

   A. 3
   B. 4
   C. 5
   D. 6
   E. 7

5. Block 5

   A. 1
   B. 2
   C. 3
   D. 4
   E. 5

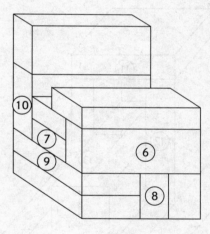

6. Block 6

   A. 4
   B. 5
   C. 6
   D. 7
   E. 8

7. Block 7

   A. 6
   B. 7
   C. 8
   D. 9
   E. 10

GO ON TO THE NEXT PAGE

8. Block 8

    A. 2
    B. 3
    C. 4
    D. 5
    E. 6

9. Block 9

    A. 2
    B. 3
    C. 4
    D. 5
    E. 6

10. Block 10

    A. 1
    B. 2
    C. 3
    D. 4
    E. 5

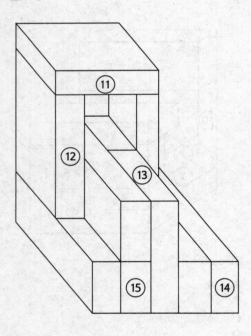

11. Block 11

    A. 1
    B. 2
    C. 3
    D. 4
    E. 5

12. Block 12

    A. 1
    B. 2
    C. 3
    D. 4
    E. 5

13. Block 13

    A. 1
    B. 2
    C. 3
    D. 4
    E. 5

14. Block 14

    A. 1
    B. 2
    C. 3
    D. 4
    E. 5

15. Block 15

    A. 3
    B. 4
    C. 5
    D. 6
    E. 7

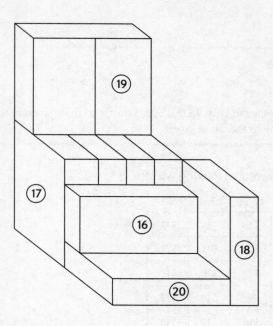

16. Block 16

   A. 3
   B. 4
   C. 5
   D. 6
   E. 7

17. Block 17

   A. 4
   B. 5
   C. 6
   D. 7
   E. 8

18. Block 18

   A. 2
   B. 3
   C. 4
   D. 5
   E. 6

19. Block 19

   A. 1
   B. 2
   C. 3
   D. 4
   E. 5

20. Block 20

   A. 2
   B. 3
   C. 4
   D. 5
   E. 6

GO ON TO THE NEXT PAGE

Part 12: Table Reading

Time: 7 Minutes

40 Questions

Directions: This is a test of your ability to read tables quickly and accurately. In this test, you are to find the entry that occurs at the intersection of the row and the column corresponding to the value given.

Money Collected In Downtown Parking Meters

		Mon	Tues	Wed	Thurs	Fri	Sat
	#1	$11	$26	$15	$25	$19	$17
	#2	$18	$30	$21	$12	$14	$21
Parking Meter	#3	$12	$13	$16	$28	$10	$14
	#4	$28	$12	$14	$8	$18	$12
	#5	$34	$22	$24	$10	$17	$18

For questions 1–5, use the preceding table to determine the amount of money collected in each parking meter for the day indicated. Choose as your answer the letter of the column in which the correct amount is found and mark that on your answer sheet.

	Parking Meter	Day of the Week	(A)	(B)	(C)	(D)	(E)
1.	1	Thurs	$12	$14	$15	$21	$25
2.	2	Wed	$15	$16	$21	$26	$30
3.	3	Sat	$10	$12	$14	$18	$21
4.	4	Tues	$12	$13	$14	$16	$22
5.	5	Fri	$8	$10	$12	$17	$18

X value

	0	1	2	3	4	5	6
6	-6	-4	-2	0	2	4	6
5	-5	-3	-1	1	3	5	7
4	-4	-2	0	2	4	6	8
3	-3	-1	1	3	5	7	9
2	-2	0	2	4	6	8	10
1	-1	1	3	5	7	9	11
0	0	2	4	6	8	10	12

Y value (label to the left of the Y column, aligned with row "3")

Questions 6–10 are based on the preceding table. Note that the X values are shown at the top of the table, and the Y values are shown on the left side of the table. Choose as your answer the letter indicating the value found at the intersection of the X column and the Y row.

	X	Y	(A)	(B)	(C)	(D)	(E)
6.	4	2	3	4	5	6	7
7.	5	1	8	9	10	11	12
8.	1	5	-5	-4	-3	-2	-1
9.	3	1	5	6	7	8	9
10.	6	6	5	6	7	8	9

Questions 11–15 are based on the following table showing housing prices in two different cities.

Housing Prices

	Center City		Springfield	
	Minimum	Maximum	Minimum	Maximum
1990	$98,000	$148,700	$130,100	$171,200
1991	$99,100	$150,200	$131,500	$171,900
1992	$99,900	$152,500	$132,200	$172,900
1993	$100,050	$153,640	$132,900	$174,200
1994	$101,200	$155,800	$134,000	$175,300
1995	$103,100	$156,700	$136,100	$176,100
1996	$104,800	$157,400	$137,200	$176,900
1997	$105,100	$159,200	$138,500	$178,200
1998	$105,950	$160,100	$139,900	$180,000
1999	$107,100	$160,700	$140,100	$181,900

GO ON TO THE NEXT PAGE

11. What was the maximum price in Springfield in 1994?

A. $101,200
B. $134,000
C. $155,000
D. $175,300
E. $176,100

12. What was the minimum price in Center City in 1998?

A. $105,100
B. $105,950
C. $139,900
D. $160,100
E. $180,000

13. What was the minimum price in Springfield in 1992?

A. $99,900
B. $131,500

C. $132,200
D. $152,500
E. $172,900

14. What was the maximum price in Center City in 1997?

A. $105,100
B. $138,500
C. $159,200
D. $160,100
E. $178,200

15. What was the maximum price in Center City in 1991?

A. $150,200
B. $152,500
C. $159,200
D. $171,900
E. $172,900

Questions 16–20 are based on the following table showing the number of phone calls received by six different people in one particular week.

Number of Phone Calls Received

		Bob	Al	Lori	Rich	Meg	Sam	Jan
	Mon	2	1	8	3	1	1	6
	Tues	4	10	7	4	1	9	7
	Wed	1	4	0	3	1	2	2
Day of the Week	Thurs	3	5	3	4	9	1	5
	Fri	0	1	2	3	2	3	6
	Sat	6	2	8	1	4	2	9
	Sun	2	1	7	9	9	6	1

16. How many calls did Rich receive on Friday?

A. 0
B. 1
C. 3
D. 4
E. 7

17. How many calls did Bob receive on Sunday?

A. 0
B. 1
C. 2
D. 6
E. 7

18. How many calls did Sam receive on Saturday?

    A. 1

    B. 2

    C. 4

    D. 6

    E. 9

19. How many calls did Lori receive on Tuesday?

    A. 3

    B. 4

    C. 7

    D. 8

    E. 10

20. How many calls did Jan receive on Saturday?

    A. 1

    B. 2

    C. 3

    D. 6

    E. 9

GO ON TO THE NEXT PAGE

Questions 21–30 are based on the mileage between the two cities represented by the following table.

Alberna	Asheboro	Ashville	Brock	Boone	Burlington	Caphat	Charlotte	Cherokee	Concord	Durham	Eliz City	Fayette	Fontana	Gaston	Goldsboro	Greensboro	Greenville
41																	
157	181																
117	132	86															
128	124	95	9														
79	39	200	149	140													
350	308	487	443	431	297												
95	54	224	174	165	26	271											
42	73	115	91	100	114	385	127										
205	224	48	134	143	259	536	272	162									
22	53	136	97	108	95	369	108	21	183								
103	67	231	184	166	34	261	12	140	283	120							
273	234	415	367	356	223	127	196	306	463	287	180						
75	80	256	210	204	82	274	67	141	299	121	72	194					
247	271	90	170	179	301	580	314	200	42	226	330	305	346				
62	93	95	82	92	132	405	147	20	143	41	159	326	162	185			
148	122	302	248	241	111	220	82	190	349	170	74	144	59	391	210		
65	26	178	128	112	21	320	48	91	227	72	54	236	91	281	112	131	

	From	To	(A)	(B)	(C)	(D)	(E)
21.	Boone	Durham	34	97	108	166	184
22.	Asheboro	Cherokee	42	54	73	95	115
23.	Fontana	Burlington	34	82	179	301	580
24.	Concord	Charlotte	12	21	127	162	272
25.	Greenville	Asheville	26	128	132	178	302
26.	Asheville	Durham	136	184	231	308	415
27.	Cherokee	Goldsboro	12	20	82	143	147
28.	Greenville	Boone	21	111	112	128	241
29.	Asheboro	Burlington	9	39	79	128	140
30.	Greensboro	Fontana	59	91	162	210	346

Questions 31–40 are based on the time of day that e-mail messages were sent between two cities as indicated by the following table.

Email Messages - Time of Day

Terminating Location

Originating Location	Portland	Seattle	Bismarck	Houston	Austin	Little Rock	Nashville	Memphis	Des Moines	Phoenix
New York	11:12 PM	3:05 PM	11:00 AM	2:15 PM	8:17 AM	9:12 PM	10:10 AM	3:28 PM	1:10 PM	4:03 PM
Boston	9:21 AM	12:18 AM	4:09 AM	2:00 PM	3:26 PM	3:04 PM	10:01 AM	1:17 PM	1:04 PM	2:17 AM
Washington	2:19 PM	8:55 PM	1:15 PM	1:15 AM	3:23 PM	9:14 PM	4:39 AM	5:45 PM	8:53 PM	9:16 AM
Cleveland	6:51 PM	3:21 PM	6:12 AM	7:55 AM	7:38 AM	8:01 AM	6:40 PM	9:10 PM	3:18 AM	10:15 AM
Las Vegas	2:14 PM	12:19 PM	2:12 PM	10:21 PM	7:22 PM	9:16 AM	4:36 AM	11:20 PM	5:12 AM	8:10 PM
San Francisco	4:14 PM	12:16 AM	1:27 PM	3:35 PM	9:00 AM	6:16 AM	12:45 AM	2:00 AM	10:15 AM	8:14 PM
Los Angeles	3:10 PM	4:06 PM	6:33 AM	4:15 AM	2:23 PM	5:20 AM	7:11 PM	1:01 PM	3:39 PM	8:22 PM
Miami	4:12 PM	8:41 AM	6:25 PM	8:19 AM	4:33 PM	3:45 PM	10:12 AM	7:30 AM	2:16 AM	8:40 AM
New Orleans	1:05 AM	9:45 PM	2:21 PM	8:00 AM	6:17 AM	9:50 AM	8:31 PM	5:01 AM	6:47 PM	10:55 AM
Denver	11:00 AM	12:13 PM	12:01 PM	11:11 AM	1:00 AM	9:51 PM	7:17 AM	2:00 PM	12:26 PM	3:00 AM
Detroit	9:41 PM	8:25 PM	4:42 PM	4:00 PM	9:14 PM	8:31 PM	11:30 PM	5:00 PM	1:12 PM	8:41 PM
Albany	9:43 PM	1:25 PM	6:00 AM	7:00 PM	8:19 PM	3:17 PM	8:14 AM	9:40 AM	10:53 AM	10:00 AM
Richmond	11:00 PM	12:05 AM	6:22 AM	11:12 AM	1:58 AM	1:52 AM	2:31 PM	3:47 PM	12:40 PM	11:30 AM
St. Louis	1:00 PM	2:00 AM	6:18 PM	4:52 PM	5:25 PM	6:14 PM	12:12 PM	9:40 PM	6:12 PM	8:30 AM

	From	To	(A)	(B)	(C)	(D)	(E)
31.	New Orleans	Memphis	2:16 AM	5:01 AM	7:17 AM	12:01 PM	8:31 PM
32.	Denver	Houston	11:00 AM	8:00 AM	8:17 AM	11:11 AM	12:23 PM
33.	Albany	Seattle	6:00 AM	6:22 AM	1:25 PM	4:42 PM	9:13 PM
34.	San Francisco	Nashville	7:11 PM	6:16 PM	5:20 AM	2:00 AM	12:45 AM
35.	Boston	Phoenix	2:17 AM	3:18 AM	10:15 AM	1:04 PM	1:17 PM
36.	Detroit	Portland	12:13 PM	1:25 PM	8:25 PM	9:41 PM	9:43 PM
37.	New York	Little Rock	3:04 PM	3:26 PM	9:12 PM	8:19 AM	10:10 AM
38.	Richmond	Bismarck	2:00 AM	6:18 AM	6:22 AM	11:12 AM	12:05 AM
39.	Washington	Des Moines	1:04 PM	1:17 PM	4:39 PM	5:45 PM	8:53 PM
40.	Los Angeles	Houston	4:15 AM	6:33 AM	9:00 AM	2:23 PM	4:33 PM

GO ON TO THE NEXT PAGE

Part 13: Aviation Information

Time: 8 Minutes

20 Questions

Directions: This test measures your knowledge of aviation. Each of the questions or incomplete statements is followed by five choices. Decide which one of the choices best answers the question or completes the statement.

1. Which of the following is NOT an aerodynamic force on an aircraft?

   A. lift
   B. drag
   C. power
   D. weight
   E. thrust

2. Which of the following is an axis of rotation in an aircraft?

   A. longitudinal axis
   B. roll axis
   C. rudder axis
   D. pitch axis
   E. yaw axis

3. The ailerons control an aircraft in what axis of rotation?

   A. vertical axis
   B. pitch axis
   C. lateral axis
   D. bank axis
   E. longitudinal axis

4. What does a flashing red light gun signal from a tower indicate to an aircraft on the ground?

   A. cleared to takeoff
   B. proceed with caution
   C. taxi clear of runway
   D. hold position
   E. airport unsafe

5. What transponder code is used in an emergency?

   A. 7500
   B. 7600
   C. 7700
   D. 7777
   E. 1234

6. Which of the following is an engine instrument?

   A. airspeed indicator
   B. manifold pressure gauge
   C. vertical speed indicator
   D. attitude indicator
   E. turn coordinator

7. How is a closed runway identified?

   A. CLOSED is printed on the runway in large letters.
   B. It has red lights positioned at the threshold.
   C. It has large yellow Xs painted on the surface.
   D. The runway markings are removed.
   E. Large orange and white flags are placed at each end.

8. Displaced thresholds are limited to what aircraft actions?

   A. takeoffs, landings and taxi operations
   B. takeoffs and taxi operations
   C. landings only
   D. takeoffs only
   E. landing and taxi operations

9. V_x is defined as the:

   A. best angle-of-climb speed
   B. stall speed
   C. flap operating speed
   D. takeoff speed
   E. best rate-of-climb speed

10. The white arc on an airspeed indicator is the:

   A. maneuvering range
   B. normal cruising speed range
   C. landing gear speed
   D. stall speed
   E. full-flap operating range

11. Angle of attack is defined as:

    A.   the angle between the relative wind and the camber of a wing

    B.   the angle between the angle of incidence and the relative wind

    C.   the angle between the relative wind and the longitudinal axis of the aircraft

    D.   the angle between the wing chord line and the relative wind

    E.   the angle between the longitudinal axis of the airplane and the ground

12. Which of the following is a component of parasite drag?

    A.   form drag

    B.   induced drag

    C.   lift drag

    D.   airflow drag

    E.   bank drag

13. Induced drag is greatest at:

    A.   high airspeeds

    B.   low angles of attack

    C.   cruise flight

    D.   low airspeeds

    E.   low lift configurations

14. Which flight instruments are gyroscopic instruments?

    A.   airspeed indicator, altimeter and vertical speed indicator

    B.   attitude indicator, directional gyro and turn coordinator

    C.   attitude indicator, airspeed indicator and directional gyro

    D.   directional gyro, vertical speed indicator and turn coordinator

    E.   manifold pressure, tachometer and airspeed indicator

15. Which is NOT a type of flap?

    A.   plain flap

    B.   split flap

    C.   grooved flap

    D.   slotted flap

    E.   Fowler flap

16. An aft center of gravity causes the aircraft to be:

    A.   less stable at all speeds

    B.   more stable at all speeds

    C.   less stable at slow speeds

    D.   no different than with a forward center of gravity

    E.   cannot be determined; changes with each flight

17. The center of pressure is defined as:

    A.   the point where the weight of the aircraft acts through

    B.   the balancing point of an aircraft

    C.   the point where thrust acts through on an airplane

    D.   the position of the drag along the wing of an aircraft

    E.   the point along the wing where lift is concentrated

18. Maneuvering speed represents:

    A.   the speed at which all flight maneuvers must be performed

    B.   the minimum speed at which an aircraft can be safely flown

    C.   the maximum speed at which full, abrupt control movements do not overstress the airframe

    D.   the speed that prevents stalls

    E.   the minimum speed at which an aircraft can be flown

19. What is the critical angle of attack?

    A.   the angle of attack that produces the greatest amount of lift

    B.   the angle of attack that produces the greatest amount of drag

    C.   the angle of attack required for a wing to produce lift

    D.   the angle of attack at which the wing stalls no matter what the airspeed

    E.   the angle of attack at which an aircraft must land

20. An aircraft turns due to:

    A.   centripetal force

    B.   the aileron and rudder

    C.   differential drag

    D.   the horizontal component of lift

    E.   the vertical component of lift

GO ON TO THE NEXT PAGE

Part 14: Rotated Blocks

Time: 12 Minutes

15 Questions

Directions: This part of the test has 15 questions designed to measure your ability to visualize and manipulate objects in space. In each item you are shown a picture of an object. Find the second block that is the same.

1.

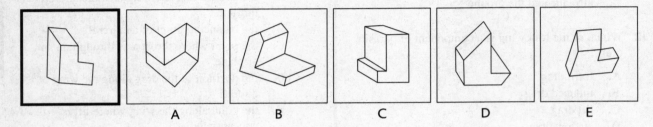

A   B   C   D   E

2.

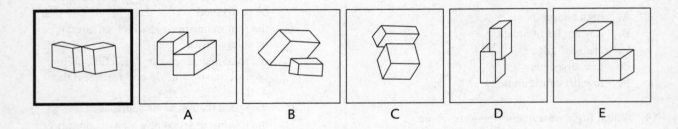

A   B   C   D   E

3.

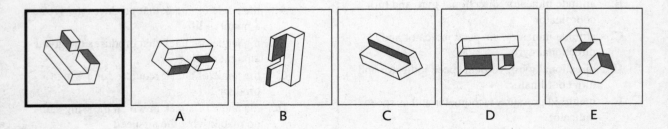

A   B   C   D   E

4.

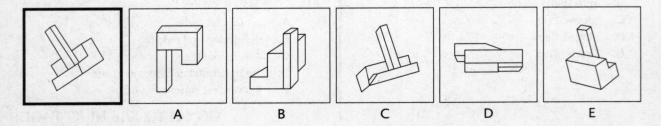

A   B   C   D   E

5.

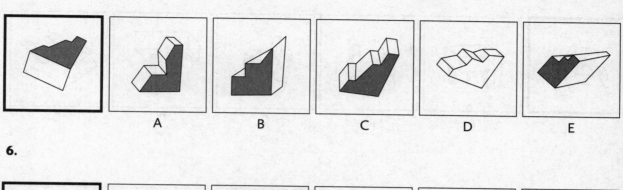

6.

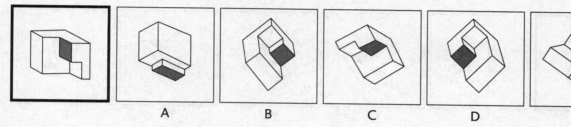

7.

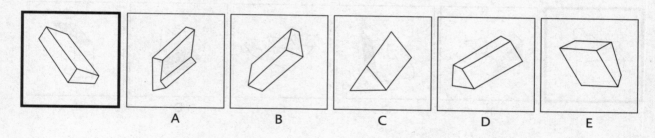

8.

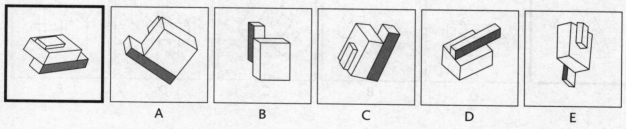

9.

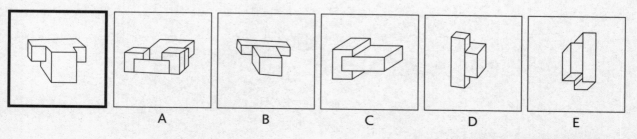

GO ON TO THE NEXT PAGE

10.

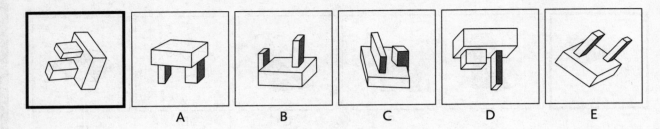

11.

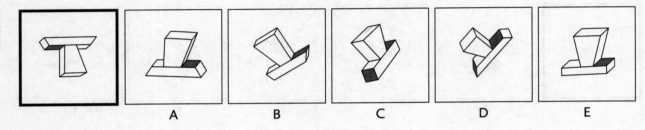

12.

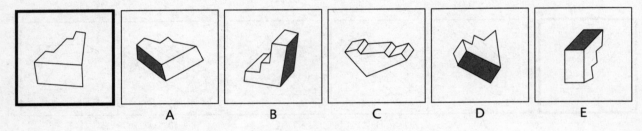

13.

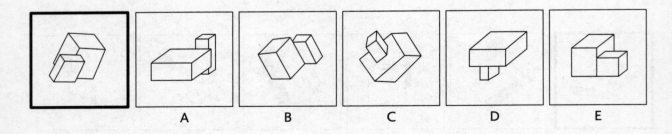

14.

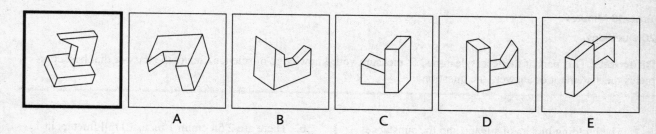

15.

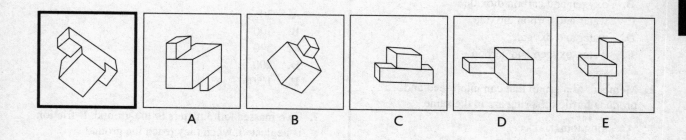

GO ON TO THE NEXT PAGE

Part 15: General Science

Time: 10 Minutes

20 Questions

Directions: This part of the test is designed to measure your knowledge of science. Select the answer that best completes the statement or answers the question.

1. The building blocks of sugars, and the substances used by plants in photosynthesis, are

   A. oxygen and nitrogen
   B. oxygen and carbon dioxide
   C. water and carbon dioxide
   D. water and oxygen
   E. water, oxygen and carbon

2. Members of a group that can interbreed and produce fertile offspring are in the same

   A. kingdom
   B. phylum
   C. family
   D. species
   E. class

3. The normal body temperature of a person is

   A. 37 degrees Fahrenheit
   B. 37 degrees centigrade
   C. 98 degrees Celsius
   D. 98 degrees centigrade
   E. 0 degrees Fahrenheit

4. A liter is about the same as

   A. a quart
   B. a gallon
   C. a pint
   D. a half gallon
   E. a cup

5. When heat is added to water, the added energy

   A. raises the electrons to a higher energy level
   B. makes the molecules move faster
   C. splits the molecules apart
   D. increases the number of electrons in the molecules
   E. decreases the number of molecules in the water

6. There are 2.54 cm in 1 inch, 10 millimeters in 1 centimeter, 12 inches in 1 foot and 3 feet in 1 yard. Approximately how many millimeters are in 1 yard?

   A. 30
   B. 300
   C. 390
   D. 900
   E. 1,500

7. Two masses fall 3 meters to the ground. If friction is neglected, when they reach the ground

   A. both masses have the same speed
   B. both masses have the same energy
   C. both masses have the same momentum
   D. the heavier mass has a higher speed
   E. the heavier mass has a higher momentum

8. The electric current in a metal conductor is carried by

   A. positive ions
   B. electrons
   C. both positive ions and electrons
   D. either positive ions or electrons, depending on the metal
   E. negative ions

9. If you were looking for DNA in a cell, you would find it in the

   A. endoplasmic reticulum
   B. nucleus
   C. vacuole
   D. plasma membrane
   E. cell wall

10. When air masses meet, why does warm air rise over cooler air often causing rain?

   A. Warm air is less dense than cooler air.
   B. Warm air is denser than cooler air.
   C. Cooling air can hold less water vapor than warmer air.
   D. Cooler air is very volatile.
   E. Cooler air holds more water vapor than warmer air.

11. The process of dividing one cell nucleus into two nuclei is called

   A. mitosis
   B. meiosis
   C. cytokinesis
   D. cell division
   E. symbiosis

12. Increasing which of the following factors would not help a plant photosynthesize faster?

   A. oxygen
   B. carbon dioxide
   C. light intensity
   D. water
   E. temperature

13. A man with O-type blood and a woman with AB-type blood could have which type of children?

   A. O
   B. AB
   C. A or B
   D. O negative
   E. all of the above

14. Summers are warmer than winters in the Northern Hemisphere because the Earth

   A. is closer to the Sun in the summer
   B. is inclined on its axis toward the Sun in the summer
   C. is tilted away from the Sun in the summer
   D. speeds up in its orbit in the winter
   E. slows in its orbit in the summer

15. When blood leaves the heart and enters the pulmonary artery, it

   A. has just left the right atrium
   B. is heading to the lungs
   C. has just left the left atrium
   D. is heading to the aorta
   E. is heading toward the left atrium

16. Jack has 100 ml of a 12 molar solution of sulfuric acid. How much of it should he put into a graduated cylinder to make 20 ml of a 1.2 molar solution?

   A. 1
   B. 2
   C. 10
   D. 12
   E. 14

17. The transformation of a solid directly into a gas is called

   A. vaporization
   B. ionization
   C. sublimation
   D. polarization
   E. condensation

18. A 50 cm long metal rod expands 2 mm when heated in an oven. How much would a 75 cm long rod of the same material expand in the same oven?

   A. 2 mm
   B. 3 mm
   C. 4 mm
   D. 6 mm
   E. 9 mm

19. The organ that is most closely associated with the digestion of proteins is the

   A. stomach
   B. liver
   C. small intestine
   D. large intestine
   E. gall bladder

20. A car is driving around a curve on a level road. The force holding the car on the curve is

   A. friction
   B. gravity
   C. tension
   D. magnetic
   E. centrifugal force

GO ON TO THE NEXT PAGE

Part 16: Hidden Figures

Time: 8 Minutes

15 Questions

Directions: This part of the test measures your ability to see a simple figure in a complex drawing. You will be presented with five figures, lettered A, B, C, D, and E. Following these figures will be several numbered drawings. You are to determine which lettered figure is contained in each of the numbered drawings. Each numbered drawing contains only ONE of the lettered figures. The correct figure in each drawing will always be of the same size and in the same position as it appears in the answer choices.

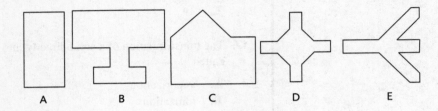

A   B   C   D   E

1.

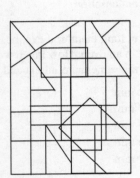

2.

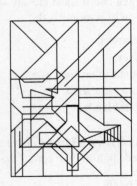

3.

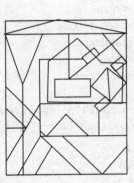

4.

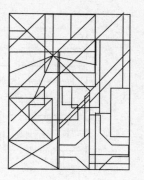

5.

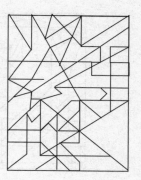

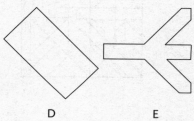

A   B   C   D   E

6.

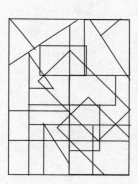

7.

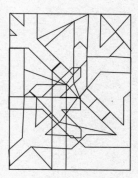

GO ON TO THE NEXT PAGE

8.

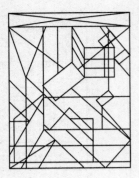

9.

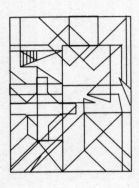

10.

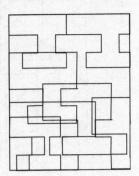

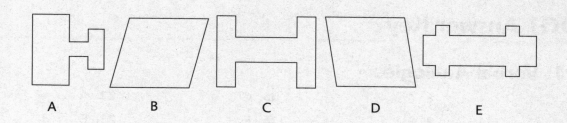

A   B   C   D   E

11.

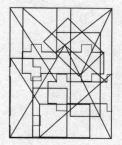

12.

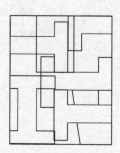

13.

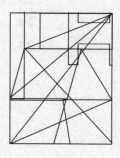

14.

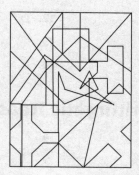

15.

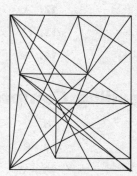

IF YOU FINISH BEFORE TIME IS CALLED, CHECK YOUR WORK ON THIS SECTION ONLY. DO NOT WORK ON ANY OTHER SECTION IN THE TEST.

AFOQT Answer Key

Part 1: Verbal Analogies

1. B	8. C	15. C	22. A
2. B	9. E	16. E	23. E
3. D	10. D	17. D	24. D
4. C	11. B	18. D	25. C
5. B	12. D	19. B	
6. B	13. C	20. D	
7. D	14. B	21. B	

Part 2: Arithmetic Reasoning

1. B	8. D	15. B	22. E
2. B	9. E	16. C	23. D
3. A	10. D	17. B	24. D
4. D	11. A	18. C	25. A
5. C	12. A	19. C	
6. E	13. C	20. A	
7. A	14. A	21. D	

Part 3: Reading Comprehension

1. C	8. C	15. A	22. D
2. D	9. B	16. B	23. C
3. A	10. A	17. A	24. A
4. B	11. E	18. C	25. C
5. A	12. C	19. E	
6. A	13. D	20. B	
7. D	14. B	21. A	

Part 4: Data Interpretation

1. E	8. E	15. A	22. B
2. C	9. D	16. D	23. E
3. C	10. B	17. D	24. C
4. B	11. E	18. E	25. B
5. A	12. B	19. C	
6. B	13. B	20. C	
7. E	14. D	21. A	

Part 5: Word Knowledge

1. B	8. C	15. C	22. B
2. D	9. B	16. B	23. A
3. D	10. D	17. B	24. C
4. E	11. D	18. A	25. B
5. A	12. B	19. E	
6. B	13. C	20. C	
7. A	14. A	21. C	

Part 6: Mathematics Knowledge

1. C	8. B	15. A	22. B
2. E	9. C	16. A	23. C
3. A	10. B	17. C	24. B
4. B	11. C	18. E	25. A
5. C	12. C	19. A	
6. C	13. B	20. C	
7. D	14. C	21. B	

Part 7: Mechanical Comprehension

1. B	6. D	11. A	16. A
2. D	7. C	12. C	17. C
3. D	8. C	13. A	18. A
4. A	9. C	14. C	19. E
5. A	10. B	15. D	20. A

Part 8: Electrical Maze

1. D	6. C	11. C	16. C
2. C	7. A	12. A	17. D
3. B	8. C	13. C	18. B
4. B	9. B	14. D	19. E
5. E	10. D	15. A	20. B

Part 9: Scale Reading

1. C	11. D	21. C	31. B
2. C	12. D	22. D	32. C
3. E	13. A	23. C	33. C
4. D	14. E	24. D	34. D
5. C	15. B	25. C	35. E
6. B	16. C	26. C	36. B
7. D	17. C	27. D	37. E
8. B	18. E	28. D	38. D
9. C	19. A	29. B	39. A
10. B	20. B	30. C	40. D

Part 10: Instrument Comprehension

1. A	6. B	11. D	16. C
2. D	7. C	12. C	17. A
3. B	8. A	13. D	18. D
4. D	9. D	14. B	19. A
5. A	10. B	15. A	20. A

Part 11: Block Counting

1. D	6. C	11. B	16. D
2. C	7. A	12. C	17. A
3. A	8. E	13. D	18. A
4. B	9. D	14. A	19. C
5. B	10. D	15. B	20. E

Part 12: Table Reading

1. E	11. D	21. C	31. B
2. C	12. B	22. C	32. D
3. C	13. C	23. B	33. C
4. A	14. C	24. E	34. E
5. D	15. A	25. D	35. A
6. D	16. C	26. A	36. D
7. B	17. C	27. B	37. C
8. C	18. B	28. C	38. C
9. A	19. C	29. B	39. E
10. B	20. E	30. A	40. A

Part 13: Aviation Information

1. C	6. B	11. D	16. A
2. A	7. C	12. A	17. E
3. E	8. B	13. D	18. C
4. C	9. A	14. B	19. D
5. C	10. E	15. C	20. D

Part 14: Rotated Blocks

1. E	5. C	9. D	13. B
2. C	6. D	10. A	14. D
3. A	7. B	11. D	15. C
4. E	8. C	12. C	

Part 15: General Science

1. C	6. D	11. A	16. B
2. D	7. A	12. A	17. C
3. B	8. B	13. C	18. B
4. A	9. B	14. B	19. A
5. B	10. C	15. B	20. A

Part 16: Hidden Figures

1. A	5. E	9. B	13. B
2. D	6. D	10. A	14. A
3. C	7. E	11. E	15. D
4. B	8. C	12. C	

AFOQT Answers and Explanations

Part 1: Verbal Analogies Answers and Explanations

1. **B.** The purpose of a place of sanctuary is refuge. Likewise the purpose of a place of imprisonment is punishment.

2. **B.** The function of bathing is to achieve cleanliness, and the function of schooling is to achieve an education.

3. **D.** The function of smiling is to convey happiness. The function of scowling is to convey displeasure.

4. **C.** Two hands comprise a whole clock. Two legs comprise a whole body.

5. **B.** A quarter is part of a dollar, and a week is part of a month. Additionally, a quarter is one fourth of a dollar, and a week is one fourth of a month.

6. **B.** A dancer is one member of a whole ensemble. A student is one member of a whole class.

7. **D.** An anarchist promotes disorder, while a pacifist promotes peace.

8. **C.** A doctor's primary action is to heal patients. An author's primary action is to write books.

9. **E.** The police characteristically uphold the law in a community. The clergy characteristically uphold religion in a community.

10. **D.** Frigid is an extreme degree of something that is cool. To detest something is to dislike to an extreme degree.

11. **B.** A puddle is a small body of water, and an ocean is an enormous body of water. A crumb is a tiny portion of bread, while a loaf is a huge amount of bread.

12. **D.** A breeze is a soft wind. A gale is a strong and violent wind. A snowflake is one solitary piece of snow, and a blizzard is an abundance of large amounts of snow.

13. **C.** A croissant is a type of pastry, while a haiku is a type of poem.

14. **B.** There are many types of novels, including the romance novel. Likewise, there are many types of music, and rap music is one type.

15. **C.** A tanker is a type of ship, and a minivan is a type of automobile.

16. **E.** Whales live in the ocean, and bees live in a hive.

17. **D.** An actor acts on the stage. A teacher teaches in the classroom.

18. **D.** An attribute of all tyrants is that they practice cruelty to achieve their ends. An attribute of all sycophants is that they practice flattery to achieve their ends.

19. **B.** To be a sloth is to be lazy, and to be an insomniac is to be sleepless.

20. **D.** Something that is hallowed is always sacred. Someone who is nomadic is always wandering.

21. **B.** Someone who is sanctimonious is very smug, and someone who is lugubrious is very melancholy.

22. **A.** If something is in pristine condition, then it is unspoiled. If something is tainted, then it is contaminated.

23. **E.** Birthing someone can result in life, while exposing someone can result in infection.

24. **D.** A state of meditation results in relaxation. A state of satiation results in satisfaction.

25. **C.** Placing a person in isolation results in loneliness for that individual. Promoting a person results in advancement for that individual.

Part 2: Arithmetic Reasoning Answers and Explanations

1. **B.** If 400 people fit in 8 subway cars, then $400 \div 8$, or 50, people fit in 1 subway car. Therefore, 50×5, or 250, people fit in 5 subway cars.

2. B. The earnings for 30 hours are $8.25 \times 30 = \$247.50$.

3. A. $3\frac{1}{4} - 2\frac{1}{8} = \frac{13}{4} - \frac{17}{8} = \frac{26}{8} - \frac{17}{8} = \frac{9}{8} = 1\frac{1}{8}$ more cups of flour.

4. D. Two dozen eggs is 24 eggs. If 3 eggs are in an omelet, then $24 \div 3$, or 8 omelets can be made.

5. C. Because two runners finish in 80 seconds, the average of 80, 80, 72 and 68 must be found. This average is $\frac{80 + 80 + 72 + 68}{4} = \frac{300}{4} = 75$ seconds.

6. E. Let n represent the number of students in the band. Then $\frac{1}{3}n = 72$, so n $= 72 \times 3 = 216$.

7. A. Add the amount of money received and subtract the amount spent. $\$30 + \$15 - \$16 = \$29$.

8. D. If an item is discounted 20%, the sale price is 80% of the original price. Let p represent the original price. Then $\$800 = 80\% \times p$, and $p = \frac{800}{80\%} = \frac{800}{.80} = \$1,000$.

9. E. For a 30-hour week with $500 in sales, total earnings are $(30 \times \$9.50) + (3\% \times \$500) = \$285 + \$15 = \$300$.

10. D. The area of the circle with a radius of 3 is $\pi r^2 = \pi 3^2 = 9\pi$. The area of the larger circle is $4 \times 9\pi = 36\pi$. Therefore, $r^2 = 36$, so $r = \sqrt{36} = 6$. The radius of the larger circle is 6.

11. A. $\$20 - \$3.95 = \$16.05$.

12. A. Using the ratio $\frac{\text{height}}{\text{shadow}}$, the proportion $\frac{3\frac{1}{2}}{6} = \frac{x}{24}$ models this situation, where x represents the height of the pole. Cross multiply: $3\frac{1}{2} \times 24 = 6x$, so $84 = 6x$, and $x = \frac{84}{6} = 14$ feet.

13. C. The overtime rate is $\$8.40 \times 1.5 = \$12.60$. Five hours of overtime were completed, so the total earnings are $(\$8.40 \times 40) + (\$12.60 \times 5) = \$336 + \$63 = \$399$.

14. A. The amount of the discount is $\$40 - \$30 = \$10$. The percent of the discount is the amount of the discount divided by the original price: $\frac{10}{40} = \frac{1}{4} = 25\%$.

15. B. The volume of the original box is $3 \times 2\frac{1}{2} \times 2 = 15$. The volume of the box with the length and depth doubled is $6 \times 2\frac{1}{2} \times 4 = 60$. The amount of change in volume is $60 - 15 = 45$. The percent change is the amount of change in volume divided by the original volume. $\frac{45}{15} = 3 = 300\%$.

16. C. The amount of commission is $10\% \times \$8,350 = \$835$. Total earnings are $\$300 + \$835$ commission $= \$1,135$.

17. B. The total number of stamps collected is $300 + 420 + 180 = 900$. The number of coins that can be collected is $\frac{900}{25} = 36$.

18. C. The proportion $\frac{1 \text{ cm}}{4 \text{ miles}} = \frac{x \text{ cm}}{10 \text{ miles}}$ models this situation. Cross multiply. $1 \times 10 = 4x$, so $10 = 4x$, and $x = \frac{10}{4} = 2\frac{1}{2}$ cm.

19. C. Let p represent the amount of the paycheck: $\frac{4}{13}p = \$26.80$, so p $= p = \$26.80 \times \frac{13}{4} = \$87.10$.

20. A. The proportion $\frac{\frac{1}{2} \text{ miles}}{4 \text{ minutes}} = \frac{x \text{ miles}}{15 \text{ minutes}}$ models this situation. Cross multiply: $\frac{1}{2} \times 15 = 4x$, so $\frac{15}{2} = 4x$, and $x = \frac{15}{2} \times \frac{1}{4} = \frac{15}{8} = 1\frac{7}{8}$ miles.

21. D. Three feet are in a yard, so a kitchen 4 yards by 5 yards is equivalent to (4×3) feet by (5×3) feet, or 12 feet by 15 feet. The area of the kitchen is $12 \times 15 = 180$ square feet. The cost to tile is $\$2.89 \times 180 = \$520.20$.

22. E. At the end of the first day, $1 - \frac{1}{8} = \frac{7}{8}$ of the magazines remain. $\frac{7}{8} \times \frac{1}{4} = \frac{7}{32}$ sold the next day. So at the end of the second day, $\frac{7}{8} - \frac{7}{32} = \frac{28}{32} - \frac{7}{32} = \frac{21}{32}$ of the magazines remain.

23. D. The interest earned in one year is $\$300 \times 5\frac{1}{4}\% = \$15.75$. The total amount in the account after one year is $\$300 + \$15.75 = \$315.75$.

24. D. Let m represent the minutes of the phone calls. The monthly charge for the first plan is 20 + 0.08m. The monthly charge for the second plan is 12 + 0.12m. When the monthly charges are the same, 20 + 0.08m = 12 + 0.12m. Solve for m to find the number of minutes after which both plans have the same rate.

20 + 0.08m − 0.08m = 12 + 0.12m − 0.08m

20 = 12 + 0.04m

20 − 12 = 12 + 0.04m − 12

8 = 0.04m, so $m = \dfrac{8}{0.04} = \dfrac{800}{4} = 200$ minutes

25. A. The perimeter of a rectangle is l + w + l + w = 48. Because l = 3w, the perimeter is 3w + w + 3w + w = 48, so 8w = 48, and w = 6. Therefore, the length is 3 × 6, or 18, and the area of the rectangle is l × w = 18 × 6 = 108.

Part 3: Reading Comprehension Answers and Explanations

1. C. Because the car is more than three years old, the free replacement guarantee does not apply. **A** is not correct because it does not tell whether the customer has to pay for the work. No information in the paragraph suggests that **B** would be what would happen. While **D** might be a true statement, the situation in the paragraph does not describe any problem with the engine.

2. D. Choices **A** and **B** are statements that describe some but not all sonnets according to the paragraph. Choice **C** is incorrect because the paragraph states that a sonnet has 14 lines.

3. A. The paragraph states that Americans travel more in the summer. You can conclude that if they travel more, they use more gasoline. The paragraph also states that when people want to buy more of a product, the price goes up.

4. B. Choices **A** and **D** are examples of facsimiles; they do not define the word. **C** is incorrect because the paragraph indicates that ways of making facsimiles are ways of making copies.

5. A. A main idea is a general statement. The other choices are specific facts.

6. A. The paragraph is written in the order of things to do, and this is the last action mentioned in the paragraph.

7. D. The paragraph explains why recycling is a good idea. The paragraph is not a story (choice **B**), and does not have a contrast (choice **C**). It does not tell what recycling is, so **A** is incorrect.

8. C. All the other choices are discussed in the paragraph.

9. B. The paragraph discusses Superman from the 1930s to the 1980s, so one can conclude that he has been popular for a long time. Choices **C** and **D** are facts stated in the paragraph. Most people would agree with choice **A**, but it is not part of the information in the paragraph.

10. A. It is the only choice that states a fact about why pizza is a nutritious food.

11. E. The details in the paragraph about standing up, staring at the sky, the exclamation, "there it is," and the applause and cheering show that the spectators are excited.

12. C. Because the paragraph gives reasons, it is explaining causes. Although the first sentence of the paragraph is a contrast, the paragraph does not explain the contrast, so **A** is an incorrect choice.

13. D. Because King's letter was a reply to the clergymen, he had to have written it after he read their letter.

14. B. This fact is stated in the second sentence of the paragraph.

15. A. From the paragraph, you can infer that a REDUNDANT expression is one in which both words have the same meaning. COOPERATE means WORK TOGETHER, so it is an example of a redundant expression. Choice **C** might look appropriate because REVIEW means look at again. But something can be reviewed more than one time.

16. B. Because both food products and beauty products are mentioned, this title best describes the paragraph as a whole.

17. A. The second sentence states that students in college classrooms are often yawning and sleepy. Thus, many college lectures might be described as dull.

18. C. The third sentence explains that snout structure is different in crocodiles and alligators.

19. E. The first sentence of the selection states that carbon has varying forms, and the paragraph develops this topic sentence further.

20. B. The selection states that environmentalists believe natural gas is a way to decrease pollution. The next paragraph states that natural gas vehicles emit up to 95% less pollution than their gasoline and diesel counterparts.

21. A. The first sentence of the second paragraph states that great emphasis is put on producing such vehicles.

22. D. Because vampire bats are thought to be ruthless bloodsuckers, many perceive them to be evil creatures.

23. C. The selection states that vampire bats' saliva might be useful in blood clotting, thus preventing heart attacks and strokes.

24. A. This selection explains what a tsunami is. It does not focus on any other Japanese words, natural disasters or the effects of a tsunami.

25. C. The first sentence discusses the fact that pyromaniacs rarely start fires. The last sentence explains what a pyromaniac is.

Part 4: Data Interpretation Answers and Explanations

1. E. There are 5,000 students at Smithfield High School and 30% of them are sophomores.

30% of 5,000 = .30 × 5,000 = 1,500.

2. C. There are 5,000 students at Smithfield High School and 22% of them are seniors.

22% of 5,000 = .22 × 5,000 = 1,100 seniors.

If 80% of the seniors are college bound, the 80% of 1,100 = .80 × 1,100 = 880 college-bound seniors.

3. C. Read the explanation for question 2 to see that there are 880 college-bound seniors. If 30% of them plan to attend schools in the east, then 30% of 880 = .30 × 880 = 264.

4. B. If clothing represents 15% of the total budget, then 15% × (total budget) = .15 × (total budget) = $192. Therefore, the total budget is $192 ÷ .15 = $1,280.

5. A. Whichever group encompasses the largest percent of the budget will be the group on which the most money is spent.

Housing and medical = 31% + 3% = 34%. Choice **A** = 34%.

Food and Clothing = 18% + 15% = 33%. Choice **B** = 33%.

Medical, entertainment and savings = 3% + 9% + 10% = 22%. Choice **C** = 22%.

Clothing and miscellaneous = 15% + 14% = 29%. Choice **D** = 29%.

Food, medical and entertainment = 18% + 3% + 9% = 30%. Choice **E** = 30%.

Thus, the largest value is 34%, choice **A**.

6. B. Food represents 18% and savings represents 10%. The difference is 18 − 10 = 8. Eight percent of $1,500 = .08 × $1,500 = $120.

7. E. Entertainment represents 9% and food represents 18%. Therefore, food is twice as much as entertainment. If $125 is spent on entertainment, then 2 × $125 = $250 is spent on food.

8. E. The monthly rental for apartment 2 is $600. If five people share apartment 2, they each pay $600 ÷ 5 = $120. The monthly rental for apartment 6 is $480. If four people share apartment 6, they each pay $480 ÷ 4 = $120. Each person pays the same amount.

9. **D.** There are two apartments that have two bathrooms. Apartment 2 rents for $600 a month, and apartment 7 rents for $560 per month. The smallest fee for a two-bathroom apartment would then be $560.

10. **B.** The total number of windows in the building is $7 + 7 + 4 + 5 + 3 + 5 + 7 = 38$. If the window cleaner charges $7.50 to clean each window, he will earn $7.50 \times 38 = $285.

11. **E.** Apartment 5 costs $400. Five percent of $400 = $.05 \times $400 = $20. A $20 increase would raise the cost to $400 + $20 = $420.

    Apartment 4 costs $480. Five percent of $480 = $.05 \times $480 = $24. A $24 increase would raise the cost to $480 + $24 = $504.

    Apartment 3 costs $460. Five percent of $460 = $.05 \times $460 = $23. A $23 increase would raise the cost to $460 + $23 = $483.

    Apartment 2 costs $600. Five percent of $600 = $.05 \times $600 = $30. A $30 increase would raise the cost to $600 + $30 = $630.

    Apartment 1 costs $520. Five percent of $520 = $.05 \times $520 = $26. A $26 increase would raise the cost to $520 + $26 = $546. This is the answer we were looking for.

12. **B.** The total number of accidents is $1 + 3 + 2 + 4 + 0 + 4 + 0 + 2 + 5 + 1 + 1 + 1 + 0 + 2 + 2 + 1 = 29$.

13. **B.** The number 0 appears three times in the table. The number 1 appears five times in the table. The number 2 appears four times in the table. The number 3 appears one time in the table. The number 4 appears two times in the table. The number that appears most often is the number that is most likely to occur in any randomly chosen week. The correct answer is 1, choice **B**.

14. **D.** At least 5'9" tall means 5'9" and above. This includes the three right-hand bars of the male-applicant graph. $75 + 60 + 35 = 170$.

15. **A.** There are 60 women in the 5'5" to 5'6" range. There are 50 men in the 5'5" to 5'6" range. $60 - 50 = 10$.

16. **D.** The total number of male applicants is $25 + 50 + 70 + 75 + 60 + 35 = 315$. If 40% are accepted, then 60% will be rejected. 60% of $315 = .60 \times 315 = 189$.

17. **D.** If 7 females are added to the 5'1" to 5'2" range, there will be 37 females in that range. If 10 females are added to the 5'7" to 5'8" range, there will be 40 females in that range. Because 37 is not greater than 40, the answer is not choice **A**. Because 37 is not equal to 40, the answer is not choice **C**. No females are added to the 5'5" to 5'6" range, which has 60 females. Because 40 is not greater than 60, the answer is not choice **B**. If 8 females are added to the 5'3" to 5'4" range, there will be 63 females in that range. Because 63 is greater than 60, the answer is choice **D**.

18. **E.** In week 2 the 40-year-old male consumed 1,800 calories. In week 4 he consumed 1,800. The increase was 0. Choice **A** = 0. In week 3 he consumed 1,600 and 1,800 in week 5. The increase was 200. Choice **B** = 200. In week 6 he consumed 2,000 and 1,800 in week 8 for a decrease of 200. Choice **C** = 200. In week 7 he consumed 1800 calories and in week 9, he consumed 2000 calories. The increase was 200. Choice **D** = 200. In week 8 he consumed 1,800 and 2,200 in week 10. The increase was 400. Choice **E** = 400. This is the greatest increase.

19. **C.** In week 9 the 30-year-old male consumed 3,000 calories. In week 9 the 40-year-old male consumed 2,000 calories. $3,000 = 1\ 1/2 \times 2,000$.

20. **C.** To calculate the average daily calories over the 11-week period, we need to add the values for all 11 weeks, and then divide that total by 11.

    $1,600 + 1,600 + 1,600 + 1,600 + 1,800 + 1,600 + 1,800 + 1,800 + 1,600 + 1,800 + 2,000 = 18,800$.

    $18,800 \div 11 = 1,709$. 1,709 is approximately 1,700, so choice **C** is correct.

21. **A.** In week 10 the 40-year-old male consumed 2,200 calories, and the 60-year-old male consumed 1,200. The difference is 1,000. Choice **A** = 1,000. In week 8 the 40-year-old male consumed 1,800 calories, and the 60-year-old male consumed 1,600. The difference is 200. Choice **B** = 200. In week 6 the 40-year-old male consumed 2,000 calories, and the 60-year-old male consumed 1,600. The difference is 400. Choice **C** = 400. In week 3 the 40-year-old male consumed 1,600 calories, and the 60-year-old male consumed 1,600. The difference is 0.

Choice **D** = 0. In week 1 the 40-year-old male consumed 2,000 calories, and the 60-year-old male consumed 1,400. The difference is 600. Choice **E** = 600. Choice **A** is the greatest.

22. B. The greatest hourly sales in menswear is $528 and the least is $49. $528 − $49 = $479.

23. E. The total sales after 4 p.m. are found in the last column.

$88 + $187 + $412 + $299 + $310 + $110 = $1,406

24. C. The average hourly sales in the notions department is found by adding the seven hourly sales figures and dividing that total by seven.

$28 + $46 + $50 + $75 + $62 + $43 + $110 = $414.

$414 ÷ 7 = $59.14

25. B. The sales in children's wear from 10–11 a.m. are $43. Looking across the row for notions we find $43 in the time period from 3–4 p.m.

Part 5: Word Knowledge Answers and Explanations

1. B. *Distraught* means deeply agitated.

2. D. *Furor* means anger.

3. D. *Trivial* means unimportant.

4. E. *Verbose* means wordy.

5. A. *Vogue* means fashion.

6. B. *Assail* means attack.

7. A. *Ruse* means trick.

8. C. *Prudence* means caution.

9. B. *Listless* means indifferent.

10. D. *Superficial* means external.

11. D. *Feasible* means possible.

12. B. *Squelch* means silence.

13. C. *Antithesis* means opposite.

14. A. *Destitute* means poverty stricken.

15. C. *Belligerent* means warlike.

16. B. *Recluse* means hermit.

17. B. *Saddled* means burdened.

18. A. *Rostrum* means speaker's platform.

19. **E.** *Inane* means silly.

20. **C.** *Pessimistic* means gloomy.

21. **C.** *Natal* means of birth.

22. **B.** *Rigorous* means demanding.

23. **A.** *Ideology* means philosophy.

24. **C.** *Lackadaisical* means lifeless.

25. **B.** *Aborigines* means native inhabitants.

Part 6: Mathematics Knowledge Answers and Explanations

1. **C.** Substitute $\frac{5}{2}$ for a. $\frac{1}{a} = \frac{1}{\frac{5}{2}} = 1 \div \frac{5}{2} = 1 \times \frac{2}{5} = \frac{2}{5}$.

2. **E.** Let n represent the number. If 12 is 15% of n, then $12 = .15n$. Divide both sides by .15. Therefore, $n = 80$.

3. **A.** Substitute -3 for x. Then $3(-3) + 7 = -9 + 7 = -2$.

4. **B.** The area of a square is s^2 where s is a side of the square. If $s^2 = 36$, then $s = 6$. The diagonal of a square forms two right triangles; d is the hypotenuse, and the two legs are 6 units long.

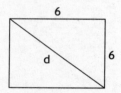

   Using the Pythagorean Theorem, $d^2 = 6^2 + 6^2 = 36 + 36 = 72$. Therefore, $d = \sqrt{72} = 6\sqrt{2}$.

5. **C.** $3a + 3b = 3(a + b)$. Because $a + b = 6$, $3a + 3b = 3(6) = 18$.

6. **C.** The hypotenuse of the triangle is the diameter of the circle. By the Pythagorean Theorem, $d^2 = 6^2 + 8^2 = 36 + 64 = 100$. So, $d = \sqrt{100} = 10$, and the radius is $\frac{10}{2} = 5$.

7. **D.** Following the correct order of operations produces:

   $(3 - 1) \times 7 - 12 \div 2 = 2 \times 7 - (12 \div 2) = 14 - 6 = 8$.

8. **B.** Factors of 24 are $2 \times 2 \times 2 \times 3$. Factors of 36 are $2 \times 2 \times 3 \times 3$. The greatest common factor is $2 \times 2 \times 3 = 12$.

9. **C.** $3m - 12 + 12 = -6 + 12$

   $3m = 6$.

   Dividing both sides by 3 results in $m = 2$.

10. **B.** Substitute 1 for p and solve for q. $7(1) + 5q = -3$, so $7 + 5q = -3$.

    $7 + 5q - 7 = -3 - 7$, and $5q = -10$. Dividing both sides by 5 results in $q = -2$.

11. **C.** Slope is found by identifying two points on the line and finding the $\frac{\text{change in } y}{\text{change in } x}$. The points $(0, 0)$ and $(5, 2)$ form the slope $\frac{2 - 0}{5 - 0} = \frac{2}{5}$.

12. **C.** $\frac{9x^2 y^3 z - 12xy^2 z^2}{3yz} = \frac{9x^2 y^3 z}{3yz} - \frac{12xy^2 z^2}{3yz} = 3x^2 y^2 - 4xyz$.

13. B.

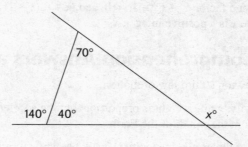

The angle adjacent to the 140° angle is 40° because supplementary angles add to 180°. The angles of a triangle add to 180°, so the angle adjacent to angle x is $180° - 70° - 40° = 70°$. Angle x and 70° are supplementary, so $x = 180° - 70° = 110°$.

14. C. Probability is $\dfrac{\text{number of expected outcomes}}{\text{number of possible outcomes}}$. Because one king was drawn and not replaced, three kings remain in the deck of 51 cards. So the probability of drawing another king is $\dfrac{3}{51} = \dfrac{1}{17}$.

15. A. There are 60 minutes in an hour, 24 hours in a day, and 7 days in a week. So,
$1 \text{ week} = \dfrac{7 \text{ days}}{1 \text{ week}} \times \dfrac{24 \text{ hours}}{1 \text{ day}} \times \dfrac{60 \text{ minutes}}{1 \text{ hour}} = 7 \times 24 \times 60 = 10{,}080$ minutes.

16. A. $\dfrac{1}{8} = \dfrac{1}{2^3} = 2^{-3}$, so $2b^{+3} = 2^{-3}$, and $b + 3 = -3$. Therefore, $b + 3 - 3 = -3 - 3 = -6$.

17. C. Angles in a triangle add to 180°. So, $3x + 4x + 5x = 180°$, and $12x = 180°$. Diving both sides by 12 results in $x = 15°$. The smallest angle is represented by $3x = 3(15°) = 45°$.

18. E. Subtraction can be changed to addition by changing the signs in the entire term being subtracted. $(2x^3 - 3x + 1) - (x^2 - 3x - 2) = (2x^3 - 3x + 1) + (-x^2 + 3x + 2)$. Combine like terms. $2x^3 - x^2 - 3x + 3x + 1 + 2 = 2x^3 - x^2 + 3$.

19. A. The area of a square is s^2 where s is a side of the square. If $s^2 = 400$, then $s = \sqrt{400} = 20$.

20. C. Translate this to a mathematical expression, and solve. $3x + 7 = 70$, so $3x + 7 - 7 = 70 - 7$, and $3x = 63$. Divide both sides by 3. Therefore, $x = 21$.

21. B. The volume of a cylinder is given by the formula $V = \pi r^2 h$, where r is the radius of the circular base, and h is the height. Because $h = r$, $V = \pi r^2 r = \pi r^3$.

22. B. Prime factors of 120 are $2 \times 2 \times 2 \times 3 \times 5$. Distinct factors are 2, 3, and 5. Therefore, there are 3 distinct prime factors.

23. C. Let p represent the unknown percent. Then, $p \times \dfrac{3}{4} = \dfrac{1}{8}$. Solve for p by multiplying by the reciprocal of $\dfrac{3}{4}$. $p \times \dfrac{3}{4} \times \dfrac{4}{3} = \dfrac{1}{8} \times \dfrac{4}{3} = \dfrac{4}{24} = \dfrac{1}{6}$. As a percent, $\dfrac{1}{6}$ is $16\dfrac{2}{3}\%$.

24. B. Divide the figure into a rectangle and triangle as shown.

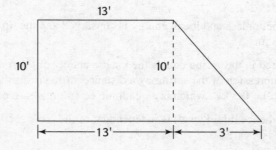

The area of the figure equals the area of the rectangle plus the area of the triangle. The area of the rectangle = length × width or $10 \times 13 = 130 \text{ ft}^2$; the area of the triangle = $\dfrac{1}{2}$ base × height or $\dfrac{1}{2} \times 3 \times 10 = 15 \text{ ft}^2$. The combined area is $130 \text{ ft}^2 + 15 \text{ ft}^2 = 145 \text{ ft}^2$.

25. A. Set the equation equal to 0 and factor. $x^2 + 6x - 16 = 0$, and $(x + 8)(x - 2) = 0$. Then, either $x + 8 = 0$, or $x - 2 = 0$, so $x = -8$, or $x = 2$. Because x is a positive integer, $x = 2$.

Part 7: Mechanical Comprehension Answers and Explanations

1. B. This is a consequence of Newton's third law of motion.

2. D. Mass is independent of gravity, while weight is proportional to the acceleration of gravity, which decreases with height or distance away from the center of the Earth.

3. D. Because only a component of the original velocity is available while turning, she must accelerate to maintain her original speed.

4. A. Each rotation of the second hand amounts to 2π radians divided by 60 seconds. Hence the angular velocity is $2\pi/60$ or .105 rad/s.

5. A. The speed is the magnitude of the velocity, so the minus sign indicates the direction of motion but has no effect on the speed.

6. D. Because acceleration is the time rate of change of the velocity,

7. C. The time required is $46.8/9.8 \approx 4.785$.

8. C. $(8 - 24 + 48)/160 = 0.2$m.

9. C. Because $\omega_f = \omega_i + \alpha t$, where ω_f and ω_i are the final and initial angular velocities, α is the angular acceleration and t is the time, and the torque $T = I\alpha$ where I is the moment of inertia, we obtain $\alpha = .625$ and $T = .625 \times 3 = 1.88$.

10. B. For equilibrium the clockwise and counter clockwise moments must be the same, that is, $F_i \times 80 = F_o \times 40$, or $F_i = 30$ N and $F_o/F_i = 60/30 = 2$.

11. A. The change in momentum ΔP equals the force F multiplied by the time increment t. Hence, we obtain $F = 40/12 = 3.33$ N.

12. C. The law of conservation of momentum requires that $80(3) + 0 = -120$ v, and hence v = -2 m/s.

13. A. Period $T = 2\pi[m/k]^{1/2}$, hence k = 40.

14. C. Because $1/2\ mv^2 = mgh$, m = 5, and h = 10, we obtain v = 14 m/s. Also, the downward force on the block is mg (sin θ), where θ is the slope angle of the inclined plane. Hence, the downward force = $5(9.8)(10/40) = 12.25$ N.

15. D. From Newton's second law, $F = m$ (mass) $\times a$ (acceleration). Because a equals the change in velocity (Δv) divided by the increment of time (Δt) and $F = \mu$ mg, it follows that $\Delta t = (\Delta v)/(\mu\ g) = [(108)(1,000/3,600) - 0]/[(.3)(9.81)] = 10.19$ s.

16. A. If the mass of the rod is assumed to be at the centroid, then the average drop height h = .5 L sin 60°. Also, the kinetic energy of the rod is .5 I ω^2, which equals the average potential energy of the rod on impact or mgh, where ω is the angular velocity in rad/sec. Solving for ω, we obtain 2.9146 rad/sec, which corresponds to a linear velocity v = L ω = 8.744 m/s.

17. C. Because the system is frictionless and ideal, energy is conserved and the tip of the rod returns to its original position at L sin 60° = 2.598 m.

18. A. The potential energy stored in the spring equals the kinetic energy of the rod upon impact plus the potential energy of the rod due to compression of the spring by a distance x (that is, further drop in height). Thus, $mgx/2 + (1/2)(1/3)(m)(L^2)(\omega^2) = 0.5\ kx^2$, which is a quadratic equation whose positive root is $x = .0954$ m.

19. E. The liquid pressure (and hence liquid level) is independent of the cross sectional area or shape of the container.

20. A. The most common is the spur gear drive system shown in Figure A.

Part 8: Electrical Maze Answers and Explanations

1. D.

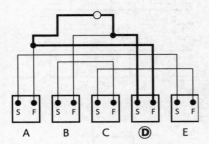

2. C.

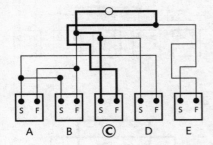

3. B.

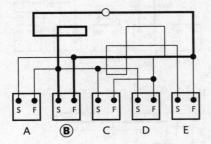

4. B.

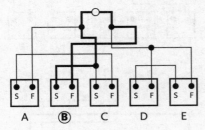

5. E.

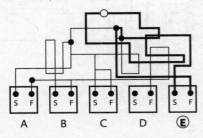

6. C.

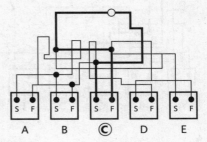

7. A.

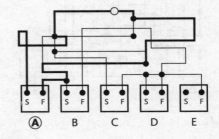

8. C.

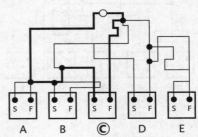

9. B.

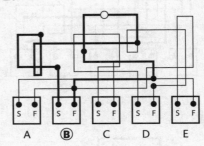

10. D.

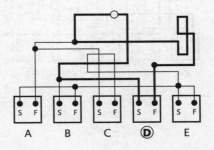

11. C.

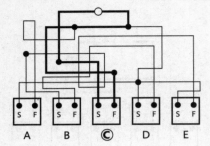

12. A.

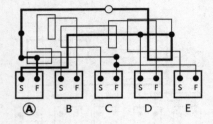

13. C.

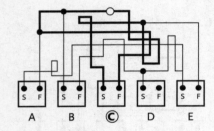

14. D.

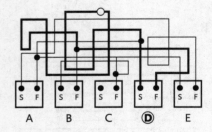

15. A.

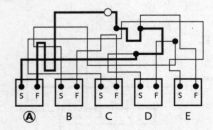

16. C.

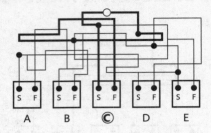

17. D.

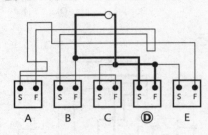

18. B.

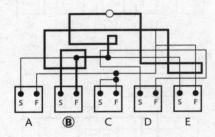

19. E.

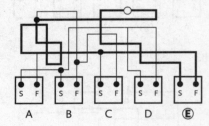

20. B.

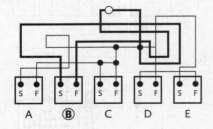

Part 9: Scale Reading Answers and Explanations

1. **B.** Arrow 1 points to the first small tick after the number 2. The scale is divided into sixteenths. Thus the answer is $2\frac{1}{16}$ or 2.0625. 2.06 would be the correct choice.

2. **C.** Arrow 2 points to a spot at $4\frac{1}{4}$, which is the same as 4.25.

3. **E.** The Voltmeter scale is divided by a zero in the middle. Numbers to the left are negative and to the right are positive. Arrow 3 is pointing to –1.

4. **D.** Arrow 4 points to a spot just beyond the tick between 2 and 4, which is 3. The only logical choice would be 3.3.

5. **C.** Arrow 5 points to a tick between 200 and 300 on the scale that runs from right to left, in increments of 2. Thus the number would be 240.

6. **B.** Arrow 6 also points to a scale running from top to bottom. The arrow is about $\frac{1}{2}$ of the way between 400 and 500. Therefore the correct answer is 450.

7. **D.** If you look at the scale you will see that the number 3 before the arrow is actually the number 30. The arrow points to the third tick — 33.

8. **B.** Arrow 8 is pointing to pi (π), which equals 3.14.

9. **C.** Arrow 9 points to the lower part of the scale and like question 7, the number 4 before the arrow is actually 40. The arrow points to the first major tick — 41.

10. **B.** The numbers run from right to left on the protractor. Arrow 10 points to 67.

11. **D.** Arrow 11 points to 118. All you have to do is start at 110 and count by ones, if you're unsure.

12. **D.** You have to read the directions of each scale on this meter, starting at the left. You count the lowest number on each, so that the first dial is 8, the second is 4, and so on.

13. **A.** Like the previous answer, start at the left and read the direction of the dials.

14. **E.** Each increment on the top scale represents one. Thus, arrow 14 points to $27\frac{1}{2}$ or 27.5.

15. **B.** You have to estimate where the arrow is pointing between 6 and 7. You should be able to see that the arrow is more than half way between 6 and 7, and the correct choice would then be 6.7.

16. **C.** The larger ticks between 1 and 2 represent .10, and between them, the smallest ticks are .02. Arrow 16 points to the first small tick, just after the fifth (.50) larger tick. Thus, the answer is 1.52.

17. **C.** The ticks represent .10, and arrow 17 points between .30 and .40, just after the number 2. Thus the answer should be 2 + .30 +.05 = 2.35.

18. **E.** Although the numbers are closer together as the numbers increase, the divisions are the same. Arrow 18 points to a tick between 4.7 and 4.8 = 4.75.

19. **A.** Each increment between 8 and 9 is .10. Arrow 19 points to 8.3.

20. **B.** On the scale, arrow 20 points to a spot closer to 100 miles. Based on the choices given in the question, you should be able to estimate the mileage at 120.

21. **C.** Arrow 21 clearly points midway between 400 and 500 kilometers. The answer can only be 450.

22. **D.** Each tick between numbers represents $\frac{1}{4}$ lb., or 4 oz. The arrow points to the third tick after 8, which is $\frac{3}{4}$ lb. or 12 oz. The answer is 8 lb., 12 oz.

23. **C.** The numbers on the scale run from right to left. Arrow 23 points to the seventh increment of .10 following the number 8. The answer is 8.7.

24. **D.** This scale runs from left to right and arrow 24 points to the first major tick (.10) after 2. The answer is then 2.10.

25. **C.** The larger ticks between 1 and 2 represent .10. The smaller ticks represent .02. Arrow 25 is between 1.14 and 1.16 and therefore the answer is 1.15.

26. **C.** Using the same scale as 25 above, the arrow is directly on the eighth larger tick. The answer is 1.8.

27. **D.** The larger ticks between 2 and 3 represent .10 and the smaller ticks represent .05. The line points between 2.7 and 2.8 = 2.75.

28. **D.** The ticks are the same as in 27. The line is directly on 4.6.

29. **B.** The line passes directly through 9.0.

30. **C.** The smallest ticks between numbers represent $\frac{1}{16}$ or .0625. The larger ticks represent $\frac{1}{8}$ or .125. Arrow 30 points to $1\frac{5}{16}$ or 1.313.

31. **B.** The arrow points to $1\frac{5}{8}$ or 1.625.

32. **C.** Arrow 32 points to $3\frac{15}{16}$ or 3.94. The closest choice is 3.95.

33. **C.** Arrow 33 points to the line at $5\frac{7}{16}$ or 5.4375. The closest choice is 5.45.

34. **D.** Despite the fact you're reading upside down, you should be able to see arrow 34 points to $3\frac{3}{4}$ or 3.75.

35. **E.** Each tick is .10. Arrow 35 points to 7.8.

36. **B.** Each increment between 1 and 2 along the bottom is $\frac{1}{8}$ of an inch (.125). Arrow 36 points to $1\frac{3}{8}$ or 1.375.

37. **E.** The scale runs clockwise and the arrow points to a spot about $\frac{3}{4}$ of the way between 7 and 8. $7\frac{3}{4} = 7.75$.

38. **D.** Arrow 38 clearly points halfway between 140 and 150, which is 145.

39. **A.** Arrow 39 points directly at the eighth tick between 90 and 100. The answer is therefore 98.

40. **D.** The dial runs clockwise and the arrow is pointing at about 52. Just remember that the scale is in mph, not km.

Part 10: Instrument Comprehension Answers and Explanations

1. **A.** Level flight, no banking, heading 180° south

2. **D.** Level flight, banking right, heading 180° south

3. **B.** Level flight, no banking, heading 225° southwest

4. **D.** Diving, banking right, heading 360° north

5. **A.** Climbing, banking right, heading 045° northeast

6. **B.** Diving, no banking, heading 090° east

7. **C.** Level flight, no banking, heading 270° west

8. **A.** Climbing, banking left, heading 270° west

9. **D.** Diving, banking right, heading 270° west

10. **B.** Diving, no banking, heading 180° south

11. **D.** Climbing, no banking, heading 090° east

12. **C.** Level flight, banking left, heading 180° south

13. **D.** Diving, banking right, heading 135° southeast

14. **B.** Diving, banking left, heading 270° west

15. A. Level flight, no banking, heading 045° northeast

16. C. Diving, banking left, heading 110° southeast

17. C. Climbing, banking left, heading 075° northeast

18. D. Climbing, no banking, heading 360° north

19. A. Level flight, banking right, heading 090° east

20. D. Climbing, banking right, heading 270° west

Part 11: Block Counting Answers and Explanations

1. D. 4. Block 1 touches one block on top, one behind, one below and one in front.

2. C. 3. Block 2 touches one block above and two below.

3. A. 5. Block 3 touches three blocks above, one below and one to the right.

4. B. 4. Block 4 touches one block to the left, and three above.

5. B. 2. Block 5 touches one block above and one to the right.

6. C. 6. Block 6 touches one block above, three below and two in the back.

7. A. 6. Block 7 touches one block above, one in back, one in front and three below.

8. E. 6. Block 8 touches three blocks above, one to the right and two to the left.

9. D. 5. Block 9 touches three blocks above and three below.

10. D. 4. Block 10 touches one block above, two to the side and one below.

11. B. 2. Block 11 touches two blocks below.

12. C. 3. Block 12 touches one block above, one to the right and one below.

13. D. 4. Block 13 touches one block in the back, one on the right and two on the left.

14. A. 1. Block 14 touches one block on the left.

15. B. 4. Block 15 touches two blocks on the right, one above and one on the left.

16. D. 6. Block 16 touches four blocks behind, one on the right and one below.

17. A. 4. Block 17 touches one block above, one to the right and two in front.

18. A. 2. Block 18 touches two blocks to the left.

19. C. 3. Block 19 touches two blocks below and one to the left.

20. E. 6. Block 20 touches four blocks behind, one above and one to the right.

Part 12: Table Reading Answers

1. E. $25	**8. C.** −3	**15. A.** $150,200	**22. C.** 73
2. C. $21	**9. A.** 5	**16. C.** 3	**23. B.** 82
3. C. $14	**10. B.** 6	**17. C.** 2	**24. E.** 272
4. A. $12	**11. D.** $175,300	**18. B.** 2	**25. D.** 178
5. D. $17	**12. B.** $105,950	**19. C.** 7	**26. A.** 136
6. D. 6	**13. C.** $132,200	**20. E.** 9	**27. B.** 20
7. B. 9	**14. C.** $159,200	**21. C.** 108	**28. C.** 112

29. B. 39	**32. D.** 11:11 a.m.	**35. A.** 2:17 a.m.	**38. C.** 6:22 a.m.
30. A. 59	**33. C.** 1:25 p.m.	**36. D.** 9:41 p.m.	**39. E.** 8:53 p.m.
31. B. 5:01 a.m.	**34. E.** 12:45 a.m.	**37. C.** 9:12 p.m.	**40. A.** 4:15 a.m.

Part 13: Aviation Information Answers and Explanations

1. **C.** The four aerodynamic forces on an aircraft are lift, weight, thrust and drag. Power is not one of these forces.

2. **A.** The longitudinal axis of an aircraft runs from the nose to the tail of an aircraft. It is one of the three axes around which an aircraft rotates. (The other two are the vertical and lateral axes.)

3. **E.** The ailerons control the aircraft around the longitudinal axis, which runs the length of the aircraft from the nose to the tail.

4. **C.** A flashing red light gun signal directed at an aircraft on the ground is an instruction to taxi clear of the active runway and await further instructions. This light gun signal should be followed with either a flashing white or green light to instruct the aircraft to taxi off the airport movement area.

5. **C.** Aircraft should squawk 7700 in case of an emergency. 7500 is the aircraft hijack code, and 7600 is used in case of communications failure. 1234 is not assigned a specific emergency code.

6. **B.** The manifold pressure gauge is an engine gauge. It displays the pressure of the fuel and air mixture as it enters the engine manifold, generally in inches of mercury. All the other gauges are flight instruments.

7. **C.** A closed runway is denoted by large yellow *X*s on the runway. They are usually painted on runways that are permanently closed or are on large lighted signs when the runway is closed only temporarily.

8. **B.** The displaced threshold can be used only for takeoffs and taxi operations. The pavement under displaced thresholds is not built to sustain the weight of landing aircraft.

9. **A.** V_x is defined as the best angle-of-climb speed for an aircraft. This speed gives an aircraft the best climb performance over a given distance across the ground.

10. **E.** The white arc on an airspeed indicator denotes the range in which full flaps can be deployed. Deploying flaps above this speed can cause damage to the flaps, while the bottom of the arc denotes the full-flap stall speed.

11. **D.** The angle of attack is created by the angle between the relative wind against the aircraft and the wing chord line of the aircraft. The pilot controls this by varying the pitch of the aircraft.

12. **A.** Form drag is a component of parasite drag. (Skin friction drag and interference drag are the other two components of parasite drag.)

13. **D.** Induced drag is greatest at low airspeeds and decreases as the velocity of the aircraft increases. Induced drag has an inverse relationship to parasite drag.

14. **B.** The attitude indicator, directional gyro and turn coordinator are all gyroscopic instruments. Generally, the attitude indicator and directional gyro are vacuum powered, while the turn coordinator is powered electrically.

15. **C.** The grooved flap is not a generally recognized type of flap. The plain, slotted, split and Fowler flap are all generally recognized flap types.

16. **A.** An aft center of gravity causes an aircraft to be less stable in pitch at all airspeeds. This is due to the reduced down force on the horizontal stabilizer as well as a less-effective elevator.

17. **E.** The center of pressure, sometimes referred to as the center of lift, is the point on the wing where the aerodynamic lifting force of the wing is concentrated.

18. **C.** Maneuvering speed is the maximum speed at which an aircraft can withstand abrupt control inputs and still maintain structural integrity. Moving at or below this speed ensures that the aircraft will stall before the airframe can be stressed beyond certified limits.

19. D. The critical angle of attack is the angle of attack at which the wing stalls no matter what the airspeed. This is a design limitation of a wing that causes airflow separation from the wing due to the angle at which the relative wind strikes the front of the wing.

20. D. An aircraft turns due to the horizontal component of lift. This is due to the component forces of lift coming out of a wing in a banked turn.

Part 14: Rotated Blocks Answers

There's not a lot of explaining that can be done on these questions. If you missed one, go back and look at the question again, now that you know the answer, and try to identify the answer in the question.

1. E.	**5.** C.	**9.** D.	**13.** B.
2. C.	**6.** D.	**10.** A.	**14.** D.
3. A.	**7.** B.	**11.** D.	**15.** C.
4. E.	**8.** C.	**12.** C.	

Part 15: General Science Answers and Explanations

1. C. The water is split, oxygen is given off as a waste product and hydrogen is combined with carbon dioxide to form sugars.

2. D. The definition of species is artificial, but conveys the idea that only members of the same species meet in the wild and mate to produce fertile offspring.

3. B. Celsius and centigrade are the same thing. Water boils at 100 degrees centigrade or 212 degrees Fahrenheit. To convert Fahrenheit to Celsius (centigrade), subtract 32 and divide by 1.8. To convert Celsius (centigrade) to Fahrenheit, multiply by 1.8 and add 32. Thus 98.6° Fahrenheit, which is normal body temperature, = 98.6 − 32 = 66.6 ÷ 1.8 = 37° C.

4. A. A liter is slightly larger than a quart; a liter is about 33 ounces.

5. B. Adding heat to water gives the molecules more kinetic energy, resulting in faster motion. It does not change the energy level of electrons or the number of electrons in the molecules.

6. D. A yard is slightly less than a meter. Because there are 1,000 millimeters in a meter, there should be slightly less in a yard.

7. A. The acceleration of objects in free fall is independent of mass, resulting in the same speed at the end of a fall. The momentum and energy are proportional to the mass.

8. B. Electrons are the only charges free to move in a metal.

9. B. DNA never leaves the nucleus.

10. C. Choice **A** is a true statement, but it does not explain rain, only the motion of the fronts. The motion of the warmer air over cooler air is due to differing densities, but it is the drop in temperature due to increased elevation and contact with cooler air (among other things) that causes the rain. As air cools, its capacity to hold water vapor decreases. As the saturation point is reached, excess water vapor condenses on particles in the air and eventually can fall as rain.

11. A. Mitosis is nuclear division, cytokinesis is cell division, meiosis is used for sex cell production, and symbiosis is where two species live in close association for long periods.

12. A. Oxygen slows down the rate of photosynthesis because most plants will use it in photorespiration, which is caused by the plant's enzymes picking up oxygen rather than carbon dioxide.

13. C. Both A and B are dominant to O and will be expressed.

14. B. The inclination of the Earth's axis causes seasons. The Earth is closer to the Sun during winter in the Northern Hemisphere. Though the Earth's orbital speed changes slightly over the course of the year, it is not the cause of seasonal variation.

15. B. Arteries carry blood away from the heart.

16. B. One should apply the equation $V_1M_1 = V_2M_2$, where V = volume and M = molarity. Solving $V_1 = V_2M_2/M_1$.

17. C. The transformation of a solid directly to a gas is called sublimation.

18. B. The amount of thermal expansion of a rod is proportional to its length for a given temperature change. Because the 75 cm rod is 50% longer, its expansion is 50% greater.

19. A. The only function for the stomach is protein digestion, while the small intestine digests all food types.

20. A. Friction between the tires and the road provide the centripetal force to keep the car in the turn.

Part 16: Hidden Figures Answers

1.

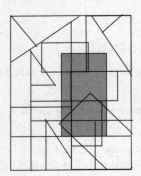

4.

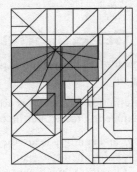

2.

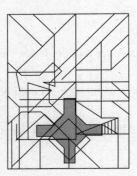

5.

3.

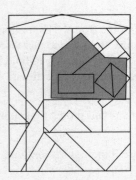

6.

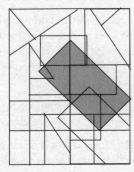

7.

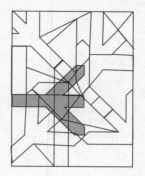

8.

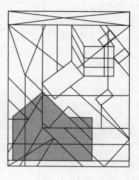

9.

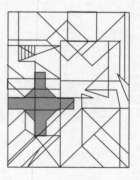

10.

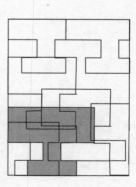

11.

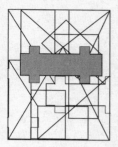

12.

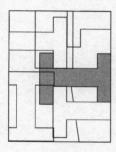

13.

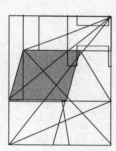

14.

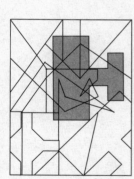

15.

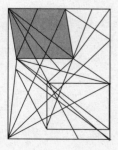

Answer Sheet for AFAST Practice Test

Subtest 1: Background Information

1 Ⓐ Ⓑ Ⓒ Ⓓ Ⓔ	11 Ⓐ Ⓑ Ⓒ Ⓓ Ⓔ	21 Ⓐ Ⓑ Ⓒ Ⓓ Ⓔ
2 Ⓐ Ⓑ Ⓒ Ⓓ Ⓔ	12 Ⓐ Ⓑ Ⓒ Ⓓ Ⓔ	22 Ⓐ Ⓑ Ⓒ Ⓓ Ⓔ
3 Ⓐ Ⓑ Ⓒ Ⓓ Ⓔ	13 Ⓐ Ⓑ Ⓒ Ⓓ Ⓔ	23 Ⓐ Ⓑ Ⓒ Ⓓ Ⓔ
4 Ⓐ Ⓑ Ⓒ Ⓓ Ⓔ	14 Ⓐ Ⓑ Ⓒ Ⓓ Ⓔ	24 Ⓐ Ⓑ Ⓒ Ⓓ Ⓔ
5 Ⓐ Ⓑ Ⓒ Ⓓ Ⓔ	15 Ⓐ Ⓑ Ⓒ Ⓓ Ⓔ	25 Ⓐ Ⓑ Ⓒ Ⓓ Ⓔ
6 Ⓐ Ⓑ Ⓒ Ⓓ Ⓔ	16 Ⓐ Ⓑ Ⓒ Ⓓ Ⓔ	
7 Ⓐ Ⓑ Ⓒ Ⓓ Ⓔ	17 Ⓐ Ⓑ Ⓒ Ⓓ Ⓔ	
8 Ⓐ Ⓑ Ⓒ Ⓓ Ⓔ	18 Ⓐ Ⓑ Ⓒ Ⓓ Ⓔ	
9 Ⓐ Ⓑ Ⓒ Ⓓ Ⓔ	19 Ⓐ Ⓑ Ⓒ Ⓓ Ⓔ	
10 Ⓐ Ⓑ Ⓒ Ⓓ Ⓔ	20 Ⓐ Ⓑ Ⓒ Ⓓ Ⓔ	

Subtest 2: Instrument Comprehension

1 Ⓐ Ⓑ Ⓒ Ⓓ Ⓔ	6 Ⓐ Ⓑ Ⓒ Ⓓ Ⓔ	11 Ⓐ Ⓑ Ⓒ Ⓓ Ⓔ
2 Ⓐ Ⓑ Ⓒ Ⓓ Ⓔ	7 Ⓐ Ⓑ Ⓒ Ⓓ Ⓔ	12 Ⓐ Ⓑ Ⓒ Ⓓ Ⓔ
3 Ⓐ Ⓑ Ⓒ Ⓓ Ⓔ	8 Ⓐ Ⓑ Ⓒ Ⓓ Ⓔ	13 Ⓐ Ⓑ Ⓒ Ⓓ Ⓔ
4 Ⓐ Ⓑ Ⓒ Ⓓ Ⓔ	9 Ⓐ Ⓑ Ⓒ Ⓓ Ⓔ	14 Ⓐ Ⓑ Ⓒ Ⓓ Ⓔ
5 Ⓐ Ⓑ Ⓒ Ⓓ Ⓔ	10 Ⓐ Ⓑ Ⓒ Ⓓ Ⓔ	15 Ⓐ Ⓑ Ⓒ Ⓓ Ⓔ

Subtest 3: Complex Movements

1 Ⓐ Ⓑ Ⓒ Ⓓ Ⓔ	11 Ⓐ Ⓑ Ⓒ Ⓓ Ⓔ	21 Ⓐ Ⓑ Ⓒ Ⓓ Ⓔ
2 Ⓐ Ⓑ Ⓒ Ⓓ Ⓔ	12 Ⓐ Ⓑ Ⓒ Ⓓ Ⓔ	22 Ⓐ Ⓑ Ⓒ Ⓓ Ⓔ
3 Ⓐ Ⓑ Ⓒ Ⓓ Ⓔ	13 Ⓐ Ⓑ Ⓒ Ⓓ Ⓔ	23 Ⓐ Ⓑ Ⓒ Ⓓ Ⓔ
4 Ⓐ Ⓑ Ⓒ Ⓓ Ⓔ	14 Ⓐ Ⓑ Ⓒ Ⓓ Ⓔ	24 Ⓐ Ⓑ Ⓒ Ⓓ Ⓔ
5 Ⓐ Ⓑ Ⓒ Ⓓ Ⓔ	15 Ⓐ Ⓑ Ⓒ Ⓓ Ⓔ	25 Ⓐ Ⓑ Ⓒ Ⓓ Ⓔ
6 Ⓐ Ⓑ Ⓒ Ⓓ Ⓔ	16 Ⓐ Ⓑ Ⓒ Ⓓ Ⓔ	26 Ⓐ Ⓑ Ⓒ Ⓓ Ⓔ
7 Ⓐ Ⓑ Ⓒ Ⓓ Ⓔ	17 Ⓐ Ⓑ Ⓒ Ⓓ Ⓔ	27 Ⓐ Ⓑ Ⓒ Ⓓ Ⓔ
8 Ⓐ Ⓑ Ⓒ Ⓓ Ⓔ	18 Ⓐ Ⓑ Ⓒ Ⓓ Ⓔ	28 Ⓐ Ⓑ Ⓒ Ⓓ Ⓔ
9 Ⓐ Ⓑ Ⓒ Ⓓ Ⓔ	19 Ⓐ Ⓑ Ⓒ Ⓓ Ⓔ	29 Ⓐ Ⓑ Ⓒ Ⓓ Ⓔ
10 Ⓐ Ⓑ Ⓒ Ⓓ Ⓔ	20 Ⓐ Ⓑ Ⓒ Ⓓ Ⓔ	30 Ⓐ Ⓑ Ⓒ Ⓓ Ⓔ

Subtest 4: Helicopter Knowledge

1 Ⓐ Ⓑ Ⓒ Ⓓ Ⓔ	6 Ⓐ Ⓑ Ⓒ Ⓓ Ⓔ	11 Ⓐ Ⓑ Ⓒ Ⓓ Ⓔ	16 Ⓐ Ⓑ Ⓒ Ⓓ Ⓔ
2 Ⓐ Ⓑ Ⓒ Ⓓ Ⓔ	7 Ⓐ Ⓑ Ⓒ Ⓓ Ⓔ	12 Ⓐ Ⓑ Ⓒ Ⓓ Ⓔ	17 Ⓐ Ⓑ Ⓒ Ⓓ Ⓔ
3 Ⓐ Ⓑ Ⓒ Ⓓ Ⓔ	8 Ⓐ Ⓑ Ⓒ Ⓓ Ⓔ	13 Ⓐ Ⓑ Ⓒ Ⓓ Ⓔ	18 Ⓐ Ⓑ Ⓒ Ⓓ Ⓔ
4 Ⓐ Ⓑ Ⓒ Ⓓ Ⓔ	9 Ⓐ Ⓑ Ⓒ Ⓓ Ⓔ	14 Ⓐ Ⓑ Ⓒ Ⓓ Ⓔ	19 Ⓐ Ⓑ Ⓒ Ⓓ Ⓔ
5 Ⓐ Ⓑ Ⓒ Ⓓ Ⓔ	10 Ⓐ Ⓑ Ⓒ Ⓓ Ⓔ	15 Ⓐ Ⓑ Ⓒ Ⓓ Ⓔ	20 Ⓐ Ⓑ Ⓒ Ⓓ Ⓔ

Subtest 5: Cyclic Orientation

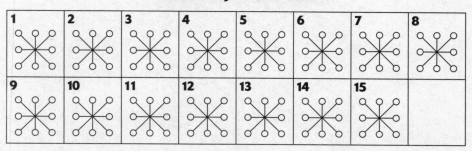

Subtest 6: Mechanical Functions

1 Ⓐ Ⓑ	3 Ⓐ Ⓑ	5 Ⓐ Ⓑ	7 Ⓐ Ⓑ	9 Ⓐ Ⓑ	11 Ⓐ Ⓑ	13 Ⓐ Ⓑ	15 Ⓐ Ⓑ	17 Ⓐ Ⓑ	19 Ⓐ Ⓑ
2 Ⓐ Ⓑ	4 Ⓐ Ⓑ	6 Ⓐ Ⓑ	8 Ⓐ Ⓑ	10 Ⓐ Ⓑ	12 Ⓐ Ⓑ	14 Ⓐ Ⓑ	16 Ⓐ Ⓑ	18 Ⓐ Ⓑ	20 Ⓐ Ⓑ

Subtest 7: Self-Description Form

Section A

1 Ⓐ Ⓑ Ⓒ Ⓓ Ⓔ	6 Ⓐ Ⓑ Ⓒ Ⓓ Ⓔ	11 Ⓐ Ⓑ Ⓒ Ⓓ Ⓔ	16 Ⓐ Ⓑ Ⓒ Ⓓ Ⓔ
2 Ⓐ Ⓑ Ⓒ Ⓓ Ⓔ	7 Ⓐ Ⓑ Ⓒ Ⓓ Ⓔ	12 Ⓐ Ⓑ Ⓒ Ⓓ Ⓔ	17 Ⓐ Ⓑ Ⓒ Ⓓ Ⓔ
3 Ⓐ Ⓑ Ⓒ Ⓓ Ⓔ	8 Ⓐ Ⓑ Ⓒ Ⓓ Ⓔ	13 Ⓐ Ⓑ Ⓒ Ⓓ Ⓔ	18 Ⓐ Ⓑ Ⓒ Ⓓ Ⓔ
4 Ⓐ Ⓑ Ⓒ Ⓓ Ⓔ	9 Ⓐ Ⓑ Ⓒ Ⓓ Ⓔ	14 Ⓐ Ⓑ Ⓒ Ⓓ Ⓔ	19 Ⓐ Ⓑ Ⓒ Ⓓ Ⓔ
5 Ⓐ Ⓑ Ⓒ Ⓓ Ⓔ	10 Ⓐ Ⓑ Ⓒ Ⓓ Ⓔ	15 Ⓐ Ⓑ Ⓒ Ⓓ Ⓔ	20 Ⓐ Ⓑ Ⓒ Ⓓ Ⓔ

Section B

1 Ⓨ Ⓝ	3 Ⓨ Ⓝ	5 Ⓨ Ⓝ	7 Ⓨ Ⓝ	9 Ⓨ Ⓝ	11 Ⓨ Ⓝ	13 Ⓨ Ⓝ	15 Ⓨ Ⓝ	17 Ⓨ Ⓝ	19 Ⓨ Ⓝ
2 Ⓨ Ⓝ	4 Ⓨ Ⓝ	6 Ⓨ Ⓝ	8 Ⓨ Ⓝ	10 Ⓨ Ⓝ	12 Ⓨ Ⓝ	14 Ⓨ Ⓝ	16 Ⓨ Ⓝ	18 Ⓨ Ⓝ	20 Ⓨ Ⓝ

Section C

1 Ⓛ Ⓓ	3 Ⓛ Ⓓ	5 Ⓛ Ⓓ	7 Ⓛ Ⓓ	9 Ⓛ Ⓓ	11 Ⓛ Ⓓ	13 Ⓛ Ⓓ	15 Ⓛ Ⓓ	17 Ⓛ Ⓓ	19 Ⓛ Ⓓ
2 Ⓛ Ⓓ	4 Ⓛ Ⓓ	6 Ⓛ Ⓓ	8 Ⓛ Ⓓ	10 Ⓛ Ⓓ	12 Ⓛ Ⓓ	14 Ⓛ Ⓓ	16 Ⓛ Ⓓ	18 Ⓛ Ⓓ	20 Ⓛ Ⓓ

Section D

1 Ⓐ Ⓑ	2 Ⓐ Ⓑ	3 Ⓐ Ⓑ	4 Ⓐ Ⓑ	5 Ⓐ Ⓑ	6 Ⓐ Ⓑ	7 Ⓐ Ⓑ	8 Ⓐ Ⓑ	9 Ⓐ Ⓑ

Section E

1 Ⓐ Ⓑ Ⓒ Ⓓ	2 Ⓐ Ⓑ Ⓒ Ⓓ	3 Ⓐ Ⓑ Ⓒ Ⓓ	4 Ⓐ Ⓑ Ⓒ Ⓓ	5 Ⓐ Ⓑ Ⓒ Ⓓ	6 Ⓐ Ⓑ Ⓒ Ⓓ

AFAST Practice Test

Subtest 1: Background Information

Time: 10 Minutes

25 Questions

Directions: The following questions pertain to your general background. If the question does not pertain to you, please skip it. Select the choice that best answers the question.

1. What is your age?

   A. under 20 years
   B. 20–25
   C. 26–30
   D. 31–40
   E. over 40

2. What has been your primary area of residence up until now?

   A. northeast United States
   B. southern United States
   C. central United States
   D. western United States
   E. outside the continental United States

If you were born in the United States, please skip questions 3 and 4, and go directly to question 5.

3. Where were you born?

   A. Australia
   B. Asia
   C. Africa
   D. South America
   E. Europe

4. If born outside the Unites States, how long have you been here?

   A. 0–5 years
   B. 5–10 years
   C. 10–15 years
   D. 15–20 years
   E. more than 20 years

5. What is your father's citizenship status?

   A. native-born American citizen
   B. naturalized American citizen
   C. legal resident
   D. not an American citizen
   E. deceased

6. What is your mother's citizenship status?

   A. native-born American citizen
   B. naturalized American citizen
   C. legal resident
   D. not an American citizen
   E. deceased

7. If your father served in the U.S. Armed Forces, in which branch did he serve?

   A. Army
   B. Air Force
   C. Navy
   D. Marines
   E. Coast Guard

8. How many years of schooling did your father complete?

   A. elementary
   B. some high school
   C. high school graduate
   D. some college
   E. college graduate

If neither parent served in the U.S. Armed Forces, please skip questions 9 and 10, and go directly to question 11.

9. If your mother served in the U.S. Armed Forces, in which branch did she serve?

- **A.** Army
- **B.** Air Force
- **C.** Navy
- **D.** Marines
- **E.** Coast Guard

10. How many years of schooling did your mother complete?

- **A.** elementary
- **B.** some high school
- **C.** high school graduate
- **D.** some college
- **E.** college graduate

11. How many years of schooling did you complete?

- **A.** high school
- **B.** some college
- **C.** college graduate
- **D.** some graduate school
- **E.** graduate degree

If you answered (A) to question 11 OR if none of your siblings served in the U.S. Armed Forces, please skip questions 12–13, and go directly to question 14.

12. What type of high school did you attend?

- **A.** public academic
- **B.** public vocational
- **C.** private parochial
- **D.** private nonparochial
- **E.** military

13. How many siblings (sisters and brothers) do you have in your family?

- **A.** 0
- **B.** 1
- **C.** 2
- **D.** 3
- **E.** 4 or more

14. If you had a job during high school, approximately how many hours a week did you work?

- **A.** less than 5
- **B.** 6–10
- **C.** 11–15
- **D.** 16–20
- **E.** more than 20

15. If you had a job during college, approximately how many hours a week did you work?

- **A.** less than 5
- **B.** 6–10
- **C.** 11–15
- **D.** 16–20
- **E.** more than 20

16. Which type of school did you attend for the majority of your academic experience?

- **A.** Liberal arts or sciences public school
- **B.** Vocational or technical public school
- **C.** Religious private school
- **D.** Non-sectarian private school
- **E.** Military school

17. What was your age at the time of your high school graduation?

- **A.** 16 years or less
- **B.** 17
- **C.** 18
- **D.** 19
- **E.** 20 or more years

18. How many years of college or other post-secondary education have you completed?

- **A.** Less than one year
- **B.** 1 year
- **C.** 2 years
- **D.** 3 years
- **E.** 4 or more years

If you did not graduate from college, please skip questions 19–21, and go directly to question 22.

19. How old were you when you completed your college degree?

   A. under 20 years old
   B. 21–22 years old
   C. 23–25 years old
   D. 26–29 years old
   E. over 30 years old

20. In what academic area did you major?

   A. Natural or physical sciences (such as biology or math)
   B. Social sciences (such as economics or psychology)
   C. Language arts (such as communications or Russian)
   D. Fine or performing arts (such as photography or dance)
   E. Other

21. What was your standing in your college graduating class?

   A. Top 2 percent
   B. Honor graduate
   C. Top third
   D. Middle third
   E. Bottom third

22. If you took the Armed Services Vocational Aptitude Battery (ASVAB), in which of the following categories did your score fall?

   A. Category I: 93rd–100th percentile range
   B. Category II: 65th–92nd percentile range
   C. Category III: 31st–64th percentile range
   D. Category IV: 10th–30th percentile range
   E. Category V: 9th percentile and below

If you did not work while attending school, please skip questions 23–25.

23. If you were employed ONLY on school days during the last four years of your schooling, how many hours did you work per week?

   A. 5 or less
   B. 6–10
   C. 11–15
   D. 16–19
   E. 20 or more

24. If you were employed on weekends ONLY or on school days AND weekends, during the last four years of your schooling, how many hours did you work per week?

   A. 5 or less
   B. 6–10
   C. 11–15
   D. 16–19
   E. 20 or more

25. What type of employment did you engage in during your last four years of schooling?

   A. Academic or clerical (research, filing, computing, and so on)
   B. Food services (waiting tables, cooking, washing dishes, and so on)
   C. Sales (telemarketing, retail sales, wholesale buying, and so on)
   D. Technical, trades, or construction (welding, plumbing, painting, and so on)
   E. Other

AFAST Practice Test

DON'T GO ON UNTIL TOLD TO DO SO. STOP

Subtest 2: Instrument Comprehension

Time: 5 Minutes

15 Questions

Directions: In this subtest, you have to determine the position of an airplane in flight by looking at two dials, one showing the artificial horizon, the other showing the compass heading. From these you determine the amount of climb or dive, the degree of bank to left or right, and the heading. Five airplane silhouettes are shown from which you choose the one that most nearly represents the position indication on the dials. **A chart of aircraft flying positions can be found on page 145.**

1.

A B C D E

2.

A B C D E

3.

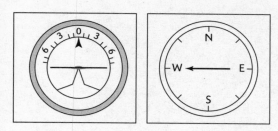

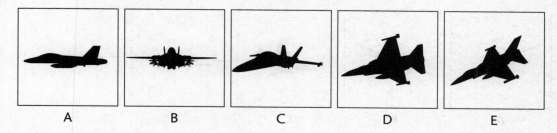

A B C D E

4.

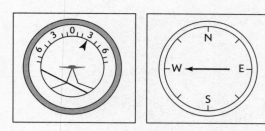

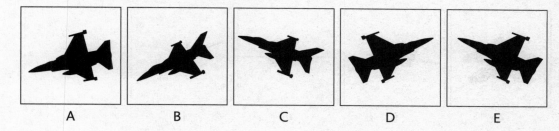

A B C D E

5.

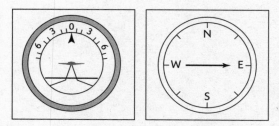

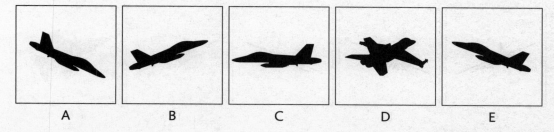

A B C D E

GO ON TO THE NEXT PAGE

6.

A B C D E

7.

A B C D E

8.

A B C D E

9.

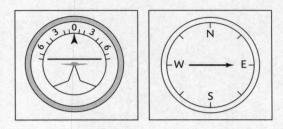

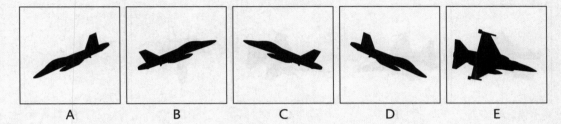

A	B	C	D	E

10.

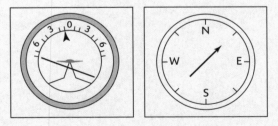

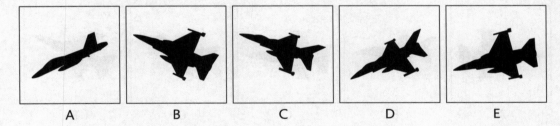

A	B	C	D	E

11.

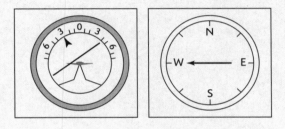

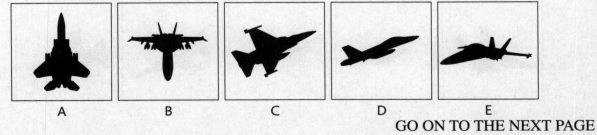

A	B	C	D	E

GO ON TO THE NEXT PAGE

12.

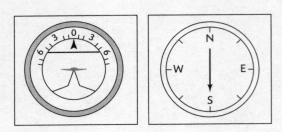

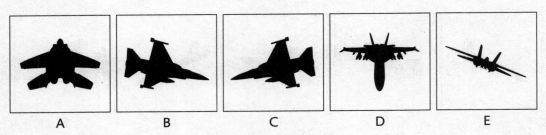

A   B   C   D   E

13.

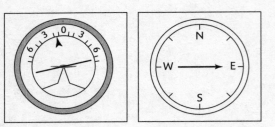

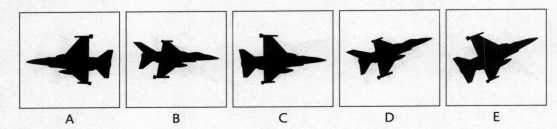

A   B   C   D   E

14.

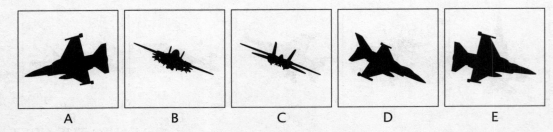

A   B   C   D   E

15.

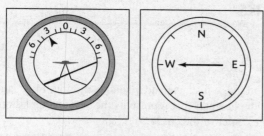

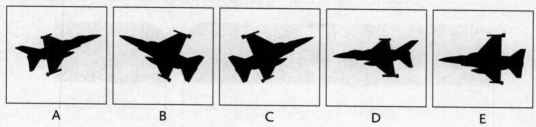

A   B   C   D   E

DON'T GO ON UNTIL TOLD TO DO SO.

Subtest 3: Complex Movements

Time: 5 Minutes

30 Questions

Directions: The questions in this subtest measure your ability to judge distance and visualize motion. Five pairs of symbols are given representing direction and distance. Choose the one pair that represents the amount, and direction of movement needed to move a dot from outside the circle into the center of the circle.

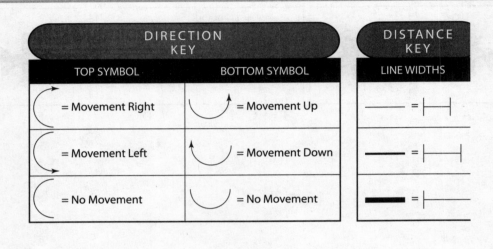

1.

2.

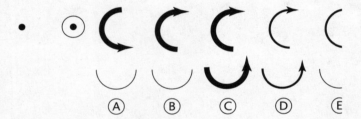

3.

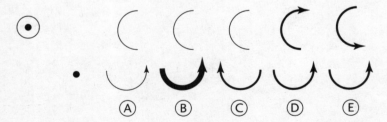

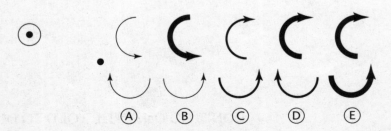

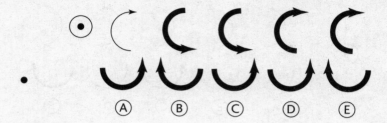
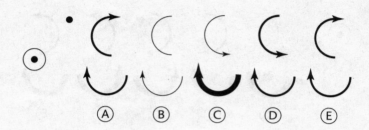
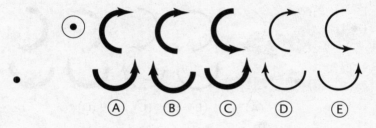
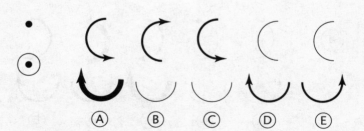
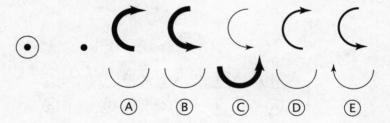
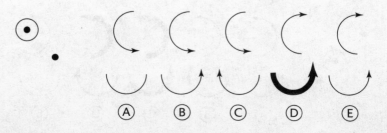

4.

5.

6.

7.

8.

9.

GO ON TO THE
NEXT PAGE

10.

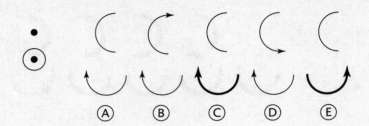

11.

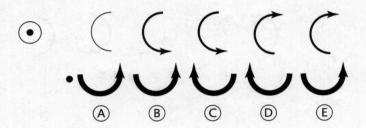

12.

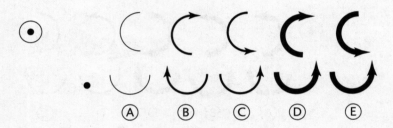

13.

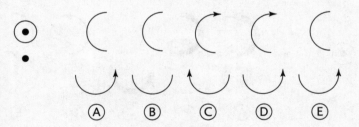

14.

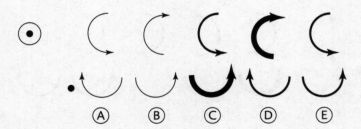

15.

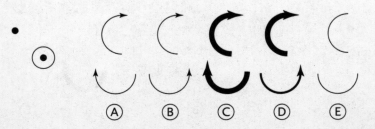

16.

17.

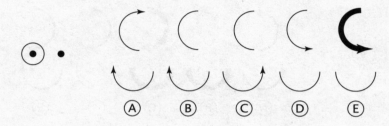

18.

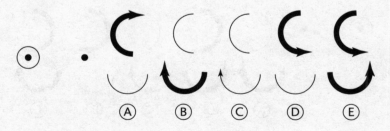

19.

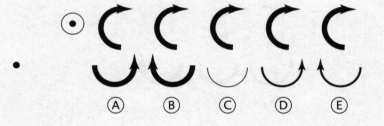

20.

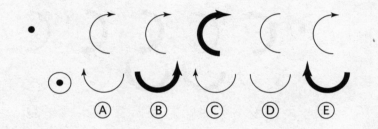

21.

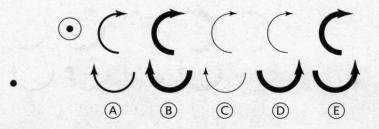

GO ON TO THE
NEXT PAGE

289

22.

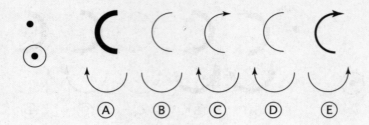

23.

24.

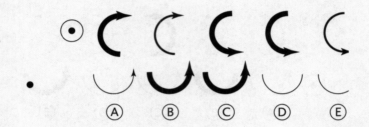

25.

26.

27.

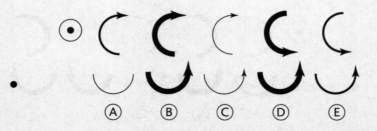

28.

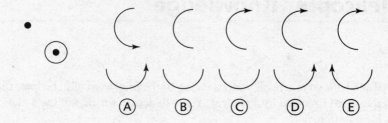

29.

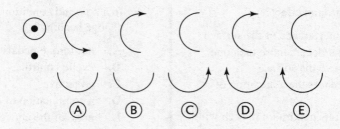

30.

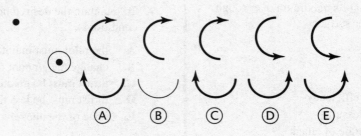

DON'T GO ON UNTIL TOLD TO DO SO.

Subtest 4: Helicopter Knowledge

Time: 10 Minutes

20 Questions

Directions: This subtest deals with your general understanding of the principles of helicopter flight. It contains 20 incomplete statements or questions followed by 5 choices. You will decide which 1 of the 5 choices BEST completes the statement or answers the question.

1. Which best describes ground effect?

    A. the result of the interference of the surface

    B. a phenomenon that occurs more than one rotor diameter above the surface

    C. an effect that increases the generation of blade tip vortices

    D. an effect that is at its maximum in high wind conditions

    E. an effect that is at its maximum over rough terrain and water surfaces

2. A stall is the result of

    A. decreased RPM

    B. decreased rotor efficiency

    C. low manifold pressure

    D. exceeding the angle of attack

    E. excessive weight

3. What is created by the motion of an airfoil through the air?

    A. lift

    B. drag

    C. thrust

    D. relative wind

    E. stability

4. Translational lift is the result of

    A. ground effect

    B. increased rotor efficiency

    C. drift

    D. ground speed

    E. drag

5. If RPM is low and manifold pressure is high, what initial corrective action should be taken?

    A. Decrease the throttle.

    B. Increase the throttle.

    C. Lower the collective pitch.

    D. Raise the collective pitch.

    E. Apply left antitorque pedal pressure.

6. In a no-wind condition, which control is used to change heading?

    A. antitorque pedals

    B. cyclic control

    C. collective

    D. a combination of cyclic and antitorque pedals

    E. none of the above

7. To maintain the desired hovering altitude (no-wind conditions),

    A. the pilot must maintain constant power

    B. change the amount of main rotor thrust

    C. thrust must be greater than actual weight

    D. thrust must be less than actual weight

    E. none of the above

8. Lift is the upward force created by

    A. airflow as it passes around an airfoil

    B. blade flapping

    C. torque

    D. thrust

    E. rotor articulation

9. Ground effect is most likely to result in which problem?

    A. inability to get airborne on a smooth surface

    B. settling to the surface abruptly during landing

    C. becoming airborne before reaching appropriate takeoff speed

    D. the creation of wake turbulence

    E. an increased amount of drag

10. When departing behind a heavy aircraft, the pilot should avoid wake turbulence by maneuvering the helicopter

    A. below and downwind from the heavy aircraft

    B. above and upwind from the heavy aircraft

    C. below and upwind from the heavy aircraft

    D. above and downwind from the heavy aircraft

    E. as close to the flight path of the heavy aircraft as possible

11. A helicopter that is improperly loaded with a CG forward of forward limits will

   A. have a tail low attitude

   B. need excessive forward displacement of the cyclic to maintain a hover

   C. have a nose low attitude

   D. need excessive rearward displacement of the cyclic to maintain a hover

   E. both C and D

12. Translational lift is the result of

   A. density altitude

   B. weight

   C. decreased rotor efficiency

   D. both airspeed and groundspeed

   E. airspeed

13. Lift differential that exists between the advancing main rotor blade and the retreating rotor blade is known as

   A. hunting tendency

   B. transverse flow effect

   C. geometric unbalance

   D. dissymmetry of lift

   E. Coriolis effect

14. During a hover, a helicopter tends to drift to the right. To compensate for this, some helicopters'

   A. tail rotor is tilted to the left

   B. tail rotor is tilted to the right

   C. rotor mast is rigged to the left side

   D. are typically loaded with an aft CG

   E. both a and c

15. The upward bending of the rotor blades resulting from the combination of lift and centrifugal forces is known as

   A. hunting

   B. coning

   C. blade slapping

   D. inertia

   E. translating tendency

16. The tail rotor produces thrust and is variable through the use of

   A. cyclic control

   B. induced drag

   C. cross wind

   D. antitorque pedals

   E. collective

17. Which action would be appropriate for confined area operations?

   A. A vertical take off must be made.

   B. A steep angle of descent should be used to land.

   C. Plan the flight path over an area suitable for a forced landing.

   D. A running takeoff is required.

   E. Both A and D.

18. What action should the pilot take if engine failure occurs at altitude?

   A. Open the throttle.

   B. Raise the collective pitch.

   C. Reduce cyclic back pressure.

   D. Lower the collective pitch control to maintain rotor rpm.

   E. Aft cyclic and raise the collective pitch.

19. To initiate a quick stop,

   A. forward cyclic and lower the collective pitch

   B. aft cyclic, and simultaneously lower the collective pitch

   C. aft cyclic, and then slowly lower the collective pitch

   D. aft cyclic, and raise the collective pitch

   E. rapid aft cyclic, and slightly lower the collective pitch

20. The primary purpose of the tail rotor system is to

   A. assist in making coordinated turns

   B. maintain heading during forward flight

   C. deflect adverse yaw

   D. counteract the torque effect of the main rotor

   E. allow coordinated flight

GO ON TO THE NEXT PAGE

AFAST Practice Test

Subtest 5: Cyclic Orientation

Time: 5 Minutes

15 Questions

Directions: This is a test of your ability to recognize simple changes in helicopter position and to indicate the corresponding cyclic (stick) movement. You will look at a series of three sequential pictures that represents the pilot's view out a helicopter windshield. The three pictures change from top to bottom, showing a view from an aircraft in a climb, dive, bank to the left or right, or a combination of these maneuvers. You will determine which position the cyclic would be in to perform the maneuver indicated by the picture.

Instructions: *You are the pilot of a helicopter with a constant power setting going through a maneuver as shown in the pictures that follow. The helicopter can be climbing, diving, banking (turning) to the right or left, or in a climbing or diving bank. Look at the pictures from TOP to BOTTOM and decide what maneuver the helicopter is performing. Next, decide which position the cyclic (stick) would be in to perform the maneuver.*

For items in this test, the cyclic is moved as follows. FOR BANKS: To bank left, move the cyclic stick to the left. To bank right, move the cyclic stick to the right. FOR CLIMBS AND DIVES: To dive, push the cyclic stick forward. To climb, pull the cyclic stick back.

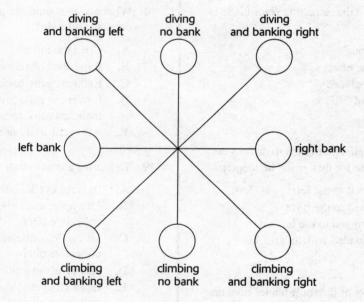

1.

2.

GO ON TO THE NEXT PAGE

3. **4.**

5.

6.

GO ON TO THE NEXT PAGE

7.

8.

9.

10.

GO ON TO THE NEXT PAGE

11.

12.

13.

14.

GO ON TO THE NEXT PAGE

15.

DON'T GO ON UNTIL TOLD TO DO SO.

Subtest 6: Mechanical Functions

Time: 10 Minutes

20 Questions

Directions: This subtest determines your understanding of general mechanical principles. In this part, pictures are shown, and questions are asked on the mechanical principles illustrated. There are 20 questions in this test and you have 10 minutes in which to answer them.

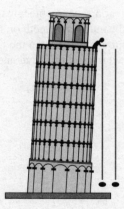

1. A stone is tied to the end of a string and swings in a circular motion. If the speed of the stone is tripled, the centripetal force of the stone will become

   A. 3 times as great
   B. 9 times as great

2. Two objects with different weights are dropped at the same moment from the top of the Leaning Tower of Pisa.

   A. Both objects hit the ground at the same time.
   B. The heavier object hits the ground first.

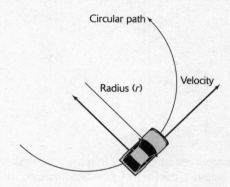

3. For a car moving around a circular track at a constant speed, the acceleration is

   A. away from the center of the circle
   B. toward the center of the circle

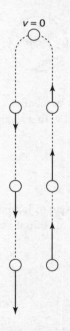

4. A ball thrown vertically upward has an initial potential energy of 100 J and an initial kinetic energy of 700 J. At the top of the trajectory, its energy in joules is

   A. 100
   B. 800

GO ON TO THE NEXT PAGE

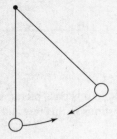

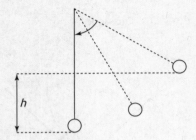

5. A simple pendulum has a frequency of oscillation f. To double f, the length of the pendulum should be

  A.   increased by a factor of 2
  B.   decreased by a factor of 4

6. The velocity of a baseball 4 s after it is thrown vertically upward with a speed of 32.1 m/s is _____ m/s.

  A.   −7.2
  B.   14.6

7. For a football player to jump vertically upward a distance of .8 m, his initial velocity must be _____ m/s.

  A.   3.92
  B.   4.27

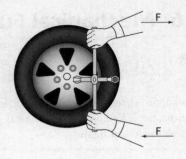

8. The torque required to loosen a nut that holds a wheel on a car has a magnitude of 56 N.m. If a .35 m lug wrench is used to loosen the nut when the angle of the wrench is 56 degrees, the force that must be exerted at the end of the wrench is

  A.   143 N
  B.   286 N

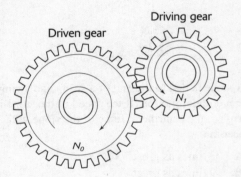

9. In the spur gear arrangement shown in the figure, the ratio of the number of teeth on the output gear (N_o) to the number of teeth on the input gear (N_i) is 2. The speed ratio of the input and output gears is

  A.   1/2
  B.   2

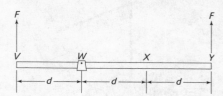

13. A massless horizontal rigid rod of length 3d is pivoted at a fixed point W, and two forces each of magnitude F are applied vertically upward as shown in the figure. To achieve rod equilibrium, a third vertical force of magnitude F is to be applied at which of the labeled points?

A. V or X only
B. X or Y only

10. The gain in kinetic energy if a 400 kg satellite moves from a distance of 3×10^6 m above the surface of the Earth to a point 1.5×10^6 m above the surface is _____ J. The mass of the Earth is 5.98×10^{24} kg and the radius of the Earth is 6.37×10^6 m.

A. 1.7×10^9
B. 3.25×10^9

11. The speed of a baseball with a momentum of 5.8 kg m/s and a mass of .145 kg is _____ m/s.

A. 1.19
B. 40

14. Two balls of different masses are thrown vertically up from the same point and at the same time. The two balls will experience the same change in

A. velocity
B. kinetic energy

12. A 24 kg skier moving with a velocity of .6 m/s collides with and sticks to a 26 kg skier moving with a velocity of .2 m/s. The final velocity v of the two skiers is _____ m/s.

A. .392
B. .184

15. An arrow is shot vertically upward. As the arrow approaches its maximum altitude, the amount of work done against gravity

A. increases and then decreases
B. remains the same

GO ON TO THE NEXT PAGE

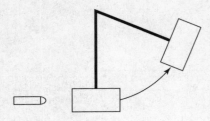

16. A 15 g bullet is fired into a 3 kg block of plastic suspended from the ceiling by a string. As a result of the impact, the block with the bullet swings 12 cm above its original level. The velocity of the bullet as it strikes the block is nearly

A. 308 m/s

B. 3,080 m/s

17. An astronaut lands on Jupiter. Which of the following is true?

A. Mass increases, but weight decreases.

B. Mass remains the same, but weight increases.

18. Ignoring air resistance, the acceleration of a person sliding down an inclined plane with a constant coefficient of kinetic friction

A. is constant

B. increases with time

19. A bicycle collides head on with a large car moving at the same speed. Following the collision, the bicycle and the car stick together. Which of the two had the larger change in momentum?

A. The bicycle.

B. The changes were equal.

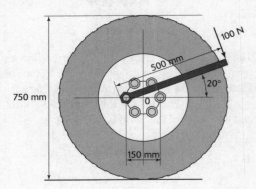

20. A force of 100 N is applied to the far end of the wrench to tighten a bolt that holds the wheel to the axle. For the position of the wrench shown in the figure, the moment produced by this force about the center point O is approximately

A. 4.32 N.m.

B. 43.2 N.m.

DON'T GO ON UNTIL TOLD TO DO SO.

Subtest 7: Self-Description

Time: 25 Minutes

75 Questions

Section A

Directions: The following questions consist of sets of five descriptive words from which you are asked to select the choice that either MOST accurately describes you or LEAST describes you. Keep in mind that there are no "correct" answers.

1. Which of the following MOST accurately describes you?

   A. happy
   B. joyful
   C. smiling
   D. content
   E. disappointed

2. Which of the following LEAST accurately describes you?

   A. happy
   B. joyful
   C. smiling
   D. content
   E. disappointed

3. Which of the following MOST accurately describes you?

   A. smart
   B. cagey
   C. sincere
   D. competent
   E. excitable

4. Which of the following LEAST accurately describes you?

   A. smart
   B. cagey
   C. sincere
   D. competent
   E. excitable

5. Which of the following MOST accurately describes you?

   A. reliable
   B. entrepreneurial
   C. facile
   D. trusting
   E. carefree

6. Which of the following LEAST accurately describes you?

   A. reliable
   B. entrepreneurial
   C. facile
   D. trusting
   E. carefree

7. Which of the following MOST accurately describes you?

   A. slow
   B. careful
   C. patient
   D. competent
   E. skilled

8. Which of the following LEAST accurately describes you?

   A. slow
   B. careful
   C. patient
   D. competent
   E. skilled

GO ON TO THE NEXT PAGE

AFAST Practice Test

9. Which of the following MOST accurately describes you?

   A. creative
   B. gifted
   C. quick
   D. skilled
   E. solid

10. Which of the following LEAST accurately describes you?

    A. creative
    B. gifted
    C. quick
    D. skilled
    E. solid

11. Which of the following MOST accurately describes you?

    A. reserved
    B. cautious
    C. outgoing
    D. friendly
    E. pleasant

12. Which of the following LEAST accurately describes you?

    A. reserved
    B. cautious
    C. outgoing
    D. friendly
    E. pleasant

13. Which of the following MOST accurately describes you?

    A. dependable
    B. open
    C. agreeable
    D. private
    E. solid

14. Which of the following LEAST accurately describes you?

    A. dependable
    B. open
    C. agreeable
    D. private
    E. solid

15. Which of the following MOST accurately describes you?

    A. careful
    B. thrifty
    C. extravagant
    D. needy
    E. satisfied

16. Which of the following LEAST accurately describes you?

    A. careful
    B. thrifty
    C. extravagant
    D. needy
    E. satisfied

17. Which of the following MOST accurately describes you?

    A. tolerant
    B. impatient
    C. touchy
    D. judgmental
    E. aloof

18. Which of the following LEAST accurately describes you?

    A. tolerant
    B. impatient
    C. touchy
    D. judgmental
    E. aloof

19. Which of the following MOST accurately describes you?

    A. attractive
    B. striking
    C. nice looking
    D. unattractive
    E. ordinary

20. Which of the following LEAST accurately describes you?

    A. attractive
    B. striking
    C. nice looking
    D. unattractive
    E. ordinary

Section B

Directions: The following items consist of questions that are to be answered either Yes or No. Again, there are no "correct" answers. Circle the choice that seems the most suitable.

1. Do you usually like to meet new people?

   Y. Yes.
   N. No.

2. Are you usually able to control your temper?

   Y. Yes.
   N. No.

3. Do you speak slowly?

   Y. Yes.
   N. No.

4. Do you regret some of the things you've done in the past?

   Y. Yes.
   N. No.

5. Do you normally rush through chores?

   Y. Yes.
   N. No.

6. Did you enjoy school?

   Y. Yes.
   N. No.

7. Have you ever flown in a jet?

   Y. Yes.
   N. No.

8. Did you every play sports?

   Y. Yes.
   N. No.

9. Have you ever tried hang gliding?

   Y. Yes.
   N. No.

10. Do you have hobbies?

    Y. Yes.
    N. No.

11. Do you usually find yourself under pressure?

    Y. Yes.
    N. No.

12. Have you ever flown in a helicopter?

    Y. Yes.
    N. No.

13. Have you ever been depressed?

    Y. Yes.
    N. No.

14. Are you often lonely?

    Y. Yes.
    N. No.

15. Do you enjoy watching movies?

    Y. Yes.
    N. No.

16. Do you enjoy reading books?

    Y. Yes.
    N. No.

17. Do you consider yourself in good physical condition?

    Y. Yes.
    N. No.

18. Are you confident when starting a project?

    Y. Yes.
    N. No.

19. Do you enjoy mathematics?

    Y. Yes.
    N. No.

20. Do you normally solicit opinions from others before beginning a project?

    Y. Yes.
    N. No.

GO ON TO THE NEXT PAGE

Section C

Directions: The following is a listing of different occupations. You might like some of them and not like others. For each of those that you would consider for a career, choose LIKE. If you would dislike the occupation for a career, choose DISLIKE.

1. Police officer

   L. like
   D. dislike

2. School teacher

   L. like
   D. dislike

3. Builder

   L. like
   D. dislike

4. Electrician

   L. like
   D. dislike

5. Lawyer

   L. like
   D. dislike

6. Physician

   L. like
   D. dislike

7. Musician

   L. like
   D. dislike

8. Clothing designer

   L. like
   D. dislike

9. Sales person

   L. like
   D. dislike

10. Pilot

    L. like
    D. dislike

11. Auto mechanic

    L. like
    D. dislike

12. Meteorologist

    L. like
    D. dislike

13. Social worker

    L. like
    D. dislike

14. Journalist

    L. like
    D. dislike

15. Computer technician

    L. like
    D. dislike

16. Carpenter

    L. like
    D. dislike

17. Software designer

    L. like
    D. dislike

18. Politician

    L. like
    D. dislike

19. Scientist

    L. like
    D. dislike

20. Accountant

    L. like
    D. dislike

Section D

Directions: The following questions consist of pairs of statements that describe personal characteristics and preferences. Select the statement that best describes you.

1. **A.** I like to work on projects by myself.
   B. I prefer working in groups.

2. **A.** I look forward to meeting new people.
   B. I prefer my own group of friends.

3. **A.** I think life is fun.
   B. I think life is often dreary.

4. **A.** I enjoy reading books and magazines.
   B. I prefer watching television instead of reading.

5. **A.** Life always offers me new challenges.
   B. Life is fairly routine for me.

6. **A.** I would like to earn a lot of money.
   B. I would like a job that I enjoy.

7. **A.** I am not worried about taking physical risks.
   B. I prefer a sedate lifestyle.

8. **A.** I believe most people enjoy my company.
   B. I believe that I sometimes offend people.

9. **A.** I like working on long-term projects.
   B. I like working on several short-term projects.

Section E

Directions: The following questions consist of a statement that might or might not be controversial. Select the choice that best describes how you feel about that statement—whether you agree or disagree.

1. All it takes is to be diligent at a job, and you will succeed.
   A. strongly agree
   B. tend to agree
   C. tend to disagree
   D. strongly disagree

2. Open communication is the key to a successful relationship.
   A. strongly agree
   B. tend to agree
   C. tend to disagree
   D. strongly disagree

3. Life should be fun.
   A. strongly agree
   B. tend to agree
   C. tend to disagree
   D. strongly disagree

4. Politics is all about who you know.
   A. strongly agree
   B. tend to agree
   C. tend to disagree
   D. strongly disagree

5. The United States should be the "policeman to the world."
   A. strongly agree
   B. tend to agree
   C. tend to disagree
   D. strongly disagree

6. Without SUVs, this country would have far less pollution.
   A. strongly agree
   B. tend to agree
   C. tend to disagree
   D. strongly disagree

AFAST Answer Key

Subtest 1: Background Information

There are no correct or incorrect answers for this test.

Subtest 2: Instrument Comprehension

1. E	**5.** B	**9.** D	**13.** B
2. B	**6.** B	**10.** E	**14.** E
3. A	**7.** C	**11.** C	**15.** B
4. C	**8.** E	**12.** D	

Subtest 3: Complex Movements

1. E	**9.** B	**17.** D	**25.** D
2. E	**10.** A	**18.** E	**26.** D
3. B	**11.** B	**19.** D	**27.** B
4. D	**12.** E	**20.** D	**28.** E
5. D	**13.** E	**21.** E	**29.** C
6. A	**14.** C	**22.** D	**30.** A
7. B	**15.** A	**23.** D	
8. D	**16.** B	**24.** B	

Subtest 4: Helicopter Knowledge

1. A	**6.** B	**11.** E	**16.** D
2. D	**7.** B	**12.** E	**17.** C
3. D	**8.** A	**13.** D	**18.** D
4. B	**9.** C	**14.** C	**19.** B
5. C	**10.** B	**15.** B	**20.** D

Subtest 5: Cyclic Orientation

1.

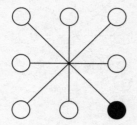

2.

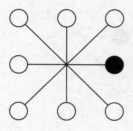

3.

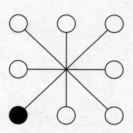

4.

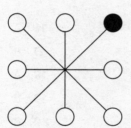

5.

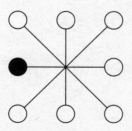

6.

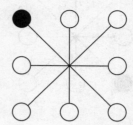

7.

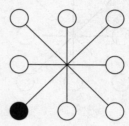

8.

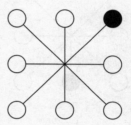

9.

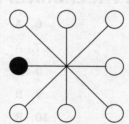

10.

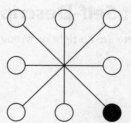

11.

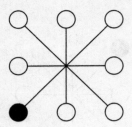

12.

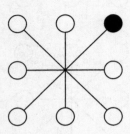

13.

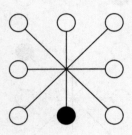

14.

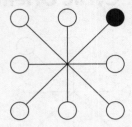

15.

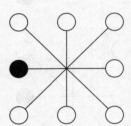

Subtest 6: Mechanical Functions

1. B	**6.** A	**11.** B	**16.** A
2. A	**7.** A	**12.** A	**17.** B
3. B	**8.** B	**13.** A	**18.** A
4. B	**9.** B	**14.** A	**19.** B
5. B	**10.** B	**15.** B	**20.** B

Subtest 7: Self-Description

In this subtest there are no right or wrong answers.

AFAST Answers and Explanations

Subtest 1: Background Information Answers

There are no correct or incorrect answers for this test.

Subtest 2: Instrument Comprehension Answers and Explanations

1. **E.** Level flight, no banking, heading 225° southwest
2. **B.** Climbing, banking right, heading 45° northeast
3. **A.** Level flight, no banking, heading 270° west
4. **C.** Climbing, banking left, heading 270° west
5. **B.** Climbing, no banking, heading 90° east
6. **B.** Level flight, banking right, heading 180° south
7. **C.** Level flight, no banking, heading 180° south
8. **A.** Climbing, banking right, heading 45° northeast
9. **D.** Diving, no banking, heading 90° east
10. **E.** Diving, banking right, heading 270° west
11. **C.** Climbing, banking left, heading 45° northeast
12. **D.** Diving, no banking, heading 180° south
13. **B.** Level flight, banking right, heading 90° east
14. **E.** Diving, banking left, heading 110° southeast
15. **B.** Climbing, banking right, heading 270° west

Subtest 3: Complex Movements Answers and Explanations

1. **E.** 1/8 of an inch left, no up or down
2. **E.** 2/8 of an inch left, 2/8 of an inch up
3. **B.** 3/8 of an inch left, 1/8 of an inch up
4. **D.** 3/8 of an inch right, 3/8 of an inch up
5. **D.** 2/8 of an inch down, 2/8 of an inch down
6. **A.** 3/8 of an inch right, 3/8 of an inch up
7. **B.** 3/8 of an inch left, no up or down
8. **D.** no left or right, 2/8 of an inch down
9. **B.** 1/8 of an inch left, 1/8 of an inch up
10. **A.** no left or right, 1/8 of an inch down
11. **B.** 2/8 of an inch left, 3/8 of an inch up
12. **E.** 3/8 of an inch left, 3/8 of an inch up
13. **E.** no left or right, 1/8 of an inch up
14. **C.** 2/8 of an inch left, 3/8 of an inch up

15. **A.** 1/8 of an inch right, 1/8 of an inch down

16. **B.** 3/8 of an inch left, 3/8 of an inch down

17. **D.** 1/8 of an inch left, no up or down

18. **E.** 1/8 of an inch right, 3/8 of an inch down

19. **D.** 3/8 of an inch right, 2/8 of an inch up

20. **D.** 3/8 of an inch left, no up or down

21. **E.** 3/8 of an inch right, 3/8 of an inch up

22. **D.** 1/8 of an inch left, no up or down

23. **D.** 2/8 of an inch left, no up or down

24. **B.** 1/8 of an inch right, 3/8 of an inch up

25. **D.** 1/8 of an inch right, 1/8 of an inch up

26. **D.** 3/8 of an inch left, no up or down

27. **B.** 3/8 of an inch right, 3/8 of an inch up

28. **E.** 1/8 of an inch right, 1/8 of an inch down

29. **C.** no left or right, 3/8 of an inch up

30. **A.** 2/8 of an inch right, 2/8 of an inch down

Subtest 4: Helicopter Knowledge Answers and Explanations

1. **A.** Ground effect takes place while hovering near the ground. **B** is incorrect because ground effect takes place LESS than one rotor diameter above the surface. **C** is incorrect because ground effect restricts the generation of blade tip vortices due to the downward and outward airflow making a larger portion of the blade produce lift. **D** and **E** are incorrect because ground effect is at its maximum in a no-wind condition over smooth surfaces.

2. **D.** An excessive angle of attack can make it difficult for air to flow smoothly across the top of the airfoil. The airflow separates from the airfoil, creating a turbulent pattern. Any increase in an angle of attack beyond this (critical angle of attack) will result in a stall.

3. **D.** For a helicopter, the relative wind is the flow of air with respect to the rotor blades, that is, the movement of air past the blades, the motion of a blade through the air, or a combination of the two. **A** is incorrect because lift is the upward force created by the effect of airflow as it passes around an airfoil.

4. **B.** Translational lift is that additional lift obtained when entering horizontal flight due to the increased efficiency of the rotor system.

5. **C.** Lowering the collective pitch decreases manifold pressure and increases rpm. In piston helicopters, the collective pitch is the primary control for manifold pressure.

6. **B.** The cyclic control is used to change heading by making a turn. In a no-wind condition, the antitorque pedals are not used to control heading.

7. **B.** You can change the amount of main rotor thrust to maintain hovering altitude. **C** and **D** are incorrect because if thrust is greater than actual weight, the helicopter will gain altitude. If thrust is less than actual weight the helicopter will lose altitude. The goal of hovering is to maintain a constant position a few feet above the ground.

8. **A.** The four forces acting on a helicopter in flight are lift, weight, thrust and drag. An airfoil is any surface, such as a helicopter rotor blade, that provides aerodynamic force when it interacts with a moving stream of air.

9. **C.** Due to the decreased amount of drag with ground effect, the helicopter will be capable of takeoff BEFORE reaching recommended takeoff speed.

10. B. Note the rotation point of the heavy aircraft, and depart prior to and stay upwind of the flight path.

11. E. The flight should not be continued in this condition. The pilot might run out of rearward cyclic control and might find it impossible to bring the helicopter to a stop. Furthermore, in the event of an engine failure, the pilot might not have enough cyclic control to flare for a landing.

12. E. Translational lift is present with any horizontal flow of air across the rotor. As the helicopter accelerates through 16 to 24 knots, rotors move out of its vortices and are in relatively undisturbed air. Additional lift or translational lift is available at these speeds.

13. D. When a helicopter moves through the air, the relative airflow through the main rotor disc is different on the advancing side than on the retreating side. The relative wind encountered by the advancing blade is increased by the forward speed of the helicopter, while the relative wind speed acting on the retreating blade is reduced by the helicopter's forward airspeed.

14. C. The rotor mast in some helicopters is rigged slightly to the LEFT side so that the tip path plane has a built-in tilt to the left, producing a small sideward thrust.

15. B. Rotor blade coning occurs as the rotor blades begin to lift the weight of the helicopter. As a result of centrifugal forces acting outward and perpendicular to the rotor mast, along with lift acting upward and parallel to the mast, the blades assume a conical path instead of remaining in the plane perpendicular to the mast.

16. D. Thrust is generated by the rotation of the main rotor system and the tail rotor system. The amount of thrust through the tail rotor system is variable through the use of the antitorque pedals and is used to control the helicopter's yaw.

17. C. Plan the flight path over an area suitable for a forced landing.

18. D. By immediately lowering the collective pitch, lift and drag will be reduced, and the helicopter will begin an immediate descent. This will produce an upward flow of air through the rotor system.

19. B. Apply aft cyclic to reduce forward speed, and simultaneously lower the collective pitch to counteract climbing tendency.

20. D. The force that compensates for torque and keeps the fuselage from turning in the direction opposite the main rotor is produced by means of an auxiliary rotor located on the end of the tail boom.

Subtest 5: Cyclic Orientation Answers and Explanations

1. Climbing and banking right

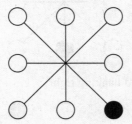

2. Banking right

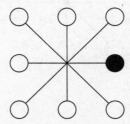

3. Climbing and banking left

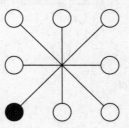

4. Diving and banking right

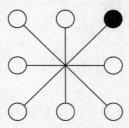

5. Banking left

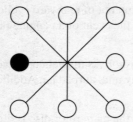

6. Diving and banking left

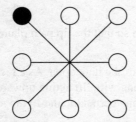

7. Climbing and banking left

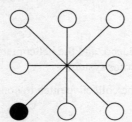

8. Diving and banking right

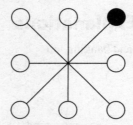

9. Banking left

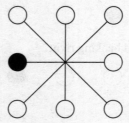

10. Climbing and banking right

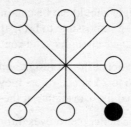

11. Climbing and banking left

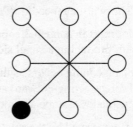

12. Diving and banking right

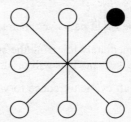

13. Climbing, no banking

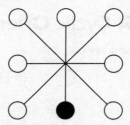

14. Diving and banking right

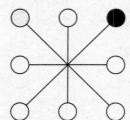

15.

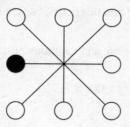

Banking left

Subtest 6: Mechanical Functions Answers and Explanations

1. **B.** The centripetal force of the stone is proportional to the square of the velocity.

2. **A.** The travel time depends on the height above the ground and the acceleration of gravity; both of which are the same for both objects.

3. **B.** From Newton's second law of motion, the centripetal force, or the inward force necessary to maintain uniform circular motion, is the product of mass and centripetal acceleration.

4. **B.** At the top of the trajectory, the ball stops and all the kinetic energy has already been converted to potential energy. Thus, the total energy is the sum of 100 and 700, or 800 J.

5. **B.** Because the frequency of oscillation is inversely proportional to the square root of the length of the pendulum, the length has to be decreased by a factor of 4 for the frequency to be doubled.

6. **A.** The final velocity is the initial velocity minus 4 times the acceleration of gravity (9.8 m/s) or −7.14 (≈ 7.2) m/s.

7. **A.** Using the expressions $s = v_o t + 1/2\ at^2$ and $v_f = v_o + at$, we obtain $t = .4$ and $v_o = 3.92$ m/s.

8. **B.** Because the torque $T = Fd\cos\theta$ where F is the force, d is the arm and θ is the angle between the force and the arm, we can solve for F to obtain 286 N.

9. **B.** The speed ratio of input to output gears equals the mechanical advantage, which is the ratio N_o/N_i, or 2.

10. **B.** $K + [(6.67 \times 10^{-11})(400)(5.98 \times 10^{24})]/[(6.37 \times 10^6 + 3 \times 10^6)] = [(6.67 \times 10^{-11})(400)(5.98 \times 10^{24})]/[(6.37 \times 10^6 + 1.5 \times 10^6)]$, or $K = 3.25 \times 10^9$ J.

11. **B.** Because the momentum P equals the mass m multiplied by the velocity v, it follows that $v = P/m = 40$ m/s.

12. **A.** Conservation of momentum requires that $.24(.6) + .26(.2) = (.24 + .26)v$. Hence, $v = .392$ m/s.

13. **A.** For rod equilibrium, the clockwise and counterclockwise torques must be equal, that is, (F at V + F at V)(d) = (F at Y)(2d) or (F at V)D = (F at Y)(2d) −(F at X)D, which means that the third force can only be applied upward at V or downward at X.

14. **A.** Acceleration will be the same for both arrows. Momentum and energy are dependent on mass and will therefore be different. Only the change in velocity will be the same for both arrows.

15. **B.** The work done does not depend on time or path of travel because the deceleration of the arrow is constant.

16. **A.** Letting the masses of the bullet and block be m and M, their initial velocities be u and U and their combined velocity be V, the conversion from kinetic to potential energy requires that $1/2(m + M)V^2 = (m + M)gh$, where h is the increment in height (12 cm). This leads to V = 1.533 m/s. The conservation of momentum requires that mu + MU = (m + M)V, where U = 0. Hence, solving for u we obtain 308.258 ≈ 308 m/s.

17. **B.** Mass cannot change because of changes in gravitational acceleration, but weight changes, and in this case increases because the gravitational acceleration is higher.

18. **A.** The acceleration is the ratio of the force and the mass. The mass remains the same, while the net force is set by the mass, acceleration of gravity, slope of the inclined plane and the coefficient of kinetic friction (which are all constant). Thus, the acceleration remains the same.

19. **B.** Because the momentum is conserved, there is no change in speed due to the collision, and the momentum of both remains the same.

20. **B.** Taking moments about O, we obtain net moment M = 100(.50 − .0725 cos 20°) = 43.187 N.m.

Subtest 7: Self-Description Answers

In this subtest there are no right or wrong answers.

Answer Sheet for ASTB Practice Test

Math/Verbal Test

1 Ⓐ Ⓑ Ⓒ Ⓓ	11 Ⓐ Ⓑ Ⓒ Ⓓ	21 Ⓐ Ⓑ Ⓒ Ⓓ	31 Ⓐ Ⓑ Ⓒ Ⓓ
2 Ⓐ Ⓑ Ⓒ Ⓓ	12 Ⓐ Ⓑ Ⓒ Ⓓ	22 Ⓐ Ⓑ Ⓒ Ⓓ	32 Ⓐ Ⓑ Ⓒ Ⓓ
3 Ⓐ Ⓑ Ⓒ Ⓓ	13 Ⓐ Ⓑ Ⓒ Ⓓ	23 Ⓐ Ⓑ Ⓒ Ⓓ	33 Ⓐ Ⓑ Ⓒ Ⓓ
4 Ⓐ Ⓑ Ⓒ Ⓓ	14 Ⓐ Ⓑ Ⓒ Ⓓ	24 Ⓐ Ⓑ Ⓒ Ⓓ	34 Ⓐ Ⓑ Ⓒ Ⓓ
5 Ⓐ Ⓑ Ⓒ Ⓓ	15 Ⓐ Ⓑ Ⓒ Ⓓ	25 Ⓐ Ⓑ Ⓒ Ⓓ	35 Ⓐ Ⓑ Ⓒ Ⓓ
6 Ⓐ Ⓑ Ⓒ Ⓓ	16 Ⓐ Ⓑ Ⓒ Ⓓ	26 Ⓐ Ⓑ Ⓒ Ⓓ	36 Ⓐ Ⓑ Ⓒ Ⓓ
7 Ⓐ Ⓑ Ⓒ Ⓓ	17 Ⓐ Ⓑ Ⓒ Ⓓ	27 Ⓐ Ⓑ Ⓒ Ⓓ	37 Ⓐ Ⓑ Ⓒ Ⓓ
8 Ⓐ Ⓑ Ⓒ Ⓓ	18 Ⓐ Ⓑ Ⓒ Ⓓ	28 Ⓐ Ⓑ Ⓒ Ⓓ	
9 Ⓐ Ⓑ Ⓒ Ⓓ	19 Ⓐ Ⓑ Ⓒ Ⓓ	29 Ⓐ Ⓑ Ⓒ Ⓓ	
10 Ⓐ Ⓑ Ⓒ Ⓓ	20 Ⓐ Ⓑ Ⓒ Ⓓ	30 Ⓐ Ⓑ Ⓒ Ⓓ	

Mechanical Comprehension Test

1 Ⓐ Ⓑ Ⓒ	11 Ⓐ Ⓑ Ⓒ	21 Ⓐ Ⓑ Ⓒ
2 Ⓐ Ⓑ Ⓒ	12 Ⓐ Ⓑ Ⓒ	22 Ⓐ Ⓑ Ⓒ
3 Ⓐ Ⓑ Ⓒ	13 Ⓐ Ⓑ Ⓒ	23 Ⓐ Ⓑ Ⓒ
4 Ⓐ Ⓑ Ⓒ	14 Ⓐ Ⓑ Ⓒ	24 Ⓐ Ⓑ Ⓒ
5 Ⓐ Ⓑ Ⓒ	15 Ⓐ Ⓑ Ⓒ	25 Ⓐ Ⓑ Ⓒ
6 Ⓐ Ⓑ Ⓒ	16 Ⓐ Ⓑ Ⓒ	26 Ⓐ Ⓑ Ⓒ
7 Ⓐ Ⓑ Ⓒ	17 Ⓐ Ⓑ Ⓒ	27 Ⓐ Ⓑ Ⓒ
8 Ⓐ Ⓑ Ⓒ	18 Ⓐ Ⓑ Ⓒ	28 Ⓐ Ⓑ Ⓒ
9 Ⓐ Ⓑ Ⓒ	19 Ⓐ Ⓑ Ⓒ	29 Ⓐ Ⓑ Ⓒ
10 Ⓐ Ⓑ Ⓒ	20 Ⓐ Ⓑ Ⓒ	30 Ⓐ Ⓑ Ⓒ

Spatial Apperception Test

1 Ⓐ Ⓑ Ⓒ Ⓓ Ⓔ	11 Ⓐ Ⓑ Ⓒ Ⓓ Ⓔ	21 Ⓐ Ⓑ Ⓒ Ⓓ Ⓔ	31 Ⓐ Ⓑ Ⓒ Ⓓ Ⓔ
2 Ⓐ Ⓑ Ⓒ Ⓓ Ⓔ	12 Ⓐ Ⓑ Ⓒ Ⓓ Ⓔ	22 Ⓐ Ⓑ Ⓒ Ⓓ Ⓔ	32 Ⓐ Ⓑ Ⓒ Ⓓ Ⓔ
3 Ⓐ Ⓑ Ⓒ Ⓓ Ⓔ	13 Ⓐ Ⓑ Ⓒ Ⓓ Ⓔ	23 Ⓐ Ⓑ Ⓒ Ⓓ Ⓔ	33 Ⓐ Ⓑ Ⓒ Ⓓ Ⓔ
4 Ⓐ Ⓑ Ⓒ Ⓓ Ⓔ	14 Ⓐ Ⓑ Ⓒ Ⓓ Ⓔ	24 Ⓐ Ⓑ Ⓒ Ⓓ Ⓔ	34 Ⓐ Ⓑ Ⓒ Ⓓ Ⓔ
5 Ⓐ Ⓑ Ⓒ Ⓓ Ⓔ	15 Ⓐ Ⓑ Ⓒ Ⓓ Ⓔ	25 Ⓐ Ⓑ Ⓒ Ⓓ Ⓔ	35 Ⓐ Ⓑ Ⓒ Ⓓ Ⓔ
6 Ⓐ Ⓑ Ⓒ Ⓓ Ⓔ	16 Ⓐ Ⓑ Ⓒ Ⓓ Ⓔ	26 Ⓐ Ⓑ Ⓒ Ⓓ Ⓔ	
7 Ⓐ Ⓑ Ⓒ Ⓓ Ⓔ	17 Ⓐ Ⓑ Ⓒ Ⓓ Ⓔ	27 Ⓐ Ⓑ Ⓒ Ⓓ Ⓔ	
8 Ⓐ Ⓑ Ⓒ Ⓓ Ⓔ	18 Ⓐ Ⓑ Ⓒ Ⓓ Ⓔ	28 Ⓐ Ⓑ Ⓒ Ⓓ Ⓔ	
9 Ⓐ Ⓑ Ⓒ Ⓓ Ⓔ	19 Ⓐ Ⓑ Ⓒ Ⓓ Ⓔ	29 Ⓐ Ⓑ Ⓒ Ⓓ Ⓔ	
10 Ⓐ Ⓑ Ⓒ Ⓓ Ⓔ	20 Ⓐ Ⓑ Ⓒ Ⓓ Ⓔ	30 Ⓐ Ⓑ Ⓒ Ⓓ Ⓔ	

Aviation/Nautical Information

1 Ⓐ Ⓑ Ⓒ Ⓓ Ⓔ	11 Ⓐ Ⓑ Ⓒ Ⓓ Ⓔ	21 Ⓐ Ⓑ Ⓒ Ⓓ Ⓔ
2 Ⓐ Ⓑ Ⓒ Ⓓ Ⓔ	12 Ⓐ Ⓑ Ⓒ Ⓓ Ⓔ	22 Ⓐ Ⓑ Ⓒ Ⓓ Ⓔ
3 Ⓐ Ⓑ Ⓒ Ⓓ Ⓔ	13 Ⓐ Ⓑ Ⓒ Ⓓ Ⓔ	23 Ⓐ Ⓑ Ⓒ Ⓓ Ⓔ
4 Ⓐ Ⓑ Ⓒ Ⓓ Ⓔ	14 Ⓐ Ⓑ Ⓒ Ⓓ Ⓔ	24 Ⓐ Ⓑ Ⓒ Ⓓ Ⓔ
5 Ⓐ Ⓑ Ⓒ Ⓓ Ⓔ	15 Ⓐ Ⓑ Ⓒ Ⓓ Ⓔ	25 Ⓐ Ⓑ Ⓒ Ⓓ Ⓔ
6 Ⓐ Ⓑ Ⓒ Ⓓ Ⓔ	16 Ⓐ Ⓑ Ⓒ Ⓓ Ⓔ	26 Ⓐ Ⓑ Ⓒ Ⓓ Ⓔ
7 Ⓐ Ⓑ Ⓒ Ⓓ Ⓔ	17 Ⓐ Ⓑ Ⓒ Ⓓ Ⓔ	27 Ⓐ Ⓑ Ⓒ Ⓓ Ⓔ
8 Ⓐ Ⓑ Ⓒ Ⓓ Ⓔ	18 Ⓐ Ⓑ Ⓒ Ⓓ Ⓔ	28 Ⓐ Ⓑ Ⓒ Ⓓ Ⓔ
9 Ⓐ Ⓑ Ⓒ Ⓓ Ⓔ	19 Ⓐ Ⓑ Ⓒ Ⓓ Ⓔ	29 Ⓐ Ⓑ Ⓒ Ⓓ Ⓔ
10 Ⓐ Ⓑ Ⓒ Ⓓ Ⓔ	20 Ⓐ Ⓑ Ⓒ Ⓓ Ⓔ	30 Ⓐ Ⓑ Ⓒ Ⓓ Ⓔ

CUT HERE

Test 1: Math/Verbal Test

Time: 35 Minutes

37 Questions

Directions: Select the answer choice that best satisfies the question.

Questions 1–5: Each of the following five questions consists of an arithmetic problem followed by four possible answers. Select the one choice that is the correct answer.

1. A machine can produce 8,000 widgets in 3 hours. How many widgets are produced in 1 day?

   A. 96,000
   B. 64,000
   C. 32,000
   D. 8,000

2. Sam buys 3 candy bars for 45 cents each and two packs of gum for 79 cents each. What is the total cost of this purchase?

   A. $1.24
   B. $2.93
   C. $6.20
   D. $6.24

3. Devin throws a football $7\frac{1}{3}$ yards. Carl throws it $2\frac{1}{2}$ times farther. How much farther did Carl's throw travel than Devin's?

   A. $2\frac{1}{2}$ yards
   B. $7\frac{1}{3}$ yards
   C. 11 yards
   D. $18\frac{1}{3}$ yards

4. This morning, Taryn drove 13 miles to the library and then returned home. In the afternoon, she drove 9 miles to the movies and returned home. How much farther did Taryn travel in the morning?

   A. 4 miles
   B. 6 miles
   C. 8 miles
   D. 9 miles

5. Jared rents 3 videos for $8.00. What would the cost of 2 video rentals be?

   A. $1.33
   B. $5.00
   C. $5.33
   D. $6.00

Questions 6–10: The following five questions consist of sentences in which one word is omitted. For each question, select the lettered choice that best completes the thought expressed in the sentence.

6. The home's _____ furnishings included French antiques, Chinese draperies, and American lamps.

   A. boring
   B. eclectic
   C. demonstrative
   D. opulent

7. Many people left after the first act of the play; their _____ opinion of it was clear.

   A. tacit
   B. verbal
   C. admiring
   D. dramatic

8. Because neither side was willing to modify its position, the negotiations were _____.

   A. delicate
   B. minimal
   C. concise
   D. stagnant

GO ON TO THE NEXT PAGE

9. Neither passionate nor monotonous, the speaker's _____ voice helped the audience understand his views.

    A. dynamic

    B. minimal

    C. sentimental

    D. temperate

10. Because the author did not use a spelling checker, the text was _____ with errors.

    A. replete

    B. charged

    C. complete

    D. read

Questions 11–15: Each of the following five questions consists of an arithmetic problem followed by four possible answers. Select the one choice that is the correct answer.

11. The basketball game starts at 8:00. If it is now 5:30, how much time is left before the game starts?

    A. 1 hour, 30 minutes

    B. 2 hours, 30 minutes

    C. 3 hours, 30 minutes

    D. 4 hours, 30 minutes

12. How many blocks 6" × 4" × 4" can fit in a box 8' × 6' × 4'?

    A. 2

    B. 48

    C. 576

    D. 3,456

13. Janice buys a quart of milk and two dozen eggs. If the milk costs $1.39 and eggs are $1.28 a dozen, how much change does Janice get back if she pays with a $10.00 bill?

    A. $3.95

    B. $5.94

    C. $6.05

    D. $7.33

14. Eight hundred employees work at a company. If 60% drive to work and 30% take the train, how many employees travel to work by car?

    A. 240

    B. 480

    C. 540

    D. 600

15. Min reads 3 hardcover mysteries and 4 softcover mysteries. She reads 3 times as many nonfiction books as she does mysteries. How many nonfiction books does Min read?

    A. 9

    B. 12

    C. 18

    D. 21

The following five questions consist of quotations that contain one word that is incorrectly used and not in keeping with the meaning that each quotation is evidently intended to convey. Determine which word is incorrectly used. Then, select from the lettered choices the word that, when substituted for the incorrectly used word, would best help to convey the intended meaning of the quotation.

16. "Destruction of the Florida panther's already increased habitat is occurring at a dangerous pace, threatening the species' future."

    A. constructed

    B. diminished

    C. fertile

    D. impoverished

17. "Before the test drive of this new model, we expected to be underwhelmed, and that initial disregard makes it all the more remarkable how much we ended up liking it after a week behind the wheel."

    A. certainty

    B. hope

    C. disinterested

    D. skepticism

18. "Families nourish us during childhood, and the values our families seek to maintain usually affect our identities in powerful ways, whether we adopt them wholly, modify them, or accept them completely."

    A. pretense

    B. reject

    C. behold

    D. deviate

19. "Some economists argue that as a result of large tax cuts, wealthy people invest their windfall, businesses thrive, jobs are created, and the new tax revenues created by these economic activities are smaller or equivalent to the amount of the original reduction."

    A. compensate
    B. regular
    C. thriftier
    D. larger

20. "After the disaster at the manufacturing plant, engineers stated that even if the safety systems had been activated, there were objections about whether they would have mitigated the damage done by the explosion."

    A. discuss
    B. observations
    C. doubts
    D. consideration

Questions 21–25: Each of the following five questions consists of an arithmetic problem followed by four possible answers. Select the one choice that is the correct answer.

21. The volume of a cube is 343 cm^3. The surface area of the cube is:

    A. 7 cm^2
    B. 49 cm^2
    C. 294 cm^2
    D. 2401 cm^2

22. Melodi eats $\frac{3}{8}$ of a pizza and divides the rest between her two friends. What percent of the pizza do her friends each receive?

    A. 62.50%
    B. 37.50%
    C. 31.25%
    D. 18.75%

23. Kim's favorite movie is 144 minutes long. Justin's favorite movie is 127 minutes long. How much longer is Kim's favorite movie?

    A. 17 minutes
    B. 23 minutes
    C. 36 minutes
    D. 44 minutes

24. Roger collects bottle caps. Each cap can be traded for 5 cents. If Roger receives $40.50, how many bottle caps did he trade?

    A. 810
    B. 405
    C. 200
    D. 8

25. A batch of cookies requires two cups of milk and four eggs. If you have nine cups of milk and nine eggs, how many batches of cookies can you make?

    A. nine
    B. six
    C. four
    D. two

Questions 26–30 are based on different reading passages. Answer each question on the basis of the information contained in the quotation.

26. "In January 2002, a person buys a car that comes with a three-year or 36,000-mile free replacement guarantee on the engine and transmission. In June 2005, the car has 34,300 miles on it. The transmission fails."

    According to the situation described in the paragraph, the car dealer will:

    A. put in a new transmission
    B. give the person a new car
    C. not fix the transmission free
    D. not replace the car's engine

27. "A sonnet is a specific type of poem. It has 14 lines. The lines must rhyme in a set pattern. Sometimes, the last 6 lines of a sonnet contrast with the first 8 lines. Many sonnets are love poems."

    To be a sonnet, a poem must:

    A. be a love poem
    B. present a contrast
    C. have fewer than 14 lines
    D. rhyme in a specific way

GO ON TO THE NEXT PAGE

28. "When many people want to buy a product, the price will probably go up. In the summer, Americans travel more than they do at other times of year. They might take planes or trains, and many families drive to their vacation spots."

From the information in the paragraph, you can conclude that

A.   gasoline prices rise in the summer
B.   gasoline prices rise in the winter
C.   gasoline prices go down in the summer
D.   gasoline prices do not change in any season

29. "When you send a document to someone by electronic means, you are faxing it. The word FAX comes from the word FACSIMILE. Earlier ways of making facsimiles included photocopying and photographing. The oldest facsimiles were hand-written versions of original texts."

The word FACSIMILE means:

A.   an electronic copy
B.   an exact copy
C.   any document
D.   a photocopy

30. "The United States Supreme Court is the highest court in the nation. Its nine judges review cases from other courts. They decide if these courts have ruled in a way that agrees with the United States Constitution. But they cannot make new laws. Their decision is based on a majority vote of the nine judges."

The main idea of this paragraph is that:

A.   the Supreme Court has nine judges
B.   the Supreme Court is the highest court in the United States
C.   the Supreme Court cannot make new laws
D.   the Supreme Court's decisions are based on a majority vote

Questions 31–35: Each of the following five questions consists of an arithmetic problem followed by four possible answers. Select the one choice that is the correct answer.

31. A right triangle has an area of 24 feet. If one leg is 3 times as long as the other, what is the length of the longest side?

A.   12.6 feet
B.   12 feet
C.   8.4 feet
D.   6.3 feet

32. Interest earned on an account totals $100. If the interest rate is $7\frac{1}{4}$ %, what is the principal amount?

A. $725
B. $1,333
C. $1,379
D. $1,428

33. William can read 2 pages in 3 minutes. At this rate, how long does it take him to read a 360-page book?

A.   30 minutes
B.   2 hours
C.   6 hours
D.   9 hours

34. Tanya's bowling scores this week were 112, 156, 179 and 165. Last week, her average score was 140. How many points did her average improve?

A.   18
B.   13
C.   11
D.   8

35. Felix buys 3 books for $8.95 each. How much does he owe if he uses a $12.73 credit toward his purchase?

A. $39.58
B. $26.85
C. $21.68
D. $14.12

Questions 36 and 37 are based on reading passages. Answer each question on the basis of the information contained in the quotation.

36. "Early British colonists in Virginia typically came from England to plant tobacco, harvest it, and then return to their homeland to sell it; however, British colonists who came to New England did so to establish permanent colonies where they could practice their religious beliefs freely."

The preceding quotation best supports the statement that motives for early colonists:

A.   sprang from a universal desire for freedom of religion
B.   determined where they located their colonies
C.   originated because of different kinds of terrain
D.   evolved from a need for more income

37. "Although many people consider Latin to be a dead language, studies have shown that a student's understanding of grammar and his vocabulary can be improved if he studies Latin and that his algebraic skills can be strengthened, especially in problem solving."

The preceding quotation best supports the statement that:

A. studying Latin can improve verbal and math skills

B. all students should study Latin

C. basic arithmetic skills can be improved for students of all levels

D. even if Latin is no longer a spoken language, everyone should be able to read it

DON'T GO ON UNTIL TOLD TO DO SO. **STOP**

Test 2: Mechanical Comprehension Test

Time: 15 minutes

30 Questions

Directions: This test is designed to measure your ability to learn and reason using mechanical terms. Each diagram is followed by a question or an incomplete statement. Select the choice that best answers the question or completes the statement.

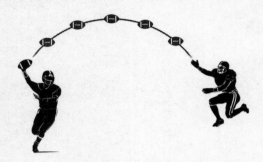

1. Which of the following best describes the path in the air of a ball after it is thrown by one player to another?

   A. a straight line

   B. a parabola

   C. a circle

2. Mr. James pushes against the wall with a force of 30 N for 30 s. If the wall does not move, then the work done on the wall is

   A. positive

   B. negative

   C. zero

3. A ball is thrown horizontally from the top of a building. At the same time, another ball is dropped from the same height. Which ball will hit the ground first?

   A. The ball thrown horizontally.

   B. The ball dropped from rest.

   C. Both balls will hit the ground at the same time.

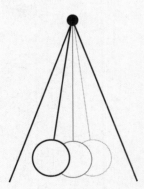

4. If a mass at the end of a simple pendulum with a small amplitude of motion is increased by a factor of 2, other things remaining constant,

   A. its period will double

   B. it will have the same frequency

   C. the frequency remains the same

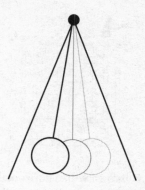

5. For an object with simple harmonic motion, simultaneously its

   A. displacement is maximum when its acceleration is maximum

   B. velocity is maximum when its displacement is maximum

   C. kinetic energy is maximum when its displacement is maximum

7. A skater is spinning with a constant angular momentum. If she pulls her arms in toward her body, her angular momentum will

   A. increase

   B. decrease

   C. remain constant

6. A wheel is rotating with a constant frequency. A point on the outside of the wheel compared to a point near the center has _____ linear speed and _____ angular speed.

   A. the same, a smaller

   B. a greater, the same

   C. a smaller, the same

8. A ball is thrown vertically upward with a speed of 14.5 m/s from the top of a building that is 50 meters tall. The ball will reach the ground after a time of _____ s.

   A. 1.48

   B. 2.96

   C. 5

GO ON TO THE NEXT PAGE

9. A 4kg ball moving at a speed of 2 m/s collides head on with another ball of 2kg mass and 4 m/s speed. If the two balls stick together, their joint speed after the elastic collision is _____ m/s.

    A. 0
    B. 1
    C. 2

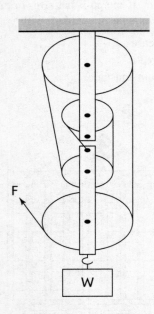

10. The input force required to lift a 200N load W in the pulley arrangement shown in the figure is

    A. 40 N
    B. 50 N
    C. 800 N

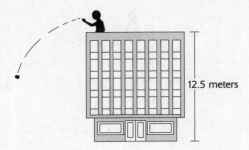

11. An object is thrown with a horizontal velocity of 10 m/s from the edge of a building that is 12.5 m above ground level. If the air resistance is negligible, the time t that it takes the object to reach the ground and the distance d from the building where it strikes the ground are most nearly

    A. 3s, 100m
    B. 1.6s, 16m
    C. 3.2s, 32m

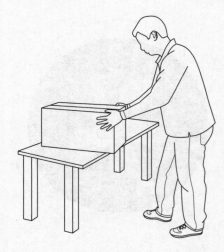

12. A block of mass 3 kg slides along a horizontal tabletop. A horizontal force of 10 N and a downward vertical force of 17.4 N act on the block at the same time. If the coefficient of kinetic friction against the table is .25, the net horizontal force exerted on the block is nearly

    A. 3 N
    B. 5 N
    C. 7 N

13. A man pulling a small box along the floor suddenly decides to raise his pulling hand. If the pulling force remains the same, the amount of work done to pull the box the same distance

   A. increases
   B. decreases
   C. remains the same

14. An ice skater is touching her waist while spinning. Suddenly the music changes and she extends her hands out so that her fingers are twice as far from the axis of rotation. Her spin rate

   A. increases significantly
   B. decreases significantly
   C. remains the same

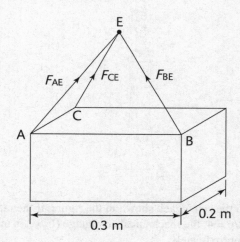

15. The box shown in the figure has uniform density and a total weight of 120 N. If the box is suspended by three cables of identical length, and if point E is 40 cm above the top surface of the box, then the tension T in cable CE is nearly

   A. 16 N
   B. 20 N
   C. 27 N

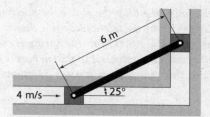

16. Two 5kg blocks are linked by a slider rod assembly as shown in the figure. If the sliding surfaces are frictionless, and if the speed of block A is 4 m/s, the speed of block B is

   A. 8.57 m/s
   B. 4.28 m/s
   C. 1.5 m/s

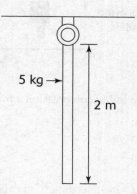

17. A 5 kg uniform rod 2 m long is suspended from the ceiling by a frictionless hinge. If the rod is free to pivot, the product of inertia of the rod about the pivotal point is

   A. 0 kg.m^2
   B. 20 kg.m^2
   C. 2.5 kg.m^2

GO ON TO THE NEXT PAGE

Consider the following diagram where the mass m equals 10 kg and is guided by the frictionless rail shown. The spring constant is k = 1,000 N/m. The spring is compressed sufficiently and released so that m barely reaches point B. Using this information, answer questions 18–21.

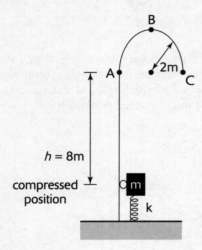

18. What is the initial compression *x* in the spring?

    A. 1.3 m

    B. 1.4 m

    C. 1.5 m

19. What is the kinetic energy of *m* at point A?

    A. 1.962 J

    B. 19.62 J

    C. 196.2 J

20. What is the velocity *v* of *m* at point A?

    A. 6.264 m/s

    B. 62.64 m/s

    C. 19.62 m/s

21. What is the energy stored in the spring if it is compressed .1 m?

    A. 100 J

    B. 50 J

    C. 5 J

22. An object is dropped from a building. If the speed of impact is to be tripled, how much higher should the object be?

    A. 3 times

    B. 6 times

    C. 9 times

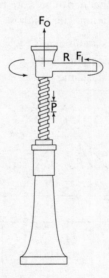

23. In the screw jack shown in the figure, if the ratio R/p = 4, the mechanical advantage (F_o/F_i) is most approximately

    A. 14

    B. 21

    C. 25

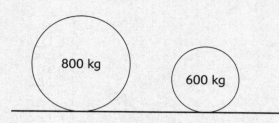

24. If the centers of a 800kg mass and a 600kg mass are separated by .25 m, then the magnitude of the gravitational force F between them is nearly _____ N.

A. 5×10^{-4}
B. 5×10^{-5}
C. 1.67×10^{-7}

25. The weight of a 70kg astronaut on the surface of a planet with a mass of 3×10^{24} kg and a radius of 5×10^{6}m is nearly _____N.

A.   686
B.   586
C.   560

26. The forces exerted on the lug wrench are to the right and left as shown in figures a and b.

A.   The nut in graph a may be loosened.
B.   The nut in graph b may be loosened.
C.   The nut in either graph a or b may be loosened.

GO ON TO THE NEXT PAGE

In questions 27 and 28, water flows inside the pipe with a circular cross section from A to B at the rate of 10 liters/second. The diameter of the pipe at A is 12 cm and 4 cm at B. Point B is 6 m higher than A, and the pressure at A is 140 kilopascals.

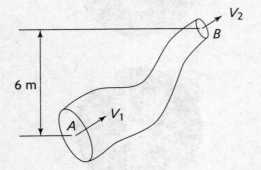

27. The velocity of the stream at point B is approximately

    A. 4 m/s
    B. 8 m/s
    C. 12 m/s

28. The pressure at point B in kilopascals is approximately

    A. 30
    B. 40
    C. 50

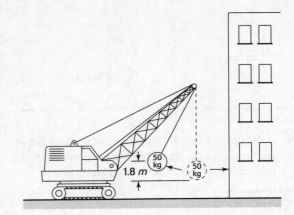

29. The 50kg ball of the demolition equipment shown in the figure is pulled to the left until it is 1.8 m above its lowest point. Its velocity as it passes through its lowest point is approximately

    A. 32.25 m/s
    B. 5.6 m/s
    C. 5.9 m/s

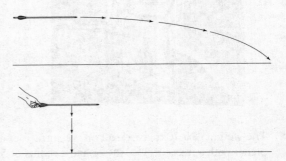

30. Consider the two arrows in the figure. The first is shot by the woman in the horizontal direction. The second is dropped by the man and travels only in the vertical direction. The two arrows originate from the same height above the ground. Which arrow arrives at the ground first?

    A. The arrow shot by the woman.
    B. The arrow dropped by the man.
    C. The two arrows arrive at the ground at the same time.

DON'T GO ON UNTIL TOLD TO DO SO.   **STOP**

Test 3: Spatial Apperception Test

Time: 10 Minutes

35 Questions

Directions: You will have 5 minutes to read these instructions before you answer the following questions.

Each problem in this test consists of six pictures: an aerial view at the upper left followed by five pictured choices, labeled A, B, C, D, and E. Each picture shows a plane in flight. The picture at the upper left (the aerial view) shows the view that the pilot has looking straight ahead from the cockpit of one of the five pictured planes. You are to determine which of the five choices most nearly represents the position or attitude of the plane and the direction of the flight from which the view is seen.

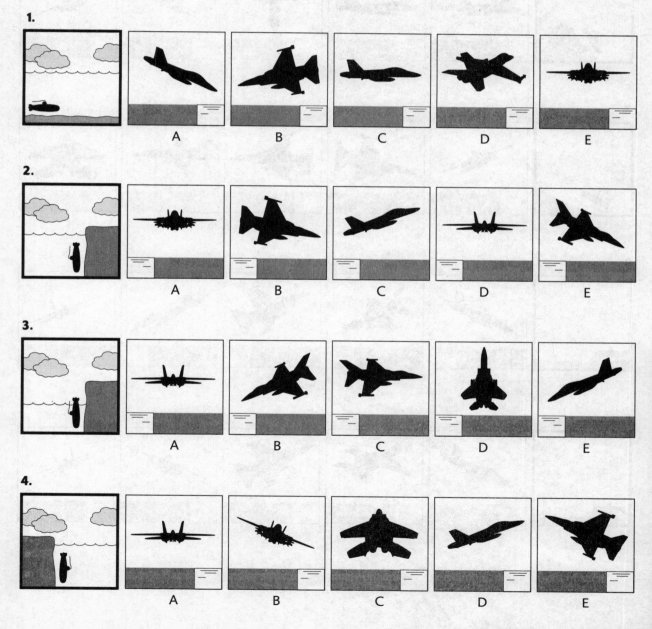

1.

A   B   C   D   E

2.

A   B   C   D   E

3.

A   B   C   D   E

4.

A   B   C   D   E

GO ON TO THE NEXT PAGE

ASTB Practice Test

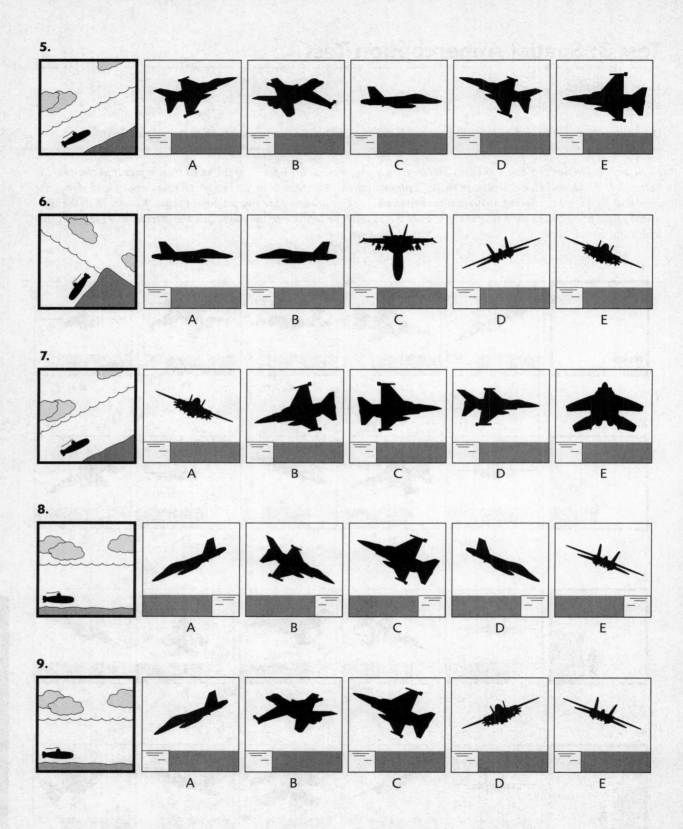

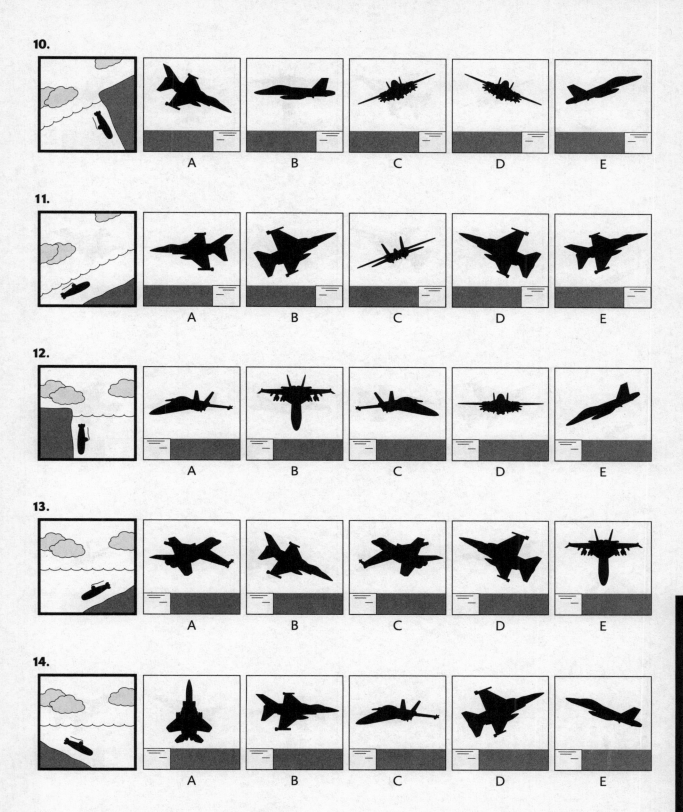

GO ON TO THE NEXT PAGE

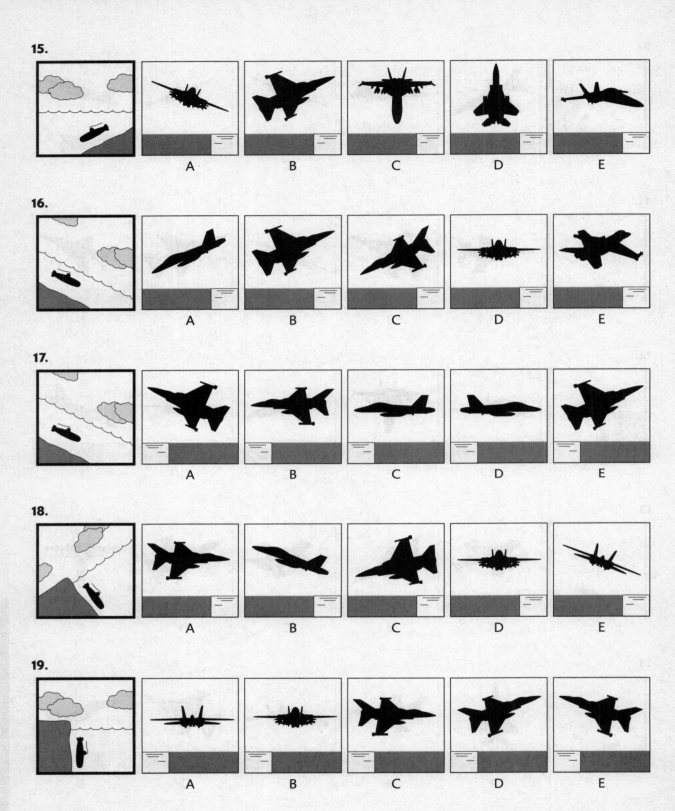

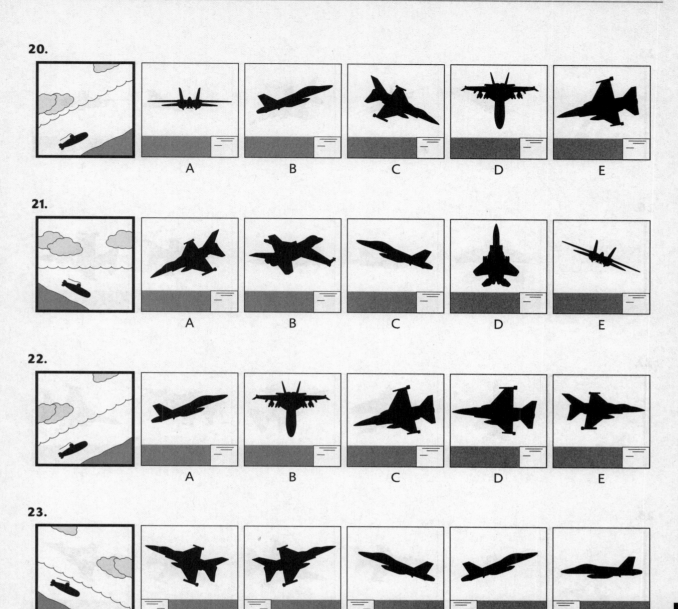

25.

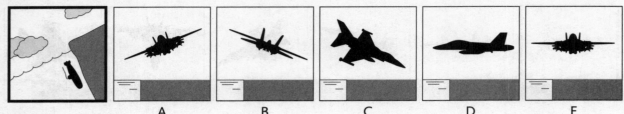

A   B   C   D   E

26.

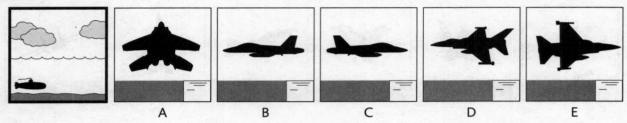

A   B   C   D   E

27.

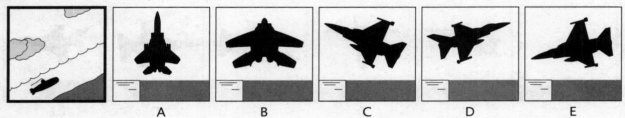

A   B   C   D   E

28.

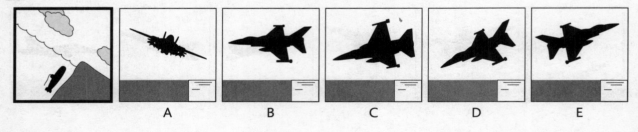

A   B   C   D   E

29.

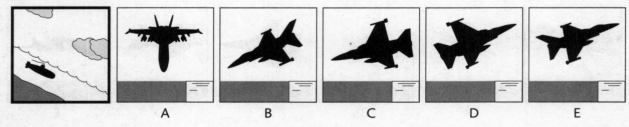

A   B   C   D   E

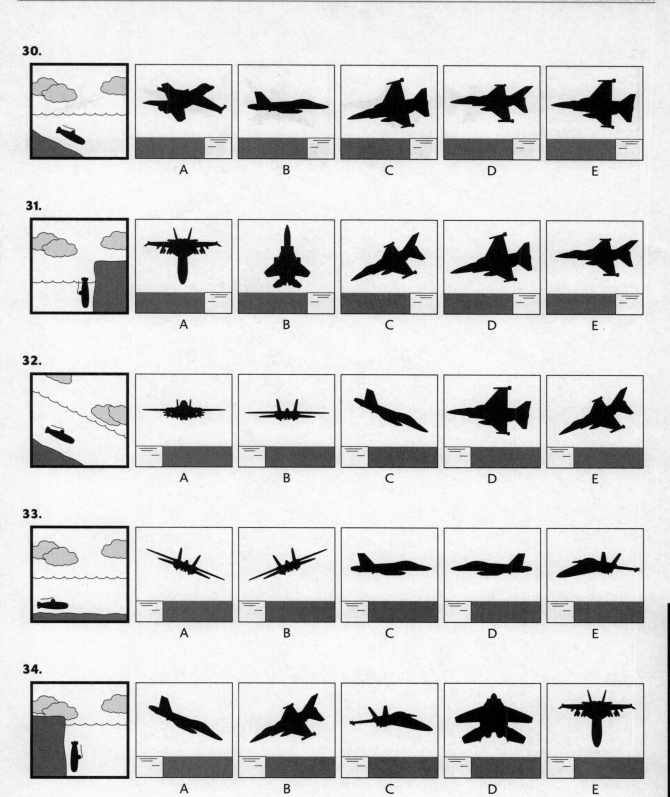

GO ON TO THE NEXT PAGE

35.

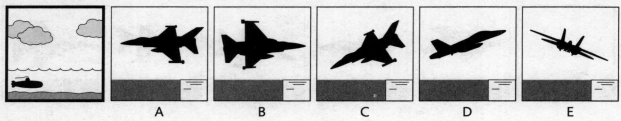

A   B   C   D   E

DON'T GO ON UNTIL TOLD TO DO SO.

Test 4: Aviation and Nautical Information Test

Time: 15 Minutes

30 Questions

Directions: Select the answer choice that best satisfies the question.

1. The pilot yaws an airplane by using the:
   A. flaps
   B. ailerons
   C. elevators
   D. trim
   E. rudder

2. The aircraft is controlled through the lateral axis with the:
   A. rudder
   B. elevators
   C. trim
   D. ailerons
   E. flaps

3. Camber is the:
   A. curvature of an airfoil between the leading edge and the trailing edge
   B. distance between the leading edge and the trailing edge of a wing
   C. distance between each wingtip
   D. angle between the chord line of the wing and the relative wind
   E. angle between the longitudinal axis of an airplane and the wing chord line

4. In steady flight, drag equals:
   A. lift
   B. weight
   C. thrust
   D. power
   E. airspeed

5. A runway is numbered 36. An aircraft lined up on the runway has an approximate heading of:
   A. 180°
   B. 270°
   C. 315°
   D. 360°
   E. 090°

6. The opposite direction runway of runway 23L on the same surface is:
   A. 18L
   B. 23R
   C. 5L
   D. 5R
   E. 6R

7. A stall is cause by:
   A. a hesitation of the aircraft engine
   B. the horizontal component of lift
   C. the separation of airflow from the wing's upper surface
   D. a change in the coefficient of lift
   E. a reduced angle of attack

8. The aspect ratio is the ratio between the:
   A. wingspan and camber
   B. length and width
   C. length and angle of attack
   D. width and height
   E. wingspan and chord line

9. Runway 13/31 is aligned in a:
   A. NW-SE direction
   B. NE-SW direction
   C. N-S direction
   D. E-W direction
   E. NNW-SSE direction

10. A rectangular wing stalls first at the:
    A. trailing edge
    B. leading edge
    C. ailerons
    D. wing root
    E. wing tip

GO ON TO THE NEXT PAGE

343

11. A takeoff with a headwind will:

   A. not be different than with a calm wind
   B. have a longer takeoff roll than in a calm wind
   C. have the same effect as a tailwind
   D. reduce the takeoff roll in relation to a calm wind
   E. cannot be determined

12. Feathering a propeller causes it to:

   A. create the most drag
   B. windmill as the aircraft moves through the air
   C. present the smallest cross section possible to the relative wind and therefore reduce drag
   D. turn easily in the wind
   E. cannot be determined

13. What is the second stroke in a four-stroke engine?

   A. intake
   B. compression
   C. combustion
   D. exhaust
   E. spark

14. A no-flap landing causes an approach and landing to be performed:

   A. at a higher speed on a longer runway
   B. at a slower speed on a shorter runway
   C. at a lower angle of attack
   D. at a lower angle of incidence
   E. at a slower airspeed on a longer runway

15. Latitude and longitude are used to compute an aircraft's:

   A. heading
   B. airspeed
   C. altitude
   D. fuel burn
   E. position

16. The rotating beacon on an aircraft is what color?

   A. white
   B. green
   C. blue
   D. red
   E. yellow

17. In the United States, altimeter settings use what unit of measure?

   A. millibars
   B. inches of mercury
   C. feet of mercury
   D. hectopascals
   E. atmospheres

18. The first controlled, powered airplane flight took place on what date?

   A. December 7, 1941
   B. October 29, 1976
   C. June 8, 1899
   D. December 17, 1903
   E. November 11, 1918

19. During a coordinated 60° banked turn, an aircraft weighs:

   A. twice as much as in level flight
   B. half as much as in level flight
   C. four times as much as in level flight
   D. one quarter as much as in level flight
   E. the same as in level flight

20. The second stage of a thunderstorm is:

   A. dissipating
   B. cumulus
   C. mature
   D. downdraft
   E. updraft

21. The vertical partitions of a ship are called the:

   A. frames
   B. hull
   C. bulkheads
   D. keel
   E. deck

22. A ship's capstan is used for:

   A. moving or handling heavy weights
   B. navigation
   C. communication
   D. refueling at sea
   E. steering

23. A nautical mile is:

    A. 2 times that of a statute mile

    B. 1.5 times that of a statute mile

    C. 1.25 times that of a statute mile

    D. 1.15 times that of a statute mile

    E. equal to a statute mile

24. Using the 24-hour basis in navigation, 2:55 p.m. is:

    A. 2.55

    B. 255

    C. 0255

    D. 14.55

    E. 1455

25. As the weight of the load carried by a ship decreases,

    A. both the freeboard and the draft increase

    B. both the freeboard and the draft decrease

    C. freeboard increases and draft decreases

    D. freeboard decreases and draft increases

    E. none of the above

26. A navigation light associated with "port" is:

    A. white

    B. red

    C. green

    D. yellow

    E. none of the above

27. Cool air pulled ashore by rising thermal air currents caused by the air inland rising as the land heats up is called:

    A. land breeze

    B. sea breeze

    C. radiation fog

    D. advection fog

    E. sea fog

28. The line in Greenwich represents the Prime Meridian of the world, meaning:

    A. longitude 0°, divides eastern and western hemispheres of the earth

    B. latitude 0°, divides eastern and western hemispheres of the earth

    C. longitude 0°, divides northern and southern hemispheres of the earth

    D. latitude 0°, divides northern and southern hemispheres of the earth

    E. none of the above

29. Two or more bearings located on a chart to determine a ship's position are called:

    A. parallel lines

    B. lines of position

    C. cross bearings

    D. longitude and latitude

    E. course lines

30. The centerline of a boat running fore and aft, the backbone of a vessel, is called the:

    A. chine

    B. keel

    C. main beam

    D. bulkhead

    E. spar

ASTB Answer Key

Test 1: Math/Verbal Test

1. B	11. B	21. C	31. A
2. B	12. D	22. C	32. C
3. C	13. C	23. A	33. D
4. C	14. B	24. A	34. B
5. C	15. D	25. D	35. D
6. B	16. B	26. C	36. B
7. A	17. D	27. D	37. A
8. D	18. B	28. A	
9. D	19. D	29. B	
10. A	20. C	30. A	

Test 2: Mechanical Comprehension Test

1. B	9. A	17. A	25. C
2. C	10. A	18. B	26. B
3. C	11. B	19. C	27. B
4. C	12. C	20. A	28. A
5. A	13. B	21. C	29. C
6. B	14. B	22. C	30. C
7. C	15. C	23. C	
8. C	16. A	24. A	

Test 3: Spatial Apperception Test

1. A	10. C	19. B	28. A
2. D	11. E	20. C	29. D
3. D	12. D	21. B	30. A
4. A	13. C	22. E	31. B
5. E	14. C	23. A	32. E
6. D	15. E	24. A	33. C
7. B	16. B	25. B	34. E
8. D	17. B	26. C	35. D
9. A	18. A	27. C	

Test 4: Aviation and Nautical Information Test

1. E	**9.** A	**17.** B	**25.** C
2. B	**10.** D	**18.** D	**26.** B
3. A	**11.** D	**19.** A	**27.** B
4. C	**12.** C	**20.** C	**28.** A
5. D	**13.** B	**21.** C	**29.** C
6. D	**14.** A	**22.** A	**30.** B
7. C	**15.** E	**23.** D	
8. E	**16.** D	**24.** E	

ASTB Answers and Explanations

Test 1: Math/Verbal Test Answers and Explanations

1. B. If a machine produces 8,000 widgets in 3 hours, it produces $\frac{8000}{3}$ widgets in one hour. Twenty-four hours are in a day, so $\frac{8000}{3} \times 24$ or 64,000 widgets are produced in one day.

2. B. The total cost of the purchase is $(3 \times \$0.45) + (2 + \$0.79) = \$1.35 + \$1.58 = \$2.93$.

3. C. Carl's throw went $7\frac{1}{3} \times 2\frac{1}{2} = \frac{22}{3} \times \frac{5}{2} = \frac{110}{6} = 18\frac{1}{3}$ yards. The difference between the two throws is $18\frac{1}{3} - 7\frac{1}{3} = 11$ yards.

4. C. The total distance traveled in the morning was $13 \times 2 = 26$ miles. The total distance traveled in the afternoon was $9 \times 2 = 18$ miles. The difference between the two distances is $26 - 18 = 8$ miles.

5. C. Using the ratio $\frac{price}{video}$, the proportion $\frac{8}{3} = \frac{x}{2}$ can be used to find the cost to rent two videos. Cross multiply $8 \times 2 = 3x$, so $16 = 3x$ and $x = \frac{16}{3} = \$5.33$.

6. B. The word ECLECTIC means composed of a variety of different elements.

7. A. The word TACIT means unspoken, or implied by action.

8. D. The word STAGNANT means showing little or no sign of action or progress.

9. D. The word TEMPERATE means moderate.

10. A. The word REPLETE means full of, or abundantly supplied with.

11. B. At 5:30, 30 minutes remain until 6:00, and 2 additional hours until 8:00 for a total of 2 hours and 30 minutes.

12. D. Convert the dimensions of the box from feet to inches: $8' \times 6' \times 4'$ is equivalent to $(8 \times 12") \times (6 \times 12") \times (4 \times 12") = 96" \times 72" \times 48"$. The volume $= 96" \times 72" \times 48" = 331,776"$. The volume of each block is $6 \times 4 \times 4 = 96$. The number of blocks that fit in the box is $\frac{331,776}{96} = 3456$.

13. C. The cost for milk and 2 dozen eggs is $\$1.39 + (2 \times \$1.28) = \$3.95$. The change is $\$10.00 - \$3.95 = \$6.05$.

14. B. Sixty percent travel to work by car, so $800 \times 60\% = 480$.

15. D. Min read a total of $3 + 4$ or 7 mysteries. Therefore, she read 3×7 or 21 nonfiction books.

16. B. The word INCREASED is incorrect. An increased habitat would not be threatening. Changing INCREASED to DIMINISHED makes the meaning of the quotation clear.

17. D. The word DISREGARD is incorrect. Having an expectation of something, even a negative one, is not disregarding it. SKEPTICISM, which means doubt, conveys the intended meaning of the quotation.

18. B. The word ACCEPT is incorrect. To accept completely is the same as to adopt wholly. The word OR indicates that the sentence intends to provide an alternative. Changing ACCEPT to REJECT provides an alternative.

19. D. The word SMALLER is incorrect. The creation of economic activities would increase tax revenues rather than reducing them. LARGER conveys the logic of the sentence.

20. C. The word OBJECTIONS is incorrect. The sentence means to convey the idea that damage might not have been lessened if the safety systems were working. Changing OBJECTIONS to DOUBTS makes this meaning clear.

21. C. The volume of a cube is s^3, where s represents the length of an edge. Surface area is $6s^2$. If the volume = 343 cm^3, then $s = \sqrt[3]{343} = \sqrt[3]{7 \times 7 \times 7} = 7$. So the surface area is $6 \times 7^2 = 6 \times 49 = 294$ cm^2.

22. C. If $\frac{3}{8}$ of the pizza is eaten, then $1 - \frac{3}{8} = \frac{5}{8}$ remains. If that is divided by 2, then each receives $\frac{5}{8} \div 2 = \frac{5}{8} \times \frac{1}{2} = \frac{5}{16} = 0.3125 = 31.25\%$.

23. A. The difference in times is $144 - 127 = 17$ minutes.

24. A. Let c represent the number of caps traded in. Then $0.05c = 40.50$, and $c = \frac{40.50}{0.05} = 810$ caps.

25. D. With nine cups of milk, $\frac{9}{2} = 4\frac{1}{2}$ or four full batches can be made. However, with nine eggs, only $\frac{9}{4} = 2\frac{1}{4}$ or two full batches can be made. At most, only two batches can be made with the given ingredients.

26. C. Because the car is more than three years old, the free replacement guarantee does not apply. Choice **A** is not correct because it does not tell whether the customer has to pay for the work. No information in the paragraph suggests that choice **B** is what would happen. While choice **D** might be a true statement, the situation in the paragraph does not describe any problem with the engine.

27. D. Choices **A** and **B** are statements that describe some but not all sonnets according to the paragraph. Choice **C** is incorrect because the paragraph states that a sonnet has 14 lines.

28. A. The paragraph states that Americans travel more in the summer. You can conclude that if they travel more, they use more gasoline. And the paragraph states that when people want to buy more of a product, the price goes up.

29. B. Choices **A** and **D** are examples of facsimiles; they do not define the word. Choice **C** is incorrect because the paragraph indicates that ways of making facsimiles are ways of making copies.

30. A. A main idea is a general statement. The other choices are specific facts.

31. A. The area of a triangle is $\frac{1}{2}bh$. Let b represent the length of one leg. Then $h = 3b$, so the area is $\frac{1}{2}bh = \frac{1}{2} \times b \times 3b = \frac{3}{2}b^2 = 24$ so $\frac{2}{3} \times \frac{3}{2}b^2 = \frac{2}{3} \times 24$ and $b^2 = 16$. $b = \sqrt{16} = 4$ and $h = 3 \times 4 = 12$. The longest side of a right triangle is the hypotenuse. Using the Pythagorean Theorem, leg^2 + leg^2 = hypotenuse^2, so $4^2 + 12^2 = c^2$. Therefore, $160 = c^2$ and $c = \sqrt{160} = 12.6$.

32. C. Interest = principal $\times$ rate. Let p represent the principal. Then $\$100 = p \times 7\frac{1}{4}\%$, so $p = \frac{\$100}{7\frac{1}{4}\%} = \frac{\$100}{0.0725} = \$1379$.

33. D. Using the ratio $\frac{\text{pages}}{\text{minutes}}$, the proportion $\frac{2}{3} = \frac{360}{x}$ can be used to find the time. Cross multiply $2x = 3 \times 360$, so $2x = 1,080$, and $x = \frac{1080}{2} = 540$ minutes. Convert minutes to hours. Sixty minutes are in 1 hour, so $\frac{540}{60} = 9$ hours.

34. B. The average is found by adding all the scores and dividing by the total number of scores. The average this week is $\frac{112 + 156 + 179 + 165}{4} = \frac{612}{4} = 153$. The amount of improvement is $153 - 140 = 13$.

35. D. The total cost of the purchase is $\$8.95 \times 3 = \$26.85$. With a $\$12.73$ credit, the amount owed is $\$26.85 - \$12.73 = \$14.12$.

36. B. Choice **A** is incorrect because it is too limited; it deals only with the New England colonists. Choice **C** is not correct because it focuses only on the Virginia colonists who chose to colonize fertile land to cultivate tobacco. Choice **D** also deals only with the Virginia colonists who sought to make money on their tobacco crop.

37. A. Choice **B** is incorrect because it is too broad; the quotation does not indicate that all students should study Latin. Choice **C** is incorrect because algebraic skills, not basic arithmetic skills, can be improved. Choice **D** is wrong because it is also too broad; everyone is not included in the quotation.

Test 2: Mechanical Comprehension Test Answers and Explanations

1. **B.** Neglecting friction with air, the velocity vector of the ball has a horizontal component that remains constant and a vertical component that suffers deceleration due to the force of gravity. Because distance is speed multiplied by time, the path gradually curves downward due to gravity.

2. **C.** Work is force multiplied by distance, which is zero in this example.

3. **C.** The horizontal component of the velocity of the first ball has no effect on the vertical travel, and initially both balls have zero vertical velocity.

4. **C.** If the acceleration of gravity is constant, the period (and hence the frequency) is determined solely by the length of the connecting cord or rod.

5. **A.** Because the direction of the vibrating body is reversed at the end point of its motion, its velocity must be zero when its displacement is a maximum. It is then accelerated toward the center by the restoring force until it reaches its maximum speed at the center of oscillation, that is, when its displacement is zero. Because the restoring force is maximum at the end point, its acceleration at that moment is also a maximum by Newton's second law of motion.

6. **B.** The farther the particle is from the axis of rotation of a rigid body, the greater its linear speed because the linear speed is 2π multiplied by the product of the frequency of rotation and the radius of rotation. On the other hand, the angular speed is the linear speed divided by the radius of rotation, thus resulting in both points having the same angular speed.

7. **C.** The total angular momentum is equal to the product of the body's angular velocity and the moment of inertia. Pulling the arms toward the body increases the first by a certain ratio and decreases the second by the same ratio, thus keeping the angular momentum the same, as the question states.

8. **C.** Using the expressions $s = v_o t + 1/2 at^2$ and $v_f = v_o + at$, we set the time of travel as the sum of t_1 to travel the distance s_1 from the top of the building to the maximum height and t_2, s_2 as the corresponding values from the maximum height to the ground. Substituting numbers, we obtain $t_1 = 1.48$ s, $s_1 = 10.72$ m and $t_2 = 3.52$s, $s_2 = 50$ m so that the total time $= 1.48 + 3.52 = 5$ s.

9. **A.** Because this is an elastic collision, momentum is conserved. Hence, $4(2) - 2(4) = (4 + 2)v$, that is, $v = 0$ m/s.

10. **A.** Because five strands support the movable load, the required force is $200/5 = 40$ N.

11. **B.** $12.5 = 1/2\ g\ t^2$, hence $t \approx 1.6$ s, while $d = 1.6\ (10) = 16$ m.

12. **C.** The net vertical force on the block $= 3 \times 9.8$ (upward reaction force) $- 17.4$ N (downward applied force) $= 12$ N. The resulting force of friction $= 12(.25) = 3$ N. Because friction acts against any motion, the net horizontal force on the block $= 10 - 3 = 7$ N.

13. **B.** Because work equals the travel distance multiplied by the component of the force along the direction of travel, the angle θ between the pulling rope and the floor increases, and hence both its cosine and the work done decrease.

14. **B.** The spin rate (or angular velocity) is inversely proportional to the distance from the axis of rotation, so as the skater stretches her hands, the distance from her hands to the axis of rotation increases and the spin rate decreases significantly.

15. **C.** From the given dimensions, BC and BE are 0.721 m and 0.616 m, respectively. Examination of the force in cable AE shows that it must be 0 because its component along the top surface of the box toward the unsuspended corner is not balanced. The remaining cables BE and CE share the weight equally so that each has a vertical component of force equal to 60 N. Hence $T = (60)(.616/.5) = 27.035$ N.

16. **A.** If the velocity vectors of the two blocks are denoted by V_A and V_B, then the instantaneous center of rotation is at the intersection of the two vectors perpendicular to V_A and V_B. If the intersection point is denoted by C, then the distance BC is $6 \cos 25°$, while the distance CA is $6 \sin 25°$. Furthermore, because the linear velocity equals the angular velocity ω multiplied by the arm of rotation, $\omega = V_A/CA$ or V_B/BC. This leads to the result $V_B = (V_A)(BC)/CA = (4)(6 \cos 25°)/(6 \sin 25°) = 8.578$ m/s.

17. A. In this case the product of inertia for the rod is 0 because the pivotal point lies on an axis of symmetry.

18. B. If the compression of the spring is denoted by x, then $.5 kx^2 = mgh$. Solving for x we obtain $x = 1.4$ m.

19. C. The total energy of the system is constant and equals potential energy (PE) plus kinetic energy (KE), that is, $PE_A + KE_A = PE_B + KE_B$. Because $KE_B = 0$, we have $KE_A = PE_B - PE_A = mg(h + 1) - mg = 196.2$ J.

20. A. Because $KE_A = 196.2 = .5 m v^2$, $v = 6.264$ m/s.

21. C. The potential energy stored in the spring $= .5 k x^2 = 5$ J.

22. C. The new height should be 9 times greater because the speed of impact is proportional to the square root of the height.

23. C. The mechanical advantage equals 2π multiplied by the ratio R/p, which is approximately 25.

24. A. $F = 6.67 \times 10^{-11} \times 800 \times 600/(.25^2) = 5.12256 \times 10^{-4}$ N.

25. C. $F = 6.67 \times 3 \times 10^{24} \times 70/(5 \times 10^6)^2 = 560.28$ N.

26. B. The forces in graph b are not in equilibrium, so the nut may be loosened.

27. B. Velocity = rate of flow/cross sectional area $= 10/[\pi(2)^2] = 7.96$ m/s.

28. A. Bernoulli's equation applied to this case yields a pressure of 30.3 kilopascals at point B.

29. C. Because the potential energy of the ball is converted to kinetic energy, the speed at the lowest point is $[2gh]^{1/2} = 5.9$ m/s, where $g = 9.8$ m/s^2 and $h = 1.8$ m.

30. C. The horizontal component of the velocity of the arrow shot by the woman has no effect on the travel time, assuming that the air resistance is negligible.

Test 3: Spatial Apperception Test Answers and Explanations

1. A. Diving, no banking, flying out to sea.

2. D. Straight and level flight, flying up the coastline.

3. D. Climbing, no banking, flying up the coastline.

4. A. Straight and level flight, flying up the coastline.

5. E. Level flight, banking right, flying out to sea.

6. D. Level flight, banking left, flying up the coastline.

7. B. Diving, banking right, flying out to sea.

8. D. Diving, no banking, flying out to sea.

9. A. Diving, no banking, flying out to sea.

10. C. Level flight, banking right, flying down the coastline.

11. E. Climbing, banking right, flying out to sea.

12. D. Level flight, no banking, flying down the coastline.

13. C. Flying straight and level, no banking, heading 45° left of the coastline.

14. C. Flying straight and level, heading 45° right of the coastline.

15. E. Flying straight and level, heading 45° of the coastline.

16. B. Climbing, banking left, flying out to sea.

17. B. Level flight, banking left, flying out to sea.

18. A. Level flight, banking right, flying up the coastline.

19. B. Flying straight and level, flying down the coastline.

20. C. Diving, banking right, flying out to sea.

21. B. Diving, banking left, flying out to sea.

22. E. Flying level, banking right, flying out to sea.

23. A. Climbing, banking left, flying out to sea.

24. A. Level flight, banking left, flying up the coastline.

25. B. Level flight, banking right, flying up the coastline.

26. C. Flying straight and level, flying out to sea.

27. C. Climbing, banking right, flying out to sea.

28. A. Level flight, banking left, flying down the coastline.

29. D. Level flight, banking left, flying out to sea.

30. A. Straight and level flight, heading 45° right of the coastline.

31. B. Climbing, no banking, flying down the coastline.

32. E. Diving, banking left, flying out to sea.

33. C. Straight and level flight, flying out to sea.

34. E. Diving, no banking, flying down the coastline.

35. D. Climbing, no banking, flying out to sea.

Test 4: Aviation and Nautical Information Test Answers and Explanations

1. E. The pilot uses the rudder to yaw the airplane about the vertical axis. No other flight control rotates the aircraft around this axis.

2. B. The elevators cause the aircraft to rotate around the lateral axis. The elevators cause the aircraft to pitch up and down.

3. A. Camber is the curvature of a wing between the leading edge and the trailing edge of the wind. The greater the curvature, the greater the lift the wing produces.

4. C. In steady flight, thrust equals drag, and weight equals lift. This results in steady-state, unaccelerated flight.

5. D. A runway is numbered in relation to the magnetic heading of the runway. Runway 36, therefore, has a magnetic heading of 360°.

6. D. The opposite direction runway to runway 23L is 5R. Runways sharing the same magnetic direction are numbered left, right and center. In this case, a parallel runway, 5L and 23R, is next to the runway in the question.

7. C. A wing stall is caused by the separation of airflow over the surface of the wing of an aircraft. This is caused by a wing exceeding its critical angle of attack or by reducing the speed of an aircraft to a point that makes it impossible for airflow to stay adhered to the upper surface of the wing.

8. E. Aspect ratio is defined as the ratio of the wingspan versus the average chord line.

9. A. Runway 13/31 is laid out on a magnetic heading of 130° for runway 13 and 310° for runway 31. This means that aircraft can take off and land in either a southeasterly or northwesterly direction.

10. D. A rectangular wing is designed to stall at the wing root first. This is ideal for a training aircraft because it allows for aileron effectiveness all the way up to a complete wing stall.

11. D. A headwind improves aircraft performance during a takeoff roll. It allows an aircraft to accelerate to rotation speed quicker and improve climb performance in relation to obstacles (more so than in a calm wind).

12. C. A feathered propeller creates the least amount of drag due to the fact that it presents the smallest cross section possible to the relative wind. A propeller is feathered most often during an engine failure.

13. B. Compression is the second stroke in a four-stroke engine cycle. It causes the fuel-air mixture to reach high levels of compression before it is ignited by the spark.

14. A. A no-flap landing causes an approach to be flown at a high airspeed due to the higher stall speed of the aircraft without flaps. This causes a longer landing roll as well due to the increased braking required to stop the airplane.

15. E. Latitude and longitude are used to compute an aircraft's position relative to imaginary lines drawn around the surface of the earth.

16. D. The rotating beacon, usually positioned on the top of the tail of an aircraft, is a pulsating red light that must be on during all aircraft operations.

17. B. Barometric pressure is expressed in inches of mercury at U.S. airports. Millibars and other units of pressure are not commonly used in aviation in the United States.

18. D. The Wright brothers made the first controlled flight at Kitty Hawk, North Carolina, on December 17, 1903.

19. A. Due to the force of gravity, an aircraft weighs twice as much in a 60° banked turn as it does in level flight. The occupants sense a force of two Gs as they move through the turn.

20. C. The second stage of a thunderstorm is the mature stage, when rain begins to fall as the storm reaches its strongest intensity.

21. C. Vertical partitions aboard a ship are called bulkheads.

22. A. A machine for moving heavy weights is a capstan. It is made up of a large drum with a cable wrapped around it.

23. D. A nautical mile is equal to 1.15 statute miles.

24. E. The 24-hour clock uses 4 digits; hours and minutes less than 10 are preceded by a 0.

25. C. As the weight of a ship decreases, it lowers the waterline, increasing the freeboard and decreasing the draft.

26. B. Red is for port; green is for starboard; white indicates the direction of the vessel; yellow is for special circumstances.

27. B. A sea breeze is the result of cool air being pulled ashore by the rising inland air as it is heated by the ground.

28. A. Longitude divides the east and west hemispheres with 0° being Greenwich, England, the Prime Meridian of the world.

29. C. Two or more intersecting bearings located on a chart to determine position are called cross bearings.

30. B. The keel is the centerline of the ship, or the backbone.